CE,

Snow White and the Seven Dwarfs

AUG 2022

ANIMATION: KEY FILMS/FILMMAKERS

Series Editor: Chris Pallant

Titles in the Series

Snow White and the Seven Dwarfs

New Perspectives on Production, Reception, Legacy

Edited by
Chris Pallant and
Christopher Holliday

BLOOMSBURY ACADEMIC
NEW YORK • LONDON • OXFORD • NEW DELHI • SYDNEY

BLOOMSBURY ACADEMIC
Bloomsbury Publishing Inc
50 Bedford Square, London, WC1B 3DP, UK
1385 Broadway, New York, NY 10018, USA
29 Earlsfort Terrace, Dublin 2, Ireland

BLOOMSBURY, BLOOMSBURY ACADEMIC and the Diana logo are trademarks of
Bloomsbury Publishing Plc

First published in the United States of America 2021
This paperback edition published 2022

Volume Editor's Part of the Work © Chris Pallant and Christopher Holliday

Each chapter © of Contributors

For legal purposes the Acknowledgements on p. x constitute an extension
of this copyright page.

Series Designer: Louise Dugdale
Cover image © Ronald Grant Archive / ArenaPAL

This work is published open access subject to a Creative Commons
Attribution-NonCommercial-NoDerivatives 3.0 licence (CC BY-NC-ND 3.0,
https://creativecommons.org/licenses/by-nc-nd/3.0/). You may re-use, distribute,
and reproduce this work in any medium for non-commercial purposes, provided you
give attribution to the copyright holder and the publisher and provide a link to the
Creative Commons licence.

Bloomsbury Publishing Inc does not have any control over, or responsibility for, any
third-party websites referred to or in this book. All internet addresses given in this
book were correct at the time of going to press. The author and publisher regret any
inconvenience caused if addresses have changed or sites have ceased to exist, but can
accept no responsibility for any such changes.

ISBN: HB: 978-1-5013-5122-8
PB: 978-1-5013-7396-1
ePDF: 978-1-5013-5120-4
eBook: 978-1-5013-5121-1

Series: Animation: Key Films/Filmmakers

Typeset by Newgen KnowledgeWorks Pvt. Ltd., Chennai, India

To find out more about our authors and books visit www.bloomsbury.com
and sign up for our newsletters.

CONTENTS

Part 2 *Snow White* in Hollywood 115

Part 3 International legacies 177

ILLUSTRATIONS

ACKNOWLEDGEMENTS

In addition to the many wonderful authors whose hard work has given shape to this collection, the editors would like to thank family, friends and colleagues, as well as Bloomsbury's editorial team, for their encouragement in getting this book over the finish line.

Huge thanks to Lyndsey for all of her support; thanks to my children Charlie and Evie for helping me to see the world through their eyes; and thanks to my dog Pixel for choosing to chew through everything except my laptop cable. As expected, the 'other Chris' proved himself to be the perfect accomplice, and I valued every moment working with him on this book.

(Chris Pallant)

I would like to first thank my terrific colleagues at King's College London for both their intellectual stimulation and moments of welcome distraction. Huge thanks are also directed at the 'other Chris' for being an incisive, generous and patient co-editor as we asked each other questions, worked out our angles and figured out exactly how this was all going to come together. Final thanks go to my parents, Frances and Robert, and to Lauren, who was not here when the idea for this book began but, to my very good fortune and enduring gratitude, is here to see its completion.

(Christopher Holliday)

Introduction: Into the burning coals

Christopher Holliday and Chris Pallant

The wicked woman uttered a curse, and she became so frightened, so frightened, that she did not know what to do. At first she did not want to go to the wedding, but she found no peace. She had to go and see the young queen. When she arrived she recognized Snow-White, and terrorized, she could only stand there without moving.

Then they put a pair of iron shoes into burning coals. They were brought forth with tongs and placed before her. She was forced to step into the red-hot shoes and dance until she fell down dead.[1]

To undertake a scholarly project on the Wonderful World of Disney, in particular one focused on the historical, cultural and artistic significance of its celebrated cel-animated feature film *Snow White and the Seven Dwarfs* (David Hand, 1937), is an endeavour that often feels like jumping headlong 'into burning coals'. Over eighty years after its initial theatrical release, Disney's adaptation of the Grimm Brothers' nineteenth-century German fairy tale[2] remains 'one of the most-discussed films in animation studies, and one of the most historically significant films of all time'.[3] *Snow White*'s unwavering durability as the emblematic Disney product, its historical contribution to the Golden Age of Hollywood animation, and its industrial and artistic relationship to the creativity of animation as an expressive medium during the first decades of the twentieth century have all combined to secure the film's overwhelming place within American – and indeed global – film history. As animation historian Leonard Maltin explains, 'There is no way to overstate the effect of *Snow White and the Seven Dwarfs* on the film industry, the moviegoing public, and the world in general.'[4] However, despite the 'staggering' number of books already published on 'Walt Disney, the Disney company, and Disney products', there nonetheless remains numerous aspects of *Snow White*'s landmark production at the Disney studio, its reception both domestically and abroad, and the strength of its cultural legacy, which have yet to receive significant critical attention.[5] *Snow White and the Seven Dwarfs: New Perspectives on Production, Reception, Legacy* seeks to address this knowledge deficit. It pushes beyond well-established areas of discussion to reveal new insights into the industrial forces shaping the production of Disney's debut feature film; the interplay between exhibition practices and the critical reception of *Snow White* in the United States; and the international legacy of a film that continues to circulate within a variety of national filmmaking cultures and traditions. The collection also counters much of the existing scholarship on the film that has tended to focus on *Snow White* in its US (and, at best, largely Western and Anglophone) contexts. Several of the chapters reclaim production histories surrounding the film that have hitherto been marginalized, while others enhance our understanding of the contemporary exhibition of *Snow White* both in the United States and overseas and, for the first time, bring together accounts of *Snow White*'s cultural impact on the global stage through a series of international case studies.

Snow White in theory

Snow White's ongoing centrality within a number of interdisciplinary fields, not least its robust place across Film, Media and Animation studies, is entirely reflective of the film's standing as one of the defining achievements of twentieth-century animation. Numerous critical accounts have situated *Snow White* as a flashpoint film where the medium's artistic credentials and development of cel-animation as a technique came firmly into contact with the hardening of animation into an industrial art form in the United States. It was *Snow White* that propelled Disney's studio from a 'Poverty Row' operation, one that employed twenty-five staff in 1929, to an ambitious studio with three hundred employees in 1936, helping to prime the identity of a studio that would next go on to produce the films *Pinocchio* (Ben Sharpsteen and Hamilton Luske, 1940), *Fantasia* (James Algar et al., 1940), *Dumbo* (Ben Sharpsteen, 1941) and *Bambi* (David Hand, 1942).[6] Within the hagiographic register of numerous company histories too, *Snow White* has often been positioned simultaneously – and paradoxically – as a launchpad for Disney's subsequent endeavours within feature animation *and* as confirmation of the studio's mastery of the then-nascent form. *Snow White* was, for J. B. Kaufman, a film that ultimately 'capped what had been a decade of remarkable expansion and development for Walt and his artists', just as much as it would go on to establish a set of working practices for the animated feature moving forward.[7] Indeed, the size of *Snow White*'s production and volume of personnel necessitated the reorganization of the company's infrastructure, including the breaking up of 'facilities into divisions that thought up and wrote stories, created initial and final drawings for those stories, inked and painted the drawings, created music and visual and sound effects, and shot and produced film', alongside the management of other administrative roles that supported the production of its animated features.[8] Nicholas Sammond notes that the labour of *Snow White* quickly became a symbol of Disney's own 'fetishistic celebration of repetition and standardization', implicated in the framing of the studio as a highly efficient and 'hypermodern industrial concern'.[9] However, many scholars have also identified *Snow White* as equally an industrial milestone within the context of broader Classical Hollywood production. Geoffrey Nowell-Smith argues that, although not the first full-length animated feature, *Snow White* 'enjoyed a phenomenal success (including a special Oscar), with serious impact on industrial animation in the US'.[10] Beyond the contribution made by the film to Disney's business evolution as a viable corporation (including the training of new animators and the hiring of Shamus Culhane, Al Eugster, Ted Sears and Grim Natwick from neighbouring studios), *Snow White*'s influence certainly reached beyond the studio's walls. The shape of this influence can be traced through the contemporaneous emergence of comparable domestic productions in the United States, which in turn has served to mythologize Walt's status as a uniquely American genius equivalent to George Gershwin, Irving Berlin, Thomas Edison and Henry Ford.[11] Nowell-Smith adds that in response to the critical and commercial success of *Snow White*, the Paramount Corporation 'insisted' that the Fleischer Brothers begin immediate work on a 'rival feature' in the form of *Gulliver's Travels* (Dave Fleischer, 1939) and, later, *Mr. Bug Goes to Town* (Dave Fleischer, 1941). The outcome of these kinds of industrial exchanges, which have been writ large into Disney's industrial history, has been the sustained framing of Walt as a 'master' or 'systems builder' who exerted his influence not solely through the efficiency of technologies, machines and processes but also through a form of entertainment that reached into 'local, national and global' spaces.[12]

It is through the significance of *Snow White* that contrasts between Disney and the Fleischers (who were themselves one of the most distinctive studios of the 1930s) are able to measure the success of the latter via their impact on the former. Mark Langer's comparison of the two studios in this

Golden Age period argues that 'By coopting the dominant feature-length format of classical Hollywood cinema, Disney differentiated his product. ... His competitors could follow, or be left with what would be perceived as a less innovative, inferior, product.'[13] In the case of the Fleischers – who had already adapted the Grimms' fairy tale four years previously with *Snow-White* (Dave Fleischer, 1933) – brothers Max and Dave 'drove themselves into insolvency by combining all of their technologies' for the ambitious *Gulliver's Travels* and *Mr. Bug Goes to Town*.[14] The outcome of this 'institutional pattern' of give-and-take and 'product differentiation' within the teleology of early animation history during the 1930s is that Disney's *Snow White* was a creative catalyst, one whose profits were invested in – and used to fund – the studio's roster of subsequent features. By comparison, this industrial narrative of competition, mimesis, progress, conflict and tension has consistently worked to frame the altogether more anxious working culture at Fleischers (not helped by the troubled production of *Mr. Bug Goes to Town*), leading to the company's failures as the industry moved headlong into the 1940s.[15]

If *Snow White* remains industrially significant to the formation of animation's Golden Age in Hollywood through the 1940s and 1950s, then aesthetically too the film has been widely credited for establishing Disney's 'hyper-realist' visual style and thematic preoccupations that have held sway over animation aesthetics throughout the twentieth century. Not only did *Snow White* popularize cel-animation within both Hollywood and internationally, but the film also initiated what would become a long-standing love affair between the animated medium and the folk tale/fairy-tale tradition. Joseph Zornado argues that the critical and commercial success of *Snow White* 'would forever link' animation with fantasy and fairy-tale storytelling structures, a connection that has come under continual scrutiny through the studio's appropriation and colonizing of the popular understanding of these tales around the world.[16] Numerous writers on Disney's animated features have interrogated this problematic process of 'Disneyfication' or 'Disneyization' as a symptom of Disney's identity as a 'globalizing force' through its reworking of source material for its animated films.[17] In his book *The Disney Fetish*, Seán J. Harrington seeks to reclaim this activity of exchange by framing it as necessary for scholars to understand the formation of Disney's animated formula. Harrington argues that 'changes in translation from folk-tale to film are inevitable', adding that 'it is the ideological differences between film and folk-tale that present the qualities that can uniquely be called Disney'.[18] Disney's mediation of pre-existing stories gives rise to a central element of the Disney 'formula', a catchall term rooted in the formal properties and formulaic identity of Disney's many multimedia products and business ventures. As Disney's feature film debut, *Snow White* has often been understood as a standard bearer of such formulaic tendencies, repeating pleasures and cycles of repetition, which have emphatically structured the studio's thematic and narrative content, character types, and high-contrast dualities between good and evil. Janet Wasko is not alone in arguing that *Snow White* 'might be said to have fully established the Classic Disney formula', while Jack Zipes agrees that the film 'laid down the prescribed formula' that has otherwise remained relatively untroubled well into the era of post-millennial Disney feature animation.[19]

Snow White's embodiment of the Disney formula has certainly guided its meaningfulness as a critical blueprint, and it is not hard to find references to the studio's founding feature within popular discourse surrounding more recent Disney animation, including their turn to digital technologies via their recent cycle of computer-animated films. To coincide with the release of the musical *Frozen* (Chris Buck and Jennifer Lee, 2013), which was inspired by Hans Christian Andersen's 1844 fairy tale 'The Snow Queen', *Variety* charted the evolution of the Disney Princess from *Snow White* to *Frozen*'s depiction of sisters Anna and Elsa (*Entertainment Weekly* ran a similar piece following the release of *Frozen 2* [Chris Buck and Jennifer Lee, 2019]).[20] Numerous reviews of Disney's other computer-animated films *Tangled* (Nathan Greno and Byron Howard, 2010) and *Moana* (Ron Clements and John Musker, 2016) also make strong connections between the organization of the fairy-tale narrative, musical numbers and gender politics of 'the studio's early years', to which *Snow White* is often cited as the defining feature and fullest embodiment of Disney's formulaic constitution.[21] Perhaps expectedly, the fairy-tale musical *The Princess and the Frog* (Ron Clements and John Musker, 2009) – Disney's momentous return to cel-animation amid a Hollywood animation landscape dominated by the digital – was also widely positioned against its own 1937 feature. Justin Chang compared protagonist Tiana to Snow White through their contradictory use of geography (the castle vs. the ghetto), while Brooks Barnes in the *New York Times* argued that Tiana is 'a hand-drawn throwback to classic Disney characters', notably Snow White.[22]

Snow White's narrative and stylistic influence upon Disney feature animation can certainly be understood through the studio's development of its own 'Disney-Formalist' aesthetic, one that according to Chris Pallant was 'forged' by the aesthetic style and pursuit of hyper-realism in *Snow White*, then continued in subsequent films *Pinocchio*, *Dumbo* and *Bambi*.[23] For Pallant, *Snow White*'s success 'profoundly altered the studio', not just in terms of financial revenue and business acumen but in its emergent role as an 'artistic paradigm' and 'aesthetic blueprint for much of the Disney-Formalist period'.[24] Foundational to this blueprint for a kind of realist representation that resisted the surrealist creativity and fluidity of form seen in Otto Messmer's *Felix the Cat* (1919–), and even Disney's own *Silly Symphonies* (1927–37) series of shorts, was the studio's engagement with technology. *Snow White* has been widely understood as the site for numerous technological developments that would ultimately impact the entire animated medium. Eric Smoodin admits that 'the story of the making of *Snow White* has been told many times', a tale that has been largely directed at its monumental influence upon animation as a technology of potentially persuasive realist representation.[25] For Annette Kuhn, who charts *Snow White*'s reception in the UK during the 1930s, the film involved 'innovative animation techniques and specially developed film-making equipment'.[26] Kuhn argues that the film ultimately marked a 'huge gamble' for the Disney studio thanks to its $1.5 million cost for new equipment, with much of the hype that surrounded *Snow White*'s release in Britain directed at 'the new cinematographic technology developed for the film, ... as well as on the intensive labour involved in making the thousands of drawings required for such an extended piece of animation'.[27] Among these 'cinematographic' developments were synchronized sound and the multi-plane camera, which Maltin defines as a device that 'enabled the camera to look through a series of animation "planes" instead of just one, so that the finished picture would have a feeling of depth and dimension'.[28] In addition to *Snow White*'s influence on the acceleration in Hollywood cartoon production (with the film signalling for Smoodin a 'new interest' in animation as it moved from the margins to the mainstream), Disney's seminal cel-animated feature also 'reconfirmed' the studio's interest in colour, thereby building upon their application of Technicolor across its previous *Silly Symphonies* series of shorts.

The boundaries of enchantment

The birth of a more ideologically focused 'Disney studies' during the early 1990s – that, perhaps not coincidentally, corresponded with the 'renaissance' of the studio's cel-animated features – once again turned to *Snow White* as fully representative of the Disney text due to its particular ideological operations. In 1994, Smoodin had already reflected on the notable resurgence in Disney literature, a shift he correlated with an increased interest in 'developing a branch of cultural studies that examines networks of power, and ... emphasises the relation of the cinema to other disciplines and particularly to the social sciences'.[29] A few years later in 2001, Wasko similarly identified a narrative of scholarly expansion that emerged throughout the preceding ten-year period, aligning the company's growth via popular tourist attractions (theme parks, holiday resorts) during this 'Disney Decade' with a 'deluge of academic studies from a variety of disciplines'.[30] Disney's position as a global media and entertainment corporation (including its links to alternate media enterprises), alongside its status as a manufacturing operation and production facility, certainly seemed to promote the company as an ideal 'network of power' for critical analysis. The same courtesy was extended to *Snow White*, with scrutiny of its carefully orchestrated marketing strategies and exhibition practices that seemed to anticipate the consumerist logic and lucrative multimedia synergy for which the Disney Corporation perhaps remains best known. As Richard Neupert explains, Disney (in collaboration with United Artists) 'provided what seems to have been one of the most successful promotional campaign of the 1930s with *Snow White*', with 'Dollarize with Disney' a common 'battle cry', signifying the film as bankable revenue within trade advertisements of the period.[31] Indeed, the index entries for *Snow White* listed in Smoodin's collection *Disney Discourse: Producing the Magic Kingdom* speak to something of a scholarly orientation towards plotting the cultural influence of the Disney phenomenon primarily through the rubric of consumerism (entries for the film include 'product tie-ins', 'production of', 'profits from' and 'promotional strategies').

That is not to say *Snow White* has not been immune to examinations of its ideological operations and gender politics. Following David Forgacs's association in the pages of *Screen* between Disney and childhood nostalgia through the workings of *Snow White*'s 'clean, nonviolent, fantasies with songs and happy endings', a closer look at Disney's ideological impact on American popular culture did begin to emerge.[32] Edited anthologies, such as *From Mouse to Mermaid: The Politics of Film, Gender, and Culture*, revisited several of the issues around the common characteristics of the Disney ideology first identified in Ariel Dorfman and Armand Mattelart's 1971 cultural analysis of the Disney comic books.[33] Originally banned under the country's Fascist regime by President Allende, Dorfman and Mattelart's seminal text – aside from being a valuable introduction to the neglected area of Disney comic books – vehemently deconstructed the Disney myth and thereby established the subsequent process by which communication studies of mass media were applied to forms of (Disney) animation. Painted with a broad brush, the aim of these accounts published in the 1990s was to 'intervene in Disney's construction of gender, identity and culture' and to enable an understanding of Disney feature animation as forms of cultural pedagogy.[34] Framed by these emergent scholarly shifts towards the identification of cultural imperialism, critical considerations of *Snow White* quickly understood the film through the question of gender. In fact, as one of the 'nest eggs' of the Disney Empire, *Snow White* (the film and the eponymous heroine who was modelled on US dancer and actress Marjorie Champion) became the locus for studies into the 'indelible images of the feminine' and the ways in which Walt himself had 'wrote his name and ownership on the folk stories of women'.[35] Since its 1937 release, *Snow White* has undoubtedly remained prototypical in the way that it presents a particularly conservative image of womanhood. For Cassandra Stover, the essentially 'voiceless' and 'conventional' heroine exemplifies 'Hollywood's trend towards passive, childish figures' and a character archetype of 'pure maiden innocence' easily mapped onto American culture of the 1930s to which Disney's commercial animated features actively contributed.[36] At the same time, Snow White's sketching as submissive and docile during the period leading up to second-wave feminism equally provides a contrast to the studio's rhetorical shift towards more proactive post-feminist princesses since the 1990s, even if – as Stover cautions – their autonomy, assertiveness and heroism do not always fulfil their narratological potential 'as a representation of agency for an American female audience'.[37] However, one of the most prescient elements of Snow White's gender politics ultimately occurs beyond the screen.

The contribution of supervising animator David Hand – who began as an animator on the Out of the Inkwell (1918–29) series for the Fleischers, before joining the Disney studio in 1930 – to Snow White has been considered alongside the various sequence directors, supervising animators, character designers, art directors and background animators that comprised Snow White's extensive production team. As Sammond explains, Snow White's division of labour among its departments, facilities, offices and studios was flaunted as 'exemplary of its [Disney's] modernity, and as proof of its commitment to a Fordist imaginary of efficiency as humanized industrial practice'.[38] More crucial to understanding the historical specificity of Disney's animated infrastructure, however, is the occlusion of women from these received industrial narratives, a discourse of erasure that entirely fits with what Jonathan Frome has called the 'frustratingly general' nature of the historical accounts into the making of Snow White. Discussing the 'heavily gendered dimension' of work on the film that 'typified' Hollywood studios at the time, Smoodin argues that 'With the exception of Dorothy Ann Blank, one of eight credited with the story adaptation, and Hazel Sewell, one of the ten art directors, men made up the credited workforce'.[39] More recent studies into the studio's female employees during this Classic period, such as Mindy Johnson's Ink & Paint: The Women of Walt Disney's Animation and Nathalia Holt's The Queens of Animation: The Untold Story of the Women, are necessary correctives to this industrial invisibility and vital spaces for reclaiming the labour of women.[40] As Patricia Zohn put it in a recent Vanity Fair article shining a light on 'Disney animation girls', the studio's talented female workforce of young women, mostly under 25, were 'inking and painting minor miracles that would become part of our collective visual consciousness'.[41] Their miraculous work included, of course, Snow White. Zohn thus continues that behind the hardened image of the 'all-male assembly line', which erroneously defined Disney's workforce, stood an extensive army of women that comprised the very 'backbone' of Disney's Snow White but whose creative contribution to the film's naturalism of background, colour palette and levels of visual detail, and artistry of expressing character movement and rhythm is a story only now being told.

In many ways, it is difficult, then, to think of a time 'before Snow White', of what popular animation in the United States looked like prior to Disney's

feature-length cel-animated debut.[42] Kaufman writes that such was the
Disney film's 'enchanting effect' that it soon 'established a precedent for
much of the subsequent production, not only of Disney films, but of all
animated features'.[43] Back in 1992, Forgacs speculated that while *Snow
White* 'may not be the highest grossing film of all time ... it must be the most
rereleased', and he suggested that Walt himself 'could not have anticipated
quite how long these films would last or how big their eventual profits
would be'.[44] Re-released theatrically in 1944, and then again in 1952, 1958,
1967, 1975, 1983, 1987 and 1993, *Snow White*'s subsequent post-cinema
afterlife on a variety of media platforms has also reflected the studio's careful
management of its animated content in the growing home entertainment
market. *Snow White* has certainly been subject to the Disney's studio's
corporate strategy to deliberately suppress certain titles, a lucrative business
model that fuels the subsequent cultural value of absent, missing or withheld
features locked in the symbolic Disney media 'vault'. David McGowan
argues that '*Snow White*, for instance, was only issued on VHS in the United
States between October 1994 and April 1995, and then finally returned to
stores on VHS and DVD in 2001 (before being removed from sale yet again
early in the following year)'.[45] The protection of *Snow White* by Disney's
Studio Entertainment division tells us as much about the esteem in which
the film is held by the company as it does about their careful gatekeeping
of its most treasured products. *Snow White*'s sporadic appearance on VHS,
DVD and now Blu-Ray platforms (as well as its availability on subscription,
on-demand and streaming services) offers an example of Disney's market
power both during and following 'the growth years of home video', if not
their broader distribution practices that serve to 'maximize revenues' and
build domestic family audiences.[46]

The extent to which *Snow White* is often situated at the centre point of
scholarly writing on the Disney Corporation is clear, a fulcrum that continues
to support sustained methodological consideration into the popularity of
studio's animated features. Given the multitude of contexts in which Disney
feature animation has been explored, it is perhaps unsurprising, then, that
Gillian Youngs speaks of the 'ghost' of *Snow White and the Seven Dwarfs*,
a film so deeply knotted together with what are now considered (and
celebrated) as the repeated archetypes of Disney's storytelling structures and
their ideological commitment to family entertainment that its very presence
'looms large' over critical and cultural understandings of the studio's
animated feature film canon.[47] The aim of *Snow White and the Seven
Dwarfs: New Perspectives on Production, Reception, Legacy* is to therefore
paint a more nuanced picture of the film's enchanting spectral quality and
to understand why its pleasures 'haunt' critics, film history and the popular
imagination. The collection is divided into three complementary parts that
chart the evolution of *Snow White* across distinct phases of ideation, design,
production, distribution, promotion, exhibition and reception. These parts

are titled 'Innovation, technology and style', '*Snow White* in Hollywood' and 'International legacies' and are intended to signpost the considerable importance of Disney's debut feature film across a multitude of competing industrial and artistic contexts. However, they are also intended to speak to how the existing critical terrain that has enveloped *Snow White* and the ways in which the film's place within academic discourse can be productively unfixed.

Innovation, technology and style

Snow White and the Seven Dwarfs: New Perspectives on Production, Reception, Legacy begins with an opening section that speaks directly to *Snow White*'s status as a feat of innovation and as a film that pioneered a multitude of formal styles, practices and technological processes as part of its landmark production. Eric Jenkins is not alone in acknowledging that immediately upon its release, '*Snow White* was praised as a wonder, a masterpiece, declared a true breakthrough, something never seen before'.[48] Jenkins attributes this rhetoric of 'wonder' to the studio's construction of a 'fantasy world' predicated on a mode of 'animistic mimesis' and the 'mimetic perception of life'.[49] The root cause of this graphic illusionism has, in turn, been widely acknowledged as emerging from not only *Snow White*'s identity as a technological marvel *as animation* (as a medium of representation) but also the film's particular mobilization of individual technologies and techniques that would formally approximate the real and its sensations of life and movement. The aim of this book's opening section is, then, to reach into the corners of the film's production history through a consideration of *Snow White*'s aesthetic novelty and modernity, elements of its character design and its organization of animated space. But its objective is also to complicate accepted and highly durable industrial narratives, and to thereby expand the ongoing scholarly fetishism with *Snow White*'s critical–functional status as the bearer of animation's technological progress.

Chapter 1, written by Victoria Mullins, discusses the legacies of German Expressionist cinema that can be traced throughout Disney's adaptation of the *Snow White* tale. Responding to a larger critical narrative that has engaged with Disney's national–cultural interpretation of European folklore, Mullins notes how Disney's film is often criticized for 'Americanizing' the Grimm Brothers' original story. However, although *Snow White*'s Expressionist aesthetic is routinely acknowledged by Film and Animation scholars, the debt that the film owes to German filmmakers has not yet been made the focus of extended academic inquiry. Mullins therefore places *Snow White* in direct dialogue with German Expressionist cinema, arguing that the characters and settings of *Snow White* should be observed as active components of the film's Expressionist tendencies. This chapter's analysis of

Snow White's multiple visual references to German Expressionist cinema, as well as Hollywood horror films of the period, builds the argument that Expressionism was initiated into the visual fabric of the film and has since remained an integral component of Disney's animated aesthetic.

The next chapter, co-written by Stéphane Collignon and Ian Friend, shifts the focus of discussion onto this subject of 'believability' within an animated context and the artistic strategies employed at the Disney studio to achieve such an aesthetic. Through the *Silly Symphonies* series, first, and then with the development of *Snow White* in mind, the studio started to improve its animation standards both on the fronts of character design and personality animation. Collignon and Friend discuss how Disney and his animators dealt with notions of reality, achieving the perfect balance of expressivity and credibility while fine-tuning a style that would become a standard for animators working all over the world. They make fruitful connections with cognitive psychology, neuroscience and ethology to explain why the specific recognizability of character design developed by the studio in *Snow White* has proved to be so efficient and still endures today, thereby extending a critical enquiry that highlights the legacy of the live-action referencing workflow pioneered in Disney's feature.

In Chapter 3, Christopher Holliday and Chris Pallant discuss *Snow White*'s pastoral graphic style through a consideration of Disney animation's long-standing investment in lush woodland settings. However, they argue that the studio's engagement with nature as both a theme and practical environment in which to set their animated features paradoxically function as highly technological, man-made spaces. The focus of Holliday and Pallant's chapter is largely directed at the patented multi-plane camera device, an imposing vertical camera system involving the spacing of horizontal planes, developed in 1937 by engineer William Garity, and first pioneered in the Disney short *The Old Mill* (Wilfred Jackson, 1937). In *Snow White*, woodland realms become worlds of increased depth and dimensionality thanks to the multi-plane's arrangement of space, allowing the film to narrativize its natural environments in ways that reinforce the Disney studio's synonymous relationship with animated technology. Yet beyond affording Disney feature animation more precise levels of reality, the multi-plane camera is also framed by a troubling industrial rhetoric, with the sustained relegation of women's labour to the extreme margins of the multi-plane narrative. This chapter therefore draws on archival research to argue that despite their historical occlusion, the studio's female workforce played an important role in ensuring the success of the multi-plane and by extension offers a space to think more closely about the place of women's labour in Golden Age Hollywood animation.

In Chapter 4, Maarit Kalmakurki reminds readers that although Disney animation is a site of intensive academic study, such studies have tended to neglect those elements that had a bearing on the costume design process, the final look of the costume and how costumes were traditionally used to enhance both narrative and character. Kalmakurki therefore focuses on the Disney animators and their process of designing costumes in *Snow White*, drawing upon the production's story meeting notes, video footage filmed during a series of motion studies and conceptual drawings that each contributed to the realization of three-dimensional animated characters. Following on from Collignon and Friend, Kalmakurki assesses how animators used rotoscoping as a tool for designing character costumes, analysing how and why some of the rotoscoping costumes were different in their construction than everyday garments. Additionally, Kalmakurki reveals how the pressures of production influenced the style of the costumes, with small details and complex constructions avoided as they would have taken too long to be drawn. Ultimately, this chapter shows the multilayered process of the character costume design, a process that resulted in *Snow White*'s iconic costume, thereby supporting the significance of characters' costume in animation as an important – yet hitherto neglected – object of study.

Amy M. Davis closes the first section of the book, offering a consideration of what makes Disney's *Snow White* so emblematic of the studio's 'magic touch'. Drawing an evolutionary line from Disney's short-form animation through to their first feature, Davis works to locate what it is that we mean when we talk about *Snow White*'s 'Disney' qualities. How is Disney's interpretation of the ancient folk tale of 'Little Snow White' uniquely *Disney*? What is the trait, or pattern, or technique, or technology, or – as Davis terms it – 'magic touch' that identifies *Snow White* as a product specifically of Walt Disney Productions other than its title card? In her chapter, Davis situates *Snow White* in context, setting the questions that drive her chapter in relation to the cultural milieu of Jazz Age America and Modernist aesthetics.

Snow White in Hollywood

The book's middle section is tasked with picking apart *Snow White*'s Hollywood connection. Chapters take into account how (and why) Disney's film established its critical and cultural reputation within the domestic arena, while also expanding new thinking into its US reception and exhibition through detailed primary research. *Snow White* was, as animation historian Michael Barrier argues, conceived by Walt as a 'Hollywood product', one that could operate successfully within the machinations of the entrenched Hollywood studio system (and, perhaps, consolidate animation's place within such an economic arrangement of production).[50] Disney's film has undoubtedly become fixed as a central component of animation's historical development in the United States, central to the medium's forward momentum and rapid acceleration towards industrial security in the first two decades of the twentieth century. Framed by this teleological project of unstoppable development that sites *Snow White* through its significant contribution to animation as an industrial art form, this section offers the opportunity to pause and move outwards, painting a more complete picture of the film's reception and its place in Hollywood during the 1930s and early 1940s.

In Chapter 6, Sadeen Elyas highlights how Disney's debut animated feature prompted a sonic revolution in US filmmaking practice through its identity as very much a Hollywood musical. As a genre, the musical had already solidified as a lucrative product within Hollywood's substantial Fordian economy (though as Barry Keith Grant notes, 'English cinema made musicals, particularly during the 1930s', though he dismisses them as 'largely undistinguished quickies').[51] However, Elyas argues that within the history of Hollywood cinema, *Snow White* was one of the first (if not *the* first) fully 'integrated' film musicals in terms of its songs and musical score. By utilizing historical sources related to the production of *Snow White* and the Hollywood musical genre, and situating them alongside material drawn from musicology, Elyas examines Disney's position among other US studios during the first major era of Hollywood's use of sound. This allows a closer critical investigation into the complexity of *Snow White*'s soundscape, one that – as a tale as old as time – has often pivoted on the studio's synchronization of sound and image that marked out Disney from its Golden Age contemporaries.

The next two chapters discuss the ways that *Snow White* was symptomatic of the culture that produced it and how the film represented a response to factors external to the Disney studio: the diminishing returns of short-form animation and the Depression of the 1930s. In Chapter 7, Pamela O'Brien discusses Disney's recognition that changing audiences and distribution agreements had limited the commercial viability of animated shorts. O'Brien details the efforts made by Walt himself to ensure a return on his investment in feature-length animation, which includes the marketing strategies adopted to promote the release of *Snow White*. Disney's increasing appetite to merchandise his studio's productions through licensing deals and ancillary consumer products was an agenda that saw Walt's adaptation of the *Snow White* fairy tale prioritize characters that would connect with audiences, while supporting broad marketing and branding efforts. O'Brien therefore shows how Disney was able to tie the film and its marketing into the sociocultural context of the late 1930s in the United States to improve the film and merchandise's chance for success. In Chapter 8, Jane Batkin situates Disney's film against the backdrop of Depression-era America, dissecting US culture of the time and the contradictions of restraint and change that defined the 1930s to identify how *Snow White* came to represent an acute expression of Americana. Batkin argues that *Snow White* spoke directly to an American identity in the 1930s as one of crisis, thereby shaping the film into a powerful cultural text that functioned as a transformative turning point in US national identity. *Snow White* is, for Batkin, a film that captures a critical moment in American history by ultimately looking back, with Disney presenting a solution rooted in a nostalgia for nature, hard work, routine and collectivism that comes together to preserve (and celebrate) the American Way.

The final chapter of this middle section anticipates those that follow by shifting critical focus, looking forward to the many afterlives of Disney's cel-animated debut. The seismic cultural impact of the film has been a mainstay of its historical narrative, and the 'standard account that *Snow White* was universally considered a masterpiece is generally accurate'.[52] In Chapter 9, Terry Lindvall charts the journey taken by *Snow White* from a landmark of 1930s Hollywood cinema to its status as a dominant catalyst for extreme parodic enquiry. Lindvall's aim is to illuminate the many animation artists working within different national contexts and filmmaking traditions that have paid regular homage to Disney's fairy-tale adaptation. This includes the work of Bob Clampett in his *Coal Black and de Sebben Dwarfs* (1943) – a film produced by Leon Schlesinger and one of the controversial 'Censored Eleven' shorts now removed from circulation – and the more recent shorts of Italian filmmakers Bruno Bozzetto and Guido Manuli. Theories of film parody have often identified its form as an imitative genre whose structures of comedic intent are rooted in a fundamental process of recontextualization that supports its achievements of 'logical absurdity'.[53] However, Lindvall argues that the many playful reinterpretations and reworkings of Disney's *Snow White* – both within and beyond Hollywood – serve to draw attention to the ideological framing and politics of identity supporting Disney's film, including its otherwise invisible discourse of whiteness. Yet the sheer volume of animated media that take the specificity of Disney's adaptation as its target equally strengthens the identity of animation as a rigorous device of parody and a medium whose mutable and subversive potential is well-matched to the implausible distortions, heightened reflexivity and intertextual charge typically required of humorous parodic action.

International legacies

It is a 'tale as old as time' that the impact of Disney's *Snow White* was felt most emphatically across Hollywood, galvanizing the studio as a major force in US animation at the same time as its influence reached beyond the filmmaking system that created it. Robin Allan argues that the release of *Snow White* 'shifted' (albeit 'slightly') the course of cinema in the US context, and he notes that 'not only was it a product of the studio system itself but it would in turn influence that system'.[54] Yet *Snow White*'s 'many waves of influence' and cultural impact across 'popular musical form, literature, art and commerce' can, of course, equally be attributed to the durability of the original fairy tale. The folkloric heritage of fairy tales, as rooted in the oral telling and retelling of stories, therefore comes to bear on the 'pleasure of recognition' that accompanies fairy-tale narratives and perhaps accounts for their modality as ahistorical, formulaic and flexible texts readily adaptable to the new conditions and historical moments that produce and re-enchant them.[55] Jack Zipes argues that, as a classical text, there has 'been a wave of fairy-tale films about Snow White' since the first adaptation by Siegmund Lubin in July 1902 (the first screen version of a Grimm story), particularly in the twenty-first century as part of a broader 'tsunami' of adaptations that have further secured the fairy tale as an ever-popular filmmaking phenomenon.[56]

The *Snow White* narrative has appeared in American productions such as *Snow White: A Tale of Terror* (Michael Cohn, 1997), *Happily N'Ever After 2: Snow White – Another Bite at the Apple* (Steven E. Gordon and Boyd Kirkland, 2009), *Mirror, Mirror* (Tarsem Singh, 2012), *Snow White: A Deadly Summer* (David DeCoteau, 2012), *Grimm's Snow White* (Rachel Lee Goldenberg, 2012), *Snow White and the Huntsman* (Rupert Sanders, 2012) – and its more recent sequel *The Huntsman: Winter's War* (Cedric Nicolas-Troyan, 2016) – and a variety of international versions too. In addition to the Italian feature *The Seven Dwarfs to the Rescue* (Paolo W. Tamburella, 1951), there are at least three live-action German adaptations released in 1955, 1959 and 1962 directed by Erich Kobler, Fritz Genschow and Gottfriend Kolditz, respectively; another German comedy titled *7 Dwarves – Men Alone in the Wood* (Otto Waalkes, 2004) that itself prompted two sequels *7 Dwarves: The Forest Is Not Enough* (Sven Unterwaldt, 2006) and the digitally animated *The Seventh Dwarf* (Boris Aljinovic and Harald Siepermann, 2014); adult French animated feature *Snow White: The Sequel* (Picha, 2007) that reinterprets the fairy tale as a broad sex comedy; Spanish black-and-white drama *Blancanieves* (Pablo Berger, 2012); *Lilet Never Happened* (Jacco Groen, 2012), produced in the Netherlands and the Philippines that examines child prostitution in the capital Manila; and the recent computer-animated film *Red Shoes and the Seven Dwarfs* (Sung Ho Hong and Moo-Hyun Jang, 2019) by South Korean animation and VFX studio Locus.

Given *Snow White*'s pervasive international circulation, part three of the collection is devoted to the specificity of Disney's animated adaptation by plotting its extensive global influence beyond the institutional parameters of Hollywood, thereby approaching and evaluating *Snow White*'s tentacular reach across discrete national borders and its movement into alternate filmmaking traditions. If recent shifts within national cinema discourse have begun to push against the fixity and coherency of 'the national' as a practice, then the aim of 'International Legacies' can be understood as similarly informed by this methodological project. Authors identify *Snow*

White's complex identity as both an American cultural product based on a European folk tale *and* a transnational feature, one whose mobility and presence within new institutional limits is intensely related to the effects of globalization on cultural production. In Chapter 10, for example, Yuanyuan Chen identifies how *Snow White* was interpreted and indigenized in China during the 1930s and 1940s, quickly evolving into a phenomenon across Chinese media culture. For Chen, *Snow White* and its characters experienced increasing visibility in local print advertising (with 'Snow White' even registered as a trademark for local products) to coincide with its 1938 release in the country. The film also exerted its influence over two Chinese features that are the main focus of the chapter: the live-action remake *Chinese Snow White* (Wu Yonggang, 1940), produced by the Xinhua Film Company, and the first Asian animated feature-length film *Princess Iron Fan* (Wan Guchan and Wan Laiming, 1941), just two examples that reflect *Snow White*'s immediate impact upon Chinese film and animation industries.

The push–pull relationship in *Snow White*'s international circulation between local and global elements is continued by Greg Philip and Sébastien Roffat, who frame a discussion of the specificity of culture and aesthetics through their own restoration project and work with private collectors to recover the original French dub of Disney's *Snow White*. In Chapter 11, Philip and Roffat present new research surrounding this first French version and how the film's Francophone release was altered to attract prospective local audiences. They discuss the original film's French release on 6 May 1938 in the Marignan cinema Paris on the Champs-Elysées alongside its less-than-favourable reception by French critics and intellectuals that targeted Disney's unwavering pursuit of 'photographic' realism. Using extensive archival material, Philip and Roffat also compare the many versions of the film to identify clear shifts in aesthetic style, including reanimated scenes and the redesign of visual elements, which served to cater to international audiences. This chapter therefore illuminates what makes this rare French version of Disney's *Snow White* so historically significant, detailing the specific technical and artistic merits that are revealed by its recent rediscovery.

In Chapter 12, authors Priscila Mana Vaz, Janderson Pereira Toth and Thaiane de Oliveira Moreira engage with the arrival of Disney's *Snow White* in Brazil, doing so through the film's contemporary recuperation by LGBTQ communities across Brazilian social media. Placing representation in Disney's animated feature films within the Vito Russo Test (that measures the prominence of LGBTQ+ characters across media products), Mana Vaz, Pereira Toth and de Oliveira Moreira argue that queer communities have begun to co-opt Disney's iconic characters as a way of reframing the studio's traditionally conservative treatment of gender and sexuality. Drawing on social network analysis and data extracted from YouTube, their analysis of *Snow White* focuses particularly on online responses to the release of

Over the Rainbow: Um Livro de Contos de Fadxs, a 2016 book written by a collective of Brazilian authors that combines *Snow White* with LGBTQ narratives, themes and identities. One of these stories – titled 'The Resurrection of Júlia' – includes the relationship between a transgender girl and her stepmother, thereby aligning LGBTQ representation with the fairy tale to radically question identity and non-normative bodies in ways not previously explored by Disney in its animated characters.

In Chapter 13, Daniël Biltereyst offers a comparative study of cross-national/cultural differences by examining both the reception and censorship of Disney's *Snow White* in the UK and the Low Countries (specifically Belgium and the Netherlands). The chapter engages specifically with material from archives in Belgium (Royal Archives, Royal Film Archive, KADOC) and the Netherlands (Royal Library, Cinema Context) as a way of mapping *Snow White*'s often problematic historical reception and press coverage. Biltereyst's aim is to chart the Disney film's censorship history across the Low Countries as a small, but significant, element of the studio's European marketing reach, using *Snow White* as a milestone in the history of children's popular culture to discuss Hollywood's internal censorship system, cultural hegemony and conflictual relationship with Europe. The chapter also seeks to connect archival material to wider issues of public morality and Disney's own commercial imperatives, identifying *Snow White* as a feature film to which issues connected to new cinema historiography (film exhibition, programming and the social experience of cinema) are particularly central.

The collection's closing two chapters each expound the international influence of Disney's *Snow White* through close textual analysis of, and comparison between, multiple adaptations within popular film and television. In Chapter 14, Irene Raya Bravo and Maria del Mar Rubio-Hernández identify very recent transformations of the Disney feature in Spain by discussing two prominent case studies – Pablo Berger's 2012 film *Blancanieves* and an episode of the television series *Cuéntame un cuento* titled 'Blancanieves' (Iñaki Peñafiel, 2014) broadcast on Antena 3 Televisión. The authors argue that while Berger's adaptation inherits the character stereotypes drawn from the generalizing 'la españolada' discourse supporting national folklore, the 'Blancanieves' episode reworks the space and gender politics of Disney's version, doing so within the media context of a generalist channel on Spanish broadcast television. The section's closing chapter, written by Zeynep Gültekin Akçay, similarly relocates Disney's *Snow White* beyond the industrial structures of Hollywood, this time situating the film firmly within the storytelling traditions of Turkish cinema. In Chapter 15, Akçay works through numerous contemporary adaptations of the film as a way of discussing transnational textual references and the hybridity of style. The focus here is three highly popular adaptations produced for Turkish audiences – *Pamuk Prenses ve 7 cüceler/Snow White and Seven Dwarfs*

(Ertem Göreç, 1971), *Komser Sekspir/Police Chief Shakespeare* (Sinan Çetin, 2000) and *Anlat Istanbul/Istanbul Tales* (Selim Demirdelen, Kudret Sabancı, Ümit Ünal, Yücel Yolcu and Ömür Atay, 2004) – that were overwhelmingly inspired by Disney's animated adaptation rather than the original Brothers Grimm story. As with many international adaptations of Disney's cel-animated film, each of these Turkish reimaginings was also interlaced with local storytelling elements (including the fictional figure of the Keloğlan typical of Turkish stories). By examining the variant combinations of Disney storytelling structures together with national folkloric traditions in Spanish and Turkish productions, these two chapters argue both for the timelessness of the Brothers Grimm original tale, and how popular and enduring fairy tales such as *Snow White* always belong to different cultural contexts and historical moments.

'Go on, have a bite ...'

Writing back in 1999 in the introduction to their book *Deconstructing Disney*, Eleanor Byrne and Martin McQuillan playfully ask, 'At this late stage in the process of 'Advanced Capitalism', the conditions of 'postmodernity', the construction of the Disney oeuvre, and the practice of 'poststructuralist' inquiry, what is there left to say about the feature-length animations of the Disney corporation?' Despite Byrne and McQuillan's initial trepidation at a time when Disney Studies was imminently poised to enter the new millennium, more recent Disney scholarship produced over the last decade indicates that the studio and its animated features have lost none of their critical purchase, with *Snow White* remaining no less rife for 'deconstruction', 'demystification', 'debate' and 'discussion'.[57] *Snow White and the Seven Dwarfs: New Perspectives on Production, Reception, Legacy* is intended to continue the paths taken by this foundational scholarship and to be emphatic in plotting new ones. It expands a consideration of the aesthetic frameworks and formal characteristics of Disney animation, while using historical and cultural analyses to locate the film's Hollywood impact. It also navigates *Snow White* through the social and political climates of its development and identifies the broader structures of global production and distribution through which Disney's feature continues to move. This book therefore traces *Snow White* from the offices and workstations of the Disney studio located at 2701 Hyperion Avenue in Los Angeles during the 1930s, to its haunting of popular cinema in Turkey. In therefore making a virtue out of both the film's domestic movement within Hollywood and its migration across – and involvement with – national filmmaking traditions, *Snow White and the Seven Dwarfs: New Perspectives on Production, Reception, Legacy* interrogates a landmark film that, like the Queen's magical metamorphosis, has always changed its shape to assume any form.

Notes

1 Brothers Grimm ending to *Little Snow-White*.

2 The phraseology of 'fairy tale', 'fairytale', and 'fairy-tale' is used interchangeably throughout this book, both by the contributing authors and also within the secondary materials cited. No connotative importance is placed on this differing presentation.

3 Jonathan Frome, '*Snow White*: Critics and Criteria for the Animated Feature Film', *Quarterly Review of Film and Video* 30 (2013): 462.

4 Leonard Maltin, quoted ibid.

5 Janet Wasko, *Understanding Disney: The Manufacture of Fantasy* (Cambridge: Polity Press, 2001), 4.

6 Anon., 'Walt Disney Comes to the Valley', *Valley Progress: Community, Commercial, and Industrial Progress in the San Fernando Valley* (October 1939): 3.

7 J. B. Kaufman, '*Snow White and the Seven Dwarfs*', *Library of Congress – National Film Preservation Board Essays* (2015): 1–2.

8 Nicholas Sammond, *Babes in Tomorrowland: Walt Disney and the Making of the American Child, 1930–1960* (Durham: Duke University Press, 2005), 116.

9 Ibid.

10 Geoffrey Nowell-Smith, *The Oxford History of World Cinema* (Oxford: Oxford University Press, 1996), 270.

11 Eric Smoodin, 'Introduction', in *Disney Discourse: Producing the Magic Kingdom*, ed. Eric Smoodin (London: Routledge, 1994), 3.

12 Ibid.

13 Mark Langer, 'The Disney-Fleischer Dilemma: Product Differentiation and Technological Innovation', *Screen* 33 (1992): 354.

14 Ibid.

15 See Ray Pointer, *The Art and Inventions of Max Fleischer: American Animation Pioneer* (Jefferson, NC: McFarland, 2017). Pointer notes the 'economic warning signs' that surrounded the troubled production of *Mr. Bug Goes to Town*, including the film's cancelled release and Paramount's attempts to 'recover the remaining Fleischer debt' that reflected then then-Paramount president Barney Balaban's desire to 'duplicate Disney's successes without totally understanding them' (240).

16 Joseph Zornado, *Disney and the Dialectic of Desire: Fantasy as Social Practice* (London: Palgrave Macmillan, 2017), 70.

17 Alan Bryman, *The Disneyization of Society* (London: SAGE, 2004), 2.

18 Seán J. Harrington, *The Disney Fetish* (New Barnet: John Libbey, 2015), 73.

19 Wasko, *Understanding Disney*, 131; Jack Zipes, *The Enchanted Screen: The Unknown History of Fairy-Tale Films* (New York: Routledge, 2011), 257.

20   Anon., 'Disney's Princesses: From Snow White to Frozen', *Variety* (26 November 2013), available at https://variety.com/gallery/disneys-princesses-from-snow-white-to-frozen/; and Sydney Bucksbaum, 'The Evolution of Disney Princesses, from *Snow White* to *Frozen 2*', *Entertainment Weekly* (21 November 2019), available at https://ew.com/movies/disney-princesses-evolution/.

21   Richard Corliss, '*Tangled*: Disney's Ripping Rapunzel', *Time* (26 November 2010), available at http://content.time.com/time/arts/article/0,8599,2033166,00.html. See also Tasha Robinson, 'Moana Review: After 80 Years of Experiments, Disney Has Made the Perfect Disney Movie', *The Verge* (26 November 2016), available at https://www.theverge.com/2016/11/26/13749060/moana-film-review-walt-disney-animation-dwayne-johnson-diversity.

22   Justin Chang, 'The Princess and the Frog', *Variety* (24 November 2009), available at https://variety.com/2009/digital/features/the-princess-and-the-frog-1200477289/; and Brooks Barnes, 'Her Prince Has Come: Critics, Too', *New York Times* (29 May 2009), available at https://www.nytimes.com/2009/05/31/fashion/31disney.html.

23   Chris Pallant, 'Disney-Formalism: Rethinking "Classic Disney"', *animation: an interdisciplinary journal 5* (3) (2010): 342.

24   Ibid., 345.

25   Eric Smoodin, *Snow White and the Seven Dwarfs* (London: Palgrave Macmillan, 2012), 30.

26   Annette Kuhn, '*Snow White* in 1930s Britain', *Journal of British Cinema and Television 7* (2) (2010): 183.

27   Ibid., 189.

28   Leonard Maltin, *Of Mice and Magic: A History of American Animated Cartoons* (New York: McGraw-Hill, 1980), 51.

29   Smoodin, 'Introduction', 4.

30   Wasko, *Understanding Disney*, 156–7. In 1999, Eleanor Byrne and Martin McQuillan cautioned against this notable increase in scholarly writing on the studio, claiming it is only a matter of time before Disney scholars adopt a 'baroque critical strategy' that links Walt Disney 'to the assassination of J.F. Kennedy and the production of anti-personnel landmines'. Eleanor Byrne and Martin McQuillan, *Deconstructing Disney* (London: Pluto Press, 1999), 1.

31   Richard Neupert, 'Painting a Plausible World: Disney's Color Prototypes', in Smoodin, *Disney Discourse*, 114.

32   David Forgacs, 'Disney Animation and the Business of Childhood', *Screen* 33, no. 4 (1992): 366.

33   Ariel Dorfman and Armand Mattelart, *How to Read Donald Duck: Imperialist Ideology in the Disney Comic* (trans. David Kunzle, New York: International General, 1975), originally published as *Para Leer al Pato Donald* (Ediciones Universitarias de Valparíso, 1971).

34 Elizabeth Bell, Lynda Haas and Laura Sells, 'Introduction', in *From Mouse to Mermaid: The Politics of Film, Gender, and Culture*, ed. Elizabeth Bell, Lynda Haas and Laura Sells (Bloomington: Indiana University Press, 1995), 2–3. See also the essays collected in Johnson Cheu, *Diversity in Disney Films: Critical Essays on Race, Ethnicity, Gender, Sexuality and Disability* (Jefferson, NC: McFarland, 2013).

35 Elizabeth Bell, 'Somatexts at the Disney Shop: Constructing the Pentimentos of Women's Animated Bodies', in *From Mouse to Mermaid*, 167.

36 Cassandra Stover, 'Damsels and Heroines: The Conundrum of the Post-Feminist Disney Princess', *LUX: A Journal of Transdisciplinary Writing and Research* 2, no. 1 (2013): 1.

37 Ibid., 5.

38 Sammond, *Babes in Tomorrowland*, 116.

39 Smoodin, *Snow White and the Seven Dwarfs*, 30–1.

40 Mindy Johnson, *Ink & Paint: The Women of Walt Disney's Animation* (Glendale: Disney Editions, 2017); and Nathalia Holt, *The Queens of Animation: The Untold Story of the Women* (London: Little, Brown Book Group, 2019).

41 Patricia Zohn, 'Coloring the Kingdom', *Vanity Fair* (March 2010), available at https://www.vanityfair.com/culture/2010/03/disney-animation-girls-201003.

42 J. B. Kaufman, 'Before Snow White', *Film History* 5, no. 2 (June 1993): 158–75.

43 Ibid., 158.

44 Forgacs, 'Disney Animation and the Business of Childhood', 367.

45 David McGowan, 'Walt Disney Treasures or Mickey Mouse DVDs? Animatophilia, Nostalgia, and the Competing Representations of Theatrical Cartoon Shorts on Home Video', *animation: an interdisciplinary journal* 13, no. 1 (2018): 54.

46 Jason Scott, 'Disneyizing Home Entertainment Distribution', in *DVD, Blu-ray and Beyond: Navigating Formats and Platforms within Media Consumption*, ed. Jonathan Wroot and Andy Willis (London: Palgrave Macmillan, 2017), 20.

47 Gillian Youngs, 'The Ghost of Snow White', *International Feminist Journal of Politics* 1, no. 2 (1999): 311–14.

48 Eric Jenkins, *Special Affects: Cinema, Animation and the Translation of Consumer Culture* (Edinburgh: Edinburgh University Press, 2014), 110.

49 Ibid.

50 Michael Barrier, *The Animated Man: A Life of Walt Disney* (California: University of California Press, 2007), 123.

51 Barry Keith Grant, *The Hollywood Film Musical* (Oxford: Wiley-Blackwell, 2012), 5.

52 Frome, '"*Snow White*: Critics and Criteria for the Animated Feature Film'," 464.

53 Dan Harries, *Film Parody* (London: BFI, 2000), 9.

54 Robin Allan, '50 Years of *Snow White*', *Journal of Popular Film and Television* 15, no. (4) (1988): 156.

55 Jessica Tiffin, *Marvelous Geometry: Narrative and Metafiction in Modern Fairy Tale* (Detroit: Wayne State University Press, 2009), 144.

56 Jack Zipes, 'The Great Cultural Tsunami of Fairy-Tale Films', in *Fairy-Tale Films Beyond Disney: International Perspectives*, ed. Jack Zipes, Pauline Greenhill and Kendra Magnus-Johnson (London: Routledge, 2016), 4.

57 Byrne and McQuillan, *Deconstructing Disney*; Chris Pallant, *Demystifying Disney: A History of the Disney Feature Animation* (London: Bloomsbury, 2011); Douglas Brode and Shea T. Brode (eds), *Debating Disney: Pedagogical Perspectives on Commercial Cinema* (Lanham, MD: Rowman & Littlefield, 2016); and Amy M. Davis (ed.), *Discussing Disney* (Bloomington: Indiana University Press, 2019).

PART ONE

Innovation, technology and style

1

From Caligari to Disney: The legacy of German Expressionist cinema in *Snow White and the Seven Dwarfs*

Victoria Mullins

Life is composed of lights and shadows, and we would be untruthful, insincere, and saccharine if we tried to pretend there were no shadows. Most things are good, and they are the strongest things; but there are evil things too, and you are not doing a child a favor by trying to shield him from reality. The important thing is to teach a child that good can always triumph over evil.[1]

From Caligari to Disney

While film scholars routinely recognize the 'expressionist' aesthetic of *Snow White and the Seven Dwarfs* (1937), Disney's fairy-tale film has thus far eluded a sustained academic dialogue with German Expressionist cinema.[2] This is largely due to the variant sociopolitical contexts that envelop each area of study. *Snow White* – and, indeed, Disney animation at large – is both applauded and admonished as a reflection of Walt's own 'conservative … middle American values'.[3] German Expressionist cinema has, on the contrary, come to represent the collectively deflated psyche that permeated the Weimar Republic in the years immediately preceding Adolf Hitler's rise to power. In much the same way that America and Germany occupied oppositional sides in the First World War, so too have Disney animation and German Expressionist cinema come to represent and embody contrasting sociocultural values and climates, if not contrasting visual styles.

Adapted from the Grimm Brothers' 'Little Snow White' (first published in 1812), Disney's *Snow White* is based on an oral folktale that was first committed to print as part of a concerted effort to recover 'a German mythology and German attitude to life [in order to assert] what was German against the French occupying forces of the Napoleonic empire'.[4] Yet, created and released during the Great Depression that plagued America in the wake of the 1929 Wall Street Crash, Disney's version of the fairy tale has become ingrained in the cultural mythology of Walt Disney as 'an avuncular Horatio Alger figure'.[5] Dubbed 'Disney's Folly' throughout its ever-extending period of production, *Snow White* not only raised the Hollywood cartoon to a platform previously reserved for live-action cinema, it also 'reinvigorat[ed] one of America's most poignant national myths'.[6] Far from simply providing escapist fantasy during a time of cultural anxiety, *Snow White* transformed Walt Disney into a living personification of the American Dream.

In stark contrast, German Expressionist cinema, known as 'the world of light and shadow', is largely understood as a 'world of distorted perspectives, dreamscapes, murder, mayhem and menacing shadows' that reflects the 'dark side' of the collective German psyche during the sociopolitical uncertainty of the Weimar Republic (1919–33).[7] As Thomas Elaesser explains, this 'potent analogy between film culture and political history' is largely the result of two scholarly texts: Lotte H. Eisner's *The Haunted Screen* (1952) and Siegfried Kracauer's *From Caligari to Hitler* (1947).[8] Eisner's work focuses on the movement's aesthetic presentation of Romantic tensions between reality and the subjective 'German soule', yet Kracauer's text interprets recurrent plotlines and symbols within Weimar cinema as psychoanalytically charged reflections of the 'general retreat into a shell' mentality that Weimar Germany had inherited from the failure of the First World War and the disastrous effects of the Treaty of Versailles. Often taken together, Eisner and Kracauer's respective analyses created what Elaesser terms 'historical imaginaries' that see German Expressionist cinema consistently aligned with German nationalism and the rise of Nazism.[9]

Although *Snow White* and German Expressionist cinema were therefore both created during times of national trauma, they have been respectively aligned to the contrasting formations of American triumphalism and German defeatism. German Expressionist cinema is hailed for its visual presentation of 'that excess of soul ascribed to things "typically German"', yet Disney's simplification of the Grimm Brothers' 'Little Snow White' has led many folklorists to conclude that *Snow White* sees 'the German quality of the original tale [give] way to media fantasy'.[10] However, as this chapter shall demonstrate, while the simplification of (and deviation from) the Grimms' 'Little Snow White' allowed Disney to imbue their adaptation with specific 'Hollywoodizations', it also provided opportunities to give clear animated form to the 'dark shadows' found across German Expressionist filmmaking.

Animation is, in many ways, the most fully realized incarnation of the great Expressionist art director Hermann Warm's oft-quoted mantra that 'Films must be drawings brought to life.'[11] Unbound by corporeal reality, Disney animation in particular held what Sergei Eisenstein called a 'plasmatic' potential that affords the medium a unique ability 'to more persuasively show *subjective reality*'.[12] Nevertheless, while German Expressionist cinema is routinely applauded for its cohesive use of stylized sets, lighting and acting to reflect the psychological depths of both its characters and its audience,[13] *Snow White* is often analysed in terms of the attainment and subsequent consolidation of the 'Disney Style': an aesthetic that, frequently parodied and often criticized, is largely defined by the pursuit of 'hyperrealist' principles that appear to undermine the 'ideological freedoms' of the animated form.[14]

By exploring *Snow White* through the lens of German Expressionism, this chapter will argue that, in crafting the 'realistic' characters of *Snow White*, Walt Disney not only recognized animation's expressive potential but also actively encouraged his animators to draw upon Expressionist techniques in the production of their animated images. As he explained in a 1935 memo to Don Graham (a highly respected art teacher tasked with leading art classes for the Disney animators), 'In our animation we must show not only the actions or reactions of a character, but we must picture also with the action … the feeling of those characters.'[15] Through a close reading of *Snow White*'s most overtly 'expressionist' sequences (Snow White's forest flight and the Queen's transformation, as well as the relationship between these pivotal characters), this chapter will demonstrate that rather than 'simplifying' and 'Americanising' the Grimms' original German tale, Disney utilized the 'expressive' potential of animation (and the visual referents of German Expressionist filmmaking) to lend visual form to the psychological depths of the Grimms' inherently German source text.

The trees have eyes: Snow White's forest flight

Snow White's deployment of Classical Hollywood narrative conventions to amplify the heroine's romance with the Prince has fuelled a common critique of the film that 'Disney's focus on Snow White appears to extend no further than her willingness to fall in love.'[16] However, such critiques often fail to analyse the character of Snow White as an intrinsic part of the film's broader cinematic landscape. In reading *Snow White* through the lens of Expressionism, we can observe that, although Disney's inaugural Princess has been routinely admonished as a 'flat and one-dimensional' heroine, she plays an integral – and, indeed, active – role in shaping the landscape that surrounds her.[17] As Kristin Thompson explains, 'Expressionism lends the expressivity of the human body to the entire visual field, while simultaneously trying to make the body a purely compositional element.'[18] The apparent simplicity of Snow White's character (and her role as a reactive heroine) not only foregrounds the highly expressionist nature of the film's visual style but also affords her a depth of consciousness arguably not found among Disney's later, more 'active,' heroines. This formal relationship between German Expressionism and the visualization of Snow White's subconscious can be readily observed in her iconic forest flight.

Disney's cinematic portrayal of this sequence conforms to – and deviates from – the Grimm Brothers' original description. In the Grimms' version, the Huntsman, unable to kill Snow White himself, tells her to 'Just run off, you poor child', while resolving to himself that 'The wild animals will devour [her] before long.'[19] His thinking is practical: he will avoid staining his own hands with the princess's blood by leaving her to the predatory whims of the forest beasts. Snow White's reaction is rather unsurprising:

> She was so frightened that she has no idea where to turn. She started running and raced over sharp stones and through thorny bushes. Wild beasts hovered around her at times, but they did not harm her. She ran as fast as her legs would carry her. When night fell, she discovered a little cottage and went inside to rest.[20]

Within the Grimms' forest, Snow White is both frightened by the Queen's vendetta and facing the genuine and constant threat of predators. In Disney's reimagining of the sequence, however, the predatory threat is presented as symptomatic of Snow White's compromised state of mind: the terrifying forest is sculpted by the heroine's fear of falling victim to the Queen's hatred. The trees with horrifying faces and snatching talons, the gaping mouth into which she falls, the snapping crocodile-logs that attack her as she dangles from a vine: they are the incarnation of Snow White's terror. Disney thus transforms the material threat of the Grimms' forest into a stylistic opportunity to demonstrate Snow White's overwhelming sense of danger.

To visually present Snow White's terror, Disney borrows heavily from the stylistic repertoire of German Expressionist cinema. Marc Davis, one of Snow White's central character animators, recalls that Walt Disney hired a cinema auditorium during the film's production, in which he and the lead animators watched:

Anything that might produce growth, that might be stimulating – the cutting of the scenes, the staging, how a group of scenes were put together … *The Cabinet of Dr. Caligari*, *Nosferatu* were things that we saw. I remember *Metropolis* … I would never want to see this film again because it had a very strong impact on me. I have built it up in my mind and want to leave it that way.[21]

Davis's account verifies how key works of German Expressionist cinema were used as vital sources of visual inspiration during *Snow White*'s production. It also evidences a strong link between Fritz Lang's *Metropolis* and Snow White's forest flight. The 'strong impact' that Lang's treatise on technology had on Davis manifests in the crescendo of predatory eyes that overwhelm Snow White, causing her to collapse in terror. The sequence parallels *Metropolis*' iconic use of an eye-montage when the imposter, robot-Maria, dances erotically in a men's club (see Figure 1.1).

A compilation of the lustful stares of the high-society males watching robot-Maria's dance, *Metropolis*'s eye-montage is – as Andrew Webber posits – 'an image of the consuming potency of the male gaze' that – thanks to robot-Maria's position as a bachelor machine 'put on show by her "father"' – can be understood as a reproduction of the 'uncanny effects of the proliferation of eyes, organic and artificial' in the German Romantic author E. T. A. Hoffman's *The Sandman* (1816).[22] In both Hoffman's short story and Lang's film, the sense of unfamiliar familiarity encapsulated in the concept of the uncanny is linked to automata, because, in blurring the boundary between human and humanoid, they lead us to question 'whether an apparently animate being is really alive; or conversely, whether a lifeless object might not be in fact animate'.[23] Snow White is, in both a literal and philosophical sense in this 'forest-flight' sequence, an *animated* figure. Although a Rotoscoped human figure rendered through a series of drawings, Snow White is not the source of the uncanny feelings in others. Instead, the sense of uncanny that pervades her is reflective of her own reactive emotional state. By therefore observing the differences between Lang's and Disney's respective eye-montages, we can come to understand how the animators moved towards striking Expressionist imagery to imbue the doubly 'animated' Snow White with the 'Illusion of Life'.

As Disney animators Frank Thomas and Ollie Johnston have explained, the 'Illusion of Life' is dependent upon the animators' ability 'to make the audience *feel* the emotions of the characters, rather than appreciate them intellectually'.[24] To achieve this audience involvement in *Snow White*, the Disney animators draw upon Expressionist techniques. By Eisner's account, Expressionism can present both 'an extreme form of subjectivism [and] the complete abstraction of the individual'.[25] As the Disney animators utilize Expressionist techniques to transform the forest landscape into an active pursuer against which the heroine can react, I suggest that both a sense of

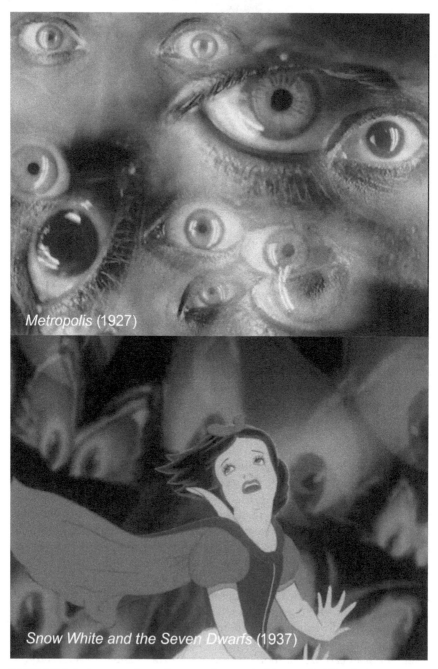

FIGURE 1.1 A comparison of composite eyes in *Metropolis* (Fritz Lang, 1927) and *Snow White and the Seven Dwarfs* (David Hand, 1937).

subjectivity and individual abstraction are inherent in Snow White's forest flight. As she reacts against the forest, her subjective fear is presented in abstracted form. Although found in preceding film movements, the use of 'montage sequences of empty landscapes [and] superimpositions to denote subjective states' is a well-established technique in German Expressionist filmmaking.[26] By superimposing gaunt faces onto the trees and logs, while intercutting point-of-view shots with images of the terrified Snow White framed using Dutch angles, the Disney animators are able to use the hostile vision of the forest to effectively dramatize the princess's inner turmoil.

As a culmination of point-of-view shots that see the terrifying tree faces quickly consume the screen as they occupy Snow White's mindset, *Snow White*'s eye-montage draws on both the notion of the consuming (male) gaze and the uncanny that Webber reads in the Expressionist imagery of *Metropolis* but employs them to contrasting effect (see Figure 1.1). Whereas Lang's eye-montage, standing alone, reinforces the control robot-Maria exerts over the lusting men, Disney's eye-montage visually overwhelms Snow White, reinforcing her victimhood. Snow White is innocent, rather than a '*femme fatale*, whore, and rabble-rouser' like robot-Maria.[27] The forest's multiplying eyes in this sequence are therefore used to reflect Snow White's all-consuming fear, as opposed to the all-consuming desire she inspires from this now animated landscape. Where the 'consumptive' gazes that fall upon Lang's robot-Maria and Hoffman's bachelor-machine Olimpia emanate from men's carnal desires, the gaze that befalls Snow White appears predatory because the eyes are animated in a style suggestive of the 'wild beasts' within the Grimms' forest. Lang's eye-montage operates as part of *Metropolis*'s Marxist critique, yet Disney's eye-montage collapses the boundary between reality and subjectivity, reflecting a tangible visualization of Snow White's horror unto the audience.

By using Expressionist techniques to transmute the forest into a monstrous manifestation of Snow White's inescapable fear, the animators are not only able to initiate the audience into Snow White's feelings of disorientating terror but also able to highlight the distinction between the heroine's subjective experience and 'reality'. As Walt Disney set out in a story meeting dated 27 June 1936,

> It would be good for her to be caught in the bushes showing these grotesque hands, then the wind and all the things that frighten her. Have it lead to things that make her think things are alive, but at the same time the audience should have a feeling that it's all in her mind … her imagination goes wild.[28]

The transition from 'subjectivity' to 'reality' is signalled as Snow White collapses onto the floor and the background turns to black. The following frame reinstates the 'reality' of Disney's animated world as Snow White, weeping on the floor, is now surrounded by several pairs of faceless eyes that, unlike those from her imagination, are not nightmarish but cartoony. As the shot pans outwards, warmth is slowly injected into the previously cold and dark colour palette, presenting this shift from interiority to 'reality' as a move away from terror and towards comfort. This is reinforced as the subsequent scenes give faces to the floating eyes: first, three shocked-looking rabbits and two chipmunks step forward into the scene's newfound light; they are followed by more chipmunks, some squirrels and deer. Where Snow White had imagined the predatory gaze of the Grimms' fairy-tale forest, Disney unveils the 'reality' of tame, jovial creatures that inhabit the forest of its own making. Snow White is soon surrounded by a flurry of the gentlest of forest inhabitants, who, learning that she is not a threat, move to comfort her. *Snow White* thus presents the uncanny through the juxtaposition of Expressionism and the familiar hyperreal 'Disneyfication' of nature. To a contemporary audience, however, the uncanny significance of the distinction between 'Expressionism' and 'Disneyfication' was much more profound.

The uncanny is derived from the German *unheimlich*: an inversion of the *heimlich*, which, in the original high German usage, means 'belonging to the house'. When understood in these terms, Disney's eye-montage is also imbued with a self-reflective sense of the uncanny. Prior to *Snow White*'s release, Disney was known primarily for its Mickey Mouse and *Silly Symphony* shorts, which – building upon the carnivalesque 'Cartoonland' in Walt Disney's earlier *Alice Comedies* short series (1923–7) – were largely characterized by anthropomorphized animals and plants that were rendered with a metamorphic, 'plasmatic' freedom of style and form. The conjunction between Disney's anthropomorphized plants and animals and their metamorphic qualities was, in many senses, not simply stylistic but a defining feature around which much of these short subjects were based. This is especially apparent in those *Silly Symphonies* based upon the springtime season. The plot structures of shorts *Springtime* (Ub Iwerks, 1929), *Flowers and Trees* (Burt Gillett, 1932) and *The Goddess of Spring* (Wilfred Jackson, 1934), for example, all used nature to mirror the cyclical state of the seasons. Harmonious nature, first abounding with images of animals, flowers and trees dancing to life in a jovial spirit, is then set upon and disrupted by disagreeable spirits – such as the arsonist snake-tongued tree, or the devilish Hades who kidnaps the goddess Persephone to be his underworld queen – that are, in turn, overthrown as the conclusion sees nature restored to its idyllic springtime state.

Within *Snow White*, however, nature and its inhabitants are largely presented in a 'hyperrealistic' or – to borrow from Paul Wells – 'neo-realistic' style.[29] While Wells uses 'neo-realism' to highlight the studio's 'constant drive' away from the inherently abstract potential of animation 'towards ever greater notions of realism', André Bazin's historical conception of cinematic 'neorealism' as style that embraces and portrays 'truth,' 'authenticity' and 'naturalness' is also a useful way to understand the set-up of this sequence. Although *Snow White* is, of course, a work of the imagination, and the animated form is inherently linked to the subjective, Disney presents its 'realistic' rendering of the natural world as a sort of 'truth'. While the metamorphoses of Disney's springtime *Silly Symphonies* offered an avant-garde reflection of the changing seasons, the transformation of *Snow White*'s forest reflects the 'unreality' of the heroine's compromised state of mind. Disney had previously employed the metamorphic potential of animation in conjunction with caricatured anthropomorphism. However, in Snow White's forest flight they draw a stark distinction between the two. As the forest's transformation is rendered through Expressionist techniques, the metamorphic potential of animation is made dependent on the heroine's fearful mindset. 'Neorealism', meanwhile, becomes the modus operandi through which nature's 'true' form is rendered. As Eisner writes, 'Expressionism sets itself against Naturalism ... and its paltry aim of photographic nature.'[30] By offering animated form to the aesthetic tensions between 'Expressionism' and 'Naturalism', Snow White's forest flight thus defines neorealism against the 'unreality' of Expressionism. The iconic sequence thus comes to stand as a sort of aesthetic watershed in which Disney's 'house' style of animation becomes the neo-realistic presentation of 'tame', 'joyful', anthropomorphized animals, while the plasmatic potential of animation, thus defined against neorealism, is made an expression of the uncanny.

As Snow White at last recognizes the 'true', non-threatening nature of the animals, she confides in them: 'You don't know what I've been through, and all because I was afraid. I'm so ashamed of the fuss I've made.' On this cue, the audience is invited to share in Snow White's sense of relief. Through the Expressionist presentation of Snow White's fear to first pervert the presentation of nature, Disney is able to offer its vision of cutely anthropomorphized animals as 'a drop of comfort, an instant of relief'.[31] By depicting Snow White as a reactive heroine to whom the audience's reaction can run parallel, Disney effectively prompts spectators to embrace its neorealism as a site of welcomed familiarity. Disney, through using the distinctive style of Expressionism, is thus able to mark the transition to neorealism as a shift from interiority to reality, from uncanny unreality to benign familiarity.

Snow White: *A Symphony of Horror*

The idea of 'nature' is evidently central to both the Grimm Brothers' tale and Disney's adaptation. Within Grimms' 'Little Snow White', Snow White's nature is linked to the queen because she likewise exhibits a destructive preoccupation with vanity. Following the folkloric rule of three, the Grimms'

Snow White suffers two additional near-death experiences. Disguising herself 'by staining her face and dressing up as an old woman', the queen first entices Snow White to try on corset staylaces tightened to the point of suffocation, then brushes a poisoned comb through her hair, before finally returning with an apple that has two sides: one red and poisoned, consumed by Snow White, the other white and un-poisoned, consumed by the queen. Exploring the symbolic significance of the shared apple, Joyce Thomas argues that Snow White and the Queen are linked in nature; the 'crucial similarities' of 'their sex, mutually dependent roles as protagonist and antagonist, beauty, vanity and association with the glass object' revealing the queen 'to be the dark shadow of Snow-White'.[32] In keeping with Carl Jung's archetypal shadow-self as the incarnation of negative personality traits from which the ego disassociates itself, the Grimms' queen stands as 'the incarnation and nightmarish exaggeration' of Snow White's own 'flaw' of vanity.[33] However, as Disney removes the queen's first two attempts to kill Snow White and justifies her consumption of the apple not by its beauty but by her belief that it is a 'magic wishing apple', the heroine's childish displays of vanity are expunged and 'the darkness of the Wicked Queen [is respectively] intensified and enlarged'.[34] Where the Grimms' Snow White is linked to the queen through her vain nature, Disney's Snow White is separated from the Evil Queen through her idyllic engagement with Disney's 'benign world of nature'.[35]

Snow White's own personal engagement with nature is evocative of the 'pastoral mode' within art and literature.[36] Although nature appears as a malevolent force throughout her forest flight, Snow White is subsequently reinvigorated through the help of her newly acquired animal helpers. As she sings and completes domestic chores alongside the animals, Snow White's purity is foregrounded, and she, like the nature that surrounds her, exists in a romanticized and idealized mode of being. The Queen, in stark contrast, is kept largely within the confines of her Gothic castle, transfixed by her vanity. Through rejecting nature, the Queen is made an 'unnatural' being. Snow White is sympathetically aligned to Disney's 'benign world of nature', but the Queen is contrastingly presented through Expressionist visuals that foreground the perverting influence of her monstrous narcissism and wicked power.

The Queen's extreme subjectivity is reflected in the architecture of her palace. This is made especially apparent in the film when a largely comical scene in which Snow White forces the dwarfs to clean themselves immediately transitions to a haunting shot of the palace's exterior, which visually recalls Dracula's Transylvanian residence within Tod Browning's 1931 film adaptation of Bram Stoker's 1897 novel. Through a series of overlaps, an image of the castle's window is overlaid upon an extreme close-up of the decorative box that holds what the Queen believes to be Snow White's heart. As the Queen learns from the mirror that Snow White is still alive, she immediately rushes down a grand and winding staircase. An architectural motif common in works of German Expressionist cinema, the staircase signifies a descent into the darkness that lurks in the 'landscape of the mind'.[37] The forbidding nature of its contents is highlighted as the perspective foregrounds the rats and cobwebs that dwell there. The Queen even goes momentarily out of shot, as the scene tracks the rats descending the stairway's hidden chains.

While *Snow White* has been critiqued for 'sanitizing' the Grimm source text, the presence of the rats not only initiates fright into the scene but also signifies the Queen's cannibalistic tendencies through aligning her with nature's 'meaner' creatures: an attribute that Stoker's Van Helsing describes as common among vampires. In particular, Disney's focus on the rats seems to visually echo an episode in F. W. Murnau's landmark German Expressionist film, *Nosferatu: A Symphony of Horror* (1922), in which both the boat's crew and the audience are made aware that the vampire Count Orlok has stowed away on a boat to Wismar by the rats that have grouped around his box-coffin. As Paul Coates suggests, the 'rats may be seen as [Orlok's] emissaries, [as they] are an aspect of the monstrous (unnatural) nature he seeks to shed so as to enter Western civilizations'.[38] However, with elongated teeth, ears and fingernails, Count Orlok has a grotesque rat-like appearance that showcases his monstrousness and obstructs him from effectively entering society. In foregrounding Orlok's unnatural existence, Murnau presented him utilizing an Expressionist aesthetic that jarringly juxtaposes the scenic shots of natural landscapes that make up the rest of the film.[39]

Disney's *Snow White* offers a similar contrast between the 'natural' and the 'unnatural' by presenting Snow White among Disney's 'benign world of nature', while rendering the Queen through Expressionist techniques and allusions that foreground her exclusion from Disney's natural order. As in *Nosferatu*, the rats function as the Queen's emissaries as they also exist outside of Disney's 'benign world of nature'. With haunting yellow eyes, they are unlike the characteristically cute anthropomorphized animals that befriend Snow White. While the Queen's monstrosity is not reflected in her appearance, her beauty is – as the Grimms' text states – 'decidedly unnatural because no simple no simple equation [is made] between the physical and the spiritual'.[40] The presence of the rats, therefore, signifies that the Queen, like Orlok, is going to shed her 'unnatural' visage so that she might enter Disney's 'benign world of nature'.

By overthrowing her coldly beautiful appearance, the Queen's transformation brings to light her monstrous nature. The scene invokes the German philosopher F. W. J. Schelling's sense of *unheimlich* as 'the name for everything that ought to have remained secret and hidden but has come to light'.[41] Within the Grimms' text, the queen descends 'into a remote, hidden chamber in which no one ever set foot' to make the poisoned apple.[42] By

Schelling's definition, the queen's chamber functions as a *heimlich* space, because it contains those things that 'good manners [have] oblige[d the Queen] to conceal'.[43] Yet, in visualizing the Queen's chamber, Disney's film necessarily amplifies the sense of *unheimlich* that is only hinted at by the Grimms, doing so by staging the chamber as a rather macabre laboratory. Adorned with a huge array of steaming flasks, skeleton imagery and a shelf of dark magic books, Disney's chamber visually recalls the laboratory setting of Dr. Henry Jekyll's iconic transformation scene in Rouben Mamoulian's *Dr. Jekyll and Mr. Hyde* (1931).

Although Mamoulian's *Jekyll* is a Hollywood production, both its cinematographer, Karl Struss, and its art director, Hans Dreier, were émigré German Expressionist filmmakers.[44] Primarily concerned with man's dualistic nature, Mamoulian's *Jekyll* employs an Expressionist aesthetic that sees 'portraits, mirror-images and shadows merged into one vision'.[45] As Mamoulian's film, in stark contrast to Robert Louis Stevenson's original novella, opens with an extended point-of-view shot from Jekyll's perspective, the first time we see him is through his mirror reflection. The first time we *truly* see Jekyll is when the camera switches to a spectator's vantage point as Jekyll delivers a public lecture in which he theorizes that 'man is not truly one, but truly two' and if the two were separated, the 'good' side would soar, while the 'evil' side 'would fulfil itself and trouble us no more'. Point-of-view shots and mirror reflections showcase Jekyll's interiority as he represses his baser instincts so that people perceive him as a charitable – even, saintly – man. Yet, as the creation of the Neanderthal-like Hyde means that Jekyll has an outlet for the 'base' behaviour he has previously repressed, Jekyll's first transformation scene offers the last instance in which both Jekyll's own point of view and reflection are shown. After he pens an apology to his love, Muriel, and walks over to a mirror, Jekyll's transformation is shot entirely from his point of view. An extreme close-up of the formula-filled glass is moved out-of-shot to unveil Jekyll's reflection (see Figure 1.2). As Jekyll walks towards the mirror, his reflection subsumes the screen and, from this perspective, we see him drink the formula, then stagger back from the mirror clasping his throat. Jekyll's disorientation is shown through a rapidly rotating camera as Expressionist superimpositions visualize a series of flashbacks in which Jekyll has fought his 'indecent' instincts.[46] As the point-of-view shot stabilizes, we hear heavy panting. When Jekyll returns to the mirror, it unveils Hyde's reflection, to which, Hyde, overcome with joy, proclaims: 'Free! Free at last!'

Walt Disney often expressed that he wanted the Queen's transformation in *Snow White* to be like 'a Jekyll and Hyde'.[47] Indeed, the sequence bears such striking similarity to that of Mamoulian's *Jekyll* that it is through exploring Disney's implementation of subtle deviations we can come to better understand the presentation of the Queen's villainy. In Disney's transformation scene, the Queen's reflection is shown directly in the

FIGURE 1.2 A comparison of reflections in *Dr. Jekyll and Mr. Hyde* (Rouben Mamoulian, 1931) and *Snow White and the Seven Dwarfs* (David Hand, 1937).

chalice containing her bubbling potion, as opposed to through a mirror (see Figure 1.2). The shot then zooms in, becoming fixed as the Queen's chalice-reflection subsumes the screen and she commands that the potion 'now begin thy magic spell'. This is the last time that we see the Queen's reflection, and its existence as a subtle deviation from Mamoulian's scene suggests that the Queen's transformed state both reflects her evil spirit and makes her feel less self-conscious. After drinking her potion, the Queen clasps at her throat. Her chalice smashes to the floor and the room begins to rotate, transforming into a swirling background that visually echoes the consumed potion. The Queen's choking visage is superimposed onto this scene, demonstrating how each frightful ingredient takes its effect. Unlike Mamoulian's *Jekyll*, the Disney animators do not utilize superimpositions to show the Queen's flashbacks, only close-up shots of her transforming hands and hair.[48] As Eisner explains, a recurrent plot device among German Expressionist films 'denies a personal life to all of the characters with whom the hero is in conflict'.[49] The Disney animators, in placing complete focus on the Queen's physical transformation, allow her only to exist insofar as she is consumed and motivated by hatred for Snow White. Thus, unlike Jekyll, the Queen does not have a 'good', or 'rational', half. Although her transformation scene bears striking similarity to that of Mamoulian's *Jekyll*, it is this departure that renders Disney's Queen a complete villain: only her appearance has transformed, not her soul.

While Jekyll came to pervert nature through science, the Queen in *Snow White* uses black magic to unveil her existence as a monstrous being. Disney concludes the Queen's transformation by focusing on the mutating shadow she casts upon the wall. As the Queen, suddenly speaking in a much older and more strained voice, exclaims, 'My voice! My voice!' the shot tracks along her mutating shadow, building up suspense before unveiling her transformed visage. Disney's focus on the Queen's shadow offers another allusion to *Nosferatu*, as it visually recalls Murnau's iconic use of *chiaroscuro* lighting to create an elongated shadow that forewarns of Orlok's presence when he enters the home of the protagonist, Thomas Hutter, to feast on the blood of his wife, Ellen (who sacrifices herself to ensure Orlok's sun-stricken demise). Disney's use of shadow thus not only heightens the suspense of unveiling the Queen's grotesque disguise, it also suggestively aligns her to cinema's inaugural vampire, highlighting her existence as the supernatural source of horror throughout the film. This is underscored as, when the scene fades to black, the Queen's eyes are left momentarily suspended (Figure 1.3). Visually piercing the screen, the Queen's eyes recall émigré Expressionist cinematographer Karl Freund's iconic use of lighting in Browning's *Dracula*. Freund, who was also the cinematographer for *Metropolis*, shone two flashlights into Bela Lugosi's eyes to give the visual impression of Dracula's hypnotic gaze (Figure 1.3).[50] Although, as Elsaesser has pointed out, it has become increasingly difficult to simply attribute the

Dracula (1931)

Snow White and the Seven Dwarfs (1937)

FIGURE 1.3 A comparison of eyes seen in *Dracula* (Todd Browning, 1931) and *Snow White and the Seven Dwarfs* (David Hand, 1937).

distinctive aesthetics of Hollywood horror and film noir to the influence of German Expressionism, we can recognize that Disney, through drawing upon Expressionist cinematographer Karl Freund's work in both Germany (*Metropolis*) and America (*Dracula*), creates a direct visual link between the Queen's looming eyes and Snow White's fearful visions. By exploring *Snow White* through the lens of Expressionist filmmaking, we can understand that the eyes proliferated in Snow White's forest flight are suggestive of the Queen's supernatural influence over the young heroine's unconscious.

The perversion of nature within Snow White's forest flight is, therefore, reflective of not only the heroine's innate fear, but also the power that the Queen wields over her as the source of that fear. As Whitley explains,

> even the branches seem to grasp at her [Snow White], their bony, finger-like structures reminiscent of the evil Queen's hands when she later transforms herself into the shape of an old hag. ... while she is in this [terrified] state Snow White's 'nature' is not just linked to the Queen's: it is subsumed by it.[51]

By understanding *Snow White*'s Expressionism through its links to the Queen's narcissism, Disney renders the Queen's existence as Snow White's 'dark shadow' in aesthetic terms. While the Grimms' queen showcased the 'evil side' of Snow White's personality, Disney draws upon the works of German Expressionism and its filmmakers to create a sense of *unheimlich* that renders Snow White a pure and familiar victim, and the Queen a complete and vampiric villain. After the Queen ultimately falls to her death, the Prince awakens Snow White with a kiss, and the pair, quite literally, ride off into the sunset. Disney's *Snow White* thus successfully showcases the morally dichotomous world that Mamoulian's Jekyll had envisioned, in which the good soar and evil extinguishes itself.

Conclusion: Walt Disney's world of light and shadow

While *Snow White*, as the 'prototype' from which all subsequent Disney animated features derived, is often taken as a milestone in its consolidation of the 'hyperrealist' principles of the 'Disney Style', their inaugural animated feature also initiated Expressionist techniques into the Disney's aesthetic repertoire. Disney film historian J. B. Kaufman states that *Snow White* (and, in particular, Snow White's forest flight) represents the studio's 'deepest foray into the world of expressionism'.[52] More recently, Disney animator Andreas Deja wrote an online piece titled 'German Expressionism and Disney', in which he playfully admitted that 'Someone needs to write a book on this topic.'[53] The influence of German Expressionist cinema on Disney animation made in the wake of *Snow White*'s success has been well-recorded,[54] particularly in relation to *Fantasia* (James Algar et al., 1940). Indeed, by giving animated form to the emotions created by classical pieces of music, *Fantasia* offers the most apparent treatment of Expressionism within Disney's animated canon. Yet, it is by no means an isolated example. Expressionism occupies a central role within Disney's animated language, providing the means through which Disney invests the often-archetypal characters of printed fairy tales with the 'Illusion of Life'. As Walt Disney himself set out, 'Story-wise, we sharpen the decisive triumph of good over evil ... in a romantic fashion, easily comprehended by children.'[55] Over eight decades since *Snow White*'s initial release, the Disney studio continues to give animated form to the time-old struggle between Good and Evil, 'familiar' and 'Other'. Given these relationships, Disney animators are consistently able to maximize the aesthetic and psychological dimensions of light and shadow, creating characters in which cross-generational audiences can invest their emotions. Through witnessing a character's hardships, we can rejoice in their triumphs. By witnessing evil, we are better equipped to embrace the good. More than simply providing a satisfying 'Happily Ever After', it is this ability to make the audience *feel* the emotions of animated figures that has made Disney such a powerful and culturally prevalent storyteller. In this way – to borrow from Walt Disney – Disney's 'moving pictures' have become 'more potent than volumes of familiar words in books'.[56]

Notes

1   Walt Disney, 'Deeds Rather Than Words', in *Faith Is a Star*, ed. Richard Gammon (New York: E. P. Dutton, 1963), 8.

2   For an example of a critical exploration of *Snow White*'s 'expressionist' aesthetic, see Thomas A. Nelson, 'Darkness in the Disney Look', *Literature/ Film Quarterly* 6, no. 2 (1978): 96.

3   David Whitley, 'Learning with Disney: Children's Animation and the Politics of Innocence', *Journal of Educational Media, Memory & Society* 5, no. 2 (2013): 75–6.

4   A. S. Byatt, 'Introduction', in *The Annotated Brothers Grimm* (The Bicentennial Edition), ed. and trans. Maria Tatar (London: W. W. Norton, 2014), xxviii.

5   Richard Schickel, *The Disney Version: The Life, Times, Art and Commerce of Walt Disney*. Revised and updated edition. (London: Pavilion Michael Joseph, 1986), 12.

6   Tracey Mollet, 'With a Smile and a Song ...': Walt Disney and the Birth of the American Fairy Tale', *Marvels and Tales* 27, no. 1 (2013): 23.

7   Thomas Elsaesser, *Weimar Cinema and After: Germany's Historical Imaginary* (London: Routledge, 2000), 61.

8   Ibid., 3.

9   Ibid., 18–60.

10 Ibid., 20; Simon J. Bronner, *Following Tradition: Folklore in the Discourse of American Culture* (Logan: Utah State University Press, 1998), 187.

11 Quoted in Siegfried Kracauer, *From Caligari to Hitler: A Psychological History of the German Film* (Princeton: Princeton University Press, 2014), 68.

12 Paul Wells, *Understanding Animation* (London: Routledge, 1998), 27 (emphasis original).

13 See Ian Roberts, *German Expressionist Cinema: The World of Light and Shadow* (London: Wallflower Press, 2008).

14 Wells, *Understanding Animation*, 3.

15 Quoted in Frank Thomas and Ollie Johnston, *The Illusion of Life: Disney Animation* (California: Disney Editions, 1984), 473.

16 Jane Batkin, *Identity in Animation: A Journey into Self, Difference, Culture and the Body* (London: Routledge, 2017), 36. For further analyses of Snow White's character, see: Elizabeth Bell, Lynda Haas and Laura Sells (eds), *From Mouse to Mermaid: The Politics of Film, Gender, and Culture* (Indianapolis: Indiana University Press, 1995); Tison Pugh and Susan Aronstein (eds), *The Disney Middle Ages: A Fairy-Tale and Fantasy Past* (Hampshire: Palgrave Macmillan, 2012); and Amy M. Davis, *Good Girls and Wicked Witches: Women in Disney's Feature Animation* (Eastleigh: John Libbey, 2006).

17 C. R. King, C. R. Lugo-Lugo and M. K. Bloodsworth-Lugo, *Animating Difference: Race, Gender, and Sexuality in Contemporary Films for Children* (Plymouth: Rowman & Littlefield, 2011), 95.

18 Kristin Thompson, *Eisenstein's Ivan the Terrible: A Neoformalist Analysis* (Princeton: Princeton University Press, 1982), 44.

19 Maria Tatar (ed. and trans.), *The Annotated Brothers Grimm* (London: W. W. Norton, 2014), 251.

20 Ibid.

21 Quoted in Robin R. Allan, *Walt Disney and Europe: European Influences on the Feature Films of Walt Disney* (Bloomington: Indiana University Press, 1999), 14.

22 Andrew Webber, 'Canning the Uncanny: The Construction of Visual Desire in *Metropolis*,' in *Fritz Lang's 'Metropolis': Cinematic Visions of Technology and Fear*, ed. Michael Minden and Holger Bachmann (Suffolk: Camden House, 2000), 266.

23 Ernst Jentsch, quoted in Freud, *The Uncanny*, 135.

24 Johnston and Thomas, *The Illusion of Life*, 22.

25 Lotte H. Eisner, *The Haunted Screen: Expressionism in German Cinema and the Influence of Max Reinhardt* (London: Thames and Hudson, 1969), 12.

26 Barry Salt, 'From Caligari to Who?', *Sight and Sound* 48, no. 2 (1979): 120.

27 Elsaesser, *BFI Film Classics: Metropolis* (London: BFI, 2000), 52.

28 Quoted in Allan, *Walt Disney and Europe*, 201.

29 Wells, *Understanding Animation*, 23.

30 Eisner, *The Haunted Screen*, 10.

31 Sergei Eisenstein, *Eisenstein on Disney*, ed. Jay Leyda, trans. Alan Upchurch (Calcutta: Seagull Books, 1986), 155.

32 Joyce Thomas, *Inside the Wolf's Belly: Aspects of the Fairy Tale* (Sheffield: Sheffield Academic Press, 1989), 73.

33 Ibid.

34 Nelson, 'Darkness in the Disney Look', 96.

35 Douglas Brode, *From Walt to Woodstock: How Disney Created Counterculture* (Austin: University of Texas Press, 2004), 201.

36 David Whitley, *The Idea of Nature in Disney Animation: From Snow White to WALL-E* (Surrey: Ashgate, 2012), 19–38.

37 Michael Walker, *Hitchcock's Motifs* (Amsterdam: Amsterdam University Press, 2014), 351.

38 Paul Coates, *The Gorgon's Gaze: German Cinema, Expressionism, and the Image of Horror* (Cambridge: Cambridge University Press, 1991), 94.

39 Count Orlok has often been interpreted as a supernatural incarnation of Weimar anxieties. For more information, see: Robin Wood, 'Burying the Undead: The Use and Obsolescence of Count Dracula' (2015), William F. Burns, 'From the Shadows: Nosferatu and the German Expressionist Aesthetic' (2016).

40 Thomas, *Inside the Wolf's Belly*, 69.

41 F. W. Schelling quoted in Freud, *The Uncanny*, 132.

42 Tatar (ed. and trans), *The Annotated Brothers Grimm*, 257.

43 Schelling quoted in Freud, *The Uncanny*, 132.

44 Hans Dreier was a long-standing friend and colleague of the iconic German Expressionist director Ernst Lubitsch, while Karl Struss had previously worked alongside both F. W. Murnau and *Caligari* co-screenwriter Carl Mayer on the Academy Award-winning film *Sunrise: A Song of Two Humans* (1927). F. W. Murnau and Carl Mayer had themselves made a German Expressionist Jekyll-and-Hyde film entitled *The Head of Janus* (1920), but it is now unfortunately lost.

45 Eisner, *The Haunted Screen*, 129.

46 The rapidly rotating camera in Rouben Mamoulian's *Dr. Jekyll and Mr. Hyde* (1931) is suggestive of F. W. Murnau's influence. Murnau, who believed that the camera is the filmmaker's pen, was known for his innovative and pioneering use of camera motion. (He famously tied a camera to a bike to achieve some footage used in *Nosferatu: A Symphony of Horror* [1922]).

47 Quoted in J. B. Kaufman, *The Fairest One of All: The Making of Walt Disney's Snow White and the Seven Dwarfs* (California: Walt Disney Family Foundation Press, 2012), 173.

48 The shot of the Queen's transforming hands is itself a reminder of Mamoulian's film, in which Jekyll consistently looks at his hands to confirm that he is transforming into Hyde. See Richard Dury's 'The Hand of Hyde' (2003).

49 Eisner, *The Haunted Screen*, 209.

50 For information about Karl Freund's use of Expressionism in *Dracula*, see Elisabeth Bronfen, 'Speaking with Eyes: Tod Browning's *Dracula* and Its Phantom Camera', in *The Films of Todd Browning*, ed. Bernd Herzogenrath (London: Black Dog, 2006).

51 Whitley, *The Idea of Nature in Disney Animation*, 21.

52 Kaufman, *The Fairest One of All*, 15.

53 Andreas Deja, 'German Expressionism and Disney', *Deja View* (12 May 2015), available at http://andreasdeja.blogspot.com/2016/05/german-expressionism-and-disney.html.

54 For a particularly in-depth reading of *Fantasia* and its use of Expressionist techniques, see Allan, *Walt Disney and Europe*, 91–174.

55 Quoted in Charles Solomon, *The Disney That Never Was: The Stories and Art from Five Decades of Unproduced Animation* (New York: Hyperion, 1995), 61.

56 Ibid.

2

From terrible toreadors to dwarfs and princesses: Forging Disney's style of animation

Stéphane Collignon and Ian Friend

As Hollywood shifted from slapstick to melodrama during the course of the 1930s, supported by the gradual addition of sound and colour, cinema audiences began to expect fuller, more believable cinematic experiences. Walt Disney's ambition was to be considered a filmmaker rather than *just* a cartoonist, and he was determined to take the challenge.[1] Throughout the *Silly Symphonies* (1929–39) series of cartoons, first, and then with the production of *Snow White and the Seven Dwarfs* (David Hand, 1937), the Disney studio began to improve and develop its animation workflow. The animation pipeline is traditionally a very complicated and time-consuming process, and character animation in particular requires a degree of labour, focused mental agility, skill and a keen observational understanding. While contemporary practitioners have at their disposal a number of digital and virtual tools designed to reduce such production times, the need for the swift execution of appealing and convincing animated performance requires more than technical proficiency and efficient animation tools. Animators have always recognized the need to draw from life, primarily as a research tool (from anatomical and motion studies to sketching) but also as a means to inform and inspire where the task at hand is the communication of a complex human emotion through modes of performance. Early animation studios were compelled to constantly innovate, contrive and develop in order to produce economically viable cartoons. However, leading the charge from the outset was the Disney studio, a collective of artists, designers and storytellers, firmly captained by the Disney brothers, who subsequently emerged as the most influential and renowned pioneers of hand-drawn character animation in the early twentieth century and beyond.

Focussing on elements of character design alongside the animation process (including, in particular, the rendition of movement), this chapter will discuss how Disney and his animators dealt with notions of reality and believability, while fine-tuning a representational style that would become a standard for animators all over the world. The first part of this chapter will therefore focus on Disney's quest for believable characters from the point of view of character design. It will explore the evolution of the studio's aesthetics from the *Silly Symphonies* to *Snow White and the Seven Dwarfs*, and the studio's desire to achieve the perfect balance of expressiveness and credibility in the pursuit of what could be described as 'emotional contagion', namely, the capacity of a character to invite the audience instinctively to feel its emotion as if by spectatorial infection. For Amy Coplan, 'emotional contagion' designates a sort of instant visual empathy independent from the knowledge of the story between viewer or perceiver and image.[2] Indeed, that capacity of the animated character to make us feel its emotion at a glance would become central to the long-standing appeal of Disney films. There is, of course, always the risk of teleology when analysing the development of the *Silly Symphonies* through to the arrival of feature-length cel-animation with *Snow White*. However, when one scrutinizes every short in the series made between 1929 and 1937, it is possible to notice that every now and then a new type of design is attempted, and that sometimes these variations become integrated into the general practice of the studio. Eventually a clear sense of the evolution of the studio's aesthetic style emerges, not a fluid linear process but as a more chaotic journey that leaps from one film to another, sometimes missing one, but ultimately keeping whatever new element that seems to improve the quality and believability of the films.

The second part of this chapter will concentrate on the legacy of the live-action referencing workflow pioneered in *Snow White* and will contextualize early rotoscoping efforts with current 'action analysis' techniques used extensively in the modern animation industry.[3] The action analysis workflow developed during Disney's first feature was initially devised to complement *Snow White*'s groundbreaking character design, allowing the animators to bring believable human animated characters to life. The technique evolved over time, developing into a house style for Disney's output that has become the centrepiece for analyses into the studio's particular style of cel-animation.

In his book on the Golden Age of Hollywood cartoons, for example, Michael Barrier cites *The Goddess of Spring* (Wilfred Jackson, 1934) as the first short film with which Disney initiated its research into creating a human character that would be credible enough to support an entire feature film.

However, the eponymous Spring Goddess is not the first human character to appear in a Silly Symphony short cartoon, neither does she demonstrate Disney studio's first engagement with representation of convincing human figures. While one must really wait until 1932, a change of distributor and a budget raise to witness a multiplication of human characters in Disney films, some attempts had already been made since the beginning of the *Silly Symphonies* in 1929 to tentatively represent human form.[4] By reviewing the shorts in the series starring a human cast, beginning with *El Terrible Toreador* (Walt Disney, 1929) up until the release of *Snow White*, it is possible to determine precisely how Disney animators progressively made the human shape in animation their own. This trajectory showcases their development of a character capable of triggering strong 'emotional contagion' and able to support the audience's attention for the duration of a feature film. As mentioned before, some may see in this attempt to draw more global trends out of the analysis of various, apparently isolated, *Silly Symphonies* a rather teleological approach towards the studio's formal evolution. However, it seems quite unlikely that a man as involved as Walt Disney was in the output of his studio, and with a true ambition to move animation forward, did not at least try to inspire a certain direction to the films. Through the works analysed here, a trend emerges in which the studio seemingly strived to create ever more verisimilar characters, capable of triggering true emotions within the audience and, certainly as of 1934, with the additional aim of maintaining this emotional state through the duration of a feature film.[5] Character design tests taking place at the Disney studio in the *Silly Symphonies* would, as this chapter argues, eventually lead to the development of the characters found in *Snow White* that became the standard for realistic animation, imposing with it a new aesthetic style still at the centre of the animation industry today.[6]

Achieving likeable human character design

Released in September 1929, *El Terrible Toreador* is the second of Disney's Silly Symphonies, but the first to explore the representation of human characters. In this short film, Disney animators still demonstrate their commitment to a 'Rubber Hose' style typical of the period, one firmly rooted in the bodily potential of slapstick humour. Character design in the film, animal as well as human, is given the same approach: a sort of potato-shaped body out of which sprout four flexible tubes (or rubber hoses) figuring the arms and legs. Only the head and clothes allow spectators to really distinguish the protagonists. Character design here is actually still placed as secondary, or at least reduced to simple visual archetypes. Movements are fluid and supple to the detriment of anatomical constraints and proportions. Bodies can inflate, stretch and distort at will. The vast majority of the gags rely on the 'plasmaticity' of the bodies, an interpretation of 'rubberhosing' put forward by Sergei Eisenstein, who proposed that an important facet of the appeal of early Disney animation was the rejection of 'once and for all' fixed constraints of shape, and a freedom from ossification and a capacity to dynamically take any form.[7] Under this principle, character design is therefore entirely subordinate to the creativity of the animation, which in *El Terrible Toreador* achieves a sort of naive purity detached from any consideration other than the spectacle of movement on screen.

One must wait until February of 1930 and the release of the film *Autumn* (Ub Iwerks, 1930) to glimpse the studio's first real departure from the 'Rubber Hose' style. Indeed, as Barrier notes, 'Disney had understood that sound could make what was on screen appear more real.'[8] The studio therefore started to develop films with more elaborated narratives, meaning that comic gags were now not solely reliant upon the humour of bodily distortion. Animators thus endowed their characters with more stable bodies in service of a coherent story, rather than a simple succession of gags relying mostly on the 'plasmatic' qualities of the character. In order to sustain these new types of story, the studio also tried to create a new type of character design aimed at triggering a more nuanced and emotional response.

Mother Goose Melodies (Burt Gillett, 1931) was the first Silly Symphony since 1929 to mostly rely on a narrative of human characters. More interestingly, the film offered a couple of archetypal representations of human characters that would be repeated in a number of subsequent episodes. These representations offer, perhaps, a glimpse into the studio's creative process in attempting to produce more believable characters. The character of Old King Cole certainly constitutes a turning point in the construction of the 'human' at Disney. His physique is still largely reminiscent of the 'Rubber Hose' style, with one big round head with a button nose on top of an oversized round body with four tube-like arms and legs. However, the treatment of the body clearly takes its distance from the old style. *Mother Goose Melodies* does not rely nearly as much on the distortion, inflation or stretching of the body. The morphology of Old King Cole remains solid, and only through his design is he to express his bonhomie and quasi-constant joyfulness. This type of character would resurface in a number of subsequent Disney shorts, including *King Neptune* (Burt Gillett, 1932), *Santa's Workshop* (Wilfred Jackson, 1932), *Father Noah's Ark* (Wilfred Jackson, 1933), *Old King Cole* (David Hand, 1933), *The Night Before Christmas* (Wilfred Jackson, 1933), among many others. However, despite the recurring use of this archetype across numerous *Silly Symphonies*, it tends to stay fixed in an expression of everlasting joviality and can scarcely express or elicit different emotional reactions.

Another bodily archetype also appears in *Mother Goose Melodies*, that of Mother Goose herself. This character is composed of a much less rounded face (moving towards slightly bony) with marked details (prominent nose and chin) atop a rather slim body. Completely contrasting with the King Cole archetype, the Mother Goose design is used for witches or, more broadly speaking, mischievous characters. The archetype appears in *Babes in the Woods* (Burt Gillett, 1932), and even as a male character in both *Lullaby Land* (Wilfred Jackson, 1933) and *The Pied Piper* (Wilfred Jackson, 1933). These two characters' ultimate designs laid the foundation for more nuanced and intelligible personalities, an essential step in eventually creating characters 'verisimilar' enough to elicit a more invested response from the audience.

A third design archetype is introduced in the following Silly Symphony, *The China Plate* (Wilfred Jackson, 1931). The character of the little girl has a body that is relatively well proportioned but covered in loose clothing, thereby hiding her true shape. Her head is slightly inflated but is not treated in the flexible 'Rubber Hose' style. Her general shape remains solid. She has neither the exaggerated bonhomie of King Cole nor the slim and caricatural aspect of Mother Goose, and her main feature is that the animators avoid a detailed anatomical representation, focussing instead on more simplified lines. The head is inflated in a neotenic exaggeration, but not as much as in the other bodily archetypes or even in the 'Rubber Hose' style of physical distortion.[9] Although this type of character is still quite far from anything leaning towards verisimilar, it does however clearly mark the moving away from the exaggeration of 'Rubber Hose' and towards something ever so slightly more 'truthful' in its appearance, even if less expressive than the two previous archetypes. Francesco Casetti argues that the expressions 'truthful' and 'likely' are preferable to the vague and ambiguous term 'realist'. For Casetti, 'likely' refers to a representation that resembles something that exists (such as a portrait), while 'truthful' relates to a representation that looks like something that 'could' exist.[10] Disney repeated this 'truthful' way of dealing with youthful character design in several films, including *Babes in the Woods*, where it is used for the two main child protagonists of the story. The archetype was slightly adapted to accommodate adult characters too, being used for beautiful female characters such as the mermaids in *King Neptune* and the wives of Noah's sons in *Father Noah's Ark*.

Another interesting film in relation to Disney's evolution of a realist visual style is *The Clock Store* (Wilfred Jackson, 1931). Here, Disney animators clearly experiment by combining archetypes and pushing the designs of their human characters further. For the first time in the *Silly Symphonies* series, Disney presents two characters with anatomically 'correct' proportions and measures, correct with regard to the representational canons developed during the Renaissance pertaining to the bodily imitation of the real.[11] Of course, the whole body structure in such Disney animation remains quite simplified, but this is the first time the studio brings us characters showcasing a certain biological or anatomical truthfulness.

In early 1932, a rise in budgets allowed Disney to devote more time and personnel to each short film, resulting in a significant increase in the number of human characters, which were more difficult to convincingly draw and animate than other non-human characters.[12] Disney soon abandoned the 'Rubber Hose' style, wanting the character's design to elicit and maintain the interest of the spectator from the beginning to the end of the film. If narration remained one of the main factors behind creating empathy for the character, it was not enough, as Leonard Maltin explains: 'One of Walt's most important pursuits was the development of personality in cartoons. He wanted audiences to respond with a variety of emotions, and he knew that character credibility was a major ingredient for this kind of success.'[13] For Disney, character design was one of the most essential elements in order to emotionally engage the audience. However, the diverse character archetypes and formulas for design used so far by the studio in its *Silly Symphonies* had hardly managed to provoke anything but feelings of joviality and amusement in the audience. When required to represent characters that one might find beautiful or cute and still communicate their affect to the audience, and that would invite a 'willing suspension of disbelief' (over, perhaps, a feature film), Disney did not yet know 'how to animated them'.[14] The studio had yet to figure out how to create characters capable of truly triggering an emotional contagion, because as Barrier notes, 'characters of that kind did not exist in 1930'.[15] Yet things would change with the arrival of a new animator in particular.

Fred Moore joined the studio in August 1930 a month before turning 19. A naturally gifted draftsman, Moore slowly progressed under Ben Sharpsteen's tutelage and began to get credited work around 1932. His first major assignment came with *Three Little Pigs* in 1933, where he eventually managed to bring a part of the charm in his characterizations that Disney was looking for:[16] with animal characters and not human ones, admittedly, but it was already part of the answer. May 1933 marks a decisive step forward in terms of character animation and brings one of Disney's most important popular successes. *Three Little Pigs* does not contain any human characters, but Moore's input revolutionized animation of the time and allowed Disney in particular to fix a series of principles to create more plausible characters with more personality.[17] According to Michael Barrier, Moore based his drawing style on round and soft shapes, immediately inciting pleasant ideas and marking a departure from previous Disney aesthetics. These round shapes, contrary to Rubber Hose, more obviously suggest flesh over bones. Barrier adds that if bodies slightly distort while bouncing to the music, they maintain their initial volume.[18] For Barrier, within a few scenes at the beginning of *Three Little Pigs*, Moore significantly extended Disney's animated vocabulary. Maltin adds too that this film 'was just the beginning for Walt; he knew that he had just scratched the surface of animation's possibilities. From this point on, the *Silly Symphonies* revealed an ever-growing mastery of the film medium.' Most of all, the studio was preparing to move on to bigger and longer projects.[19]

Going for feature length

The early 1930s presents a turning point in the Disney studio's aesthetic research and evolution in its visual style. From the end of 1933 and into 1934, Disney clearly marked his intention to produce a feature-length film.[20] But for a feature film to be conceivable, Disney animators had to provide characters that were able to withstand comparison with successful 'live' actors and performers. The studio's animators therefore had to learn how to depict the whole range of human affects and emotions if they wanted to be able to grasp the attention of the audience for the duration of a feature film.[21] To that aim, Disney hired Don Graham, an art instructor from the Chouinard Art Institute in California, who since 1932 had been giving art classes to the animators. Disney hired Graham with the aim of not only training new animators but also sharpening the skills of the existing team of staff artists. Graham organized live model drawing classes, seminars, field trips to the zoo and improvement sessions for various specialized animators of the studio. Despite all this, however, a film like *The Flying Mouse* (David Hand, 1934) demonstrates how Disney perhaps still struggled with the credible representation of human characters. Contrary to the mouse – pleasing and triggering empathy – the fairy (a human character except for butterfly wings) feels stiff and unattractive.[22]

While the production of *Snow White* effectively got underway, Disney increasingly relied on the *Silly Symphonies* to give its teams the chance to develop new techniques. The greater sophistication achieved by the studio in layout and backgrounds was quickly matched by their ability to create new and sympathetic characters.[23] But Disney also needed truly credible characters, not just those that could be interpreted as cute or funny by the child audience. The studio's short *The Goddess of Spring* therefore became the first with a main human cast since *The Pied Piper*, and perhaps the first real attempt made by Disney at creating 'truthful' and credible human characters.[24] However, the characters in the film are almost inexpressive, especially the goddess, and their design is completely incoherent with that of the secondary cast. Indeed, the devil and the goddess are portrayed with realistic and anatomically correct proportions, albeit with a caricatural face for the devil, while the rest of the spring 'gnomes' and hell minions all showcase highly neotenic and altogether more 'cartoony' designs.

It was with non-human anthropomorphic characters that Disney animators took their next step forward. In November of 1934, Disney poached Grim Natwick from Ub Iwerks' studio with a view of working on *Snow White*. Natwick had first earned his stripes on one of the most interesting Silly

Symphonies of 1934–5 under the direction of Ben Sharpsteen, namely a film about anthropomorphic cookies titled *The Cookie Carnival* (Ben Sharpsteen, 1935). Although the story exclusively revolves around strongly anthropomorphic non-human characters, and even if the Sugar Cookie Girl first appears as a flat cookie, during her makeover into the future cookie queen she suddenly becomes so anthropomorphic and humanlike that one can hardly still see a cookie. From one frame to the next the anthropomorphic cookie becomes a human character marking the studio's progression towards realistic character representation. Natwick himself was responsible for this long makeover scene. He managed to imbue the Sugar Cookie girl with all the grace and charm that *The Goddess of Spring* was lacking. The character has more solidity and weight to her body and a lot more credibility, even though she remains a little 'cartoony' in her design, and as such she marks Disney's first attractive and expressive character.[25]

In February 1936, Fred Moore, who had started to bring more charm into the studio's animation with *Three Little Pigs*, began to fix the definitive design for *Snow White*'s dwarfs. In his original model sheets for the characters, they display button noses, large bellies and a physiognomy that barely resembles that of real dwarfs (though strongly reminiscent of the King Cole archetype). Indeed, until they were eventually provided with individual personalities, the dwarfs' highly neotenized features were unmistakably cute. Barrier adds, 'The dwarfs were prime material for an animator like Moore, whose work made its strongest impression through charm and cuteness. ... The dwarfs went through a neotenic evolution, growing younger (despite their white beards and jowls), cuddlier, and more immediately appealing.'[26] After spending the first half of the 1930s experimenting with several human character archetypes, the studio was now able to achieve satisfying results when animating children or cute characters. Disney began to experiment with the creation of more visually and behaviourally 'truthful' characters, working towards an increasing expressivity to the characters as a way to overcome their artificiality.

In the spring of 1936, Natwick also was transferred to work on *Snow White*. Around that time, all the talented artists of the studio began to work with Natwick in a special unit devoted solely to the character of Snow White, and for two months all they did was practice drawing her. However, the image of a very drawn and highly stylized Snow White remains.[27] According to Natwick, some 2,000 different drawings were made during the development of the character, before the animators began even starting to animate her movements.[28] The main difficulty presiding over any definitive design for the character lay in the fact that she was intended to be beautiful. However, studies in cognitive psychology, ethology and neuroscience seem to indicate that a certain level of exaggeration and simplification may increase the expressiveness of a character, and therefore its ability to convey emotional reactions. Gillian Rhodes states that in the field of ethology, research has shown that exaggerated signals are highly effective for a variety of recognition systems.[29] Patrick Power also explains that neuroaesthetic concepts such as the 'Peak Shift Effect' indicate how an aesthetic that he describes as 'expressive' (whose characteristics are isolated and exaggerated) can facilitate cognitive, creative and emotional engagement in the spectator.[30] Beauty however, for many scholars, lies in anti-caricature and averageness.[31] Anyone seeking to create a character that needs to be both beautiful and expressive is therefore faced with an impossible paradox, as beauty seems to rely on averaging out distinctive features, while heightened expressiveness requires the exact opposite.

Disney animator Hamilton Luske eventually reworked the rotoscoped image of Snow White to give her more caricatural proportions, with a larger head and therefore more youthful appearance, thus opting for a design tending towards neoteny rather than fidelity to a certain kind of pictorial realism.[32] Indeed, contrary to beauty, neoteny (that triggers cuteness and caring) can be enhanced and supported by caricature.[33] The character of Snow White finally took on lightly caricatural and neotenic traits (smaller size, larger head, bigger eyes). The Prince's design, however, remained more truthful and quite anti-caricatural in order to be charming. His representation is, perhaps, less expressive and is devoid of the degree of liveliness imbued into the *Snow White*'s other human characters.

Over the course of the 1930s and leading up to the release of *Snow White*, Disney reached a character design paradox: an over-simplified and caricatural design is not efficient because its artificiality is too obvious to allow for a true 'emotional contagion' of the audience. But each attempt at creating a truthful design proved a failure in terms of expressiveness, eventually revealing its own artificiality. Character designs such as those of the dwarfs, who were caricatural but not in such extremes as in the 'Rubber Hose' era of the shorts, held a certain consistency. As characters, they manage to clearly and immediately express a wide range of emotional reactions.

From the 'Rubber Hose' heroes of *El Terrible Toreador* to the prince of *Snow White*, the evolution of human figures in Disney's films suggests that in order to be affective, the character's design needs to tend towards some degree of visual truthfulness yet retain an element of caricature. The trick therefore is to create a human design 'verisimilar' enough to trigger 'emotional contagion' within the audience but one that is simultaneously caricatural enough to benefit from the expressive strength particular to caricature, and from animation as a creative medium. These issues explored by Disney in his visual designs gave him animated characters that reflected the dramatic tone of *Snow White* as the studios new feature project. However, the animation team still needed to develop and utilize a variety of methods, in conjunction with shifts in design, to create believable movement and styles of character animation quickly and economically for such a pioneering production.

Disney's search for 'believable' animation – live-action footage

Successful character animation often relies on a good understanding of pose, weight, timing and, especially, performance. Consequently, a cornerstone of animation skills development, even as far back as Disney's production of *Snow White*, is the recognition of a long and intense study of human movement. Life drawing is a widely accepted and established method of documenting a character's performance and developing the required skills. During the process of life drawing the animator's perception and documentation of the model is subjective. The animator can adapt and modify the subjects' pose as they see fit in order to improve the animated characters' performance. The process can be slow, lack spontaneity and require considerable time to organize. Time has always been an animator's worst enemy, if not their greatest challenge, and too much time taken in the planning of an animated performance will result in less time to create the final character animation.

During the studio era of Hollywood animation, recorded live action was quickly recognized as an efficient way to stage a refined performance which could be shared across large teams, with the added advantage that film and subsequently video footage could easily be paused, slowed down or replayed by an individual animator. The process gained particular prominence in the 1930s and was utilized in animated works such as *Snow White* and the Fleischer Studio's *Betty Boop's Bamboo Isle* (Dave Fleischer, 1932). The most popular techniques have been commonly acknowledged as rotoscoping and action analysis (also known as Live-action Video referencing). Rotoscope work generally takes place in front of the camera, while action analysis is used behind the camera during a film's pre-production. Each process produces a very different result in spite of their similar techniques. The process of rotoscoping traces the live-action footage precisely, providing the animator with an almost exact replica of the live-action performance.[34] It is economical and efficient, and creates smooth and successful character animation, but it can disconnect an audience from an animated character due to the overly naturalistic proportions.

By comparison, 'action analysis' allows the animator to adapt and consider movement, timing and performance rather than just slavishly copying the live-action footage as is demonstrated during the rotoscope process. It is therefore more interpretational, allowing the animator to study the live-action footage in great detail, but still include their own ideas of timing and pose to the performance. The action analysis process pioneered by Walt Disney's studio on *Snow White* certainly enabled the animator to manipulate and interpret the live-action footage to their own needs. This process operates as similar to the more subjective and interpretive process of life drawing, rather than working to 'constrain' the animated character to the recorded movement as evidenced in the rotoscope workflow.

The process of action analysis is discussed comprehensively in Chris Webster's book *Action Analysis for Animators*, where he examines both its merits and the relevance of including it in modern character animation workflows. Webster states that action analysis can be broken down into four separate actions:

1. *Activity*

    Describe the position of an object in time and space, either controlled or random.
2. *Action*

    Describe the movements and behaviours that are attributable to a specific object or material.
3. *Animation*

    Describe the movements that are generated internally either purposely or instinctively by an animated object.
4. *Acting*

    Describe actions and behaviour performed by an object that are driven by psychological and emotional conditions.[35]

Disney ultimately favoured the more evaluative action analysis method as described above. One of the key animators who worked on *Snow White* as one of the studio's famous 'Nine Old Men,' Frank Thomas, explained that Walt felt the realistic movement created using the rotoscope process was too complex and lacking focus.[36] However, trainee animators can often blur the lines between rotoscoping and action analysis, tending to view this form of assistance as cheating, rather than acknowledge the benefits that each process can potentially offer. They believe that a talented professional animator should be able to fully comprehend pose, weight and timing automatically, or as if by magic. Animation students (in particular) will always recoil in horror at the notion of recording themselves as reference, rather than consider the technique of recording movement as an important element of the animation pre-production process. Walt himself believed that practicing live-action referencing techniques could speed up the animation workflow considerably and lend weight, purpose and uniformity to an action or scene.[37] In turn, this would sustain successful and economically produced character animation regardless of the experience of the animator involved.

The method of using rotoscoped live-action footage to complement animated work has been practiced since the early days of animated production, not just during the production of *Snow White*. Initially the process was devised as a way to bring lifelike human animated characters to life. Realistic characters are often perceived as difficult to animate convincingly due to the viewer's familiarity with the human body. The original iteration of the rotoscope process was devised by Max and Dave Fleischer in 1915 and later patented in 1917. Rotoscoping allowed animators to create smooth and natural realistic human character animation in a similar style that Disney desired for the human characters in *Snow White*. Live-action footage was projected frame-by-frame onto a transparent drawing board. Animators were then able to follow the movement to create smooth realistic animation. The process was not practical for most character work at the time due to the early adoption of a less physically realistic aesthetic, particularly in the case of Disney and the transforming, 'plasmatic' quality to their *Silly Symphonies*.

The rotoscope process was used extensively in the Fleischer's *Betty Boop's Bamboo Isle*. The film begins with a live-action segment starring the Royal Samoan Orchestra, featuring a dancer named Miri. Animators rotoscoped (or traced) the live-action footage of Miri to create the dance performed by Betty at the end of the short. This was possibly due to a more carefully observed application of realistic anatomy, action and proportions. The Fleischer Studios would later use the rotoscope process on its first feature-length production, *Gulliver's Travels* (Dave Fleischer, 1939), a film that was produced in response to the success of Disney's *Snow White*. The main naturalistic human character Gulliver was heavily rotoscoped, while the other supporting characters were animated in the traditional style due to their more abstract design. Fleischer's smooth rotoscoped character animation used for Gulliver appears out of place when compared to the traditional animated characters throughout the piece, a common result of mixing heavily rotoscoped action with more lively and stylized characters.

Todd James Pierce argues that, perhaps expectedly, the animators working on *Snow White* were initially overwhelmed, as Disney presented them with such a hugely ambitious debut feature-length project.[38] The animators lacked confidence faced with such radically different character design and animation style, as up to this point they had been roughing out characters largely based on simple geometric shapes, the circle and the oval (exactly the kinds of character archetypes repeated at length in the Silly Symphonies). As a result, Disney turned to the potential of action analysis. Following their training by the Chouinard animators – including the newly appointed Graham – their confidence grew as they attended these new skills classes. One session involved analysing live-action footage that had been considerably slowed down, thereby allowing the animators to study pose and timing in ways that departed from the practice of Rotoscoping. Rather than use Snow White's voice actress Adriana Caselotti, Disney hired a young dancer Marjorie Belcher to inhabit the role of Snow White for the feature, and she would also later perform other characters for Disney including the Blue Fairy in *Pinocchio* (Ben Sharpsteen, 1940) and Hyacinth Hippo in *Fantasia* (James Algar et al., 1940). The animators were able to analyse the nuances of movement and capture Belcher's performances, rather than slavishly trace the footage as was demonstrated in Fleischer's rotoscope technique. Thomas animated the dwarfs during Snow White's 'death' scene, and it was he who believed that animation was not a technical pursuit, but that a good animator must have an advanced technical knowledge of movement.[39] Thomas stated that successful character animation must adapt and synthesize real live-action performance and produce 'believable' animated movement. Real action is highly complex, but an abbreviated interpretation of believable movement would allow an audience to accept all manner of fantastical characters. To be believable the character's performance must be initially based on real-life movement. This is why the animators on *Snow White* studied motion and movement, including the performances of vaudeville acts, film, art, and attended classes in action analysis. Although anthropomorphic, Disney's characters would always retain natural proportions in order to utilize the reference material successfully. This allowed Disney to continue to use and refine the action analysis process, creating a large library of referenced movement and performance. The studio would occasionally recycle the reference material and use the same movements for several different projects. Reusing the same reference footage again and again can be perceived as cheating, but the recycled animation equally gave the studio its distinct characterful style. The recycled live-action footage thus afforded the animators with a bank of recognizable, believable performances that the viewers would be able to recognize instantly as a Disney product. The shift to the possibilities enabled by action analysis therefore allowed the animators to break from the 'plasmatic' form of the *Silly Symphonies* and instead reorient their cartoon images towards a graphic illusionism. This would ultimately lead towards the 'hyperrealist' house style demonstrated in the character animation and contained in the majority of Disney's early theatrical work.

Conclusion

The Disney studio evidently did much to establish the tradition of utilizing and experimenting with live action for animation. The particular process of 'action analysis' pioneered by Disney and the animators working on *Snow White* is still viable and utilized throughout the animation industry today. Many contemporary American animation studios such as Pixar, DreamWorks and Sony Animation still use the action analysis workflow, and viewings of any show reels of animators employed by these studios display a strong use of Disney's pre-production pipeline. Contemporary Disney character animator Jose Gaytan's own show reel likewise evidences Disney's use of live-action video reference, which adapts and works with human movement rather than simply tracing over the live-action footage.

In 2006, UK-based animation studio Aardman released their inaugural computer-generated animated feature *Flushed Away* (David Bowers and Sam Fell, 2006) in partnership with DreamWorks. Due to various production issues the entire shoot was relocated from the Aardman studios in Bristol to DreamWorks' studio in Los Angeles. Senior production staff from Aardman were sent to LA to ensure that the established Aardman studio style was acknowledged and preserved during its all-important first feature-length computer-generated production. It was during this time that the production team from Aardman (including Animator/Director Jay Grace) became exposed to the Disney style of 'action analysis' technique in practice. Grace was heavily influenced by DreamWorks' character animation workflow, which was influenced by the production of *Snow White* many years earlier. Grace eventually brought the action analysis technique to Aardman's studio in the UK, and it is now an integral part of the studios' pre-production pipeline, where it has revolutionized the studio's feature output.

The Live-action Video reference has established a fast and efficient 'roadmap' for directors and animators, and has drastically reduced approval times for the animated shots. Feature directors can now work with their animators to create live-action video reference for most character animation shots, allowing the director and animator to interpret and refine performance, plan, time and organize shots quickly before they are animated. Due to advances in modern technology, action analysis remains easily available to every animator with a smartphone or digital tablet. Live-action footage can now be appropriated anywhere at any given time. Speed will always be an issue for all animators and animated film producers, no matter the skill and experience they possess. The action analysis technique can enable all animators to considerably speed up their own process. This, in turn, allows them to enjoy the nuances of the character's performance and create the 'believable' animation that Walt Disney had desired so much during the early stages of production on *Snow White*.

Notes

1   See Michael Barrier, *Hollywood Cartoons: American Animation in Its Golden Age* (Oxford: Oxford University Press, 1999).

2   Amy Coplan, '"Catching Character's Emotions: Emotional Contagion Response to Narrative Fiction Film",' *Film Studies* 8 (Manchester: Manchester University Press, 2007), 31.

3   Chris Webster, *Action Analysis for Animators* (Independence: CRC Press, 2012).

4   Barrier, *Hollywood Cartoons*, 86. From 1928 to 1930, Disney films were circulated through Celebrity Pictures (also proprietor of the Cinephone sound system used to add sound to *Steamboat Willie* [Ub Iwerks, 1928]). However,

from 1930 to 1932 the release of Disney films was secured by Columbia, then United Artists until 1937. *Snow White and the Seven Dwarfs* was released by RKO, which officiated until 1953 when Disney opened its own distribution company, Buena Vista.

5   Based on the work of Roger Scruton in 'Photography and Representation', in *Philosophy of Film and Motion Pictures: An Anthology*, ed. Noel Carroll and Jinhee Choi (Oxford: Blackwell, 2006), 20. The concept of 'verisimilarity' is borrowed from Karl Popper's philosophy of science and designates here a character whom we know is not realistic but elicits a 'realistic enough' response that we accept it as if it were realistic.

6   The word 'character' is used to refer to the body of the character as opposed to its role in a distinction similar to that between an actor/ress and the character s/he portrays.

7   Sergei Eisenstein, *Walt Disney* (Circé: Strasbourg, 1991), 28–9.

8   Barrier, *Hollywood Cartoons*, 70.

9   Neoteny is defined in biology as the retention of youthful features in an adult. In character design it is the use of those feature to give a character a youthful and cute look. See Stephen Jay Gould, 'Mickey Mouse meets Konrad Lorenz', *Natural History* 88 (1979): 30–6.

10 Francesco Casetti, *Les théories du cinéma depuis 1945* (Paris: Nathan, 1999), 46–7.

11 Circa 1400, the harmonious man is defined as that whose vertical proportion is equivalent to 8 and 2/3 face lengths, while the stretched arm span equates the height. According to Nadeije Laneyrie-Dagen, if this model does not quite reflect reality, this canon, as elaborated by Giotto and later theorized by Cernini, marks a considerable progress from the point of view of the imitation of the real. Nadeije Laneyrie-Dagen, *L'invention du corps. La représentation de l'homme du Moyen Age à la fin du XIX* (Paris: Flammarion, 2006), 120. Other proportion ratios, such as the equivalence between the length of the foot and that of the forearm, or the fact that there is three times the length of the hand in that of the arm (from shoulder to wrist), are also present in many of Disney's character designs.

12 According to the theories of Konrad Lorenz, the weakness of distinctive human signals for social release mechanisms has forced us to become experts in the recognition of the human forms. One must therefore be much more precise to create an efficient human character than a non-human one. See Konrad Lorenz, *Essais sur le comportement animal et humain* (Paris: Seuil, 1970).

13 Leonard Maltin, *Of Mice and Magic: A History of Animated Cartoons* (New York: McGraw-Hill, 1980): 40.

14 Barrier, *Hollywood Cartoons*, 70.

15 Ibid.

16 Ibid., 87.

17 Maltin, *Of Mice and Magic*, 40; Barrier, *Hollywood Cartoons*, 89–90.

18 This principle will later be known as 'Squash and Stretch'.

19 Maltin, *Of Mice and Magic*, 41.

20 Ibid., 42; Barrier, *Hollywood Cartoons*, 124–5.

21 Barrier, *Hollywood Cartoons*, 106.

22 Maltin, *Of Mice and Magic*, 42.

23 Ibid., 51.

24 Barrier, *Hollywood Cartoons*, 124.

25 These ideas were first brought to our attention by the lectures of Charles Solomon at UCLA in 2008.

26 Barrier, *Hollywood Cartoons*, 202.

27 Ibid., 197.

28 Maltin, *Of Mice and Magic*, 56.

29 See, for example, Niko Tinbergen, *The Study of Instinct* (Oxford: Clarendon Press, 1951); B. T. Gardner and L. Wallach, 'Shapes of Figures Identified as a Baby's Head', *Perceptual and Motor Skills* 20, no. 2 (1965): 135–42; S. H. Sternglanz, J. L. Gray and M. Murakami, 'Adult Preferences for Infantile Facial Features: An Ethological Approach', *Animal Behaviour* 25, no. 1 (1977): 108–15; and Gillian Rhodes, *Superportaits: Caricatures and Recognition* (Hove: Psychology Press, 1996).

30 Patrick Power, 'Character Animation and the Embodied Mind–Brain', *animation: an interdisciplinary journal* 3 (2008): 115–21. The 'Peak Shift Effect' implies that if a stimulus causes a specific neurological reaction, then an enhanced stimulus will cause a stronger reaction. See V. S. Ramachandran and William Hirstein, 'The Science of Art: A Neurological Theory of Aesthetic Experience', *Journal of Consciousness Studies* 6, no. 6–7 (1999): 15–51.

31 Tim Valentine, Stephen Darling and Mary Donnelly, 'Why Are Average Faces Attractive? The Effect of View and Averageness on the Attractiveness of Female Faces', *Psychonomic Bulletin & Review* 11, no. 3 (2004): 482–7.

32 Barrier, *Hollywood Cartoons*, 198.

33 See Sternglanz, Gray and Murakami, 'Adult Preferences for Infantile Facial Features'.

34 See Joanna Bouldin, 'The Body, Animation and The Real: Race, Reality and the Rotoscope in Betty Boop', paper presented at the 'Affective Encounters: Rethinking Embodiment in Feminist Media Studies' conference, Turku, 2001.

35 Webster, *Action Analysis for Animators*.

36 Frank Thomas, 'Can Classic Disney Animation Be Duplicated on the Computer?' *Computer Pictures* 2, no. 4 (July 1984): 20–5.

37 Barrier, *Hollywood Cartoons*, 120.

38 Todd James Pierce, 'Wow, We've Got Something Here: Ward Kimball and the Making of *Snow White*', *New England Review* 37, no. 1 (2016): 123–36.

39 See Andreas Deja, *The Nine Old Men: Lessons, Techniques, and Inspiration from Disney's Great Animators* (Boca Raton, FL: CRC Press, 2015).

3

The depth deception: Landscape, technology and the manipulation of Disney's multi-plane camera in *Snow White and the Seven Dwarfs* (1937)

Christopher Holliday and Chris Pallant

Across its animated feature films, the Walt Disney studio has developed a strong affinity with the narrative possibilities of the natural landscape as both an idyllic, tropical paradise and a darker, more malicious milieu. Beyond simply backdrops for the movements and actions of its animated characters, Disney's landscapes are often shifting and sentient in their storytelling functions, turning between antagonistic 'wild' spaces and more bucolic environments that provide seductive realms into which spectators are repeatedly drawn.[1] David Whitley argues that such is the repeating presence of 'wild nature' as holding 'central importance' to the studio's feature animation canon that Disney 'work[s] to sensitize the viewer to a particularized forest environment'.[2] Offering the creative opportunity for richly designed and visually lush backdrops, such landscapes have traditionally been exploited as a theatricalized setting where the studio can showcase the details of its pastoral graphic style and signature 'hyperrealist' aesthetic. This chapter takes its cue from *Snow White and the Seven Dwarfs* (David Hand, 1937) as a Disney animated feature in which the spaces of the wood and the forest play a pivotal role, and examines how Disney's woodland environments as a site of narrative drama function as highly technological, *man*-made spaces. Within this broader industrial–technological narrative, *Snow White* remains particularly significant within the history of Disney feature animation, one that combined natural imagery with technological innovation to reorient the geography of the forest location as a testing ground for their proprietary animation techniques.

The lushness of *Snow White*'s imposing wooded landscape was, most significantly, achieved through the patented multi-plane camera device, a high-rise structure that allowed a mounted camera to film vertically through a series of colourful backdrops. The spatial arrangement of the trees, branches, leaves and bushes allowed each layer to be painted onto separate background plates of the apparatus, thereby giving Disney animators 'new ways of investing space with meaning' and 'of balancing it against the lure of character'.[3] The net effect was a threatening and haunted woodland of increased depth and dimension, through which the film could draw narrative distinctions within the forest as a place of shelter, sanctuary and sinister activity. By examining the production of *Snow White* and its construction of a forest environment, this chapter argues that Disney's landscapes are wholly rooted in animation's status as a highly industrial art form. With the wooded wilderness and luscious landscape of *Snow White* the product of combining cel-animation with revolutionary multi-plane camera techniques, the film crafts an imposing and visually unbridled woodland realm in ways that have reinforced the Disney studio's synonymous relationship with animated technology. Indeed, accompanying this aesthetic history of Disney's cel-animated features produced during the Classic Disney phase is a comparable tale of innovation that no less supports the studio's drive towards a natural articulation of animation in three dimensions. The development and promotion of the multi-plane camera as an industrial innovation provides, however, a highly gendered historical narrative of animated labour, one that overwhelmingly favours the creativity and contribution of men. Yet by considering the discourses that enveloped the arrival of the multi-plane camera into cel-animated feature-film production, this chapter identifies how the studio's female workforce played an important role in ensuring both the success of the multi-plane as a technology of animation and, by extension, the formation of Hollywood animation in its Golden Age.

Illusions of nature

If nature has always presented 'a conundrum in cultural logic' within the context of American national identity in its questioning of 'our role in nature and nature's in our lives', then the trajectory of the Disney studio similarly asks how we might examine and reflect upon the many woods, woodlands and wildernesses that occupy the studio's animated feature films.[4] From Bambi's woodland den and the undergrowth of *The Sword in the Stone* (Wolfgang Reitherman, 1963) to the Sherwood Forest setting of *Robin Hood* (Wolfgang Reitherman, 1973) and the 'ravishing landscape shots' of *Brother Bear* (Aaron Blaise and Robert Walker, 2003), Disney has continued to present nature as a multifaceted space of dramatic signification and negotiation.[5] The natural world in the studio's feature films (both cel and now CG) often embodies a realm of chaos as much as it is depicted as a pastoral, lyrical paradise. Nature is both a competitor and an adversary, vulnerable but also a place of escape and adventure, and a luscious nirvana largely undisturbed by the imposing threat of humanity. Such landscapes provide protection and sanctuary in their guise as 'pristine' and 'serene glades' or, in the case of the dense African junglescapes of *Tarzan* (Kevin Lima and Chris Buck, 1999), a dynamic habitat that fully nurtures the physical exuberance of its feral protagonist.[6] Whitely is certainly not alone in identifying Disney's sustained engagement with 'the theme of wild nature', an affinity that grounded and bound up their storytelling preoccupations with fantasy and fairy tale together with natural creatures, forms and environments.[7] For Douglas Brode, it was Walt Disney's own passion for nature, and his claims that 'we must make the effort to reintegrate ourselves into the natural world', which perhaps explains the filmmaker's investment in understanding and reimagining the natural world in animated media.[8] As the dually daunting and reassuring woodland in the studio's feature-length debut *Snow White* makes clear, Disney – both the man and the studio – was immediately energized by nature as a motivating force, offering up a sublime and positivist vision of natural environments that were well-suited to communicating the machinations of what would come to be Disney's thematic and narrative formula.

The chaos and calmness of ecology in Disney represents a rhetorical commitment to the idea or very 'cultural logic' of nature in all its excess, lushness and detail.[9] As a locus for such regular animated action, the natural environments that feature within numerous Disney animated films offer a space to think through what constitutes the natural, if not 'the feelings and the ideas that we bring to bear on our relationship with the natural world'.[10] Disney feature animation frames nature as 'temporal, as existing not now, but in the past (the vanished wilderness) or the future (the restored wetland)'.[11] These are cartoons that ask questions about culture and conservation, the 'intrinsic ecological value' of unspoiled nature and the 'protection of natural resources for human use in a sustainable way'.[12] In Disney's hand-drawn natural landscapes and their emphasis on degrees of visual authenticity and believability, then, resides the potential to interrogate the historical shape, awe and beauty of 'nature' as a shifting set of values.

It was not just within Disney feature animation, but across other production arms of the studio, that the role and image of nature also became fully realized. A central element of Disney's emphatic relationship to the natural world that was solidified during the late 1930s and early 1940s was the studio's *True-Life Adventures* (1948–60). With titles that included *Nature's Half Acre* (James Algar, 1951) and *The Living Desert* (James Algar, 1953), the series comprised fourteen full-length educational documentary films that focused on specific elements of the natural environment. Alongside the Disney studio's theatrically released cel-animated films that popularized their own 'anthropomorphized depictions of nature', the particular rhetoric of the *True-Life Adventure* series 'served as the hegemonic template for virtually every natural history film made by Discovery, National Geographic and the BBC since'.[13] This influence extended to the specific industrial structures of the Disney studio too. Indeed, the *True-Life Adventure* series would come to anticipate the independent 'Disneynature' film unit of the studio that was founded in April 2008 and which remains a division of the company charged with the production of nature documentaries. The first three titles produced under the Disneynature banner were *Earth* (Alistair Fothergill and Mark Linfeld, 2007) – a companion film to the BBC/Discovery series *Planet Earth* (2006) – as well as *African Cats* (Alistair Fothergill and Keith Scholey, 2011) and *Chimpanzee* (Alistair Fothergill and Mark Linfeld, 2012), and in their subject matter all recall the original *True-Life Adventure* series' focus on the scope and strangeness of the natural landscape.

It is clear, then, that Disney animation has been invested time and time again in the pleasures of nature and natural imagery, both in its feature-length animated cartoon canon and within ancillary multimedia products. That is not to say the studio's focus on the environment has not attracted degrees of criticism. In particular, the *True-Life Adventure* series – whose articulation of the natural world was loosely 'marketed as education media' – quickly became controversial on account of their 'inaccurate depictions and staged scenes'.[14] Nicholas Sammond argues that the very structure of the series 'was as reassuringly invariable as nature itself.'[15] Sammond points to the animated sequences that began each film, which helped to situate viewers 'firmly in the realm of natural history'. These devices formed part of a broader rhetoric of 'observation and revelation' that supported the narrative's investigation into the habits and habitats of the unpredictable natural world, largely with a child audience in mind.[16] More recently, Disney's articulation of natural landscapes has drawn the attentions of contemporary eco-criticism and the emergent critical field of 'Enviro-toons'. In her survey of such environmental animation, Nicole Starosielski argues that in the late 1960s, 'environmental themes in animated film became explicitly and consciously aligned with mainstream environmentalist discourses, and environmental animation coalesced as an identifiable genre'.[17] At the same time, such ecologically themed animation *can* be traced back to before this date by considering

Disney's ongoing engagement with the political positioning of nature and natural spaces. The interplay and exchange between nature and culture within films such as *Snow White* and *Bambi* (David Hand, 1942), as well as later Disney features *The Aristocats* (Wolfgang Reitherman, 1970), *The Rescuers* (Wolfgang Reitherman, John Lounsbery and Art Stevens, 1977) and *The Fox and the Hound* (Ted Berman, Richard Rich and Art Stevens, 1981), specifically 'valorize an "irrational" uncontrollable non-human nature as a space for both adventure and creativity'.[18] The framing of Disney animation as types or modes of 'environmental cartoons' therefore involves the ideological interpretation of their sentimental romanticization (if not the design styles) of trees, moss, branches and leaves as allegories of wider cultural anxieties around the sanctity of natural space. This metaphorical treatment of Disney's animated landscapes serves to present their feature films as a form of environmental activism, which in turn invites a spectatorial awareness of the material contexts shaping the cultural construction of Disney's many animated landscapes.

There are several industrial reasons why woodland – with their concentration of vertical trees and branches, and horizontal spatial expanse – became the most common backdrop in Disney animation. A teleological perspective framing the representational agenda of the studio's animated features might see their preference for pastoral settings as a strategic choice made with long-term symbolism in mind: culture/technology; people/nature; built/organic; ordered and 'civilized'/wild and 'untamed'. Such ideological pairings have ultimately come to support precisely the kinds of contemporary environmental readings of Disney animation, and the shift towards eco-criticism, through which the studio's animated features are often examined. In their comparison between Disney's *Bambi* and *Mr. Bug Goes to Town* (Dave Fleischer, 1942) – the second cel-animated feature produced at the Fleischer Studios and co-directed by ex-Disney animator Shamus Culhane – Robin L. Murray and Joseph K. Heumann offer an ideological critique rooted in a nature-versus-modernity division. They argue that both *Bambi* and *Mr. Bug Goes to Town* effectively utilize organic landscapes to highlight both the independence and interdependency between nonhuman nature and the modern world 'that threatened stability'.[19] Beyond such eco-critical interpretations, there are just as many – if not more – practical motivations for the repeated preference for wooded environments as a central visual component of Disney's animated narratives. Such motivations have their roots in the solidification by the Disney studio of animation as a commercial media practice in the 1930s. For example, the realm of the fairy tale appealed to Disney, in no small part, due to the lack of copyright restriction. A complexity of landscape was therefore needed to match the inventiveness of the subject matter. A backdrop of overlapping trees, leaves and woodland fauna brings other advantages over a built/urban setting, namely a softer detailing, with an emphasis on complementary colour tones and shading rather than precise, modernist angularity, that constructs the illusion of depth and dimension. Consequently, the drawn or painterly woodland holds the ability to represent the universal nowhere: a space immediately recognizable as a wooded space, though one that is equally free from the specificity of drawn built/urban space. The natural landscape responds to the question of 'where is this story taking place' and instead offers a generic milieu within which Disney can tell its fantasy and fairy-tale stories.

On a practical level, it is also much easier to continually reuse a woodland background compared to a built/urban background, given the greater risk of viewers recognizing repeated buildings and becoming confused versus the acceptable uniformity of a treeline. Disney was not immune to reusing graphic material in this way, particularly during the 1960s and 1970s when it was both an 'artistic choice' and an economic cost-cutting imperative.[20] In the case of *Snow White*, many of its characters would reappear in ulterior guises in *Robin Hood* (a film largely comprised of recycled animation), while visual elements of *The Jungle Book* (Wolfgang Reitherman, 1967) and its forest environment were recycled in *Robin Hood*, and later for *The Rescuers*. *Bambi*'s backdrops were similarly reused in *Alice in Wonderland* (Clyde Geronimi, Wilfred Jackson and Hamilton Luske, 1951) and *The Fox and Hound*. Disney animators traditionally 'painted backgrounds with tremendous attention to detail', with heightened levels of pictorial realism in both colour and perspective.[21] Beyond any cost-cutting measure, the recycling of cel-animated environments therefore offered the forest as a repeating pleasure of graphic verisimilitude, which in turn has allowed spectators a return to painted environments that fully support the studio's narratives invested in intricate anthropomorphic ecosystems.

Into the woods

The convergence of these factors, related to aesthetic, economic, practical and symbolic choices, resulted in the treeline becoming a mainstay of Disney feature animation. In this way, the studio's natural hand-drawn landscapes not just mark the highest animated achievements of pristine illusionism but are often technological (and technologically contested) spaces, as their production often heralds moments of technological intervention where the Disney studio showcases its latest industrial innovation. In the case of *Snow White* and its luscious wooded environments, one agenda came to dominate the production of the film's natural backgrounds and setting: depth. Indeed, the introduction and development of the multi-plane camera facilitated the separation of multiple tree layers behind (and in front of) each other, thereby simultaneously introducing a visual depth and greater opportunity to mix-and-match and repeat tree drawings on different planes. Developed in 1937 by US engineer William Garity and first pioneered in the short *The Old Mill* (Wilfred Jackson, 1937), the multi-plane camera reworked animated space against the cartoon's prior tableaux-style movement (influenced by comic strips and panels in the case of early cartoons), while offering new expressive possibilities for the cel-animated landscape. As Paul Wells explains,

> Simply, four vertical struts were constructed to accommodate six panes of glass spaced at various intervals with the camera looking down from the top. The pane of glass closest to the camera would have foreground imagery placed or painted upon it, and each succeeding pane would have images in perspective until reaching the final pane, which would have the distant background. Each pane would effectively be a different 'plane' of action, and could move from side to side, and back and forth to facilitate the maximum degree of authentic movement through space.[22]

While a number of individuals had developed earlier methods of achieving this kind of animation depth effect – including Lotte Reiniger's multi-plane set-up of the mid-1920s, Ub Iwerks' horizontal multi-plane camera built from old Chevrolet car parts and the 'setback' horizontal rig patented (US 2,054,414) by Max Fleischer in 1936 that could combine stop motion and cel animation – the multi-plane camera patented by Garity (US 2,198,006, awarded 1940), on behalf of the Disney Studio, represented a significant advancement with regard to the type of realism that Walt coveted at that time.[23] The multi-plane was certainly a device that permitted the action of *Snow White* to move within (and through) the forest scenery, following characters as they travelled deeper and deeper into the cel-animated screen world.

Snow White's first shot, for example, recalls that of *The Old Mill* (which started production after *Snow White*, but was released a month earlier in November 1937) in negotiating the visual possibilities afforded by the multi-plane camera's movement in exhibiting advances in spatial realism. For Richard Schickel, *The Old Mill* 'has no real plot, and it consisted, not unnaturally, of a succession of tracking shots that showed the activities of the animal inhabitants of a deserted windmill'.[24] *Snow White* opens on a similar moment of bravura camerawork, as the spectator is taken closer via a tracking shot to the Queen's castle, here neatly framed by trees and foliage that are painted and arranged on alternate layers of the multi-plane. The sequence then dissolves into another (closer) image of the castle with the camera continuing its forward movement as it tracks through the space, before it dissolves again to take spectators inside where the Queen echoes the camera's movements by moving forward in her approach to the Magic Mirror. The effect is one of a fantasy of dimension, with space becoming a graphic effect that demonstrates both the 'stylistic enhancements' afforded by the camera and also the film's organization of its animated environments for both 'narrative and thematic capital'.[25]

The early technological evolution of hand-drawn animation, in the case of the multi-plane camera resulting in greater efficiency through the separation of layers, points to the 'technologized' identity of Snow White's construction of its natural spaces in ways that reinforced the Disney studio's synonymous relationship with innovation.[26] Technology and technological culture immediately became central to the stability of animation as a viable commercial industry, and for many Disney scholars marks out the studio's primary contribution to the Golden Age of American cartoon tradition. Amy Foster argues that Disney himself embodied an excitement for the future (grounded in his wider interest in space travel), yet notes a 'contradictory fascination with the medieval era and his technological enthusiasm'.[27] This ideological ambivalence cleaves the fantasy of the studio's fairy-tale features from the medium used to create them, suggesting a possible tension between subject matter (past) and form (future). It also positions the popular Disney narrative of technological innovation within a framing discourse of nostalgia that underscores the studio's narrative formulae.

Snow White's formal exploitation of the multi-plane apparatus (not only in its opening sequence but also in the 'layered' shots that establish the pastoral location of the dwarfs' cottage) represents a more vexed and ambivalent experimentation with convincing three-dimensional landscapes. J. P. Telotte argues that the multi-plane device emerged at 'a kind of transitional point for Disney animation – a point at which its modernist impulses were so much tamed by a conventional realism as already seeming to be looking beyond'.[28] Within the context of Snow White, the impact of the multi-plane camera has certainly become a central component of the animated medium's 'realist' evolution and, alongside three-strip Technicolor, key to how Disney crafted imposing and visually unbridled realms in three dimensions.[29]

The prosperity of 'Golden' periods within Disney's animated history is critically understood through discourses of industrial stability, which in turn foster artistic, creative growth and the (re)emergence of the regularized Disney formula. Disney's desire to innovate and harness technology certainly contributed to many of the formalizing principles of hyperrealism, and the classicism of the Disney aesthetic honed during the 1940s and 1950s period.[30] More recently, the post-1989 Disney 'Renaissance' era – credited among Disney scholars as the 'Second Golden Age' – as well as the studio's successful computer-animated feature films released post-2005 have again been represented through an interplay between industrial harmony and formal, formulaic stability. In the case of Snow White, the film has been likewise understood as part of a wider outcome of industrial and artistic coherence. Katie Croxton argues that Snow White 'solidified Disney as a skilled interpreter of the Grimms' works and its success propelled him and the Walt Disney Studio into a popular culture staple'.[31] As a studio too, Disney's work during the production of *Snow White* coincided with a progressively more stable set of working conditions. J. B. Kaufman's account of the production of the film argues not only that it 'played a decisive part in determining the studio's future direction' but also that its success partly corrected something of an 'unstable atmosphere' at Disney during the early 1930s when they were working to produce a feature-length version of Lewis Carroll's *Alice in Wonderland*.[32] As the studio's landmark first feature, *Snow White* has therefore been conceptualized as a symptom of this growing industrial security. However, a closer look at the landscapes in *Snow White* and the application of the multi-plane camera reveals that the critical framing of three-dimensional natural environments as storytelling elements without metamorphic potential is not fully resolved by the film. Indeed, there are moments where the depiction of the wooded landscape appears to recall Disney's early cartoon history, seemingly operating outside certain hyperrealist levels of verisimilitude.

During the scene in which Snow White hurriedly escapes from the Woodsman and runs frantically deep into the woods, the camera follows her movements from right to left as she passes behind and in front of the trees. In this sequence, the organization of space in the multi-plane camera fully supports the narrative drama of the sequence. With the action obscured by branches that intrude into the spectators' field of vision, Snow White's escape *from* the Woodsman *into* the woods becomes visualized through the spatial realism and the character's movement back through clearly defined levels. However, once Snow White shifts direction as she runs, an ulterior visual style begins to emerge. The jagged edges of the trees mutate into recognizable 'arms' that check her movements, while floating wooden logs transform into crocodiles that snap ferociously to add further jeopardy to her plight. This sequence from *Snow White* suggests a more expressive play with landscape that belies the studio's hyperrealist agenda, showcasing the momentarily formal alignment between multi-plane aesthetics and a more metamorphic sensibility. *Snow White*'s wooded landscapes become lively landscapes that reflect moments of clear formal/stylistic experimentation, emblematic of a transitional film in which the metamorphic (or what Sergei Eisenstein would call 'plasmatic') charge of the *Silly Symphonies* and the emergent turn to the hyperreal forces coexist.[33] *Snow White* might therefore be considered as stylistically deciduous – shedding (though not completely) its prior states in the pursuit of pictorial realism. Telotte labels this negotiation between naturalism and modernity as a 'combinatory approach' (evoking, perhaps, Foster's description of Walt's own 'contradictory fascination').[34] Such an approach identifies how aesthetic values visible onscreen in the animated features themselves were equally matched by an industrial push–pull behind the scenes. The emergence of 'measuring dimension and producing parallax' leading to (and as a consequence of) the innovative development of the multi-plane too suggests that, as with the non-human/human collisions in the themes and narratives of *Bambi* or even *Mr. Bug Goes to Town*, the tension of nature and modernity held in delicate balance played out artistically in *Snow White* as much as it did industrially.

'Man is in the Forest!'

Whenever story director Perce Pearce would announce, 'Man is in the forest!' (a line from *Bambi* meaning 'danger') it meant Walt was down the hall.[35]

Despite the studio's involvement with technology as part of its evolution and expansion into a multimedia entertainment conglomerate, it is an element of animated feature-film production that is both made visible *and* consciously veiled. Telotte argues that 'technological supports or developments' are 'often unseen' and 'unconsidered' within the company's synergistic strands that reach across film, television, theme parks and other ancillary income streams.[36] This is, in part, due to tensions between the industry of animation and its reception as an art, coupled with the central role of 'magic' within the wider cultural experience of Disney products. Telotte argues that a narrative of Disney's industrial invention is wrought with conflict because 'technological underpinnings' are often hidden to create the illusion that characters and worlds are charmed and enchanted, thereby adding to the 'magical atmosphere that Disney sells'.[37] Although these conclusions are drawn against the literal mechanics of Disney's theme parks that seemingly 'work by magic', they equally apply to their animated features. This masking of technology suggests two competing contexts. First, it provides a broader corollary to animation as a creative medium whereby the industrial activity of its production occurs within moments that remain invisible to the spectator, and occluded from their view. As Norman McLaren defined it, 'what happens between each frame is much more important than what exists on each frame'.[38] Animation is, for McLaren, 'the art of manipulating the invisible interstices that lie between the frames'.[39] Second, however, is that the occlusion of labour incites a more gendered set of conditions that surround *Snow White*'s production and the terms of its workforce.

Allegedly uttered as a warning to Disney animators that their autocratic leader was an imminent arrival into the corridors of Disney's headquarters in Burbank, California, 'Man is in the forest!' is a phrase that usefully stands for the 'combinatory' meeting of nature and culture in *Snow White*. It also playfully gestures to the impact of a 'foreign' technological presence that permitted the studio's teleological shift towards depth and dimension. Yet however apocryphal its origins, the phrase also raises to a higher pitch of emphasis the issue of gender and the historical relegation of women's labour to the margins of the multi-plane narrative. Indeed, Disney has struggled to shake the impression of being something of an old boys' club, though this is a concern that the studio is belatedly seeking to address, perhaps most effectively through the promotion of Jennifer Lee to the role of Chief Creative Officer of Walt Disney Animation Studios, following the acrimonious departure of the previous Chief Creative Officer John Lasseter. Lee's appointment is far from tokenistic, and the co-director (with Chris Buck) of *Frozen* (2013) and *Frozen* 2 (2019) has already signalled her intent to promote gender equality through her decision to strategically partner Disney with the United Nations Foundation's 'Girl Up' programme. During Walt Disney's stewardship, however, the studio repeatedly failed to convey a sense of gender equality in the workplace, whether through masculine promotional photographs; through the public championing of his 'Nine Old Men' as the key creative individuals responsible for driving the studio's animation; or through the words chosen for recruitment adverts, such as the one posted in the April 1936 issue of *Popular Mechanics*: 'Walt Disney WANTS ARTISTS[.] Walt Disney, creator of Mickey Mouse and Silly Symphonies offers exceptional opportunities to trained male artists. Write for particulars, giving age and occupation.' However, nowhere is the issue of gender and its imbalance more visible than in the discourses that enveloped the implementation of the multi-plane camera into cel-animated feature-film production.

Reviewing the staged, promotional photographs and footage of the multi-plane in operation, presented in the 'Tricks of Our Trade' (13 February 1957) episode of *Walt Disney's Disneyland*, we encounter a conspicuously male workspace. This multi-plane sequence in 'Tricks of Our Trade' begins with Walt Disney presenting the viewer with a framed blueprint containing eight drawings showing various aspects of the multi-plane camera. These drawings do not correspond with the drawings contained in Garity's 1938 patent application, nor does Disney reference Garity's contributions at any point in this sequence. However, given that 'Tricks of Our Trade' broadcast on television with a mixed-age audience, airing almost twenty years after the submission of Garity's patent, Disney's simplified account of the multi-plane's origin, stating that 'it came out of school of self-improvement here at the studio', makes sense. Disney, with the help of cutaways to a camera operator recording a Mickey Mouse sequence with a regular rostrum camera set-up, and subsequent cutaways to the animated Mickey Mouse sequence (demonstrating depth illusions pre-multi-plane), articulates the challenge of believably animating not just the illusion of depth, but also dynamic perspective. After the Mickey Mouse sequence, Disney then describes a scene whereby the camera tracks down a country lane at night, noting how the moon increases in size at the same rate as the farmhouse on the horizon and the fields in the foreground: 'the problem was: how to take a painting and make it behave like a real piece of scenery under the camera?'. The solution was the multi-plane and, for the first five minutes of this 'Tricks of Our Trade' feature, Disney follows closely the problems and solutions articulated by Garity in his 1940 patent without actually naming the engineer who left the studio in 1942.

The final few minutes of the multi-plane feature are focussed on the camera in operation, using the opening sequence from *Bambi* as a case study, with Disney introducing this by saying 'here we see the multi-plane camera crew preparing to shoot that scene'. The following dialogue is heard in this sequence:

Dick [Borden]
Camera Operator
Everything's OK except the bottom level. What's wrong down there, Alan?

Alan
Crank Operator
I was moving it the wrong way, Dick, I'm taking it back now. How's that?

Dick
Camera Operator
Looks fine now. Ok, we've got that frame, let's get set for the second exposure.[40]

This is a staged sequence, as many of the 'behind-the-scenes' features for Disney's television venture were, and it is clear from many of the promotional photographs that were taken in more authentic production contexts that the camera crew were typically required to wear plain white overalls.

While Disney promoted an exaggeratedly male vision of the multi-plane's operation, there is conflicting photographic evidence that suggests women also had an important role in the successful recording of multi-plane sequences. In Mindy Johnson's book, *Ink & Paint: The Women of Walt Disney's Animation* (2017), we find an image depicting several women working alongside several men in the multi-plane room. Johnson's caption notes: 'Inkers and Painters touch up cels for the multiplane camera while in production, circa late 1930s.'[41] The involvement of the Ink and Paint team here, around the time of *Snow White's* production, was, perhaps, to correct or add colour, or perhaps to fix a cel to compensate for the carelessness of one of the men tasked with loading or cranking. Perhaps it was even to exaggerate a colour to compensate for the inability of the camera to adequately record the colour of a cel positioned at a lower order in the stack. What is clear is that these women – an exclusively female 'support' team – did play an important role in ensuring the success of the multi-plane camera.

Sadly, this reality is not often captured in accounts of the multi-plane's operation, both from within and outside the studio. Disney's own views on why women had not been able to make the transition from the Ink and Paint department to other divisions of his studio are certainly a key factor for this lack of visibility. Quoted in a 1946 column written by Bob Thomas from the Freeport, Illinois' *The Journal Standard*, Disney remarks: 'I have found that very few women are good cartoonists … There have been many good women artists, but cartooning by women is inevitably too fine and dainty.'[42] Thomas then attempts to offer some balance:

> Disney cited one or two exceptions to his contention that women can't cartoon. He also declared that he employs many women, but as artists. 'As artists, they often have a better knowledge of color than men, he said.'
>
> 'Another thing,' he added, 'too often we have put a girl through our long and expensive training, only to have her marry and retire. She lets her husband earn the money, whereas a male cartoonist has to stay at his job.'

If we look beyond the casual misogyny, Disney is failing to recognize his own professional prejudice, whereby he has predestined any female Disney employee's creative potential. His remarks are ultimately a key reason why women could often feel disadvantaged working under his stewardship and, as a consequence, end up becoming disillusioned by their career prospects and leaving the studio earlier than they might have previously anticipated.

Disney is not alone in speaking the language of patriarchy. Richard Schickel's *The Disney Version: The Life, Times, Art and Commerce of Walt Disney* adopts an equally uncritical register when describing the scaling up of Disney's studio during the production of *Snow White*:

> Unlike most growing industrial enterprises, the largest number of new employees were not in executive or administrative work, but were, instead, animators, assistant animators, breakdown *men*, and in-betweeners (the last being the traditional starting point for a young *man* learning the art, and whose work, logically enough, consisted of doing the drawings that come 'in-between' the drawings of the main action. Executed by the *men* above *him* on the ladder). There is no doubt that the animators were the glamorous figures of the infant industry, the *men* who drew the best salaries ($150 to $200 a week) and among whom were a few who came to work wearing polo clothes, ready to ride with the boss at the end of the day.[43]

While Schickel is undoubtedly seeking to reflect the professional world that his research revealed, he actively upholds the patriarchal register favoured by Disney, excluding at the time of his writing the work undertaken by at least two generations of women at the Disney studio working in the Ink and Paint division.

The work that has followed on Disney has done much to probe the wider technological picture surrounding the evolution of their multi-plane technology, as well as considering the aesthetic implications of Disney's pursuit of multi-plane realism.[44] Yet has it done enough to adequately reshape the historical record? By focussing on the headline figures, such as Walt Disney, Ub Iwerks, Max Fleischer and William Garity, these otherwise useful contributions allow the received (masculine) characterization of the multi-plane's operation to go unchallenged. The promotion of the multi-plane workspace as a strongly *male* workspace is emblematic of the wider marginalization of the female workforce during Disney's lifetime, a workforce that helped contribute greatly to Disney's success across its animated features. Thankfully, more work is now being done to reclaim and represent the personal, professional and industrial histories of women in animation, both at the Disney studio and beyond.

Conclusion

The forest that pervades *Snow White* and envelops its characters is anything but an inanimate backdrop. Against the flattened action and movements of earlier animated cartoons, the spectacle of 'realistic' spatial organization in *Snow White* afforded by the emergent multi-plane technology crafts persuasive depth cues and convincing perspective that illuminates the film's moments of narrative drama. Its arrangement of foreground to background space can be understood historically and formally as central to the studio's pursuit of graphic illusionism and the rapid hardening of its influential 'hyperrealist' principles. It also functions as a highly 'technologized' place in which spectators can encounter sanctuary, solitude and shadowy threat, while encouraging them to reflect upon their own curated relationship with nature in the modern world. These trees, in their static movement – being simultaneously painted on cels and frozen on celluloid, but subject to the roaming demands of the multi-plane camera – draw attention to the mechanical and technological ambition of *Snow White*. However, these trees, through their muted, yet precise, colours, also point tantalizingly at a history of the studio yet to be fully reclaimed: the work of Disney's women employees during Disney's 'Golden Era', which, as this chapter has argued, requires even greater depth and dimension.

Notes

1 For an extended discussion of environments as active ingredients within the animated realm, see Chris Pallant's *Animated Landscapes: History, Form, and Function* (New York: Bloomsbury, 2015).

2 David Whitley, *The Idea of Nature in Disney Animation: From Snow White to WALL-E* (Hampshire: Ashgate, 2008), 1, 6.

3 J. P. Telotte, *Animating Space: From Mickey to WALL-E* (Lexington: University Press of Kentucky, 2010), 139.

4 Margaret J. King, 'The Audience in the Wilderness: The Disney Nature Films', *Journal of Popular Film and Television* 24 (1996): 60 (60–8).

5 Whitley, *The Idea of Nature in Disney Animation*, 94.

6 Katherine Coyne Kelly, 'Disney's Medievalized Ecologies in *Snow White and the Seven Dwarfs* and *Sleeping Beauty*', in *The Disney Middle Ages: A Fairy-Tale and Fantasy Past*, ed. Tison Pugh and Susan Aronstein (London: Palgrave Macmillan, 2012), 191 (189–207).

7 Whitley, *The Idea of Nature in Disney Animation*, 1.

8 Douglas Brode, *From Walt to Woodstock: How Disney Created the Counterculture* (Austin: University of Texas Press, 2004), 140.

9 King, 'The Audience in the Wilderness', 60.

10 Whitley, *The Idea of Nature in Disney Animation*, 1.

11 Kelly, 'Disney's Medievalized Ecologies in *Snow White and the Seven Dwarfs* and *Sleeping Beauty*', 191.

12 Ibid., 194.

13 Jennifer A. Sandlin and Julie C. Garlen, 'Introduction: Feeling Disney, Buying Disney, Being Disney', *Disney, Culture, and Curriculum*, ed. Jennifer A. Sandlin and Julie C. Garlen (London: Routledge, 2016), 11; Ronald B. Tobias, *Film and the American Moral Vision of Nature: Theodore Roosevelt to Walt Disney* (Michigan: Michigan State University Press, 2011), xix.

14 Sandlin and Garlen, 'Introduction', 11.

15 Nicholas Sammond, *Babes in Tomorrowland: Walt Disney and the Making of the American Child, 1930–1960* (Durham: Duke University Press, 2005), 202.

16 Ibid.

17 Nicole Starosielski, '"Movements That Are Drawn": A History of Environmental Animation from *The Lorax* to *FernGully* to *Avatar*', *International Communication Gazette* 73, nos 1–2 (2011): 152 (145–63).

18 Robin L. Murray and Joseph K. Heumann, *That's All Folks?: Ecocritical Readings of American Animated Features* (Lincoln: University of Nebraska Press, 2011), 141.

19 Ibid., 42–3.

20 Chris Pallant, *Demystifying Disney: A History of Disney Feature Animation* (New York: Continuum Books, 2011), 12.

21 Newton Lee and Krystina Madej, *Disney Stories: Getting to Digital* (New York: Springer, 2012), 59.

22 Paul Wells, *Animation: Genre and Authorship* (London: Wallflower Press, 2002), 9.

23 Katharina Boeckenhoff and Caroline Ruddell, 'Lotte Reiniger: The Crafty Animator and Cultural Value', in *The Crafty Animator: Handmade, Craft-Based Animation and Cultural Value*, ed. Caroline Ruddell and Paul Ward (London: Palgrave Macmillan, 2019), 85 (75–98); and J. P. Telotte, 'Ub Iwerks' (Multi)Plain Cinema', *animation: an interdisciplinary journal* 1, no. 1 (July 2006): 16 (9–24).

24 Richard Schickel quoted in J. P. Telotte, *The Mouse Machine: Disney and Technology* (Urbana: University of Illinois Press, 2008), 65.

25 Telotte, *The Mouse Machine*, 65.

26 Contemporary reviews of *Snow White* make conspicuous reference to Disney's technological sophistication, in particular the studio's ability to create the illusion of depth. See John C. Finn's review of the film for *Variety* (28 December 1937) and Kate Cameron's review for *New York Daily News* (14 January 1938).

27 Amy Foster, 'Futuristic Medievalisms and the U.S. Space Program in Disney's *Man in Space* Trilogy and *Unidentified Flying Oddball*', in *The Disney Middle Ages: A Fairy-Tale and Fantasy Past*, ed. Tison Pugh and Susan Aronstein (New York: Palgrave, 2012), 154 (153–70).

28 Telotte, *Animating Space*, 139.

29 For a discussion of Disney and colour, see Natalie M. Kalmus, 'Color Consciousness', *Journal of the Society of Motion Picture Engineers* 25 (August 1935): 139–47; Telotte, *The Mouse Machine*, 42–55 [chapter 2 – Minor Hazards: Disney and the Color Adventure].

30 See Pallant, *Demystifying Disney*, 35–53.

31 Katie Croxton, 'Snow White, the Grimm Brothers and the Studio the Dwarfs Built', in *Walt Disney, from Reader to Storyteller: Essays on the Literary Inspirations*, ed. Kathy Merlock Jackson and Mark I. West (Jefferson, NC: McFarland, 2015), 29 (21–30).

32 J. B. Kaufman, 'Before Snow White', *Film History* 5, no. 2 (June 1993): 172; 160 (158–75).

33 Sergei Eisenstein, *Eisenstein on Disney* (trans. Jay Leyda, London: Methuen, 1988).

34 Telotte, *Animating Space*, 139.

35 Disney animator Marc Davis quoted in John Canemaker, *Walt Disney's Nine Old Men and the Art of Animation* (New York: Disney Editions, 2001), 275.

36 Telotte, *The Mouse Machine*, 2.

37 Ibid.

38 Norman McLaren quoted in Charles Solomon, *The Art of the Animated Image: An Anthology* (Los Angeles: AFI, 1987), 11.

39 Ibid.

40 https://www.youtube.com/watch?v=YdHTlUGN1zw.

41 Mindy Johnson, *Ink & Paint: The Women of Walt Disney's Animation* (Glendale: Disney Editions, 2017), 130–1.

42 https://www.newspapers.com/newspage/3995083/.

43 Richard Schickel, *The Disney Version: The Life, Times, Art and Commerce of Walt Disney* (New York: Simon & Schuster, 1968), 171; italics added for emphasis.

44 See Michael Barrier, *Hollywood Cartoons: American Animation in Its Golden Age* (Oxford: Oxford University Press, 1999), Telotte (2008) and Pallant (2011).

4

Character costume portrayal and the multilayered process of costume design in *Snow White and the Seven Dwarfs* (1937)

Maarit Kalmakurki

Without the requirement of dialogue, costumes function as a significant visual tool providing certain leads and guidance for spectators about a character's status and personality. An effective way to establish a connection between a character and the audience is by utilizing costumes in a manner that enables quick identification and empathy. In traditional hand-drawn animation, the process of costume design is integrated firmly into the development of the character, rather than executed separately by a costume designer. Nevertheless, costume plays a key part in the spectatorial identification of the character, portraying also the figure's body form and silhouette, and is therefore a fundamental element of their overall design.

For the analysis of how the costume designs evolved during the production of *Snow White and the Seven Dwarfs* (David Hand, 1937), this chapter will combine the story meeting notes, video footage filmed during the production of 'motion studies', character development and conceptual drawings alongside the design of the characters in the final animated feature film. Story meeting notes provide important information about the conversations that Disney artists had during the production of *Snow White*, which are useful in examining the design of costumes, including their shape, structure and details, and the connection that is crafted with the character's specific personalities. The story meeting notes produced during *Snow White* indicate that most of the characters' costume development seems to have been made at the end of 1934 and throughout 1936. Only a few meetings are documented during 1935. The special editions of *Snow White and the Seven Dwarfs* DVD provide a variety of bonus materials (video footage filmed during the motion studies), while others include several character development and conceptual design drawings, which share valuable visual evidence of the evolving costume design. With this analysis, I wish to highlight the different ways in which costume design is visible throughout the Disney animators' character design process, from initial concept designs to final character realization. With the examples shown in this chapter, I argue that costume design is an important part of the character design in the identification of the character's personality and their connection with the narrative. This chapter is therefore a welcome addition to the number of scholarly publications on animation, given that costume design has been a noticeably underrepresented area that discusses the character development in Disney's hand-drawn animated feature films.[1]

Costume design as part of the character development

During the production of *Snow White*, character development, including costume design, was executed through collaborative labour. Story meetings between the animators were an important part in the evolution of characters and their costumes. However, Walt Disney himself had his own strong visions for the visual outcome of the film, which guided the story and style of character animation. At that time, the Disney animation studio did not have a separate costume department that would have been responsible for areas related to character costume design, including their research for visual inspiration or for providing material references. The notes and the literature sources indicate that Walt Disney wanted the film to be set in no specific era. For this reason, most likely, early concept and character development designs show a variety of costumes that include many elements of different historical dress styles, all blended together in one costume. This is visible also in the finished animation, in which the characters' costumes are a striking combination of fashions from different eras.

The Queen's costume design was mostly created through the collaborative effort of Disney, Art Babbit and Joe Grant. Babbit was the lead animator of the character, while Grant focused on animating the Queen's transformation into the Witch.[2] However, Grant did create several sketches of the Queen, thereby contributing to her overall design.[3] In a story meeting that took place on 30 October 1934, Disney suggested the following as an action item for the Queen's character development: 'Questions of the queen's portrayal; fat cartoon type or as a stately beautiful type. Sketches to be submitted, and story sections constructed for either angle.'[4] These two different styles, proposed by Disney, can be observed in the Queen's early character designs.[5] Most of the designs for the 'fat cartoon type' present the Queen in sixteenth-century dress styles visible in the shape of her bodice, skirt and dress as well as her headdresses, whereas the 'stately beautiful type' Queen is portrayed in late medieval fashions. Several of the early designs clearly show the Queen wearing a Medici collar, introduced to the French court by Marie De Medici and typical of late-sixteenth-century fashion. For the proposed designs for the Queen, the style of this high Medici collar evolved towards a considerably simpler shape and texture. A remnant of the Medici collar is visible in the Queen's costume in the film in which she wears a cape with a white, high stand-up collar (Figure 4.1).

In the same meeting in which Disney directed the animators of the Queen's portrayal, he also requested the animators 'to draw the Queen

FIGURE 4.1 The high collar on the Queen's cape in the final animation evolved from a decorative accessory to a much simpler style.

Source: Screen grab from *Snow White and the Seven Dwarfs* (1937).

along the lines of the Benda Mask type'.[6] The Queen's black headdress and pale facial appearance are clearly inspired by this note. The style and name of Benda mask refer to the Polish artist Wladyslav Teodor Benda, who was actively working in the United States during the time of *Snow White's* production. Benda designed and produced theatrical masks, as well as other forms of art, and the designs of his masks were oval in shape, pale in colour and sometimes included a headdress.[7] Disney's reference to the Benda mask is not visible in the character design drawings in which the Queen is depicted as a 'fat cartoon type'. On the contrary, in the majority of the designs showing the Queen as a 'stately beautiful type', her face appears to be similar to someone wearing a white Benda mask. This reference also remained in the final animation, in which the Queen's crown rests on a black, tight headdress, almost like a tight hood, providing a great contrast as it frames the Queen's chalk white face. In this way, her facial appearance functions like a pale mask. The black tight headdress in between her pale face and the white stand-up collar prevents the two elements of the costume from blending together.

The visual portrayal of the Queen's character, including her costume design, evolved during the production. Her comic features and the 'fat cartoon type' were dismissed and replaced, revealing her as a tall, severely thin and fearless character. The story meeting notes from 15 October 1934 indicate that the style of the Witch that the Queen transforms into was at first described as 'a Fat Peddler Woman', to better suit the Queen's design option of the 'fat cartoon type'.[8] Interestingly, the meeting date indicates that the character design of the Witch was discussed prior to that of the Queen. On 16 November 1934, another description of the Witch was agreed upon, this time as 'a thin hawk faced old witch-type', that more obviously connects with the 'stately beautiful' characteristics of the Queen.[9]

This note certainly impacted the final design of the Queen's costume, as all the character development designs for this type portray her wearing a medieval dress. As a result, in the film the Queen wears a medieval-style long tunic with full-floor-length sleeves. No discussion from the story meetings indicates why a medieval dress style was chosen for the Queen. However, there is a connection between the 'stately beautiful type', medieval dress styles and the 1930s women's fashion and beauty standards. This connection is visible in the Queen's body shape, supported by her long dress that highly resembles the consumer and high fashion of the mid-1930s: it was popular for women to have a fitted, bias cut dress with a long, draped hemline, established by fashion designer Madeleine Vionnet.[10] Robin Allan argues that the Queen's facial appearance is inspired by a Hollywood actress Joan Crawford, and her visual look was a combination of the 1930s femme fatale and a 'figure from an older world'.[11] Film stars became trendsetters starting from the 1920s, and it was natural to choose an actress as inspiration for the character. Furthermore, the medieval dress style connects with the costumes of the male characters in the film, whereas Snow White and the dwarfs' costume designs cannot be associated with any specific era.

The story meeting notes for *Snow White* also indicate that the majority of the discussions regarding the nature of the characters as linked with their costumes were discussions concentrating on the dwarfs. The distinction between the diverse personalities of similar looking dwarfs was achieved by paying attention to the 'wearability', proportion and details of their costumes. The story meeting notes for *Snow White* refer to several discussions in which the costume portrayal is compared with each character's personality. Their character development therefore included topics which are related to the principles of costume design, even though costume design was not considered a separate entity from the character design. As an example, on 3 November 1936, animator Bill Tytla suggested in discussions regarding Dopey's costume that he is the 'sort of character that is dressed up in the cast off clothing of the others'.[12] Dopey's characteristic movements through his costume are noted many times in later meetings. For instance, in the same November 1936 meeting, animator Perce Pearce comments that 'Dopey's actions are loose, in keeping with his clothes.'[13] Later on 9 December 1936, Walt Disney remarks, 'I think we want to work Dopey as a fellow with long sleeves – like Mickey in the Band Concert [sic]. It makes him look young to have on somebody else's clothes.'[14] This comment supports Disney's analysis of Dopey a week later, in which he wants him to express that 'he hasn't grown up'.[15] These comments clearly suggest that costume was a significant element in the character design of Dopey, fully supporting the representation of his identity. The ways in which costumes are utilized to portray the characters' diverse personalities, or to connect with the specific movements of the character, strongly belong to the theory and practise of costume design.

Costumes were also utilized to support the comedic elements in *Snow White*'s narrative. The earlier description of Dopey having oversized sleeves and a long length coat impacts both the movement and the walking style of the character. Mickey Mouse's coat in the film *The Band Concert* (Wilfred Jackson, 1935) is very similar to Dopey's coat design, as both garments have long sleeves and the hemline drags along the floor, giving the impression that they are wearing someone else's clothing. For example, in Snow White Dopey's costume reinforced the comedic scene in which the dwarf Sneezy hides underneath his long coat when he is dancing with Snow White.[16]

Another note related to costume design in the story meetings for *Snow White* between the animators concentrates on whether the dwarfs' hair should be seen or not. On 3 November 1936, Pearce emphasizes that the dwarfs' hair is seen only when they take off their hats.[17] About a month later, in a story meeting dated 15 December 1936, Disney remarks that Sleepy's hat should be limp.[18] Using different headdresses for the dwarfs is an important and decisive detail for depicting their different personalities.

This is clearly visible in the animation, such as in the way Dopey holds his loose hat on his head to prevent it from constantly dropping down. This detail is a significant addition to his costume. Dopey's big hat, together with his long coat, accentuates the appearance of oversized clothing. In the case of Sleepy, his hat's tip is limp, not the entire hat, to differentiate this from the similar headdress of Dopey.

The Disney animators' discussions regarding Sleepy's physical and visual appearance contain similar remarks to clothing and the design of costume as those that occurred in relation to Dopey.[19] Sleepy is described as a 'tremendously sleepy person. His body is heavy, which causes him to move slowly, completely relaxed at all times – everything hanging clothes, hands and his knees bent.'[20] The difference between these two characters is achieved in the finished animation by making Sleepy's coat material hang over his belt, rather than having a long coat hanging on the floor as is the case with Dopey's costume. Sleepy is constantly falling asleep, his movements are sloppy and therefore the clothing represents this untidy appearance by hanging down over his body. Animator Bill Tytla supports this idea by suggesting that for the character of Dopey his 'belt line is quite low and things drag after him a bit'.[21] The beltline is an easy way to visually represent the weight and proportion of the body and to signify the character's mood.

The beltline within the design of the dwarfs is also used to differentiate the personalities for the characters of Doc and Happy. In a meeting at the Disney studio on 15 December 1936, both of these characters' visual appearances are described similarly as either 'round' or 'fat'.[22] Their personalities, though, are different, as Doc is described several times as a dignified person with a pompous attitude, whereas Happy has the personality of a comedian, bubbling with joy.[23] Doc's personality is shown through his beltline hanging low and with his stomach sitting big and high on top of it. The costume creates the impression of a big chest rather than of a big stomach, as he should be 'chesty in order to distinguish him from Happy who is also large and fat'.[24] On the other hand, Happy's beltline is high and his vest is short, which makes his lower body longer and the weight of his big stomach visible in his large round trousers.

Though every dwarf's costume was remarkably similar, the minor yet decisive details in the design of each costume differentiated their visual appearance. These small nuances in costume might be unnoticed, yet each dwarf had their own distinct costume style that functioned to convey the specific character's personality. The animators' numerous in-depth discussions on the dwarf's costumes is an example of the costume design practice that was a fundamental part of the character development at the Disney studio during the 1930s production of *Snow White*.

Snow White's costume was developed in parallel with the other characters and she wears two different costumes in the film. The visual materials available concerning the film's production, such as the character development drawings and filmed motion study footage, largely present versions of the blue-yellow gown she wears for most of the film. Only one design, a finished costume drawing, can be found depicting the costume that she wears for a short time at the beginning of the film. As the development of this costume cannot be traced, the analysis of Snow White's costume design development in this chapter concentrates predominantly on her signature blue and yellow gown.[25]

Snow White's characteristics were described in a meeting that took place at Disney on 11 November 1936, as slender, cute and dainty, for which the animators designed several versions of her costume.[26] An attempt to portray Snow White's sensitive nature can be seen in one of the early costume design examples, in which she wears a dress with an Empire silhouette that has a waistline placed just below the bosom. This design has an element that is almost like a fine layer of tulle over the skirt, a possible reference to a story meeting in which Hamilton Luske explains how she wears a dress 'made of tulle – more or less transparent'.[27] The material depiction of tulle refers to her personality, how a lightweight, delicate fabric would interpret the sensitive nature of Snow White as a character.

The animators who worked the most on the character of Snow White were Natwick and Norman Ferguson. Prior to working at Disney, Natwick had worked at the Fleischer animation studio developing the character of Betty Boop.[28] Some of the early character development drawings of Snow White highly resemble Betty Boop's design, particularly her facial expression, the shape of her head and style of hair. However, these similar character designs differ in terms of costume design, as Betty Boop often wore a mini-length skirt based on a 1920s flapper dress, while Snow White is always portrayed wearing a long dress. This difference can be observed in one of the early designs, in which Snow White is depicted in a dress similar in style to the one featured in the final cel-animated feature, but her face and hair have the Betty Boop appearance, although her hair is blond.[29] This is an addition to many other early character designs of Snow White where, interestingly, she has been designed with blond hair (Figure 4.2), thereby contradicting the film's dialogue in which the Mirror describes her as 'hair black as ebony, skin white as snow'. The blond appearance might derive from the illustrations with Scandinavian influence by Swedish illustrator Gustaf Tenggren, who worked in *Snow White*'s production.

Nearly all of the early character designs of Snow White show her in a dress with slashed puffed sleeves, just as she is portrayed in the final film, although the shape of the dress and its style vary. None of the research materials indicate why the slashed puffed sleeves were chosen for the character. Slashing refers to a popular fashion starting from the Italian Renaissance and lasting until the sixteenth century and was a style often included in several parts of garments for both men and women. Even though the slashed puffed sleeves are visible in several versions of Snow White's costume designs, the

FIGURE 4.2 One of Snow White's character designs, in which she is depicted with blond hair, although the Mirror describes her as 'hair black as ebony, skin white as snow'.

Source: Screen grab from the bonus material of *Snow White and the Seven Dwarfs* 2002 DVD release.

rest of her dress includes styles and fashions from many historical periods. For example, one of her costume versions includes features from the 1830s gowns, containing a tight-fitting bodice with an oval neckline and small puffed sleeves attached to a dropped shoulder line. On the other hand, a few designs depict Snow White in a dress resembling late-medieval style, having a one-piece dress with a long train and extra fine fabric hanging down from the puffed sleeves.

While analysing Snow White's character development drawings, it is difficult to trace the original animators, as it was not a common practice for artists at Disney to sign their work. According to the story meeting notes, however, animators Albert Hurter and David Hand were heavily involved in designing and animating Snow White's costumes, as well as those of the other characters. Hurter controlled the keying of the character, in addition to dressing them, before the characters were handed over to the animators.[30] Hurter also undertook some conceptual designs similar to those drawn by Tenggren. In one of the rare signed conceptual designs by Tenggren, Snow White is depicted in a dress similar to, yet not exactly the same as, the version in the finished film. Based on these materials, the assumption is that all of these men, Hurter, Hand, Natwick, Ferguson and Tenggren, together with Disney, had contributed to Snow White's costume design. It was a collaborative work in which they all acted as costume designers.

In the final animated feature film, Snow White's costume ensemble becomes a combination of design styles and details visible in several of the development drawings. Her bodice remained tight fitting with a white stand-up collar attached to it. The shape of the collar and the neckline is rounded for a much softer feel and to better suit the sensitive characteristics of Snow White. Her skirt had less fullness in the hem than what is seen in many of her costume development designs. The style of her hair has elements from the 1930s beauty standards and was designed to follow the hairstyle of Rochelle Hudson, a famous film actress of the era.[31] The red ribbon was a decisive accessory for breaking down the hair and to avoid the impression of her having a high forehead.[32] The bow in the ribbon is an addition that emphasizes the nature of Snow White as 'slender, cute, and dainty', despite this being a strikingly stereotypical detail in the representation of feminine characters. The red colour of the ribbon connects well with the red fabric visible in the slashing on the sleeves.

Costume design was evidently an important part of the character design development process and story meetings that took place between animators during the production of Snow White. Costumes assisted in character differentiation and the definition of personalities, and costume design development was connected with the development of story. The costume colouring for all characters, aside from Snow White, was decided during the development of the character design. The initial colouring for Snow White's dress was light-yellow, visible from some of the character designs and in the dress made especially for motion study purposes. However, her dress colours were changed during the motion study filming, demonstrating that this phase of the production was also part of the costume design process.

Motion, colouring, light and shadow: Finalizing realistic costumes

In parallel with the first year of the production of Snow White, the Disney studio released the short films The China Shop (Wilfred Jackson, 1934) and The Goddess of Spring (Wilfred Jackson, 1934), which were early attempts at introducing human characters. Disney used pre-filmed footage, named motion studies, to teach animators to understand human movement and to enhance their skills at adapting these movements to animation.[33] The filmed footage assisted the animators not only with drawing the characters realistically through fidelity to authentic bodily movement but also in depicting garments, materials and their movement with a greater degree of accuracy.

Disney selected the daughter of a Hollywood choreographer, a young dancer Marge Champion (née Belcher), to act the part of Snow White during its production. Motion study filming started during the very early stages of *Snow White* as Champion was called to a costume fitting for her motion study dress in 1934.[34] The structure and silhouette of Snow White's motion study dress resembled the animated version in the film, and therefore her costume had seemingly already been defined in such early stage. This is significant, as according to the story meeting notes the character development also took place two years later. However, the creator of the motion study dress remains unknown, as at the time there was no special costume department at Disney who would have provided this dress for the filming. Someone at the studio might have sewn the dress for that purpose, as animator Kelly Kimball recalls: 'Sometimes they had somebody just sew them up ... they could get somebody working there to sew something.'[35] Members of the studio might have sewn the garment, or perhaps a family member, as, for example, during the production of *Sleeping Beauty* (Clyde Geronimi, 1959) when animator Marc Davis's wife, fashion designer Alice Ester Davis, made Princess Aurora's dress for the motion study filming.[36]

Based on examination of the filmed motion study footage, the dress that Champion wore, including its material weight and drape, resembled the character costume of Snow White in the final animated film.[37] However, the construction of the dress differed from other kinds of mundane clothing, as a dark ribbon was sewn on top of the seams, edges, the centre-front as well as the details of her light-yellow bodice and skirt (Figure 4.3). The ribbon had most likely been sewn to clearly highlight the structure, detailing and seam-lines of the costume.[38] Another purpose for this ribbon is to indicate the correct place for the black ink outline in the animation cels. Its presence assisted the animators in perceiving the important details of the costume when they drew the actor in movement. Furthermore, as the ribbon easily indicated the costume structure, it accelerated the animating process and rotoscoping some parts of the live-action footage.[39] The unusual construction of this garment verifies that it was especially made for the motion study purpose.

During the motion studies of *Snow White*, other performers were also filmed and requested to bring particular clothes with them to the studio. Whenever Champion was absent, animator Ward Kimball's wife Betty who worked in Disney's Ink and Paint department acted as a motion study model for the character of Snow White. She was asked to wear a top with short

FIGURE 4.3 The dress that Marge Champion wore for her role as motion study actress for Snow White had a dark ribbon sewn on top of the details, seams and edges of the costume. Despite its initial function to highlight these details for animation purposes, the ribbon on the centre-front of the bodice remains an easily recognized detail of Snow White's iconic costume.

Source: Screen grab from the bonus material of *Snow White and the Seven Dwarfs* 2002 DVD release.

puffed sleeves and a long skirt for the filming, resembling the silhouette of Snow White's costume.[40] Furthermore, vaudeville actor Eddie Collins was asked to bring baggy clothes to the filming, similar to Dopey's costume. In addition to her role as Snow White, Champion also acted as Dopey during the film's production by wearing a long coat. The footage of these motion studies reveals that the coat that Champion wears is a lot bigger than her body, visible in the way her sleeves hang and the length of the coat drags along the floor.[41] This matches well the description of Dopey's character in the story meeting notes, in which the animators stated several times that Dopey should wear clothes which are too large for him. These examples show that it was important that the motion study costumes represented their animated versions, especially in their structure and silhouette. They assisted the animators to examine the garment fit and material behaviour during the motion study performance.

Motion study filming was also strongly connected to the final stages of animation, assisting in adding colour, light and shadow in the correct areas on the characters and their costumes. Disney remarked that 'You can make a good drawing of a girl, but to get all the shadings and all the things ... and make it move and turn, and keep it simple enough that it can be duplicated – we went through quite a bit of experimenting to do that.'[42] Furthermore, 'the introduction of shadows added dimension to a character and depth to a scene'.[43] Once the animators understood the meaning of the material weight, movement and drapery, they were able to indicate the correct places for the light and shadow to achieve more realistic animation and more authentic character costumes.

The 'certain depth and realism' Disney was aspiring to for the film's aesthetics was achieved by the shadow painters and workers at the Paint Lab Studio.[44] The shadow painters added the light and shadow to the animation, creating the three-dimensional style of the garments and animating the correct flow of the material. This is especially important in the depiction of different fabrics, to create authenticity in the diverse ways in which they moved. The Paint Lab Studio was responsible for the character colouring, including accurate depictions of the costumes' fabric textures. Colours were mixed and painted to illustrate different materials. For example, linen material was chosen for Snow White's costumes and woven, textured linen for the dwarfs.[45] Textured material was achieved by adding different coloured patches on the coat elbows. Doc also has this particular visual detail in the design of his socks. The patches seem like they are hand sewn with long stitches, giving the illusion of an old, used garment. Linen material is difficult to copy with hand-drawn animation, and so the depiction of the linen material for Snow White's costume relies mostly on the recognizability of the fabric's movement and not the textured finishing. In Snow White's costume, the addition of light and shadow is very limited when the costume moves, which would have further enhanced the impression of a three-dimensional form. This visual effect is visible in scenes where there is a strong contrast with light or darkness shown in the costume, such as the sunlight in the field when Snow White picks flowers and in the dwarfs' cottage during moments where the light comes from the fireplace and in candlelight.

Colour choices also assisted in the different material depiction. Although the film is not strictly tied to any specific era, the costumes in *Snow White* tend to refer to the late Middle Ages or the early Italian Renaissance. At that time, flax seed was grown largely in Europe and therefore linen was common fabric to use as both household and clothing material. Earthy colour shades were easy to achieve by colouring the fabrics using natural dyes. An earthy, light-yellow colour was therefore chosen for Snow White's dress, as it creates an image of linen better than a brighter colour. Additionally, brown shades were chosen for the dwarf's costumes to connect with the linen. Each dwarf has its own colour combination, which is used as one way in costume design to assist in the distinction of similar dwarfs. Snow White's costume colours differ from the dwarfs' brown shades, making her appearance stand out from the other characters and the milieu.

For the Queen's costume, a velvet effect was given to her cape and satin finishing for her collar.[46] When analysing the Queen's cape in the final film, the velvet material is achieved by placing sharp white lines on the highest part of each crease the material makes when it is moving. On the other hand, the same lines on top of each crease in her purple gown have a grey tone. The fabric in movement seems heavy in relation to the character movement, which enhances the depiction of velvet, rather than a lightweight fabric. A different effect of black velvet is seen when the Queen transforms into the Witch. The Witch's black cape clearly has some grey textured finishing on the material creases, instead of the sharp white lines. This stylistic effect on the black costume surface delivers the feel of velvet more accurately than the one used on the Queen's cape, while also making the Witch's cape livelier in appearance.

The Queen's costume colours also signify the status of her character. Purple colour dye was traditionally time consuming and expensive to produce and, due to its high cost, was restricted from use by the lower classes. Sumptuary laws also controlled the use of purple colour and, for example, its use was limited to the highest classes in the Byzantine and medieval periods. The presence of purple in the costume design of the Queen connects with regal clothing and expensive materials, such as velvet or silk, and therefore the colour is well utilized as a sign of the character's social identity.

Conclusion

The design of the costumes for each character during the production of Disney's *Snow White* was a process that included several animators and artists working across production departments. The analysis of the research materials surrounding *Snow White*'s production did not indicate that there was a principal or lead animator who designed the character's costumes.[47] The costume designs were achieved with contributions from several artists, driven by Disney's vision. Costume designs were developed during collaborative story meetings, which assisted the artists in making revisions in order to achieve the best possible design that served both the character and the story.

Even though human character animation was in its early stages during *Snow White*'s production, the character design process demonstrated that the animators were able to understand that costume can function as an indicator of a character's personality. Additionally, they recognized that costume can also provide comic elements and can therefore be used as part of the development of character's performance and as a visual cue for the narrative. As evident in the design of the seven dwarfs, costume assisted in the differentiation of characters that are otherwise similar in appearance. The many possibilities of costume were therefore not undermined in the character design process but served to support and reflect the personalities, identities and movements of *Snow White*'s animated cast. There is ultimately an important connection to be found between 'characterization' and the design of costume as central components of character animation, despite the fact that there is an absence of critical studies of costume design within the scholarship of animation. However, this chapter's analysis of *Snow White* and its costumes design identifies the effect of costume upon the longevity of animated characters, with Snow White herself continuing to be depicted wearing her iconic costume throughout the twentieth and twenty-first centuries.[48] The legacy of *Snow White* is therefore, perhaps, entirely connected to a memorable visual image that is itself rooted in the powerful effect of costumes and the ability of dress to establish the personalities of its animated characters.

Notes

1   See publications by Robin Allan, *Walt Disney and Europe* (London: John Libbey, 1999); John Canemaker, *Before the Animation Begins: The Art and Lives of Disney Inspirational Sketch Artists* (New York: Hyperion, 1997); Richard Holliss and Brian Sibley, *Snow White and the Seven Dwarfs & the Making of the Classic Film* (New York: Simon & Schuster, 1987); and Rebecca-Anne C. Do Rozario, *Fashion in the Fairy Tale Tradition* (London: Palgrave Macmillan, 2018).

2   Allan, *Walt Disney and Europe*, 55.

3   Each animator had their own list of 'Outline of Characters' and Grant's personal copy of the list includes several sketches of the Queen, confirming that he also contributed to her character design. The list was dated 22 October

1934. According to Disney Story Conference Notes relating to *Snow White and the Seven Dwarfs*.

4   Disney Story Conference Notes relating to *Snow White and the Seven Dwarfs*, 2.

5   The early character development designs of the Queen can be found on the Special Edition DVD of *Snow White and the Seven Dwarfs* (2002) bonus material, disc 2.

6   The story meeting took place on 30 October 1934. Disney Story Conference Notes relating to *Snow White and the Seven Dwarfs*, 2.

7   Allan, *Walt Disney and Europe*, 52–5; and Maarit Kalmakurki, '*Snow White and the Seven Dwarfs*, *Cinderella* and *Sleeping Beauty*: The Components of Costume Design in Disney's Early Hand-Drawn Animated Feature Films,' *animation: an interdisciplinary journal* 13, no.1 (2018): 11, 18.

8   Disney Story Conference Notes relating to *Snow White and the Seven Dwarfs*, 2.

9   Story Conference Notes relating to *Snow White and the Seven Dwarfs*, 3.

10 The bias-cut technique was introduced by fashion designer Madeleine Vionnet in the early 1930s. Bias cut refers to a way of cutting fabric in diagonal directions, instead of in a straight grain. This method allows the fabric to stretch, making the garment accentuate the body's shape and drape beautifully.

11 Allan, *Walt Disney and Europe*, 52, 55.

12 Disney Story Conference Notes relating to *Snow White and the Seven Dwarfs*, 6.

13 Ibid., 7.

14 Ibid., 15.

15 Ibid., 18. From a story meeting on 15 December 1936.

16 To further develop the idea of Dopey being childish in appearance, Bill Tytla also suggests for Dopey that 'His coat sleeves are much too long and hang over his hands. Everything gives him this sloppy feeling.' From a story meeting on 3 November 1936. Disney Story Conference Notes relating to *Snow White and the Seven Dwarfs*, 6.

17 Ibid.

18 Ibid., 16. This was an additional note made by Walt Disney in the list of 'General Characteristics and Personalities of All Dwarfs', dated 15 December 1936.

19 Ibid., 15. A list of 'General Characteristics and Personalities of All Dwarfs' was handed out in a story meeting on 15 December 1936.

20 Ibid.

21 Ibid., 6. A discussion of the personalities of the dwarfs in a story meeting on 3 November 1936.

22 Ibid., 16. Both characteristics appear in a story meeting notes on 15 December 1936.

23 This description can be found in the list of 'General Characteristics and Personalities of All Dwarfs' in Disney Story Conference Notes relating to *Snow White and the Seven Dwarfs*, 16.

24 Ibid., 16. From a story meeting on 15 December 1936.

25 It is unclear why the DVD bonus materials only present the development of one of Snow White's dresses. One possibility is that the designs of her first dress have been lost. Another possibility is that as the screen time for this dress was very short and Snow White is remembered by her blue and yellow gown, there was no point in spending too much time on costume development for her first dress.

26 Disney Story Conference Notes relating to *Snow White and the Seven Dwarfs*, 7.

27 Ibid. In a story meeting discussing Snow White's personality on 11 November 1936.

28 Allan, *Walt Disney and Europe*, 59; Holliss and Sibley, *Snow White and the Seven Dwarfs & the Making of the Classic Film*, 30.

29 These designs can be found in Holliss and Sibley, *Snow White and the Seven Dwarfs & the Making of the Classic Film*, 20.

30 See Canemaker, *Before the Animation Begins*, 22–3; Allan, *Walt Disney and Europe*, 46; Kalmakurki, 'The Components of Costume Design in Disney's Early Hand-Drawn Animated Feature Films,' 10.

31 The dress style of Disney princesses in later classic Disney films such as *Cinderella* and *Sleeping Beauty* was also heavily influenced by the late 1940s and 1950s fashions. During these times both of the film's productions took place. Both of Cinderella's costumes contain features from Dior's New Look, established in 1947. Additionally, even though *Sleeping Beauty* was set in the medieval period, Princess Aurora's dresses have 1950s fashions combined with some elements of the medieval style.

32 In a story meeting discussing Snow White's personality on 11 November 1936. Disney Story Conference Notes relating to *Snow White and the Seven Dwarfs*, 7, 9.

33 This process involved a real person acting as a model of the animated character.

34 Kalmakurki, 'The Components of Costume Design in Disney's Early Hand-Drawn Animated Feature Films,' 11.

35 Kelly Kimball is a distinguished animator and daughter of Ward Kimball, one of Disney's Nine Old Men. Kelly Kimball, interview by the author, 25 August 2017.

36 Kalmakurki, 'The Components of Costume Design in Disney's Early Hand-Drawn Animated Feature Films,' 16; Charles Solomon, *Once Upon a Dream* (New York: Disney Editions, 2014), 51; Charles Solomon, interview by the author, 6 April 2016.

37 Kalmakurki, 'The Components of Costume Design in Disney's Early Hand-Drawn Animated Feature Films,' 11.

38 Ibid.

39 Kimball interview.

40 Ibid.

41 As with her dress, her coat also has the black ribbon, however, only sewn on the centre back seam.

42 Johnson, *Ink & Paint*, 134.

43 Ibid., 121.

44 Ibid.

45 Ibid., 136.

46 Ibid.

47 During Disney's later film productions, for example, *Cinderella* or *Sleeping Beauty*, character and conceptual designs indicate that the principal animator Marc Davis designed the costumes for the characters he was animating. Kalmakurki, 'The Components of Costume Design in Disney's Early Hand-Drawn Animated Feature Films,' 13, 15.

48 Moving examples of this can be found in the drawings from the Theresienstadt concentration camp during the Second World War, in which children drew pictures of Snow White wearing the same dress as in the film. The animated film also inspired the creation of a theatrical performance at the Children's Block of the Family Camp in Auschwitz, where the character of Snow White was painted on the walls of the children's barracks by a professional painter. Sofia Pantouvaki, 'Experiencing Visual Metaphors: The Perception of the Theatre and Imagery by Children and Youth in Oppressive Situations', in *Engaging Children Creatively and Critically*, ed. Mary A. Drinkwater (Oxford: Inter-Disciplinary Press, 2013), 52–3.

5

Making it Disney's *Snow White*

Amy M. Davis

Since the 1930s, the name – the word – 'Disney' has become rather more than just the name of a studio or of the brothers who founded it. 'Disney' can be invoked (and often is) as an adjective – largely as a catch-all, generic term – that implies a particular kind of cuteness and innocence, one that its detractors might prefer to describe as a 'saccharine' quality that highlights the sentimental falseness of a Disney entertainment product, but which is undeniably popular with large portions of the public. For many animation fans and scholars, 'Disney' denotes top-quality animation and might even be used to describe and compliment (in its adjectival form, 'Disneyesque') a non-Disney animated film that is of a particularly high visual and/ or narrative standard. The sum of these two ideas, then, is that Disney is habitually used as both a compliment *and* as an insult, depending on how and to what it is applied. But historically, and especially for those working in the US animation industry, it has meant a very specific – and yet oddly difficult to pin down – approach to filmmaking that is so recognizable, some even speak of it as if it were a genre, despite numerous changes and evolutions in Disney's look, style and subject matter throughout its history. In looking at Disney's first animated feature-length film, *Snow White and the Seven Dwarfs* (David Hand, 1937), the goal of this chapter is to attempt to locate what it is that we mean when we talk about its 'Disney' qualities. How is Disney's interpretation of the ancient folk tale of 'Little Snow White' uniquely *Disney*? What is the trait, or pattern, or technique, or technology, or 'magic touch' – or, perhaps, the ratios for each of these – that identifies *Snow White* as a product specifically of Walt Disney Productions other than its title card? This chapter may attempt to answer these questions, but it is unlikely to do so. After all, critical accounts of the history of the American animation industry reveal that multiple individuals at multiple studios have sought, at one time or another, to capture a bit of that Disney magic for their own films, hiring Disney animators and borrowing Disney production techniques, only to find that their effort to emulate Disney had not succeeded.[1] Having celebrated *Snow White*'s eightieth anniversary in December 2017, the 'Disney factor' (not unlike the so-called 'It factor') that makes Disney's *Snow White* a uniquely 'Disney' film is still a struggle to determine – I doubt very much that I have succeeded in doing so in this chapter – but the discussion is nonetheless an important one, and hopefully will contribute in some way, big or small, towards determining what we mean, ultimately, when we describe something as being 'Disney'. In my attempt to uncover what the 'Disney factor' is, I have decided to identify Disney in terms of its themes/narratives, its aesthetics (both artistically and industrially/technologically, as each of these informs the other, particularly at the studio during the 1930s) and how, in an ideological sense, Disney has always walked a narrow path between Modernity and Nostalgia – two competing ideas that Disney has long vied between, and which (I argue) it combines in such a way as to create a popular and successful brand identity out of the tensions that lie between these two opposing concepts.[2]

Is it subject matter and/or narrative and/or character development?

Walt Disney presented movie audiences with adaptations of folklore, mythology, fables and fairy tales almost from the very beginning of his career as a filmmaker. We see this in the Laugh-O-Gram 'Jazz Age Fables' of 1922 (among them, 'Cinderella', 'Puss in Boots' and 'The Four Musicians of Bremen'), and we see it in particular a decade later in the *Silly Symphonies* series that ran from 1929 to 1939 and which depicted such traditional stories as *Mother Goose Melodies* (Burt Gillett, 1931), *King Neptune* (Burt Gillett, 1932), *Three Little Pigs* (Burt Gillett, 1933), *Father Noah's Ark* (Wilfred Jackson, 1933), *The Pied Piper* (Wilfred Jackson, 1933), *The Goddess of Spring* (Wilfred Jackson, 1934), *The Grasshopper and the Ants* (Wilfred Jackson, 1934) and *The Wise Little Hen* (Wilfred Jackson, 1934). Of the seventy-five or so *Silly Symphonies* made during this ten-year period, at least twenty-nine are based on traditional tales of one type or another. It is clear (and well documented) that the *Silly Symphonies* served the Disney studio in part as training ground that led to *Snow White and the Seven Dwarfs*, both visually and narratively; how Disney told a story – how the studio structured a narrative – was devised over the course of the *Silly Symphony* series, and the basic structures of story and character development found in the *Silly Symphonies* are likewise found in Disney's early narrative-based features, especially *Snow White*, *Pinocchio* (Ben Sharpsteen and Hamilton Luske, 1940), *Dumbo* (Ben Sharpsteen, 1941) and *Bambi* (David Hand, 1942).

This approach to character development is discussed by Russell Merritt and J.B. Kaufman in their book *Walt Disney's Silly Symphonies*, as they link the eponymous child characters of *Pinocchio* and *Dumbo* to such *Silly Symphony* characters as the leads in *Elmer Elephant* (Wilfred Jackson, 1936), *Ferdinand the Bull* (Dick Rickard, 1938) and both versions of *The Ugly Duckling* (released in 1931 and 1939) when 'the child "proves" himself by becoming a rescuer or an avenger'.[3] Ultimately, or at least by their narrative's end, these are characters who (to slightly paraphrase Merritt and Kaufman, and to borrow a bit from Billy Joel) like themselves just the way they are, even if they began their narratives feeling either out of step with their peers or unsure of their own worth (except for Ferdinand, of course, who was always happy to sit just quietly and smell the flowers). For these films, both shorts and feature length, characters spend their narratives engaging in some activity/solving some crisis that helps them and/or those around them to realize their own strengths and worth, and thereby develops the character's personality in service of emotional realism. This idea is further supported by comments made by Frank Thomas and Ollie Johnston in their seminal work *The Illusion of Life* (1981). Here, they note how Disney's thoughts about story underwent a fundamental change during the production of *Snow White*:

> Prior to 1935, [Walt's] storymen had been trained to look for the fresh, the unexpected, the different, and to think in terms of caricature and exaggeration – which they interpreted as meaning bizarre, wild, and impossible. The more outlandish, the better they liked it. To them, anything real or sincere meant 'straight' and automatically would be dull. Now [by 1935, during *Snow White*'s pre-production phase], since the animators could do so much more, Walt had to pull his storymen back and teach them new values of warmth and believability. He still wanted fresh situations and funny predicaments, but he also wanted his characters to achieve maximum identity with the audience.[4]

This is enormously significant and shows one of the key characteristics that set Disney apart from its competition. Whereas many animation studios in the 1910s–1930s (such as Bray, Terry and Fleischer) favoured rather looser structures when it came to story, plot and the actual craft of animation, Disney as a studio very quickly became more concerned with story development than was to be seen elsewhere in the animation industry. Though narrative had always been important at Disney, this further tightening and compartmentalizing of the animation process as a whole becomes apparent with the formation of a defined Ink and Paint department (created by Hazel Sewell in 1927). Later in 1932, a distinct Story department further emerged at Disney thanks in part to the work of Ted Sears and Web Smith, whose roles as gag men eventually became more defined once they claimed a permanent office, rather than relying on finding temporary/occasional space in various music rooms.[5] This emphasis on story was significant, as seen in the quotes above, when it came to how Disney thought about animated film production as a whole. Improving the quality of their stories – which inherently meant improving their approaches to character development, as character development is central to how Classical Paradigm narrative structure functions – meant that Walt and his animators saw an increasing need to improve their skills as artists in order to allow the images on screen to carry the narrative and depict believable characters. Increasingly in the early 1930s, what we can see from an examination of the *Sillies* is the growing conviction that 'believable' meant a combination of both how a character looked and also – or, perhaps, more importantly – how a character *felt* to the audience. Certainly, when it came to the story, narrative and character development for their version of *Snow White*, Disney went to unprecedented lengths to get everything right. This is documented not least by the ongoing Story Conference meetings that took place throughout *Snow White*'s production, which continued well into 1937 and which constantly examined and re-examined every aspect of the story so that it was as focused as possible. This has been discussed extensively in Johnston and Thomas's *The Illusion of Life* (1981), Michael Barrier's *Hollywood Cartoons* (1999) and Kaufman's *The Fairest One of All* (2012). The upshot is that Disney's story department strove to create a lean, simple narrative that was rich in understated emotion. As Walt himself put it during a Story Conference meeting for *Snow White* on 22 December 1936,

> In our version ... we follow the story very closely. We have put in certain twists to make it more logical, more convincing, and easy to swallow. We have taken the characters and haven't added any. The only thing we have built onto the story is the animals who are friends of Snow White. ... We have developed a personality in the mirror and comic personalities for the dwarfs.[6]

This is a kind of *emotional* realism that is even more significant, ultimately, than the strides being made towards a form of visual realism at Disney during this period. The realism of emotion can be attributed largely to the character and narrative development Disney was engaging with at least as much – I would argue more – than the visual realism Disney was beginning to incorporate by the early 1930s.

But ... saying that, is it the style of visual realism that Disney developed?

It is stating the obvious to say that, visually, Disney's animation changed extensively over the course of the 1930s. The animation produced at the end of the decade was so radically different that it might well have come from another studio entirely. Though there are many potential ways to illustrate this argument, I think the best approach is to compare the two adaptations of 'The Ugly Duckling' that were produced for the *Silly Symphonies*: the first was released in 1931 (and directed by Wilfred Jackson), the other in 1939 (directed by Jack Cutting and Clyde Geronimi). The 1931 version was made before Disney's approach to animation production begins to differ (at least to any great degree) from that of its competitors. The 1939 version – coming as it does at the end of a decade which saw Disney's animation production methods depart from those of both its competitors and itself at the start of the period – is the work of a group of artists and technicians who approach animation differently in every possible way and shows how shorts production had likewise benefitted from the many advances made in the service of producing *Snow White*. This is the only instance where we see the Disney studio producing a remake of one of its earlier animated films and so makes the perfect case study for discussing Disney's revolution in visual realism. This can likewise be said of its narrative realism and emotional realism. Ultimately, it is artificial to separate these aspects of the films, but it is useful as part of our discussion of what makes Disney – and *Snow White* – Disney if we look at these aspects separately as well as together. The 1931 short, among other things, is black and white, with a very flatland aesthetic. There is the kind of classical use of plasticity (for instance, rubber-hosing) that characterizes most American animation in the 1920s and 1930s (though this will begin to fade from Disney animation during the early 1930s). The setting is a Midwestern barnyard; we can assume it is the Midwest given the fact that a tornado arrives to give us various visual gags and to give the Ugly Duckling and his would-be adoptive family, a small flock of chickens, the necessary crisis that allows the Ugly Duckling (who, in this version, is literally a duckling) to become the hero and win his family's affection. The 1931 short's narrative ultimately bears only passing resemblance to Andersen's 1843 tale; this story is played largely for laughs, and though the Ugly Duckling is generally a sympathetic character, the audience are never really invited to invest in him emotionally. By the time the 1939 remake was released, however, we get a cartoon so different that the only things they have in common are their title and their mutual association with the *Silly Symphony* series (Figure 5.1). In the later short, we have a sophisticated use of Technicolor on display; though the multi-plane camera is not utilized, the imagery is nonetheless rich, with a greater illusion of depth and complexity – not to mention beauty and artistry – than was employed in the 1931 short. The main character – who this time is an actual cygnet – has a far more expressive face, and faces a journey that is characterized with enough trauma, rejection and heartache that, far from simply laughing at the character's mishaps, we are also moved to feel his pain and disappointment. This is so that, when a mother swan and her cygnets arrive and adopt him into their bevy, the mother's embrace of the orphan is sufficiently emotionally

FIGURE 5.1 Comparison of *The Ugly Duckling* (Wilfred Jackson, 1931) and *The Ugly Duckling* (Jack Cutting and Clyde Geronimi, 1939).

heightened as to move the audience (a reaction likewise emphasized by the music). Though Disney placed enormous emphasis on the story and characters, Walt and his artists certainly believed that, for a full emotional impact, the visual realism of their films was hugely important.

Disney's commitment as a studio to improving the artistry of animation is most visible when looking not just at how Disney focused on honing its animation but also by examining how Disney's competition demonstrated no real interest in their animators' skills nor in the beauty or narrative complexity of their films. One way of thinking about what makes Disney unique is to think about their competitors and how the studio's approach to its work differed from that of the other studios. In the 1930s, this means looking primarily at the Fleischer studio. Max Fleischer began working in the animation industry when he was hired by Bray sometime around 1917, but soon formed his own studio (along with his brother, Dave Fleischer) in 1921.[7] Over the course of the 1920s and 1930s, the Fleischer studio produced several successful series (including Koko the Clown shorts/*Out of the Inkwell* series, the *Betty Boop* series and the *Popeye* series). Although Max Fleischer would invent a number of new technologies/animation processes (to include the Rotoscope, patented in 1917, and the Setback, patented in 1933), there was no interest at Fleischer in moving beyond the kind of rubber-hose character animation typical of the era. Indeed, in contrast to Disney, those overseeing the studio's animation production were more likely to discourage staff from pursuing further training and artistic innovation than they were to encourage (let alone incorporate) innovation. As one former Fleischer employee remembered it,

> Those people who were quite content with the raw, peasant humor, the bad drawing, the kind of not-too-thought-out timing, and the simpleminded stories ... that bunch stayed [at Fleischer]. The more adventurous, who wanted to learn to do a better movie, left. Every one of them. Nobody stayed who had that urge, because there was no way to make such a picture in New York.[8]

Even by the mid-1930s, as Barrier notes,

> For all that the Fleischers emphasized a sort of cartoon engineering on the screen, they were reluctant to embrace advances that were more than just mechanical. For instance, they did not allow animating on twos until sometime after 1935, even though Disney's [*sic*] and other studios had long since realized that the uniform projection speed that came with sound meant that many scenes could be animated on twos without risking jerkiness on the screen.[9]

This is not to imply that Fleischer was interested in new devices/technologies more so than Disney. Disney, too, adopted and implemented numerous technological devices intended to enhance its films' visual impact, including its adoption of emerging sound technology in 1928, the then-new 3-strip Technicolor (which it began using in 1932 in a three-year exclusive deal with Technicolor, debuting with its short *Flowers and Trees* (Burt Gillett, 1932) that same year) and its refinement and use of the multi-plane camera beginning in 1937 (which debuted in its Oscar-winning short *The Old Mill* [Wilfred Jackson, 1937]). In addition to the differences in production approaches and priorities between Disney and Fleischer, there are further contrasts: the settings of Disney tend to be rural or suburban, whereas Fleischer tends to favour more urban settings. The ways that characters are structured, as well as the kinds of characters chosen, are likewise very different. Whereas

Disney tended to rely primarily on anthropomorphized animal characters, Fleischer's stars were human: Koko the Clown, then Betty Boop, then Popeye.[10] Furthermore, most Fleischer character designs tend to be cartoony/caricature in nature, without any evidence that they were interested in the kind of 'Realism' that came to characterize Disney during this period. Max Fleischer started out in animation thanks to his inventing the Rotoscope (certainly Koko was a rotoscoped character in his earlier/solo years), and he eventually embraced a more Disney-esque style of animation beginning with the feature film *Gulliver's Travels* (Dave Fleischer, 1939). By the time *Gulliver's Travels* was released, its form of visual realism seems to evoke the Disney style of animation, particularly in the designs for Princess Glory and Prince David, designed and animated by Grim Natwick, who was hired (from Iwerks' studio, to which he'd been enticed from Fleischer) to work on *Snow White* before being lured back to Fleischer to work on *Gulliver's Travels*.

Ultimately, however, the thing that most separates Disney and Fleischer at this time was the freedom – or lack thereof – as well as the respect that each gave to their animators and artists, particularly when it came to allowing animators to work on their skills and not only maintain but also continuously improve their animation. Charles Solomon notes that

> Most studios [during the 1930s] required animators to produce about thirty feet (or about 20 seconds of screen time) per week. At Disney, the footage requirements were much lower, and Walt paid bonuses for exceptional animation. Natwick recalls getting a $600 bonus for his work on 'Alpine Climbers' (1936); [Art] Babbitt received $1,500 for his animation on the title character in 'The Country Cousin' (1936).[11]

This is in marked contrast to the restrictions placed on innovation and improvement at Fleischer. Barrier quotes a lower-ranking animator at the studio, Ed Rehberg, who described Fleischer director Seymour Kneitel as having 'a stock formula for walks and runs, and you either did it his way or it was wrong. There was never any experimenting. He'd say, "You're stupid if you do it that way. Don't you have any more sense than that?" He was that crude.'[12] By comparison, Walt Disney's support – both moral and remunerative – for experimentation made Disney's staff want to push themselves in ways that made them both artistically and technically capable of producing a film as complex and demanding as *Snow White*. Fleischer (and Iwerks) studio alumnus Natwick, who came to work at Disney beginning in late 1934 and was part of the team working on *Snow White*, would paint a very different picture of working at Disney than the situation he had experienced at his previous studios. In a 1988 interview where, in part, he talked about his experience of *Snow White*, Natwick described the early-stage work on the animation for the film:

The first scene Walt gave us, he said, 'Take a whole month on this one scene. Just [take your time]. Everything you find that doesn't work tell us and we'll change it.' ... He [Walt] gave us a whole month, and we didn't ever have to submit one inch of animation to go into the picture. We could work them over or do anything we wanted to.[13]

Barrier's research on Fleischer studio working practices supports this: 'What had become central to Disney animation by the late thirties, the exploration of character through animation, was incidental at best in the Fleischer scheme of things because of the threat it posed to the steady flow of production.'[14] Later in the 1930s, when Fleischer, in the midst of production on its first feature, *Gulliver's Travels*, had on its payroll animators who had worked at Disney (such as Natwick), the studio still seems to have incorporated Disney's production techniques only in a half-hearted way, which demonstrates Fleischer's failure to understand either the usefulness of these techniques or the notions that lay behind them. In short, it shows a lack of genuine commitment to improving animation as a cinematic art form and is the reason why, ultimately, *Gulliver's Travels* is inferior to *Snow White* both visually and – most crucially, I would argue – narratively.

Behind all of this is the greater willingness to spend time on the pre-production planning that narratives enjoyed at Disney, a fact which was crucial to *Snow White* in both its pre-production and production phases. Barrier, in his discussion of Disney during the early 1930s, quotes Ben Sharpsteen's descriptions of when he first joined the Disney staff, saying that 'Working at Disney's "was just a complete reversal" of his New York experience.' Sharpsteen noted that 'This business of planning and having exposure sheets that spelled out to the very drawing, that was entirely new. And the synchronization of sound.'[15] Barrier goes on to note that, as early as 1930, Walt was making a point of hiring people (some of them Fleischer studio alumni such as Ted Sears) who were known for their strong story ideas and skill in shaping narratives for animation. Likewise, the practice of using what they called 'pencil tests', where rough animation was photographed onto film and the negative film then played to check over the animator's progress on a particular movement or sequence, was likewise instrumental, according to Barrier, in giving the animators a method through which they could, via trial and error, find ways of rendering more complex movements. In his discussion of the work for the short *Just Dogs* (Burt Gillett, 1932), for example, Barrier discusses how these pencil tests allowed for much more complex movement – movement which carried with it a stronger feeling of realism – than could be seen previously. He argued that:

Just Dogs was the first Disney cartoon to benefit from advances in animation and drawing of exactly the kind that could be expected to flow from the use of rough pencil tests. ... [Norm] Ferguson's earlier animation, although more lifelike than the animation that proceeded it, did not invite direct comparison with real life; the animation in *Just Dogs* did.[16]

Another lower-ranked animator at Fleischer, Bob Bemiller, had no recollection, according to Barrier, of Disney-style 'pencil tests', for example, becoming anything like standard practice at Fleischer: 'If you had some kind of an action that you weren't sure about, they'd let you make a test on it.'[17] The implication is that such techniques, used for problem solving rather than general improvement, refinement and innovation, were deemed to be largely superfluous to standard production methods. Likewise, general attitudes towards their work seem to have stood in marked contrast. In his 1988 interview with David Johnson, Natwick talks about a tour of the Hyperion studio Walt gave him in 1934 just before Natwick joined the Disney studio (by this stage, Natwick had been working at Ub Iwerks' studio since 1932, having been enticed there from Fleischer with the promise of more money):

> [Walt] stopped in on a couple of animators and showed me what they were doing – working on Mickey – particularly an animator who finished his work beautifully. I was always kind of a slapstick man. I liked to rough things out quickly and roughly. But this guy was a brilliant clean-up man [Dick Huemer]. ... I thought: 'Christ, if I have to draw like this ...' I'd been knocking out Flip the Frog and stretching him and flattening him out and doing things with him but, golly, it pretty near scared me, actually. But I thought I would risk it.[18]

These descriptions of the contrasts between Disney and Fleischer (and even between Disney and Iwerks' studio, from what Natwick implies was tolerated there) illustrate clearly that, beyond the training that came to characterize Disney thanks to the classes run by Don Graham and Phil Dike beginning in late 1932, the Disney studio gave much greater freedom – and much greater respect – to its artists than could be found elsewhere. This respect, as is supported by many accounts of the studio in this period, led its employees to work even harder and strive for newer, better techniques and approaches to all aspects of their film production methods, from story, to character animation, effects animation (which evolved as a separate specialization at Disney during this period), to the creation and/ or modification of various forms of animation and film technologies (such as sound/music, colour and the camera equipment used to photograph the cels). This attitude pushed Disney forward and, in contrast, is what made its competitors look increasingly behind the times when it came to the look and feel of their films. Disney's visual style in the 1930s took on a very distinctive look and feel. This happened as a result of the work on *Snow White*, coupled with Walt's willingness to allow his artists to experiment, to take their time and to improve their abilities as animators, as storytellers and how they incorporated sound, voice and music.

Or … is it how Disney combines the tensions between Modernity and Nostalgia?

'Disney' has often been understood as the perfect blend of Nostalgia and Modernity. Certainly, this element of Disney's cultural identity has been discussed by Richard deCordova in his essay 'The Mickey in Macy's Window' in relation to the popularity of Mickey Mouse.[19] It is not difficult to see these two seemingly opposite qualities embodied in the visuals of *Snow White*. Indeed, the very contrast between the ancientness of the story itself and the Art Deco aspects of the visuals is one site where Modernity and Nostalgia cross paths in Disney animation of the 1930s. After all, what we get with *Snow White and the Seven Dwarfs* is an ancient story being told in the form of an animated film, which is itself very much a modernist medium (especially in the 1930s). Even in its more mainstream incarnations, Animation is in fact a surrealist art form, and the most familiar of animated shorts and films can deal heavily in fantastic, surrealist qualities. Yet this Modernity (or the Modernist aspect to *Snow White*) is undercut by a number of devices employed by the film: it begins (following the opening credits) with a shot of a (live-action) book, which opens to reveal (and thereby ushers in what functions as) an opening title sequence for the film, written in a calligraphic-style print meant to echo a medieval illuminated manuscript. The text itself sounds very much like a classic story book, beginning with 'Once upon a time, there lived a lovely little Princess named Snow White.' We even get a page turning so that, as the overture music ends and the screen fades to black before the animation begins, we in a sense are entering into a storybook. Also, the text in these pages already hints at the story's moralistic elements (an idea typically associated with the fairy tale), particularly as regards the 'vain and wicked Stepmother the Queen' and the jealousy of Snow White's beauty that leads her to dress 'the little Princess in rags and force … her to work as a Scullery Maid'. In other words, the structure of the film, right from its opening shots, strives to bring a very traditional feel to the story. Once the animation begins, the levels of artistry and detail in the animation have the feel of storybook illustrations coming to life. The first two scenes of the film are of what we have just read in the 'storybook' pages that introduce the film's narrative to the audience. In other words, *Snow White* may be a Modernist technological and artistic achievement for the Disney staff in 1937, but its formal elements give it the feel of traditional storybooks as well as traditional tales, complete with the moralistic and didactic elements considered essential to the fairy tale since at least the nineteenth century.

Another way that Modernity and Nostalgia function together in *Snow White* is the contrast in the discourse on the innovative technologies and modern entertainment surrounding the film (and Disney animation as a whole in the 1930s) with the ways that Disney films of the period echo what were, by this time, traditional elements of childhood toys and children's book illustrations. As deCordova noted in his discussion of the merchandising of Mickey Mouse in the early 1930s, the linking of animals and childhood – so key to much of the merchandising that surrounds Disney shorts (and *Snow White*) in this period – goes back to the Romantic era and is part of a rejection of the sociocultural changes brought on by the Industrial Revolution. This idea – and its linking of childhood innocence with nature/animals – is an 'ideology implicit in the iconography of toys, an iconography shared by animation'.[20] Merritt and Kaufman likewise note the many similarities in the colour *Silly Symphonies* with the colour illustrations of the American children's book artist Harrison Cady.[21] While a reliance on anthropomorphic animal characters is an important part of animation in the 1920s and 1930s and happens for all sorts of reasons, it is nonetheless important to stress that, even though *Snow White* was significant as an early animated film attempting to depict 'realistic' (as opposed to 'cartoony' or caricatured) human figures, animal characters are to be found throughout the film despite the fact that they are nonessential to the film's plot. True, the animals do help Snow White to find the Dwarfs' cottage, and later they alert the Dwarfs when the Wicked Queen arrives at the cottage and gives Snow White the poisoned apple, but other ways to do this could have been found. I argue that, regardless of whether or not those involved in *Snow White*'s production thought about it consciously, the fact remains that the presence of the cute bunnies, birds, deer, racoons, chipmunks and turtles (among others) serves to highlight Snow White's innocence while simultaneously undercutting the (for the time) heightened use of technological and artistic innovation that characterize the production of *Snow White*.

Yet Snow White's innocence was itself a contentious point during the film's production. In the Grimms' version of this very ancient tale, Snow White is very young – hardly more than a child – yet by the end of the tale, after some time (how much time, one can speculate) has passed, she marries the prince. Naturally, by the 1930s, making Snow White of a plausible age to marry meant that the character needed to begin the story as at least a teenager. It is important to bear in mind that a young woman still in her late teens being married was acceptable during the 1920s and 1930s; according to US census figures, the median age for women to marry in 1930 was 21.3, which indicates that many women would have married at ages 17 to 19.[22] In his book *The Fairest One of All* (2012), Kaufman discusses the contradictions inherent in Snow White as a character, in particular the so-called 'Girl/

Woman' tensions she possesses. As Kaufman notes, these tensions can be found in various aspects of the character, most prominently in her visual depictions – as animated by Hamilton Luske and Natwick – and in her voice, particularly when the childlike voice performed by Adriana Caselotti is singing about Snow White's longing for her prince. Kaufman discusses this at some length, arguing that whereas Luske's animation – which Walt favoured overall – depicted a more childlike character, Natwick's animation gives us a more womanly, comparatively mature figure. Though Kaufman ties this with the idea of the Girl/Woman character type so popular in the 1920s (as can be seen in performances by actresses such as Mary Pickford and Marguerite Clark, who played the role of Snow White in the 1916 live-action film directed by J. Searle Dawley for Paramount), he claims that the popularity of this character type had largely faded by the 1930s.[23] Though Kaufman concludes his discussion by stating (without supporting evidence) that Disney's Snow White retained this Girl/Woman dichotomy because Margaurite Clark's performance had made this 'an inextricable part of Snow White's cultural legacy', I would argue that there are potentially other factors at work here.[24]

Walt Disney wanted his studio's film to stick to the basics of the Grimms' version of 'Snow White' as much as possible, and no doubt this desire played an important role in shaping Show White as a character. But Kaufman's claim that the Girl/Woman character had largely faded by the 1930s is problematic given the popularity of such actresses as Shirley Temple, Judy Garland and Deanna Durbin. Durbin was even considered at one stage to voice Snow White, though ultimately she was rejected because her voice was deemed to be 'too mature'.[25] But more importantly, the Girl/Woman functions in many respects as a sanitized version of the Madonna/Whore dichotomy, an ancient idea of womanhood found throughout culture, including Hollywood cinema. Indeed, one might point out that, by the late 1930s, the Girl/Woman and the Madonna/Whore were everywhere in cinema, and Disney was no exception in incorporating such a depiction of Womanhood. Snow White and the Queen replicate the Madonna/Whore, and the sexual innocence that can be part of some versions of the Madonna is suitably expressed by the ever-popular Girl/Woman type. By invoking these archetypes in ways that so obviously reference popular Hollywood stars of the period, Disney once more plays out the tensions between the modern – the New Woman, the Emancipated Woman and the Twentieth Century's version of the Girl/Woman – and the ancient Madonna/Whore and (in the evil Queen) the Femme Fatale.

Ultimately, this balancing act between Modernity and Nostalgia in all its forms – the cultural, the technological, the narrative and the archetypal – has come to characterize many of Disney's cultural products throughout the studio's history, beginning with the juxtaposition of a child's dreams with modern technology in the *Alice Comedies* (1923–7), through the rise of Mickey Mouse and his crew, the favouring of folklore and fairy tales in cinematic forms, up to and including its theme parks beginning in 1955 with the opening of Disneyland. After all, the theme park concept was well positioned by the mid-1950s to take up the mantle of modernity in entertainment just as cinema generally – and animation specifically – had begun to lose its feeling of newness as more and more people had no memory of a time before the existence of cinema. As Dorene Koehler notes in describing how the Disney parks appeal to their audience, '[Disney] balances itself on the tightrope that is the tension between tradition and invention.'[26] The same can be said of television and Disney's engagement with it as a modern technology that allowed the studio to bring audiences, in its first television special (*One Hour in Wonderland*, broadcast on NBC on Christmas Day, 1950), reminders of *Snow White* and glimpses of *Alice in Wonderland* (Clyde Geronimi, Wilfred Jackson and Hamilton Luske, 1951), the studio's animated version of the beloved Victorian novel, via what was at the time the latest in entertainment technology: broadcast television. We still see it in the theme parks (in the forms of entertainments utilized if not in the concept of the theme park itself, now well over half a century old), but we likewise see these same ideas at work in Disney's more contemporary films, its acquiring of such franchises as the Star Wars and Marvel universes, and in its use of the latest tablet and smartphone technologies to interact with its fans and customers. That this interplay between the old and the new – between Nostalgia and Modernity – continues to play itself out within Disney shows what an effective – and intrinsic – component it is to characterizing what makes something *Disney*.

Conclusions ... such as they are ...

As to the question of what it is that makes Disney's animation inherently *Disney*, and specifically what makes *Snow White and the Seven Dwarfs* inherently *Disney* – what we now might refer to as 'Disney Magic' – ultimately, the only thing that can be stated definitively is that there is no single element that can be identified as the secret factor in the equation. Certainly the first to search for Disney's 'secret' were his competitors in commercial animation in Hollywood's Golden Era studios, all of whom went so far as to lure Disney animators away in the hopes that these Disney alumni would bring the 'Disney Touch' – not unlike the Midas Touch – with them. For various reasons, as has been discussed, it never worked. During the 1930s, Disney's most serious competitor was the Fleischer studio in New York City (later in Miami). As the Fleischers' involvement in their studio ended and Paramount took it over, the animation units at Warner Brothers and MGM rose to prominence, in particular with their *Bugs Bunny* (WB) and *Tom & Jerry* (MGM) cartoon series in the early 1940s. But aside from Fleischers' (comparatively modest) successes in feature-length animation with *Gulliver's Travels* and their two-reelers such as *Raggedy Anne & Raggedy Andy* (Dave Fleischer, 1941), ultimately Fleischer never equalled Disney's quality or its success. Despite their own eras of prominence, neither did either Warner Bros or MGM; unlike Disney and Fleischer, neither Warner Bros nor MGM ever engaged with feature-length animation during the Golden Era.

Though various reasons can be posited as to why Disney's competition never succeeded in capturing its magic, the real question here is not why other studios could not replicate Disney; rather, the question is what it is that makes Disney's earliest animated features – specifically its first feature, *Snow White and the Seven Dwarfs* – inherently and unquestionably *Disney*. I argue, ultimately, that it was how Disney conceptualized story selections, narrative structures and character development; how it combined those in the 1930s with the emerging cinematic technologies of sound and colour (technologies it helped to shape); as well as technologies such as the multi-plane camera that were specific to animation production. These factors came together to create an aesthetic that, though not new in and of itself, was revolutionary in a cinematic context, given that it relied upon the familiarity of the aesthetics of late-nineteenth-/early-twentieth-century children's book illustrations and ancient, well-known stories to counterbalance the modernism that was cinematic entertainment in the 1930s. But what I struggle with are (1) Were there other factors that have not yet stood out as important? (2) In what ratios did the factors discussed here come into the equation? Was one of these more important than the others? Did they all weigh equally into the outcome? As we approach Disney's centenary in October 2023, we can now look at this question – this series of questions – from an advantageous position not available to those who sought to find out back in the 1930s what it was that made Disney different from its competitors. But as animation historians, Disney studio historians and scholars of film aesthetics, we can come together to debate the importance and weight of these (and other) factors. Whether we can finally pinpoint what it is that makes Disney … *Disney* … well, that remains to be seen. Hopefully, others will join in with the discussion.

Notes

1 In *Hollywood Cartoons: American Animation in Its Golden Age*, Michael Barrier notes several instances of Disney's rivals luring away his animators (often with promises of larger salaries and/or greater authority) in the hopes of tapping into the source of Disney's success for themselves. Just a few key examples of this are when Hugh Harman and Rudolf Ising went with Charles Mintz and George Winkler to form the short-lived Winkler Studio in 1928 (p. 153); when Pat Powers signed up Ub Iwerks in 1930 (pp. 63–7);

and when Burt Gillett (best known for directing *Three Little Pigs* [1934]) went to work at Van Beuren in 1934 (pp. 169–70). For more, see Michael Barrier, *Hollywood Cartoons: American Animation in Its Golden Age* (New York: Oxford University Press, 1999).

2   I am using the word 'Modernity' here in its usual sense of 'the contemporary', rather than as a specifically animation studies meaning (which, for some, has become associated with the idea of the 'Hollywood Flatlands', but which somehow – and peculiarly – divorces the idea from the twentieth-century notions of an aesthetic and philosophical movement that are crucial to Esther Leslie's arguments). For Disney, I would argue that 'Modernity' means a continuing reference to the Contemporary/the Modern. This can be seen literally, for example, in their naming their flagship 1971 hotel at Walt Disney World the Contemporary Hotel, and can also be seen figuratively (and even more recently) in the ideologies that lie at the heart of their most recent films and television shows, such as the emphasis on female leadership in *Moana* (Ron Clements and John Musker, 2016) (2016, the year most believed the United States would get its first female president, until it didn't) and its self-reflexive commentary on its princess characters (among many other things) in the 2018 film *Ralph Breaks the Internet* (Rich Moore and Phil Johnston, 2018).

3   Russell Merritt and J. B. Kaufman, *Walt Disney's Silly Symphonies: A Companion to the Classic Cartoon Series* (Glendale: Disney Editions, 2016), 12.

4   Frank Thomas and Ollie Johnston, *The Illusion of Life: Disney Animation* (New York: Hyperion Press, 1981), 376.

5   Barrier, *Hollywood Cartoons*, 93–5. On page 94, Barrier notes that, before late 1932, the gag men, who had 'moved like gypsies from one music room to another, now had an office of their own'.

6   Extracts from Story Conference Notes Relating to *Snow White and the Seven Dwarfs* in the Disney Archives, Burbank, California. Copied by David R. Williams, August 1987, and held in the Collections of the British Film Institute Library, London, 21.

7   There seems to be a lack of certainty as to when Max Fleischer went to work for the John R. Bray Studio. Dates in various publications, including Donald Crafton's *Before Mickey* (1982) and Michael Barrier's *Hollywood Cartoons* (1999), seem to range between 1916 and 1918, though the first instalment of his *Koko the Clown* series would not premier until September 1919.

8   Leonard Maltin, *Of Mice and Magic: A History of Animated Cartoons* (New York: McGraw-Hill, 1980), 83.

9   Barrier, *Hollywood Cartoons*, 186.

10   While of course you do get characters such as Betty Boop's friend Bimbo (who seems to be a dog, but also humanoid), the overwhelming majority of central characters in Fleischer tend to be humans, as do many of the secondary characters who feature in the *Betty Boop* and *Popeye* series.

11 Charles Solomon, *The History of Animation: Enchanted Drawings* (New York: Wings Books, 1994), 50.

12 Barrier, *Hollywood Cartoons*, 295.

13 David Johnson, 'Interview with Grim Natwick', in *Snow White's People: An Oral History of the Disney Film Snow White and the Seven Dwarfs*, ed. Didier Ghez (USA: Theme Park Press, 2017), 63.

14 Barrier, *Hollywood Cartoons*, 295.

15 Ibid., 60.

16 Ibid., 81.

17 Ibid., 294.

18 David Johnson, 'Interview with Grim Natwick', 60.

19 Richard deCordova, 'The Mickey in Macy's Window: Childhood, Consumerism, and Disney Animation', in *Disney Discourse: Producing the Magic Kingdom*, ed. Eric Smoodin (London: Routledge, 1994), 203–13.

20 deCordova, 'The Mickey in Macy's Window', 211.

21 J. B. Kaufman, *The Fairest One of All: The Making of Walt Disney's Snow White and the Seven Dwarfs* (London: Aurum Press, 2012) 12, 16, 229–30.

22 By 1940, the median age for women at the time of their first marriage had risen only marginally, to 21.5. By the late 1940s, however, this number had dropped to 20 years, where it would remain until the early 1970s. Figures found at https://www.census.gov/population/socdemo/hh-fam/tabMS-2.pdf.

23 Kaufman, *The Fairest One of All*, 48–9.

24 Ibid., 49.

25 Ibid., 48.

26 Dorene Koehler, *The Mouse and the Myth: Sacred Art and Secular Ritual of Disneyland* (East Barnet: John Libbey, 2017), 137.

PART TWO

Snow White in Hollywood

6

With a smile and a song: *Snow White and the Seven Dwarfs* as the first integrated musical

Sadeen Elyas

Walt Disney has made the 20th century's only important contribution to music. Disney has made use of music as language. In the synchronization of humorous episodes with humorous music, he has unquestionably given us the outstanding contribution of our time. In fact, I would go so far as to say it is the only real contribution.[1]

The Disney studio has been widely positioned as central to the ways in which the auditory aspects of cinema could be successfully combined with imagery in shaping the spectators' experience. In 1934, *Fortune* magazine stated that 'Most competitors are in this business for the money; but Disney (although he keeps a shrewd eye on the costs and revenues) is an artist and craftsman. His films are painstakingly made, by a large and expensive organization. Disney allows himself no delusions of artistic grandeur, but he believes in the fine quality of his work.'[2] The view of *Fortune* is significant, illustrating how Disney was perceived by the public and within the popular press at the time, when the studio decided to take a major step towards making their first feature-length animated film *Snow White and the Seven Dwarfs* (David Hand, 1937). A central element of the film's 'fine quality' was its innovative application of sound and music.

Following the success of Disney's Mickey Mouse shorts that debuted with the release of *Steamboat Willie* (Ub Iwerks, 1928) as the first successful use of synchronized sound film in animation and Hollywood, and the subsequent success of the *Silly Symphonies*, it is not surprising to see Disney approach the use of sound and music as they did in their debut feature. During the 1930s, the inclusion of music in a film was still considered to be something of a novelty. However, *Snow White* reconfigured the use of music within the broader context of Hollywood musicals of the period. The film is heavily driven by a musical rhythm, particularly visible in the ways that characters and additional story elements interact with the music.[3] *Snow White* represents a phenomenon of audiovisual synchronization where music *adds* to the story rather than simply *enhancing* it so as to signify and be fully involved with the animated imagery. This presents the film as a rich case study for thinking about the interplay between sound and music within animation, and across cinema history more broadly.

This chapter examines how *Snow White and the Seven Dwarfs* contributed to the history of film music and the musical film genre and focuses on the way the film uses music as a key component of conveying the narrative, becoming a space where music shapes our understanding, directs our attention, confirms the existence of a specific fictional reality and encapsulates our awareness of a given truth that is depicted in the film's fantasy world.[4] In particular, this chapter argues that within the history of Hollywood cinema, *Snow White and the Seven Dwarfs* was one of the first (if not *the* first) *fully* integrated film musicals in terms of its songs and musical score. By utilizing historical sources related to sound film (such as interviews with various film producers and composers such as Max Steiner, and story meeting notes from Disney's production notes on *Snow White*) and the evolution of the musical film genre, as well as film sound/music theory, the chapter examines Disney's position among other competing studios during the first major era of Hollywood's use of sound. The Disney studio not only followed but also led how films and their narratives could successfully incorporate sound and music. Although there has been relatively little research on Disney's music, as well as on sound and music in animation more generally, this chapter seeks to encourage a discussion of Disney's use of auditory (including speech/dialogue, sound effects, music, ambient sound and silence as part of a film's 'sonic fabric') and visual (imagery) aspects as parallel (yet vital) storytelling agents of the film.[5]

Sound and music evolution in Hollywood (1920s–1930s)

Disney's *Snow White* sits firmly within a particular historical moment in which the Hollywood film industry was transitioning to sound. Many Hollywood studios embraced the sound throughout the technology's gradual evolution, from synchronized sound to the rise of the musical film genre, and as mere novelty to the enhancing of the aesthetics of films, with music offering a fantasy break from the dramatic focus of the narrative. The film musical reflected a better world than the real one, with Richard Dyer describing the genre as a 'utopian place' that the audience could 'escape into', rather than serving as an *integrating* and *storytelling* component that advances the narrative.[6] By 1928–9 when synchronized sound began to emerge with more force across Hollywood cinema, most of those working at Hollywood's major studios, among them Nicholas M. Schenck (American film studio executive and businessman), regarded sound as 'a kind of spice to be sprinkled on judiciously, as needed'.[7] Early synchronized sound films, such as Warner Brothers' *The Jazz Singer* (Alan Crosland, 1927), Fox Movietone's *The Air Circus* (Howard Hawks, 1928) and Paramount's *Warming Up* (Fred C. Newmeyer, 1928), were advertised as through the novelty of spectators being able to '*Hear* and *See*' the players talk their parts.[8] However, those films were only *part-talkies, goat glands* or *dual versions*, largely due to the temporal limitation of the sound-on-disc system. This means that the entire film was silent, but included a handful of scenes and sequences that used synchronized sound. To call attention to the sound/musical content, filmmakers relied on the trend of justifying sound's inclusion via the 'backstage plot'. Hollywood filmmakers regularly and reflexively exploited the relationship between sound and music alongside an actor's stardom, such as Al Jolson, to show off the performer's vocal skills and to reinforce emotional content through musical sequences, at the same time attracting larger audiences familiar with some of these acts from vaudeville stage routines.[9]

Although contemporary audiences may look back upon Hollywood's early synchronized sound films and film musicals in the late 1920s/early 1930s with a nostalgic fondness, many of those first efforts in sound cinema were heavily derided by audiences and critics for numerous reasons, as Donald Crafton explains.[10] These include questions over the poor quality of sound and recording; an inadequate story and plot execution; the lack of dialogue or, conversely, excessive use of dialogue (as one film critic, Mordaunt Hall, complained).[11] Likewise, there were often issues with the synchronization of both speech and sound effects, so that the sound either anticipated or followed the action to which it should have been tied. Some audience members (and some filmmakers) also had problems with the actors' voices. Films such as *Caught in the Fog* (Howard Bretherton, 1928) and *State Street Sadie* (Archie Mayo, 1928) were perceived as incompatible with an actor's appearance and/or persona.[12] Other critics noted that, in some cases, 'musical accompaniment [was incorporated into the film] without regard to logical pattern'.[13] During this technological moment, Hollywood was evidently uncertain with regard to the future of synchronized sound/ musical films, with even Warner Bros. announcing that it would make 'no more all-talking films'.[14] Within these teleological histories of sound and music that focus largely on this experimental late 1920s–1930s period, and despite the central role Disney played within Hollywood's cartoon industry, the studio's importance to film sound and music is largely neglected within both popular and academic film discourse. This is certainly the case with regard to *Snow White*, which is hardly ever mentioned as an innovative film musical, let alone as the first fully *integrated* musical film. Part of the reason for this is, perhaps, the long-standing critical neglect of animation within film history. However, this omission of *Snow White* is exacerbated further by the sidelining of the history of animation's use of sound/music, yet no less surprising given Disney's contribution to film sound technology. Some of the film scoring techniques that Disney had developed, such as 'Mickey Mousing' (a term which is mysteriously elusive in its origin, as scholars are still unsure of its inventor), were heavily adopted by film composers in the 1930s–1940s, especially by Steiner, who employed the technique in many of his films such as *King Kong* (Merian C. Cooper and Ernest B. Schoedsack, 1933), *The Informer* (John Ford, 1935) and *Gone with the Wind* (Victor Fleming, 1939).[15]

The 'narrative reality' of *Snow White and the Seven Dwarfs*

By 1934, Disney had decided to take a major step towards making a feature-length animated film musical. Although he disliked the way that film musicals of the period were structured (the interruption of the narrative with a musical number), during the early planning stages of *Snow White* he said to his staff that 'it's still the influence from the musicals they have been doing for years. Really we should set a new pattern, a new way to use music – weave it into the story so somebody doesn't just burst into song.'[16] Walt believed, unlike many of his fellow studio heads in the 1930s, that through such 'weaving' music could be an integral part of storytelling in a film – that it could be used to deliver exposition, develop characters and situations and, most importantly, as a tool to advance the plot, rather than incorporating music by interrupting the narrative musically.[17] *Snow White* was one of the first (if not *the* first) fully integrated film musicals in terms of its songs and musical score. According to David Tietyen, *Snow White* was 'the finest example of the total creative integration film and music, and it is better constructed than any musical picture of that era'.[18]

To examine the structures of an integrated or non-integrated musical, it is first essential to define the narrative reality or 'classical realist narration' and the musical reality of a film. John Belton defines the former as a 'world that is consistent and coherent; that world obeys a stated or unstated set of rules that give it credibility'.[19] This is also known as a form of 'realism', which, as a concept, influenced story and narrative at Disney and involves the suspension of disbelief even if a world contains unrealistic elements and invites the spectator into an animated world. On the other hand, Belton defines musical reality as a reality that interacts with two sets of worlds and two sets of laws, which switch back and forth between one another from the grounded fictional reality world to a musical spectacle. As a result, 'musical reality' registers new laws and incorporates characters who surrender themselves to a song mood. These films operate as an act within an act because the actors in the film would suddenly move into singing and dancing, freeing themselves from 'the laws that govern the mundane world of the fiction'.[20] This is how a large number of early Hollywood musicals operated, as a spectacle to transport the audience, together with the characters, into a world of fantasy, escapism and utopia. The reason early sound films in Hollywood were musicals was that it was easier to exploit popular music financially and technologically. Popular music was the sound of Hollywood films, though there was yet to be an appreciation of utilizing music for its storytelling potentials.

Snow White might therefore be considered as the first *fully* integrated musical of its kind. John Mueller identifies six levels of 'integration' in film musicals. He explains the first category as musical numbers that are 'completely irrelevant to the plot'.[21] The final category is 'numbers which advance the plot by their content', meaning that without these numbers, there would be a gulf or space in the story.[22] According to Mueller, when Fred Astaire arrived in Hollywood in 1933, Astaire was the first one to integrate dance numbers into musicals prior to the term's very popularization.[23] However, although Astaire believed that he was integrating musical numbers into his film's plots (and was, to a degree), Mueller further argues that Astaire was only integrating these scenes in a limited way; in fact, according to Mueller,

> While Astaire may have been attempting integrated dances in the 1930s, it is argued that the rise of the 'fully integrated dancing musical' – a 'unity of expression' where 'a story is told *through* songs and dance, not despite them' – had to wait until the 1940s and early 1950s for the arrival of Gene Kelly and the emergence of the big MGM musical.'[24]

Regardless, integrated/non-integrated Hollywood musicals of the 1930s circulated around *dance*. In other words, Hollywood filmmakers found that one way to integrate musical numbers was to create a musically oriented film narrative, where singing and dancing activities would naturally take place within, such as a Broadway or backstage plot. However, Disney had demonstrated a different approach to musical integration, one in which songs and music manifest naturally within the created reality of the film – one that breaks away from the dancing framework and ecstasy lift of *sudden* song and dance mood to become a truly integrated film musical.

'Into a song before you know it': Walt's approach to musical integration

Disney seemed to be conscious of giving *Snow White* a characteristic musical theme that the audience would be able to relate to and associate with aspects of the story. After the opening credits, the story is introduced through the song (albeit without its lyrics, at this stage) 'Some Day My Prince Will Come'. From the start of the film, Disney provides a key marker that will guide the audience through the film's narrative. Although we are yet to associate that musical theme/leitmotif with any element of the story, we are learning the film's language in the ways it establishes its characteristic cinematic laws of the story's created world. 'Some Day My Prince Will Come' is a significant song within the story's development; it captures the true essence of the narrative because it informs the audience of Snow White's dearest wish. As Belton argues of the scene in which Snow White sings this song, the number functions as 'a window that opens into the psychology of [her] character'.[25] The idea of a musical number functioning as a window is also seen in other songs such as 'The Silly Song' and 'Heigh Ho', which are used to establish the dwarfs' characters. As Roy M. Prendergast states, music in animation 'can give definition to the screen action and it can invest the drawn characters with personality'.[26] When Snow White opens up to the dwarfs about her dreams and wishes later in the film, the song clearly demonstrates the character's romantic desires in a more poetic, less expositional manner. Snow White expresses herself with dignity and hope, rather than sorrow – she keeps repeating the phrase 'some day': '*some day* my prince will come ... *some day* we'll meet again ... *some day* when spring is here', believing that '*some day*' her 'dreams will come true'. This repetition hints at the bleaker side of Snow White's story – although she is hopeful, she does not, at this stage in the film, have any guarantee that things will work out. In fact, although she has found friendship and a haven following her escape from the huntsman, the dwarfs – Grumpy in particular – are keenly aware that she is still very much in danger from the Queen, and that she may never see the Prince again. This is shown in the scene where Grumpy worries that the Queen will find Snow White through her use of black magic, and again later when the dwarfs leave the cottage for their day's work, and Grumpy warns Snow White, 'Don't let nobody or nothin' inside the house!'

Moreover, this song flows directly from the dialogue, allowing the musical number to blend and integrate with the story. Frank Thomas and Ollie Johnston argue that 'Walt insisted that the only use for song would be to pick up the tempo of the story and to tell it in another way, while adding to the emotional content of the sequence. A good song should make the audience feel more deeply about the situation.'[27] In a story meeting for *Snow White* on 27 June 1936, supervising animator Hamilton Luske stated that 'I feel that instead of the song being operatic that it should work from conversation to the song.' Disney responded, 'A good pattern that strikes me as good, you are into the song before you know it. She is telling them that she fell in love and they are asking her questions that lead right up to the song – it all should lead right up to the song.'[28] The music of 'With a Smile and a Song' can also be heard accompanying two scenes in the film, first sung by Snow White when she is out from the dark, terrifying woods and later as a musical theme, without lyrics, accompanying the scene in which Snow White is being guided by the animals to the dwarfs' house. 'With a Smile and a Song' signifies hope and good fortune. By showcasing this song after – and as part of – Snow White's recovery from her terrifying flight through the woods, the song and the scene emphasize the film's optimism that there will always be a happy ending. By observing the music of *Snow White* and many other Disney films, the idea of using some songs' melodies without the words as a musical scoring to accompany certain scenes emerges as a technique for which Disney utilizes music as a storytelling agent. This is also similar to the industry's use of musical leitmotifs during the 1930s (which was first established in operas, especially in those by German composer Richard Wagner), which as a technique was 'still new'.[29] In that scene, even when Snow White talks before she begins to sing 'With a Smile and a Song', she speaks poetically and in a musical way so that some of her words rhyme:

I didn't mean to frighten you,
But you don't know what I've been through!
And all because I was *afraid* –
I'm so ashamed of the fuss I *made*. [Italics mine]

The approach to creating a musical element to the dialogue that leads into a character's performance of a song was one that was integral to how the music was incorporated into (and helped to convey) elements of the narrative. During a story conference for *Snow White* in October 1935, Disney stated:

Have our dialogue not rhymed or [with a] definite beat rhythm, but [instead, let it] have meter and at the right time tie in with the music, so the whole thing has musical pattern – dialogue and music work together and use dialogue to lead into song naturally … out in the woods she picks up words from the birds and it suggests song to her … avoid breaking into song, lead into songs instead.[30]

The songs throughout *Snow White* were used to progress the narrative (its content and story-motive), rather than incorporating them as 'stand-alone' song-motivated numbers that pause the narrative to add a fantasy or spectacular musical break. The idea of *being into a song before you know it* is key to distinguishing Disney's approach towards musical integration and Hollywood's approach. The utilizing/integrating of music and songs into the narrative is also mentioned by Barrier, who describes music as 'an organic part' that manifests itself within Disney's film narrative.[31] For example, 'The Silly Song' is a musical number during which we see the dwarfs spending some quality time with Snow White, singing, dancing and playing music. The number is neither integrated nor forced into the story as such, but rather functions simply to show the dwarfs and Snow White's unity and friendship – they are enjoying each other's company and bonding through music.

Mickey Mousing: Involving characters to making music

While in some cases the source of a sound/music is apparent in *Snow White* (and particularly 'The Silly Song'), it is not always embodied by, or made visible through, a musical instrument. Disney and his staff had created a scoring style/technique that would become known as 'Mickey Mousing', which demonstrates what William Paul describes as 'the closest possible marriage of sound and imagery'.[32] Mickey Mousing is still a term used today in the film industry and is widely known as an academic term in Film Studies and Film Musicology. The true innovation in *Snow White* was not simply Disney's ability to synchronize sound and imagery perfectly. It was also not the existence/presence of the 'eye and ear' novelty on screen that made Disney's work remarkable. Rather, it was *how* Disney *synthesized* what we see and hear to become a 'phenomenon of audiovisual synchronization'.

In 'Whistle While You Work' (that occurs when Snow White finds and enters the Dwarfs' house after coming out from the woods), a deer uses its tail to pump the water in order to clean the dishes. With every pump, the music reaches a higher note in synchronization with the tail, as if the lifting of the deer's tail is the source of the music. Similarly, the squirrels sweep the floor with their tails; again, with every sweep, the music rises and falls, mimicking the physical action of the sweeping. This use of animals acting as musical catalysts from within the world of the film also applies to other characters. In 'Heigh Ho', when Sleepy whips the donkey, the donkey jumps up three times and the music repeats with every beat of his jump. In another scene, Doc hammers diamonds to excavate them and, with every hammering motion, the music dings, again suggesting that the music is created by the characters' actions. In a *Snow White* story meeting dated 27 June 1936, Disney stated,

> The melody is so pretty I wouldn't want to hear so many words with it. During the song all animals could come out. You still have that song going on. Try some words on it, Larry, but try not to put in too many … The most important thing in a song is a chorus – utilize the verse to prepare for it … Could you have some cute thing for the animals to applaud S.W after she sings? A beaver could beat his tail and rabbits beat tails. A buck could come up eating something and hears the tune and out to him looking through. Little raccoons could be at the stream trying to catch a fish and they hear the tune and look up to listen. The turtle's head could just come out of the weeds and listen, then back into the shell. Introduce all the animals. This song could serve to warm everything up.[33]

Walt wanted to *involve* and saturate every story element and character with music and sound, demonstrating how 'Mickey Mousing' was one of the processes by which Disney used to create a musically integrated film. The musical score (when 'Mickey Moused') does not only occupy the characters in a parallel mood (where movements and actions would be in synchronization with the music) or showcase the characters that submit themselves to the music by singing or dancing along with the music. On the contrary, the characters themselves contributed to orchestrating the music and physically produced musical sounds in the realization of the final song. Disney's character-musical-involvement in the construction of songs creates *Snow White*'s particular levels of musical integration.

Music as an invisible character

The use of music in *Snow White* is not only part of the narrative's construction but functions as the narrative itself. This is what theatre composer Jerome Kern refers to as 'the use of music as language', without which the story would lack coherency.[34] In *Snow White*, the music *reacts* and *responds* to story elements as another *invisible character*, functioning in a 'call and response' mood. For example, when Snow White knocks on the door of the dwarfs' house, it is the music that responds to her action (Figure 6.1).

While the music reacts and responds to story elements, it provides *expectation and confirmation* for the characters and the audience. David Huron has pointed out that sounds and music are forms of expression that involve mimicry of some natural emotional expressions and expectations that are conjured up by biology, culture and emotion.[35] In the same way, musicologist Leonard Meyer argues that 'the principle source for music's motive power lies in the realm of expectation'.[36] When Snow White receives

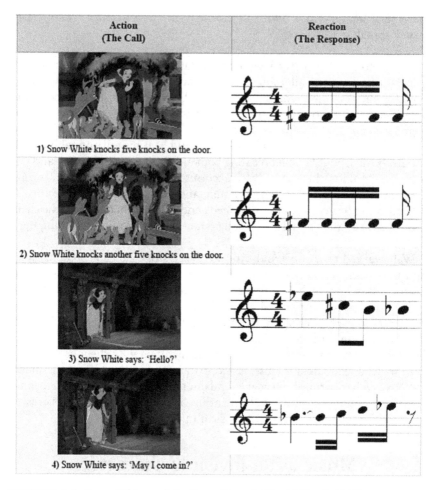

FIGURE 6.1 *Snow White and the Seven Dwarfs* (David Hand, 1937).

the musical reaction after knocking on the door, the music is confirming her initial action and her sense of curiosity by reacting/responding back as an invisible character.

The audience engages in the 'game of watching', and the ways in which music and sound effects are used in *Snow White* confirm the fictional reality constructed in the film.[37] The sound of the 'knock' meets and rewards both spectator expectations and those of Snow White as a character. Audiences expect to hear someone's voice if they speak and to hear someone's clap if they strike their hands together. Expectation is a safe confirmation of a specific reality. Indeed, this idea of sound functioning in such 'hyperrealist' terms is something that Paul Wells argues with a particular focus on the application of sound in Disney animation.[38] Bill Cottrell (sequence director in *Snow White*) stated that 'each flash should be accentuated by a chord in the music – a very modern music effect, then out back to her as she faints'.[39] In *Snow White*, the sound of music is used to confirm and affirm events in the fantasy animated world of the film, providing an element of sonic realism that specifically belongs to the *created* animated world onscreen.

Creating worlds with music: Music as the sound of sonic ambience

The approach of integrating music was a large part of the Disney studio's focus on achieving a degree of formal realism. What I mean by realism here is what Belton has referred to as a 'narrative reality', which enables spectators to suspend disbelief and be invited into the animated story world. In *Snow White*, Disney's main aim was to achieve the highest possible degree of realism because they had a deep concern that audiences would not, or would struggle to, sit through a full feature-length *animated* film.[40] The Disney studio was able to achieve this by providing the animators with intensive training to work on the quality of the animation and the drawings.

Typically, animation is a silent canvas (with the exceptions such as animator Norman McLaren's film *Synchromy* [1971] where audiences can effectively *see* the sounds that they are hearing as imagery through his process of direct animation[41]) which requires sonic ambience. This includes elements such as speech, sound effects, music and ambient sound, which can all bring depth and layers of texture to the reality of the animated world. The way in which Disney musically scored *Snow White* (the longest musical silence in the film is about twenty seven seconds long, the scene where the dwarfs realize that a stranger is in their home, after coming back from work) not only functions as a technique of drama but also brings a sense of motion, space and continuity, together creating an atmosphere and believable environment. Speech, sound effects and music are sonic components of the sonic space that exists in the ambient space. As Rebecca Coyle points out, we cannot freeze sound as we can freeze images, arguing that 'Sound fidelity and spatiality for both cinema and home has increased audience awareness and expectations of sonicity'.[42] The spectators' first glimpse of Snow White is her action integrated with the music while she is wiping the floor – she is not singing and neither should she be aware of a *musical* presence in the background; she is aware of the natural sonic ambience. In this moment, Snow White is reacting naturally to the music in the background by humming along with it, as if music is the sound of the air (recalling traditions in 1930s Hollywood, especially 'passed-along-song' influenced by the operetta) and the sonic ambience of the world in which she lives. The music is here in *Snow White* used as a way to establish atmosphere and ambience; it does this throughout the entire film, which suggests the presence of a fantasy animated realm that does not exist in the real world.

Most importantly, the use of music in *Snow White* blurs the distinction between the diegetic and the non-diegetic, which according to Claudia Gorbman 'puts music in a position to free the image from strict realism'.[43] The music in *Snow White* keeps crossing the boundary between what the characters should hear (diegetic) and should not hear (non-diegetic), demonstrating that all sound (including speech, music, sound effects, ambient sound and silence) exists in the sonic space of the *story world*. Robynn Stilwell and James Buhler describe that crossing activity as sound falling into a liminal space or 'fantastical gap'.[44] However, Stilwell argues that the crossing activity is 'not so much an event as a process, not simply crossing, or even passing through distinct intermediary states, but a trajectory, a vector, a gesture. It unfolds through time, like film, like music. Even when the transition is acknowledged, it is often suspiciously cast as "transgression" – which it can be, but isn't always.'[45] These comments suggest that, rather than assigning music, speech and sound effects to fixed categories (diegetic and non-diegetic), we can claim that the 'sonic fabric' components exist along a spectrum. The idea of a spectrum acknowledges that different sound components function differently, according to the way they are utilized in the narrative, but all belong to the *story space*.[46]

Conclusion

The cinematic medium experienced struggles and challenges as filmmakers working in the Hollywood film industry began a new era with sound and music. The musical film genre evolved from 'disintegration to integration' and from formats such as the revue, the operetta and the book musical.[47] The energetic lift and ecstasy that transfer the audience from an ordinary mood into a fantasy and escapist mood are the musical's reasons for being. However, Disney took an extremely innovative approach to integrating sound and music into his animated motion pictures, where music led the narrative in an 'organic' way without being the prime focus of attention. Musical numbers were driven by story-motives rather than song-motives, which includes musically oriented activities such as dancing and singing for musical purposes. The singing activities that took place within *Snow White's* musical numbers such as 'Heigh Ho', 'Whistle While You Work' and 'Someday My Prince Will Come' do not seek to show any musical intentions, abilities or talents of the characters, unlike other musical numbers which were musically intended (such as 'The Silly Song'). Music in *Snow White and the Seven Dwarfs*, both in terms of songs and its innovative treatment of background sound, was used to manifest the story and capture its animated details. Music is not secondary, it is the narrative itself, which would otherwise be incomplete. This synthesizing music with the imagery creates new meanings that cannot be obtained without one another. *Snow White* is a striking example of this practice.

The application of sound within popular Hollywood cinema was seen by many critics and the audiences as particularly advanced in the work of the Disney studio. Kern stated unequivocally that -Walt Disney has made the 20th century's only important contribution to music.' The use of sound and music certainly enabled Disney to create a completely new form of art. *Snow White* builds a world that combines both reality and fantasy together, one that immerses the spectator into the reality of the story. Sound functions as the bridge between these elements. Among its many contributions to histories of sound cinema, the film was narrated not only with spoken dialogue and the incorporation of songs, but also through the language of music that was expressed independently (music-occupied characters, responded and interacted with story elements): with and without spoken/ sung words. Charlie Chaplin, who was present at *Snow White*'s Hollywood premier, stated that it 'even surpassed our high expectations'.[48] Filmmaker Sergei Eisenstein likewise praised *Snow White* (which was the first film soundtrack to even be released as a recording) by referring to it as 'true cinematography of sound-and-sight consonance'.[49] As Walt stated, the idea of being 'into a song before you know it' and character-musical-involvement are key besides other aspects to Disney's contributions to the Hollywood musical, and it is what distinguishes *Snow White and the Seven Dwarfs* as the first fully integrated musical of its kind.

Notes

1   John Culhane, 'Snow White at 50: Undimmed Magic', *New York Times* (12 July 1987): 243–55. Available at https://www.nytimes.com/1987/07/12/ movies/snow-white-at-50-undimmed-magic.html (accessed 8 July 2018).

2   'The Silly Symphony'. *Fortune* 10, no. 5 (November 1934): 88–95.

3   Leonard Maltin stated that Snow White was 'planned out to a musical beat' in James Bohn, *Music in Disney's Animated Features: Snow White and the Seven Dwarfs to the Jungle Book* (USA: University Press of Mississippi, 2017), 68.

4   David Bordwell, and Kristin Thompson, *Film Art: An Introduction*, 10th edn (1979; repr., New York: McGraw-Hill, 2013), 268.

5   The term 'sonic fabric' is borrowed from an abbreviated version of a chapter included in a book: Scott D. Lipscomb and David E. Tolchinsky, 'The Role of Music Communication in Cinema', in *Musical Communication*, ed. Dorothy Miell, Raymond MacDonald and David J Hargreaves

(New York: Oxford University Press, 2005). https://pdfs.semanticscholar.
org/7bbf/34f4766a424d8fa934f5d1bda580e9ae814c.pdf.

6 Richard Dyer, 'Entertainment and Utopia', *Movie*, 24 (Spring 1977): 2–13.

7 Donald Crafton, *The Talkies: American Cinema's Transition to Sound 1926–
   1931* (London: University of California Press, 1997), 249.

8 Ibid., 280–1.

9 Ibid.

10 Ibid.

11 Ibid.

12 Ibid., 277–8.

13 Richard Barrios, *A Song in the Dark: The Birth of the Musical Film*
   (New York: Oxford University Press, 1995), 42.

14 Ibid., 55.

15 James Buhler, Rob Deemer and David Neumeyer, *Hearing the Movies: Music
   and Sound in Film History* (New York: Oxford University Press, 2010), 85.

16 Tietyen, *The Musical World of Walt Disney*, 37.

17 Ibid., 37.

18 Ibid.

19 John Belton, *American Cinema American Culture*, 2nd edn (1990; repr.,
   New York: McGraw-Hill, 2005), 151.

20 Ibid., 152.

21 John, Muller, 'Fred Astaire and the Integrated Musical', *Cinema Journal* 24,
   no. 1 (1984): 28–30.

22 Ibid.

23 Ibid., 28–31.

24 Ibid., 31.

25 Belton, *American Cinema/America Culture*, 152.

26 Roy M. Prendergast, *Film Music: A Neglected Art*, 2nd edn (1977; repr.,
   New York: W. W. Norton, 1992), 190.

27 Thomas and Johnston, *The Illusion of Life: Disney Animation*, 297.

28 Allan, 'The Fairest Film of All', 88.

29 Claudia Gorbman, *Unheard Melodies: Narrative Film Music* (London: Indiana
   Jones University, 1987), 28; Bohn, *Music in Disney's Animated Features*, 66.

30 Ibid., 69.

31 Barrier, *Hollywood Cartoons*, 206.

32 Tietyen, *The Musical World of Walt Disney*, 24.

33 Allan, 'The Fairest Film of All', 88.

34 Jerome Kern, quoted in John Culhane, 'Snow White at 50: Undimmed Magic'.

35 David Huron, *Sweet Anticipation: Music and the Psychology of Expectation* (London: MIT Press, 2007), 2.

36 Ibid.

37 Ben Winters, 'The Non-Diegetic Fallacy: Film, Music, and Narrative Space', *Music and Letters* 91, no. 2 (2010): 224–44.

38 Paul Wells, *Understanding Animation* (Oxon: Routledge, 1998), 25.

39 Ibid.

40 Thomas and Johnston, *The Illusion of Life: Disney Animation*, 90.

41 Crystal Chan, 'How to Write a Film on a Piano: Norman McLaren's Visual Music', *BFI*, 23 November 2016. Available at https://www.bfi.org.uk/news-opinion/sight-sound-magazine/features/how-write-film-piano-norman-mclaren-s-visual-music (accessed 31 December 2019).

42 Rebecca Coyle, 'Audio Motion: Animating (Film) Sound', in *Drawn to Sound: Animation Film Music and Sonicity*, ed. Rebecca Coyle (London: Equinox, 2010), 3.

43 Gorbman, *Unheard Melodies*, 4.

44 Robynn J. Stilwell, 'The Fantastical Gap between Diegetic and Nondiegetic', in *Beyond the Soundtrack: Representing Music in Cinema*, ed. Daniel Goldmark, Lawrence Kramer and Richard Leppert (Berkeley: University of California Press, 2007), 184–202.

45 Ibid., 184–5.

46 The distinction between Diegetic and Non-diegetic sound, which was initially theorized by Gorbman in her book *Unheard Melodies*, is something that I've been re-theorizing as part of my PhD research.

47 Belton, *American Cinema American Culture*, 154–5.

48 Culhane, 'Snow White at 50: Undimmed Magic'.

49 Ibid.

7

Dwarfland: Marketing Disney's folly

Pamela C. O'Brien

In the days leading up to Christmas in 1937, a strange construction project was occurring along Wilshire Boulevard, near the Carthay Circle Theatre in Los Angeles, California. Small cottages with water mills and oversized mushrooms began to materialize. Outside of the theatre large display boards were erected. While passers-by may have been curious, film critics were dismissing it as just another piece of 'Disney's folly', the negative descriptor they had taken to use when discussing *Snow White and the Seven Dwarfs* (David Hand, 1937).[1] By 1937, the film had amassed a budget exceeding 1.5 million dollars, and Hollywood insiders and critics were unsure of whether or not audiences would identify with and embrace animated characters and the full-length story they were telling.[2] Ward Kimball, one of Disney's key animators, admitted that when he was working on it people would tell him that nobody would sit still for a seven-reel cartoon, because the bright colours would hurt their eyes.[3] In fact, Walt Disney and his employees shared these concerns. In an interview after the release of the film, Walt commented, 'We started out gayly, in the fast tempo that is the special technique of short subjects. But that wouldn't do; we soon realized there was danger of wearing out an audience. There was too much going on. A feature-length picture has to deal in personality and character development instead of trying all the time for slapstick and belly-laughs.'[4]

Disney needed to find a way to branch out from short subjects as they were facing changing audiences and changing distribution agreements, which meant the animated shorts would no longer support the company. Disney knew the way for his company to continue to make a profit with animation was to take advantage of the distribution revenue that only feature-length films could generate. While the idea seems simple in retrospect, neither audiences nor Disney's animators were familiar with animation as a feature film. The challenge that Disney faced was to find a story that would highlight the production techniques that the company was developing while appealing to wide audiences. Audiences already equated the name Walt Disney with family friendly entertainment, and the company was building upon this by emphasizing Disney himself as the embodiment of family values. The stylized signature of the name Walt Disney that has become symbolic of the company and its products is one example of the creation of the Uncle Walt persona. Equally important, Disney needed characters that could tie into the company's increasingly profitable merchandise franchise. The fairy-tale adaptation of *Snow White* was developed to highlight characters that would connect with audiences while supporting broad marketing and branding efforts. This chapter will explore the marketing and merchandising techniques used by Walt Disney to prepare audiences for a feature-length animated film that built upon the expectations that filmgoers already held for Disney products. In addition, the chapter will show how Disney was able to tie the film and its marketing into the sociocultural context of the late 1930s in the United States to improve the success of both the film and its ancillary merchandise.

The years in which the Walt Disney Company was creating *Snow White* were fraught with economic, political and social upheaval. The collapse of the stock market and the resulting panic on the banks from the 1929 Great Depression marked the most difficult economic period in the history of the United States. Only one-quarter of wage-earners were able to find work, and a fourth of the nation's farmers were losing their land. Industry was at a virtual standstill, and the resulting Depression impacted Hollywood. When Disney announced that he was planning to create a feature-length animated film, his rivals declared that he must have bought a sweepstakes ticket. Roy E. Disney, however, in analysing the film's estimated budget, described it more appropriately as 'We've bought the whole damned sweepstakes.'[5]

Consumers were also growing suspicious of business due to the prevalence of misleading or false advertising.[6] Perhaps this is one reason the PR department at Disney was careful to indicate that both Walt and Roy put all of their profits into improvements for their workers and studio so that they could create better films.[7] Film quality took on new importance in 1937, as theatres wanted good films to increase audience size even if the films were not from the companies with which the theatres were affiliated.[8] RKO, Disney's distribution company, was able to use this attitude to their advantage by charging high fees for showing *Snow White and the Seven Dwarfs*, and the publicity for the film played up the quality of the animation and the story. For example, Disney indicated in an interview that he would have destroyed the film if he did not think it lived up to the studio's standards. While this does speak to Disney's desire for perfection, it also is a shrewd marketing ploy to begin to convince audiences that a longer animated film is still of high quality.[9]

Disney creates a 'classic'

In the spring of 1934, however, Disney decided on *Snow White* as the company's first feature-length film. Most of the company's animators were against the idea.[10] However, the only way to control the entire box office, not just pieces of it from shorts and PSAs, was through feature films, because even the most successful of the shorts made very little money for the company.[11] For example, *Three Little Pigs* (Burt Gillett, 1933), which was the most successful short in terms of bookings in 1934, only earned $64,000, while it cost $60,000 to produce. This was because theatres were paying only $6 a booking for a Mickey Mouse or a *Silly Symphony* short, and most of the extra revenue was being used to make more prints of the shorts to supply the theatres' demand.[12] Disney was growing increasingly frustrated with American theatres, because they did not want to pay commensurate rentals for cartoons, even though cartoons often brought in more people than features.[13] In 1936, when distributor United Artists insisted on future television rights to Disney's products, Roy approached RKO Radio and received an incredible deal. RKO would underwrite production costs for *Snow White* while taking less than 30% of the gross.[14] Therefore, in May 1937, Disney switched alliances to RKO.[15]

As part of the deal, Disney began his tradition of taking audiences behind the scenes of his studio, to show how the films were created in order to heighten anticipation and excitement for the projects. The release of the newsreel, 'Trip through the Hyperion Studio' which showed animators working on *Snow White*, acted as early marketing for the January 1938 release of the film. For the animators, their hard work meant that Disney, for the first time, bought advertising space in trade journals to publicly credit the heretofore anonymous animators and production staff.[16]

One audience that was particularly important, but also worrisome, for Disney to reach was the international market. In August 1935, Disney went on a tour of Europe to assess the popularity of his shorts. After this trip, he made the decision to remove most dialogue, while relying on more sight gags.[17] Disney believed that many of these comedy bits would not be accepted by audiences if they were done by human characters. As he points out, 'Portrayal of human sensations by inanimate objects such as steam shovels and rocking-chairs never fails to provoke laughter. Human distress exemplified by animals is sure fire.'[18] By beginning with a familiar storyline, the fairy tale of *Snow White*, Disney was able to add humorous side characters and anthropomorphized animals to enhance the audiences' connection to the characters without having to rely on dialogue. In addition, Disney's marketing and merchandizing strategy for the film relied heavily on the promotion of these additional characters.

Disney utilized the concept of anthropomorphism, giving non-human characters human traits and emotions, for the development of the personalities of the forest animals and the seven dwarfs. Disney was able to create animal characters that could convey a tremendous amount of emotion without coming across as false or overly done. For example, in *Snow White* audiences can identify with the little blue bird who hits a sour note during its song, thus damping its parent's pride. The animals also push the story forward with no reliance on dialogue. The animals comfort Snow White when she is frightened and lead her to the dwarfs' cottage. They are the ones who do much of the cleaning of the cottage and provide that long sequence with its humour.

The *Los Angeles Times* asked a family, the Millers, to write a review of *Snow White*, and the responses of the family's children captured the strong reaction audience members had to the animals and the dwarfs. Miller's 11-year-old daughter described her favourite part of the movie: 'The things that pulled the whole show together were the dear little animals. Such complete little darlings I could dream of them forever.'[19] Her older sister concurred, explaining: 'Of course, for my money, the Walt Disney animals took top honours. That one little cottontail can convey more meaning with a bounce of his ear, than can Gable, Garbo or Mae West all combined into one uncensored show.'[20] This is exactly the effect that Disney hoped for.

The only characters who are able to upstage the animals in *Snow White* are the dwarfs. While the dwarfs in the traditional tale do play an important role in the story, Disney gives each of the dwarfs a name and distinct personality. The dwarfs supply most of the slapstick humour in the film, while also translating emotions to the audience, such as Grumpy showing his softening heart towards Snow White as he waits to get kissed. While Walt Disney expressed some concern that the dwarfs would steal the picture from Snow White, he still chose to make them the centrepiece of the film's marketing campaign, with each dwarf receiving his own advertisement to introduce him to audiences.[21] Walt himself posed with dolls of the dwarfs for the cover of *Time* magazine, and in a coming attractions promotion for the film introduced each dwarf by name to help audiences understand their characteristic. Disney's highlighting of the presence and personalities of the dwarfs is indicative of the importance of secondary characters to story and merchandising at the expense of the human heroes and heroines.

Disney did, however, play up the character of the evil Queen. In July 1937, one animator sent Walt a memo warning that the Queen was too frightening. In fact, when the film opened in February at New York's Radio

City Music Hall, a story spread that the Queen was so scary that the first few rows of seats had to be reupholstered.[22] To address these concerns, Disney removed a scene with the Queen at her cauldron after the film premiered.[23] Oversees, British film censors decided to not allow anyone under the age of 16 to see *Snow White* unless they were accompanied by an adult, because they feared British children would receive nightmares from some of the scenes with the witch.[24] Without a universal certificate, RKO estimated they would lose between $100,000 and 200,000.[25] In the end, the British censors were overruled, and the film was shown without any cuts.[26] Children in Holland even boycotted a local candy company's *Snow White* chocolate bar until Dutch censors lifted the restrictions on children under 14 being able to see the movie.[27]

The marketing of *Snow White*

While *Snow White and the Seven Dwarfs* was based on a culturally known fairy tale, Disney still had to get audiences familiar with their version of the story before the movie was released. To this end, *Good Housekeeping* magazine ran a two-part serial of the story, complete with colour pictures, in its November and December 1937 issues. This would coincide with the December premier and the wide release of the film in February. The serial begins with exposition that 'This is the story the new full-length moving picture will portray. Basically, it is the old loved fairy tale, but Snow White must have had a lot of adventures the Brothers Grimm did not tell about, and these Walt Disney's fertile imagination has supplied.'[28] The stage was thus set for the fact that the story Disney would be telling is not the same as the one that audiences may know. What is also interesting about the two-part story is that there are many differences between the serialized magazine story and the film, some of which establish important backstory. For example, the magazine indicates that Snow White's father was busy being king and did not have much time to play with his daughter. The King's new wife, the evil Queen, ignored both Snow White and the King, who worked so hard he died. Overall, the article gives the audience important narrative and exposition while also providing a deeper look into many of the characters' motivations and, of course, also beginning the marketing push for the film.

In addition, *Good Housekeeping* is a magazine targeted at homemakers, and Disney was trying to generate adult interest in the film by highlighting the themes of love and jealousy rather than focusing on the animation. Disney needed adults to come on their own or come with their children to earn the highest possible profit. The early marketing strategy worked, as before the film premiered in Los Angeles, the press was already giving it high praise. Disney did not want *Snow White* to be seen as a children's film. In fact, Walt believed that children were too excitable to have anything produced specifically for their tastes, but he knew that children would be a large part of the market for the film.[29] One way to help ensure that children knew the story and were excited for the film was a volume of *Photoplay Studies* about the film that was used in elementary and high schools. Released by Educational and Recreational Guides, Inc, the materials taught students how to understand and appreciate films. As the foreword notes, 'Walt Disney's unique photoplay makes a happy contribution not only to the art of the screen but also to the art of gracious, kindly living.'[30] With publications such as these the audience was prepared for the film.

Prior to *Snow White*'s opening on 21 December 1937 at the Carthay Circle Theatre, the *Los Angeles Times* announced that Disney had created new stars and that there would be an unusual premiere.[31] Other articles explained that Disney's own staff had not seen the complete film, and even they were paying $5 to buy tickets to the premiere.[32] Years later, Adriana Caselotti, the actress who voiced Snow White explained that she and the Prince, voiced by Harry Stockwell, were not given tickets and had to sneak into the premier.[33] While the staff may or may not have seen the whole picture, it is certainly clever marketing to say that the company's staff and other celebrities were so excited over the picture that they were spending their own money to see it. All elements for the marketing of *Snow White* were carefully planned to build audience expectation for the film and its merchandise, as Disney could not afford to fail. In the week before the movie premiered, there were numerous articles in the *Los Angeles* Times describing the party that was planned. These articles discussed the celebrities that would be in attendance or the prices people were paying for tickets or the fact that it was standing room days before the premiere.[34] A 20 December article describes the premiere thus: 'every seat has been taken and the list of celebrities who purchased $5 tickets is one of the most formidable ever announced for a Hollywood event'.[35] Spectators were promised appearances by Mickey and Minnie, the Seven Dwarfs, and the Disney recording orchestra playing the movie's songs.

The most lavish aspect of the film's premiere, however, occurred outside of the theatre and remained as an attraction to future audiences: Dwarfland (Figure 7.1). Dwarfland was a life-sized recreation of the dwarfs' forest in the parkway from Wilshire Boulevard to the entrance to the Carthay Circle Theatre. In the afternoon and evening, theatregoers could walk through Dwarfland and encounter all of the seven dwarfs. In addition, the entrance to the theatre displayed art work that was used in the creation of the film. These two exhibits were hailed in advertisements as 'educational and fascinating' while also explaining that it was Walt Disney's Christmas present to the viewing public.[36] Articles next to the ads further described how many families and parties had made reservations to view the film on Christmas Eve.[37] In other words, Disney wanted to make sure that audiences

FIGURE 7.1 Dwarfland.

knew that this was a film for the whole family to be excited about, so much so that they would include it in their seasonal holiday plans.

The advertising for the movie was further enhanced by coverage of the premiere on NBC's Blue Network. The 30-minute broadcast was hosted by Don Wilson and Buddy Twain, and preceded the movie's 9.15 p.m. start. It featured voices from the film and other Disney stars.[38] Disney also used radio to advertise the movie through commercials and song rotations. In the week prior to the film's nationwide opening on 13 January, 'Whistle While You Work' was the sixteenth most heavily plugged film song on WEAF, WJZ and WABC.[39] By the first week in February, when the film was setting attendance records in Los Angeles and New York at Radio City Music Hall, the song moved up to the second most plugged, with 'With a Smile and a Song' and 'Someday my Prince will come' added to the list.[40] Overall, the premiere was a success. Reporters described the overflowing audience as being enraptured by a film that 'is a triumph of technical craft, disclosing the finest artistic feeling of its impresario and his assistants'[41] According to animator Ward Kimball, everyone in the theatre was crying at the end and gave the film a standing ovation.[42] When discussing the faults of the film, mostly the reality of the human characters, reviewers still described *Snow White* as being a miraculous victory.[43]

Disney used this positive publicity from reviewers and even celebrities in later advertisements for *Snow White*. One series of ads in *The Los Angeles Times* showcased the words of prominent reviewers such as Jimmy Fidler, Edwin Schallert and Louella Parsons. They played up the fact that the movie was not just for children, while in another series of ads, Disney used quotations from celebrities, such as Irving Berlin, Mary Pickford and Harpo Marx, discussing their *Snow White* viewing experiences. Charlie Chaplin commented that 'in dwarf Dopey he [Disney] has created one of the greatest comedians of all times'. The successful premiere of the film would create a great deal of excitement around the film and its well-organized tie-ups, as part of the film's unprecedented and carefully orchestrated marketing campaign.

Mirror, mirror on the wall, who has the best merchandise of them all?

The financial life blood of the Walt Disney Company has always been merchandising and licensing, rather than its short- or feature-length films. Just four years after *Steamboat Willie* (Ub Iwerks, 1928) Disney licensed with fifteen manufacturers.[44] In 1934, over six hundred items based on characters from Disney's short films were sold globally.[45] These ranged from clothes, books, briefcases, soap, food, chinaware, hot-water bottles, banks, napkins, dairy products, music, balls, dolls and clocks. Disney's products were creating fortunes for themselves and the licensing companies. For example, in just eight weeks, Mickey Mouse watches restored the financial stake of the Ingersoll Watch Company, which allowed them to add 2,700 employees after selling 2,000,000 watches.[46] In 1935, General Foods distributed 6,000,000 Mickey Mouse cereal bowls as box-top premiums.[47]

From 1932 to 1936, Disney, along with Kay Kamen Ltd, Disney's head of Walt Disney Enterprises, had increased the merchandising phase of Disney's operations by 10,000 per cent. This equates to a turnover of several million dollars a year.[48] The success of Walt Disney Enterprises can best be seen, however, in the fact that the royalties from its toy and related merchandise sales were what pulled the Walt Disney Company through the bank holiday panic when theatres were being forced to cancel contracts.[49]

Disney clearly established strong merchandising and marketing tactics for its products, and they employed a number of these to heighten interest for *Snow White*. In early 1937, Disney released a trailer for the film that was a tease for the audience and a way of judging interest in the project. In the trailer, Disney did not show any of the animated scenes from the movie, but showed only stills, covers of magazines discussing the film such as *Time* and *Photoplay*. It ended with Walt at his desk introducing the dwarfs by showing their dolls. There are a number of possible reasons for not including any animated footage. One of the most likely is that Disney had been unhappy with some of the early animation, such as refining Snow White's look away from a Betty Boop-style caricature or improving the animation due to new technology, and threw out a great deal of the early work on the film.[50] However, in just these few minutes, he was able to position the film as appealing to adults, show that it was being received well by popular press and introduce the early merchandising pieces for the movie.

Merchandising for *Snow White and the Seven Dwarfs* was extensive and set a pattern for other films to follow. *Snow White*-related merchandise was, for the first time, available the day that the film premiered. It was also the first time that a feature film's soundtrack was released on phonograph records.[51] Sheet music for the songs was also available for purchase. Additional tie-ups with the film were tremendous. They ranged from cloth and china dolls to puzzles to soap to balloons to metal tea sets to mechanical postcards to cereals to lunch pails to ladies clothing, such as shoes, hats and dresses. There were even *Snow White* hams and bacon.[52] In addition to being able to buy almost any branded item a person could think of, Disney used give-aways, such as the *Snow White* Jingle Club, as enticements to see the film. If a fan could sing a song from the movie, they would receive a small lapel pin featuring an image of Snow White or one of the dwarfs. Audiences were also able to win free tickets if they solved a puzzle or wrote in a line of a Snow White limerick.[53]

One of the most involved tie-ups was with Post Toasties cereal boxes. On the back of the boxes children would find images from *Snow White* that they could cut out and stand up to create all the characters and forest scenes. There were also games to play. The copy read, 'There's fun on every box. Ask Mother always to get Post Toasties – the only cereal with these wonderful toys. And be sure to see the movie, "Snow White and the Seven Dwarfs," when it comes to your neighbourhood theatre.' The images on the boxes reinforced the ideas of Snow White's kindness and the 'proper' behaviours of cleaning, cooking and bathing.

Merchandising efforts for *Snow White* were a tremendous success for Disney. In total, 147 concerns were granted licenses to manufacture 2,183 different *Snow White* products. From just the first of January 1938 until 1 May 1938 over $2,000,000 of *Snow White* toys alone were sold from 117 licensees. In that same time period over $2,000,000 of *Snow White* handkerchiefs were sold (often sold in packs with a dwarf embroidered on each handkerchief). These figures are impressive, especially considering this was after the holiday buying season.[54] Overall, Disney's merchandising efforts proved to be a boom not only for its company but also for the companies producing the items. While many rubber plants were closed through 1938 due to the Depression, a rubber company in Akron, OH, that manufactured toy rubber dwarfs was running twenty-four hours a day.[55] One report exclaimed, '*Snow White* is Disney's first full-length picture. What is going to happen when he really gets into his stride? Industrialized fantasy? It should be industrially fantastic.'[56] Even vendors who did not have a license to sell Disney paraphernalia were able to profit from the film by selling coffee and sandwiches to patrons standing in lines waiting to see it.[57] The publicity that resulted from Disney's gains for other industries was in many ways more significant, although not as extensive, as the company's advertising campaign for the movie.

Advertising the fairest one of all

There were many facets to the advertising campaign for *Snow White and the Seven Dwarfs*. Not only did Disney need to make people aware of the film, including when and where it was playing, but the company had to get audiences familiar with a new style of animation. One way in which this occurred was to include in advertisements for the film the coverage popular press magazines were giving the movie. For example, Disney included the cover image from *Time* in one of its ads for the film. This ad declares, 'Never before has *Time* paid such lavish tribute to any picture or any producer. Read it ... See ... Walt Disney's *Snow White and the Seven Dwarfs*.'[58] Disney was banking on audience trust in high-profile news publications to draw them into the theatre for a different type of film than they had seen before.

The second aspect of the advertising campaign, and the most involved, was the advertisements Disney created to educate audiences to the story and its characters. While it had become common for a film to have a few different ads over the course of its campaign, Disney created a new ad for each day of the film's initial run in Los Angeles (similar ads were then used in other cities). These ads started on 12 December 1937 and primarily highlighted the Dwarfs, as well as the effort that went into creating the film. The ads also played up the excitement surrounding the film, calling it, 'The most anticipated picture in 20 years', while also indicating that ticket demand was extremely high and advanced purchases were required. One of the more amusing ads indicated that if you could not get Rose Bowl tickets then you should come and see *Snow White*.[59]

Only one advertisement in the early ads showed Snow White or the Queen. This ad, which was one of three theatre posters for the film, was placed on 11 January 1938 and then used more heavily in New York starting 13 January 1938. The ad shows Snow White standing in the centre, but slightly behind, the row of dwarfs and forest animals. Behind Snow White are images of the Queen, the Huntsman and a stylized Prince. Behind that is the castle. This ad and the ones in New York that frame the whole image with larger drawings of the dwarfs indicate who the stars of the film are, namely the dwarfs and the animals. They are the ones that audiences are led to identify with. In addition, Snow White is shown in a curtsey to the dwarfs. This indicates that it is the dwarfs who are the true heroes of the film and deserve Snow White's, and the audience's, gratitude.

The third aspect of the advertising of *Snow White* did not come directly from Disney. During the wide release of the film, which occurred on 15 February 1938, Disney was able to use free advertising rather than conduct a large-scale advertising campaign on their own. Department stores, drug stores, grocery stores, radio stations and newspapers were so eager to tie into the success of the film that they ran large articles or had window displays of the film's merchandise, which was described as being unsurpassed by any picture in recent years.[60] *The Daily News* in Washington, DC, sent a reporter to New York by plane in order to get an early review of the film.[61] Such a rush on the part of merchants and journalists to tie-in to the film is the reverse of how it often is, where the distributor must work to get companies interested in the tie-ins.[62] This type of tie-in and limited advertising helped to make the movie a success. *Snow White and the Seven Dwarfs* broke non-holiday opening records in most cities.[63] This was helped by the increased ticket prices for juveniles and the extra showings of the film.[64] The combination of the national and local ad campaigns was described by *Variety* as 'Terrific local campaign of exploitation to keep alive the national publicity'.[65]

What also helped Disney at the time was the lack of other family-oriented films. *Snow White* competed with films such as *Man-Proof* (Richard Thorpe, 1938), the story of a woman still in love with her best friend's husband, and who turned away from men altogether. Released during the same time period was *True Confessions* (Wesley Ruggles, 1937), whose ad shows Carole Lombard and John Barrymore pulling each other's hair with ad copy that discusses Lombard using lies. Such adult themes meant that parents could not bring their children to the theatre with them.

Audiences had become familiar with Disney's shorts that utilized slapstick humour, showed the perseverance and hard work of the hero and always had good triumph over evil. Even Mickey Mouse, if he was ever bad to another character, would be 'punished' by the end of the short. Also, Mickey led a puritanical life: abhorring swearing, tobacco and liquor. Nor was he ever allowed to be cruel or arrogant. These story elements became part of the formula that Disney would employ in his feature films. Disney's extensive marketing and merchandising campaign around *Snow White* highlighted the family-friendly, classic nature of the story, which worked to excite adults and children to the film and its merchandise. At the same time, Walt was continuing the development of his own star image that would be used to market all of his company's products. Disney often is quoted as thanking the people who work on his films, but he also is careful not to give everyone credit. The reason, according to Disney himself, was that there were just too many, but it also works to make his image the one that people associate with the company's products. While sixty-two names are credited at the beginning of *Snow White*, reviewers always focus on Disney's importance in the creative process. As the reviewer for *Variety* states, 'Highest praise must go to Disney himself for collating all the diverse efforts into a conception of single purpose which bears the mark of one creative imagination.'[66] The result of the star image of Walt Disney is the idea of a friendly Uncle Walt who makes movies for the whole family to enjoy. This image is beneficial for the long-term success of the company and its products.

I'm wishing (I'm wishing) for a success

Walt Disney's image and bankability paid off very quickly in the case of *Snow White and the Seven Dwarfs*. Even before the film was released, demand was impressive. The William Morris Agency, acting for either itself or an unnamed client, offered Disney $1 million for the rights to the English showings. Disney turned it down, which was a wise decision.[67] In the first week of showings at LA's Carthay Circle Theatre, *Snow White* earned $19,000.[68] The film would go on to break all previous records for the theatre and be the most successful holiday release up to that time.[69] At New York's Radio City Music Hall, *Snow White and the Seven Dwarfs* became the first film to play more than three weeks, with grosses increasing each week of its run.[70] This was helped by the advertising campaign that was sponsored by RKO and the Music Hall. In fifteen months from its wide release date, *Snow White* earned more than $6,740,000, with an additional $2,000,000 expected from overseas markets.[71] Not only did *Snow White* save the Disney Company, but the success of the film was a boon to theatres that had been showing films averaging one-third less than *Snow White*.[72] This helped out theatres struggling from the Depression and bolstered the desire to show other Disney products. The only theatres not helped by Disney, either directly or from spill over of audiences, were vaudeville. These theatres suffered their greatest period of inactivity during *Snow White*'s run.[73]

The international market, which Disney relied on and cultivated, was also crucial to the film's success. *Snow White* was shown in more than forty-one countries and dubbed into twenty languages, including Russian and Arabic.[74] In a unique marketing move, Disney created custom artwork for each language so that the film flowed seamlessly with the dialogue. For example, in the scene where the dwarfs' names appear on the footboards of their beds, the names were seen in the language of the country that the film was playing.[75] The effort placed on such changes for each market was well received. In Czechoslovakia, the tax on tickets was removed as a sign of appreciation for dubbing the film into their native language. In France, Disney was allowed exhibition rights for the entire country rather than the normal five theatres in Paris, and ten in outlying provinces. *Snow White* ended up playing for a record-breaking thirty-one weeks in Paris.[76]

Thanks to the box office and merchandising profits of the film, Disney was able to pay off all of their debts and have over $2 million in the bank just six months after the film's release. This money also allowed Disney to build a new studio in anticipation of creating a feature-length film every year.[77] However, the success was not just monetary. Disney was awarded a special Oscar, and the New York Film critics voted on the first ballot to award it a special prize.[78] The cel showing the vultures getting ready to soar down after the Queen carrying the poison apple was accepted as part of the collection of the Metropolitan Museum of Art.[79] Disney used the inclusion of his work in the Museum as a way to keep some of his staff busy during the slack season by having them cut up cels and mount and wrap them for sale in the Museum shop where some sold for over $200.[80]

While *Snow White and the Seven Dwarfs* began the family-friendly style of animated feature-length films that Walt Disney and his company would perfect in the coming years, its success came in large part from the telling of a good story. This is exactly the reason that fairy tales have brought people together for centuries. The tales contain familiar elements that highlight the values and morals that are dominant during the time the story is told. Or, as one journalist put it when reviewing *Snow White*, the story and its characters represent and reflect society's moral and emotional stance by exposing 'worthwhile themes'.[81] Another reviewer called the changes that Disney made to the Grimms' fairy tale 'necessary modernizations'.[82] However, the most important lesson learned in the adaptation of *Snow White* to the screen was, perhaps, the studio's participation in consumerism. Audiences seemed not to be bothered by the overt merchandising of the film, but instead eagerly embraced the story, its merchandise and the company. Thus, Disney's folly became 'a thing of beauty and joy forever'.[83]

Notes

1   Anon., 'Mouse & Man', *Time* (27 December 1937): 19.

2   Ibid.

3   Walt Disney Productions, 'Making of a Masterpiece: Snow White and the Seven Dwarfs', *Walt Disney Home* video (1994).

4   Paul Harrison, '"Snow White', $1,600,000 Disney Screen Creation, Now Ready for Public', *Washington Post* (9 January 1938): 1, sect. 6.

5   Anon., 'Mouse & Man', *Time* (27 December 1937): 19.

6   E. I. Raitt, 'What Can Business Do to Remove Consumer Suspicion?', *Journal of Home Economics* 28 (January 1936): 5.

7   Martin Stillwell, 'The Story Behind Snow White's $10,000,000 Surprise Party', *Liberty* (9 April 1938): 39.

8   Douglas Churchill, 'Now Mickey Mouse Enters Art's Temple', *New York Times* (3 June 1934): 12, sect. 6.

9   Ibid.

10   Frank Daugherty, 'Mickey Mouse Comes of Age', *Christian Science Monitor* (2 February 1938): 8.

11   Steve MacQueen, 'Walt Disney's Unseen Animation: Rare Treasures from the Vault', *Smithsonian Institution* (14 March 1998): speech given at the National Museum of Natural History.

12   Anon., 'M. Mouse Poorly Paid', *New York Times* (12 March 1934): 20; Churchill, 'Now Mickey Mouse Enters Art's Temple', 13.

13   Ibid.

14   Anon., 'Mouse & Man', 21.

15   B. R. Crisler, 'Film Gossip of the Week: Walt Disney and His Galaxy of Fauna', *New York Times* (30 May 1937): 7.

16   Douglas Churchill, 'Walt Disney Signs for More Whirls', *New York Times* (9 January 1938): 5, sect. 10.

17   Anon., 'Walt Disney Returns: Creator of "Mickey Mouse" Back from Tour of Europe', *New York Times* (2 August 1935): 15.

18   Churchill, 'Now Mickey Mouse Enters Art's Temple', 13.

19   Miller family, 'The Entire Family Reviews "Snow White"', *Los Angeles Times* (2 January 1938): 1, part III.

20   Ibid.

21   Harrison, '"Snow White', $1,600,000 Disney Screen Creation, Now Ready for Public'.

22   MacQueen, 'Walt Disney's Unseen Animation'.

23   Ibid.

24   Anon., 'British Fear "Snow White" Will Cause Nightmares', *New York Times* (6 February 1938): 37.

25   Anon., 'Unusual Re-Playdating Demand for "Snow White" before It Opens', *Variety* (9 February 1938): 7.

26   Anon., 'London OK's "Snow White"', *Variety* (23 February 1938): 5.

27   T. M. Pryor, '"Snow White" Sidelights: Censors Toppled and Business Boomed as the Dwarfs Went Round the World', *New York Times* (5 February 1939): 4, sect. 9.

28   Anon., 'Walt Disney's Snow White and the Seven Dwarfs: Adapted from Grimm's Fairy Tales', *Good Housekeeping* (November 1937): 35.

29   Frank Daugherty, 'Mickey Mouse Comes of Age', *Christian Science Monitor* (2 February 1938): 9.

30   Filmic Light, *Snow White School Study* (1938), http://filmic-light.blogspot.com/2013/03/1937-snow-white-photoplay-school-study.html. Accessed 30 August 2020.

31   Anon., '"Snow White" Premiere Due Tonight', *Los Angeles Times* (21 December 1937): 10.

32   Anon., 'Disney Creates New Stars', *Los Angeles Times* (17 December 1937): 11, part II.

33 Adriana Casel, 'Snow White Speaks', *People Weekly* (18 May 1987): 104.

34 Edwin Schallert, 'Dwarf Dopey Hailed as Newest Scene Stealer', *Los Angeles Times* (11 December 1937): 7, part II; Edwin Schallert, 'Cartoon Actors Claim Spotlight', *Los Angeles Times* (12 December 1937): 1; Anon., 'Disney Creates New Starts', *Los Angeles Times* (17 December 1937): 11, part II.

35 Anon., 'Gala Premiere Assured for "Snow White"', *Los Angeles Times* (20 December 1937): 9.

36 Anon., '"Snow White" Timely Fare for Christmas', *Los Angeles Times* (25 December 1937): 14, part II.

37 Ibid.

38 Anon., 'Gala Premiere Assured for "Snow White"', 9; Anon., '"Snow White" Premiere Due Tonight', 10.

39 Anon., 'Breakdown of Network Plugs', *Variety* (12 January 1938): 45.

40 Anon., 'Breakdown of Network Plugs', *Variety* (2 February 1938): 47.

41 Edwin Schallert, '"Snow White Achievement in Film Art', *Los Angeles Times* (22 December 1937): 11.

42 Aljean Harmetz, 'Disney's "Old Men" Savor the Vintage Years', *New York Times* (4 July 1993): H9; Richard Coons, '"Snow White", Disney's First Full-Length Film, Rated "Movie of the Month" for Artistry and Charm', *Washington Post* (9 January 1938): 1, sect. 6.

43 Schallert, '"Snow White' Achievement in Film Art', 11; Churchill, 'Disney Signs for More Whirls', 5.

44 Anon., 'M.M. Is Eight Years Old', *Literary Digest* 22 (3 October 1936): 19.

45 Churchill, 'Now Mickey Mouse Enters Art's Temple', 12.

46 'M.M. Is Eight Years Old', 19; L. H. Robbins, 'Mickey Mouse Emerges as Economist', *New York Times Magazine* (10 March 1935): VI, 8.

47 'M.M. Is Eight Years Old', 19.

48 Ibid.

49 Crisler, 'Film Gossip of the Week', 7.

50 MacQueen, 'Walt Disney's Unseen Animation'.

51 Walt Disney Productions, 'Making of a Masterpiece', 1994.

52 Stillwell, 'The Story Behind Snow White's $10,000,000 Surprise Party', 40.

53 Anon., '"Snow White" Advertisement', *The Household* Magazine (June and July 1938): 12.

54 Anon., 'New Dwarf Industry', *New York Times* (2 May 1938): 16.

55 Ibid.

56 Ibid.

57 Pryor, '"Snow White" Sidelights', 4.

58 Anon., '"Snow White' Advertisement', *Los Angeles Times* (27 December 1937): 12.

59 Anon., '"Snow White' Advertisement', *Los Angeles Times* (31 December 1937): 14.

60 Anon., 'Disney $42,000 Will Be the New Hub Record', *Variety* (16 February 1938): 8; Anon., '"Snow White' Panics L'ville, Wow $15,000', *Variety* (16 February 1938): 8.

61 Anon., '"Snow White" OK $17,000', *Variety* (16 February 1938): 8.

62 Anon., '"Snow White" $100,000 on 5th N.Y. wk: Out of Town B.O. Astonishes Trade', *Variety* (16 February 1938): 11.

63 Anon., 'Disney $42,000 Will Be the New Hub Record', 8.

64 '"Snow White" Panics L'ville, Wow $15,000', 8.

65 Ibid.

66 Anon., 'Film Reviews: "Snow White and the Seven Dwarfs"', *Variety* (29 December 1937): 17.

67 Harrison, '"Snow White', $1,600,000 Disney Screen Creation, Now Ready for Public', 1.

68 Anon., 'Cartoon Characters Score Hit', *Los Angeles Times* (2 January 1938): 10, part 1.

69 Douglas Churchill, 'West-Coasting Along', *New York Times* (30 January 1938): 5, sect. 10.

70 Anon., 'Snow White $110,000 Bigger 3rd Week', *Variety* (2 February 1938): 9.

71 Anon., '"Snow White' Sets Mark with $6,740,000 Gross', *Los Angeles Times* (2 May 1939): 29.

72 Anon., '"B'dcast', Vaude Good $18,000 in Wash', *Variety* (2 March 1938): 7.

73 Anon., 'Disney's Big B.O. Kayoes Vauders', *Variety* (23 February 1938): 1.

74 Pryor, '"Snow White" Sidelights', 4.

75 Walt Disney Productions, 'Making of a Masterpiece', 1994.

76 Pryor, '"Snow White" Sidelights', 4.

77 Walt Disney Productions, 'Making of a Masterpiece', 1994.

78 Anon., 'Film Critics Here Vote Year's "Best"', *New York Times* (3 January 1939): 18.

79 F. S. Nugent, 'Disney Is Now Art–But He Wonders', *New York Times* (26 February 1939): 4; Anon., 'Disney Joins the Masters in the Metropolitan', *New York Times* (24 January 1939): 21.

80 Ibid., 5.

81 Douglas Churchill, 'Disney's "Philosophy"', *New York Times* (6 March 1938): 9, 23.

82 Anon., 'Movies: Walt Disney Goes Feature Length', *Literary Digest* (22 January 1938): 23.

83 J. P. Cunningham, 'The Play and Screen: "Snow White and the Seven Dwarfs"', *The Commonwealth* (28 January 1938): 386.

8

Framing *Snow White*: Preservation, nostalgia and the American way in the 1930s

Jane Batkin

The Past is still with us in this land. At best, the Present is a feeble growth.[1]

– WALDO FRANK

If the reach of the past pervades the present, it seems to be within American culture that it is fully embraced, as part of the composition of life. The power of memory has seeped into US thought and discussion about nationhood and has created a nostalgic framework within which society, politics and philosophy sit. As cultural historian Warren Susman states, 'not only do Americans believe they cannot escape history; few seem to want to'.[2] The period between the 1920s and 1930s represented a transition that was stark and shocking and, from a decade of decadence and selfhood, came an era of hunger and fear. Robert Harrison suggests that 'the Depression of the 1930s bit into the fabric of American life'.[3] In this challenging climate, the nation turned away from hedonism and embraced what became coined as the 'American Way', forming a collective society to support Roosevelt's New Deal politics.[4] The 1930s represented a critical turning point for America; while its politics signalled a new age of thinking, the overriding feeling was one of nostalgia for what had been lost – not the recklessness of the 1920s and its obsession with consumer wealth and stock markets but a time before, where Puritanism and self-restraint were markers of a Victorian sensibility. The 1930s was therefore a period of change and reflection, and cinema became a mirror to the struggles and achievements of the everyman. Hollywood told stories of escapism, of the ability to rise up out of the Depression, yet was condemned by some critics for not addressing reality. Margaret Thorp, writing in 1939, asserted that audiences wanted escapism, to be 'cheered up' by cinema rather than seeing 'the squalor and misery of which there was all too much at home'.[5] Conversely, Lawrence Levine argued that cinema was 'deeply grounded in the realities and the intricacies of the Depression'.[6] Then Walt Disney Studios stepped into the void in 1937 with *Snow White and the Seven Dwarfs* (David Hand, 1937), a feature film that captured the sensibilities and struggles of an entire decade within its animated looking glass. It had a curious power to frame the 1930s in terms of cultural and political contexts and became a critically important work to view on many different levels. How exactly, then, do we frame *Snow White* within these wider contextual, historical and ideological paradigms?

This chapter will explore the US landscape within which Disney's first feature-length animation sat: from Depression to New Deal politics, to the idea of collective memory and nostalgia. It will dissect culture and the contradictions of restraint and change that defined the 1930s, and journey into the film itself to discover how *Snow White* reflected America and came to represent Americana. The chapter presents an ideological reading of *Snow White* as a product of its time; there is much at stake in focusing on the film symptomatically in this way, but I believe that the politics of the era and the shifting identity of its nation and people are clearly, strikingly, reflected in Disney's work. The 1930s depicted the Hooverville kids, living in makeshift shelters after being displaced by the country's worst droughts, which led to an exodus of 2.5 million from the Great Plains. This era revealed the folly of optimism and selfish individualism, and illustrated, visually, how hunger and unemployment became the new Fear. Significantly, the 1930s represented a violent shift from self to society and a re-emerging puritanism within an inherently conservative country. Within the dusty, drought-ridden landscape of a shocked and struggling nation, and amid snapshot faces of hungry, destitute families, Disney captured a critical moment of American history and presented its own solution to the American 'problem': collectivism, hard work and, above all, preservation of the Past.

Disney's response to the Great Depression

Films can be vital sources of cultural identity and they enable mirrored encounters that provide escapism from reality, but, paradoxically, they can also offer looking-glass exposure to a society's concerns, issues and politics. John Belton states that 'in the American cinema, individual classic styles exist in the context of a larger, national style'.[7] Mainstream cinema, therefore, leans towards a national collectivism. Belton goes on to discuss American comedy (which was particularly popular during the 1920s and 1930s) as a 'cultural safety valve' that occasionally let off steam and offered a release from life's pressures; Hollywood during this time became the gateway for escapism, often through folly and laughter.[8] In 1931, cinema takings slumped dramatically as the Depression took hold and this slump continued into the middle of the decade with studios 'in a state of heightened financial sensitivity'.[9] David Eldridge states that the implementation of the Hays Production Code was believed to be part of the solution to this sensitivity; the flutter of films' financial woes was met with sensible, muted regimentation. Films that applauded hedonism were punished in what became a censorship frenzy and this reflected the changes in society at the time and the turning of the enforced production code towards conservatism. Film during the fallout of the 1920s crash, however, was also attempting to address what exactly was happening to America.

Disney's response was direct and active, and it served as a looking glass into the temperament of US politics and society at the time. Walt Disney, himself, was a staunch supporter of Franklin Roosevelt. He was quoted as saying, 'work is the real adventure of life', and certainly the work ethic of the seven dwarfs in his 1937 feature reflects this ideal.[10] Mining in the wilderness, they appear to enjoy their work routine and, at the same time, acknowledge the benefits of capitalism:

We dig dig dig dig dig dig dig in our mine the whole day through
To dig dig dig dig dig dig dig is what we really like to do
It ain't no trick to get rich quick
If you dig dig dig with a shovel or a pick

The song points to honest work that reaps rewards, a return to a simple way of life and repetition of manual labour tasks. Disney's way mirrored what became known as 'the American Way' in the 1930s, a phrase that was acknowledged and defined through art, literature and articles that united a people through core moral values.[11] Novels such as Margaret Mitchell's *Gone with the Wind* (1936) and John Steinbeck's *The Grapes of Wrath* (1939) were examples of this, as was Roosevelt's Public Work of Arts

Project which encouraged artists to depict 'the American scene', promoting values of American life and hard work.[12] Disney's view reflected this, but was tinted with what Steven Watts calls a 'politics of nostalgia'.[13] Disney was a futurist, embracing technology and innovation, yet simultaneously was forever glancing backwards into Victorian America (as has been documented and discussed by animation scholars Leonard Maltin, Esther Leslie, Norman Klein and Michael Barrier). Memory becomes fundamental to the Disney canon: Janet Harbord suggests that the studio was 'a form of memory-wiping' through its Disneyfication of a violent century, and Henry Giroux comments on Disney's films being able to 'powerfully influence the way America's cultural landscape is imagined'.[14] Thomas Inge focuses on Disney's ability to reshape the stories it told so that they deliberately reflected Walt's own vision of America and its ethical values.[15] Memory and nostalgia for an idealistic America remain at the core of Disney's cinema and *Snow White*, read ideologically, is a clear example of this, with its attachment to, and argument for, traditionalism.

In the United States, the 1930s represented a reattachment with the country's own distant past, within the work ethic of a newly collective society that ultimately rejected individualism. Amid Hays Code censorship and radically shifting politics that supported a sort of reimagined Victoriana, Disney's own natural traditionalism became aligned with this identity. America and Disney, together, captured the spirit of the time through the collective work ethic of real individuals and fictitious characters. The dwarfs are rigid in their routine of going to work in the mines, despite the distraction of the princess hiding in their home, and they reflect the heroes of the time, reaffirming status through masculinization. The struggle of the breadwinner in the 1930s, in an era of horrific unemployment and hunger, meant that masculinity had lost its past link with financial gain (such as the wealth achieved through stock market trading in the 1920s). Masculinity was instead stripped back to reflect the hard labour necessary for the nation to recover from the Great Depression. This idea ties in with Roosevelt's New Deal policy of introducing a Civilian Conservation Corps aimed primarily at young, fit men who were unemployed, to repair the soil erosion and declining timber resources in America. The men built new roads, repaired telephone lines and planted millions of trees across the nation. Hard labour defines these activities and reflects what had happened to masculinity amid the crisis. The work ethic of the dwarfs in *Snow White* resonates with the New Deal and a back-to-nature ethos: hard work creates rewards, but at the heart of this was the morality of thrift – a Puritan ethic – that working made a man a better person. The *New York Times*, in 1938, stated that the seven dwarfs 'had been the most valiant miners and sappers against recession whom the moving picture magnates have hired this year'.[16] The commercial success of *Snow White* sent a clear message not only about the potential of animated film as an artistic medium but also of the benefits of honest hard work and capitalism, again reflected within a Disney studio that, itself, created a product of the animation industry.

Popular film implied the paradoxes of the 1930s, as a time of change and of the struggle between modernity and the past. As well as gazing into history, Eldridge argues, Hollywood seemed to be saying 'return to the basics of the American tradition'[17] and therein lies the solution to the American problem. Disney's *Snow White* belonged to this cluster of socially and politically aware films that can be viewed through this ideological lens. Charlie Chaplin's social commentary within *Modern Times* (1936) also reflects the New Deal message of work and honesty as he struggles to survive in an industrial environment, often bewildered by events and the workplace itself. While Chaplin struggles to move forward, he always has one eye on the past with a melancholy sense of longing that reflects Disney's own traditionalism. In *Mr. Smith Goes to Washington* (Frank Capra, 1939), James Stewart plays an ordinary man who becomes employed by the Senate, amidst political corruption, and who represents the voice of the people in an extraordinary twist of events that enables the empowering of the everyman.

Disney's *Snow White* functioned as a similar signpost to collectivism and traditionalism, as well as being a mirror of 1930s society and politics. The themes of greed and Self are clearly represented as evil: the Queen/ wicked witch wants to erase Snow White's beauty so that the mirror will pronounce one beautiful image in the kingdom. This hedonistic display can be applied to 1920s US politics (perhaps more clearly than Europe in a previous century). Snow White's own individualism – running away, straying from the path and moving into the dwarfs' home – is resented and viewed suspiciously by Grumpy, who asserts that she is a harbinger of trouble. Those viewed as being on the 'outside' (Snow White/the Queen) are depicted in a negative light. The pessimism about individualism within society at the time was reflected in Disney's film. Tracey Mollet states that animation, as 'an overwhelmingly visual medium', was able to connect and 'correspond' with the American people during the Depression years through the myths and symbols that were prevalent in Hollywood cinema at the time.[18] Such national messages are veiled in *Snow White*, making them more intriguing. Animation's ability to 'do' ideology in a covert way is evident here, and there is a political undertone that is important. Animation, as an 'innocent' but strikingly visual medium, allows it to play with representations and political messages. Viewed through an ideological lens, *Snow White* reveals the stark truth about life in 1930s America.

The images of food being prepared for the hard-working dwarfs in *Snow White* can be viewed as particularly important symbols of 1930s America. The Hooverville children, displaced through dust storms or by their parents' failed mortgage payments, lived in makeshift shanties and stared out from the camera lens, reaffirming worker Joseph Pizza's message that the 1930s was about survival: 'people have to go through an era like

FIGURE 8.1 Destitute Pea Pickers in California: Migrant mother.
Source: https://www.loc.gov/item/2017762891/ (accessed 20 June 2018).

that to understand what it is, and what it was to be in that position'.[19] Displaced families struggled to survive (see Figure 8.1). In the American Life Histories collection 'Looking Around with a Hay Farmer' in 1938, Leonidas Cockrell laments, 'the crops are mighty little' and 'everybody is in a bad fix'.[20] Food preparation in *Snow White* is a reward offered for the absent inhabitants of the cottage and while she prepares it, she imagines she is feeding children who must be hungry, rather than dwarfs returning from work. She makes a simple pie, certain that this will be received with appreciation and that the inhabitants of the cottage will let her stay and look after them (see Figure 8.2). The honest, simple food cooked and eaten (and celebrated) in *Snow White* is symbolic of the time, as is her concern about being homeless and alone in the wilderness. Disney seemed to tap into the 1930s as a moment of suffering and survival and captured the basic needs of its people, with this American interpretation of the Grimm story. While the film deviates from the true European roots of its folklore, *Snow White* certainly seems to reflect America's own return to its Puritan past.

FIGURE 8.2 Snow White preparing food in *Snow White and the Seven Dwarfs* (David Hand, 1937).

Self-restraint, community, morality, industry and thrift defined Puritanism in US history, and Puritanism, itself, has become a marker for many of the characteristics of the nation.[21]

Snow White depicts the rejection of wealth and the immoral Self for a return to the land and its unspoiled innocence. Nature is a force in the film: it nurtures and destroys and demands respect. Perhaps this reflects the nation's preoccupation with nature's law during the 1930s, such as the dust storms that brought trauma and displacement to so many. This representation of nature as power aligns itself with Margaret King's view that Disney had an almost 'Jeffersonian bond to the land', wherein nature and nurture represent a moral path and that this is fundamentally the right path to take.[22] In believing in the quest of the common man and his sense of belonging within a simple, collective community, Disney revealed his politics of nostalgia and his own view of the American Way through *Snow White*.

Nostalgia and memory

The idea of reclaiming and preserving what has been lost seeps repeatedly into American politics and culture. As Michael Kammen states, America's collective memory links it to tradition in a never-ending dialect, that 'the past is vital, rather than dead'.[23] What is most interesting, perhaps, is how the film reveals its own nostalgia and memory and emerges as a symbol of Americana. Disney's first feature is an artefact of cultural and historical importance, a mirror of a bygone time, its reflected surfaces spilling in different directions, but always presenting a nation's culture. Nostalgia becomes key to the representation of *Snow White* as artefact of Americana, but nostalgia opens itself up to many different interpretations. It is a word that is not bound by any one era, but remains malleable and ever-changing with each interpretation.

Richard Gross and Rob McIlveen stress the importance of memory, that without it we would be 'servants of the moment'.[24] Looking backwards is regarded as memory preservation with great psychological value. Karen Wheeler's essay *Nostalgia Isn't Nasty* is interesting in its discussion of the individual moving from alienation to a state of being non-alienated and as being known by others 'in the commonality of the community which is identified as "home"'.[25] This idea complements the notion of collectivism in American society. Svetlana Boym views nostalgia as twofold. For her 'a cinematic image of nostalgia is a double exposure, or a superimposition of two images – of home and abroad, past and present, dream and everyday life'.[26] Boym finds nostalgia elusive yet alluring, a 'time-out-of-time of daydream and longing'.[27]

Memory and nostalgia are at the core of Disney animation. Through our understanding of New Deal politics and Walt Disney's stance within such politics, we can see how the puritan ideals of the past influenced this cinema and how the very nature of puritanism and the American Way point to nostalgia. Susman suggests that few Americans want to escape history, arguing that they 'could find in history a way to become immortal'.[28] He explains how early settlers interpreted history as a vital part of life and studies in America, and how the Puritan past continues to impact on the American present. For Susman, the search for the 'real' America and the American Way in the twentieth century was something that could create a new nationalism and sense of conformity.[29] Memory becomes preservation in the United States and is examined through its cinema. Hollywood casts an eye to the past and reaffirms the importance of traditional values. Within the 1930s, this was critical and became the message of the decade. Nostalgia for the innocent simplistic past – of hard labour, belonging and nature – became the symbol of the 1930s.

Snow White's nostalgia is all-pervasive. While critical interpretations of the film's messages suit the argument of social change and New Deal politics, the themes of nostalgia and preservation of the past remain dominant. Of course, these become visible through the struggles of social change and politics of the time, such as Snow White cooking and cleaning and the dwarfs engaging in hard labour. Film has always reflected culture and society and the 'real' is always implicitly or explicitly revealed within cinema. Film constructs meaning and truth from life, while shaping it to suit film's own individual message, and the United States has seen its cinema evolve into a national style. America found itself being reflected at the dawn of film: 'the possibility of showing the entire American population its own face in the mirror screen' had arrived.[30] American film documents American history and its very nature is to preserve this. The 1930s' cluster of ideological films that can be read symptomatically, such as *Snow White*, also includes *Stagecoach*

(John Ford, 1939) and *Gone with the Wind* (Victor Fleming, 1939). Where cinema at the time looked to the present, it largely did so through comedy (e.g. with Howard Hawks' 1938 screwball comedy: *Bringing Up Baby*). The past pervaded Hollywood filmmaking, partly in search of the solution to the problem of what had happened to America in the Depression.

Disney's *Snow White* invites its audience to preserve the American Way and its puritan roots. Nostalgia in the film is for nature, hard work and routine, for cooking and eating and celebrating the simple life. The past and present are at conflict; Snow White flees the palace and civilization, which have become corrupt. The present is represented as untrustworthy, a place of hedonism and vanity that embodies evil (such as the 1920s and its ideals of Self). The Queen sits alone within a hierarchical kingdom as a tyrannical ruler; collectivism is absent in this civilized world and the Queen, on hearing that Snow White is the most beautiful maiden in the land, issues a death warrant. When she is told that the princess is still alive, the Queen assumes a poisoned apple will provide the solution to her problem. Her actions are solitary and celebrate the Self; in the Brothers Grimm story, the Queen visits Snow White on three occasions and lives long enough to attend Snow White's wedding to the prince, until forced to dance to her death. Disney's version of the Grimm story is sanitized for its younger audience, and significantly the kingdom and its Queen are depicted as isolated, with only one meeting taking place between the heroine and villainess. The kingdom exists in a vacuum devoid of noise or people, the present stifled by stillness and silence (in Waldo Frank's terms, above, the present is 'feeble'). The State in *Snow White* is elusive and points more to a Stateless, empty space which, in turn, reflects the crisis occurring within politics at the time of production. The beginning of the film reaffirms Susman's views of America and its search for its history amid its rejection of the individual, rather than that of European folklore, and the film's identity and message lie more in its embracing of American traditional values than anything else.

The return to nature and to the land in *Snow White* is a strong rhetoric for nostalgia and the past. Disney strives for non-nationalism through his reimagining of a folk tale, and the film is representative of modernism in many ways, such as the innovation of technology and the use of artistic images within the film's landscape. Disney's multi-plane camera accentuates the strikingly real backgrounds in the film, at the same time signposting the studio's ability to embrace technical change, while the attention to detail of the animated characters is vividly representative of the artistic supremacy of the studio. However, at *Snow White*'s heart lies a desire to return to a pre-modern age, symbolized by nature and the collective, conservative ideals of its characters. Watts suggests that Disney's aesthetic heart 'continued to beat to an internal rhythm of nineteenth-century sentimental realism'.[31] *Snow White* seems to imply that the answer to America's woes lies within its Victorian and puritan past, realized through its own themes of nature, nurture, hard work and family values. The past represents the American Way and, for Disney, the American Dream.[32]

Family in *Snow White* mirrors society's struggle to revert to traditionalism at the time. Identity shifts from the Self (of the 1920s) to the family unit. The film's representation of family implies an unnatural one, with Snow White becoming home maker and 'mother' to the dwarfs; perhaps this in itself is a symbol of the very paradox of home. The roaring 1920s empowered women to achieve their own goals and have a voice that mattered, yet the Depression represented something of the 'punishment' of the Self. Snow White is a rural girl/woman who believes that her main goal is to feed the 'children', clean the house and be a good mother (while dreaming of marrying a Prince). Disney's message is clear and firm, alluding directly to nineteenth century sensibilities where family was the centrepiece of American values and the American home. Home itself must also be defended and the princess must learn her lesson when she fails to identify danger. It falls to the prince to rescue her because patriarchy is the lynchpin of Disney's early cinema, and patriarchy also reflects the politics of Victorian America. Snow White's journey into the wilderness is undertaken haphazardly and is fuelled by fear and trepidation. When the forest creatures discover her inert body on the ground, however, she quickly recovers, remarking how silly she was to be afraid. Nature is preferable to the cruelty of civilization. As David Whitley states, Disney's attention to the pastoral and the natural landscape within the film establishes and emphasizes 'the relationship of the heroine to the natural environment that both surrounds, and in a sense, defines her'.[33] Here, Snow White can feel safe and achieve belonging in a collective society, albeit one that is steeped in fantasy. Nostalgia is for a bygone time, or as Boym coins it, 'a time-out-of-time' that belongs neither in the real world nor in the dream world but is a combination of both.[34] Nostalgia is difficult to place because it means different things to different people. On a national scale, however, it recalls important events and values. The dwarfs' home and workplace are represented as icons of 1930s memorabilia in their values and beliefs, despite their origins in European folklore. As Snow White tries to connect the inhabitants of the cottage to her own knowledge of families, she struggles and fails. Are they children without a mother? Do they need one? The truth is stranger than her imaginings. *Snow White* is situated at the intersection of the fantastic and the political, of home and dreaming, enabling visions of nostalgia to infiltrate it through its dreamy moods and landscapes that are both real and fictional.

Disney himself shaped the stories he told to reflect his beliefs about family life, the work ethic and the American Dream back to the people through cinema. In line with the New Deal of the 1930s, the Disney studio seemed, perhaps unknowingly, to address the need for the American public to fall in line and adhere to a doctrine of puritan, good behaviour. In reshaping *Snow White* to reflect what was important to America at the time, Disney created a piece of memorabilia of the era that resonated with both the 1930s audience and audiences to come. The film is an important relic within Hollywood cinema, animation history and national US history and yet is one that contains many inconsistencies and paradoxes: it is outwardly non-nationalistic yet it echoes with nationhood, it challenges society and politics yet depicts fantasy and folklore, its characters wander from isolation to collectivism in search of 'home', as well as in and out of nature. *Snow White* Americanizes its European folklore origins as part of this process. The conflicts within Disney's film have become mirrors of society at the time. The first animated feature needed to forge a strong connection with its audience, doing so not just because of its medium specificity but also perhaps because of what it represented about US society and nostalgia. The American Way can be linked to the frontier world, to unchartered land and budding civilizations in the face of great adversities, to individual dreams and goals and Disney's *Snow White* becomes a magnifying glass into American identity.

Americana

National identity, cultural heritage and the American Dream are fragments that fit together to form the 'Americana' of the United States. Typically, they are artefacts that have become symbols of this heritage that embody America and being American. The Route 66 sign, diners, Cadillacs and the Statue of Liberty are, for example, all visual signposts of this history preservation but point more to material `things' and artefacts than an overall sense of the meaning of this national place. More focused is the relationship between Americana and nostalgia, and this ties in with the discussion above about the preservation of the past. Kammen calls America a 'land of the past, a culture with a discernible memory'.[35] It is a land of people that do not relinquish the past easily: the present is viewed as inferior while the past is seen as something alive and longed for. Traditionalism and patriarchy inform ideas of national identity in a country that submerges itself in its own nostalgia. The American Dream began with the conquering of frontiers before transforming into the quest for capitalism. The American Way alludes more to the land than its material wealth. Nostalgia and memory have shaped the United States through its tumultuous past, with preservation enabled through the capturing of images and sounds of bygone eras that we can view and listen to online today, thus tapping into the vaults of history. The past never dies.

Disney's *Snow White*, situated in a period of extreme transformation, has become part of this identity and an integral part of Americana. It forms part of the American experience of the 1930s and also represents memory preservation of the American past. Watching the film in the twenty-first century, themes of a collective culture and strong work ethic, as well as issues of simple hunger, isolation and fear that pervade it all seem to connect the film to the decade of its production. These are more profound and more directly alluded to than the European heritage of the Grimm story in Disney's adaptation. The film becomes a relic to be preserved as 'Americana', a form of national and individual identity from the vaults of history, as do the documentaries surrounding it.

In the film *American Experience: Walt Disney*, Carmentina Higginbotham makes the connection between Snow White and the 1930s, suggesting that the heroine is the perfect embodiment 'of 1930s culture' and uses her skills and trades in the best way she can, reflecting the women who gained entry to the workplace during the Great Depression. Snow White, she suggests, is completely rooted in a '30s aesthetic'.[36] Historian Susan Douglas, however, describes Disney's vision of America as something of a false mirror that projects a very idealized image of the United States back to itself. While this is viewed as a criticism because of Disney's lack of representation of difference and diversity during its classical era – and many theorists have commented on the sanitization of the Disney studios, among them Giroux and Watts – this false mirror itself aligns with the definitions and ideas of nostalgia that this chapter has discussed as pervading *Snow White*. If Disney is accepted as projecting a certain ethos through his cinema, and that ethos is nostalgia, his films must be viewed through a nostalgic lens. Boym tells us that nostalgia is 'an affective yearning for a community with a collective memory, a longing for continuity in a fragmented world'.[37] Within the troubled landscape of 1930s America, Disney used the Brothers Grimm folk tale to tell a story of a lost princess and her adventures in the wilderness. Shaping the story to reflect his own views on the world and platforming the American Way as part of those beliefs, Disney offered a solution to the American problem at the time: the Great Depression of the 1930s. *Snow White* has become Americana, a cultural snapshot of a certain period in history and one that, itself, looks back in time into a deeper history. There, it seemed to find the answer to the question 'what happened to America in the 1930s?' As Joseph Pizza reflected, above, people have to go through an era like that to understand it and to grasp the fundamental importance of pure survival, above all else. The solution to the problem of survival, Disney's *Snow White* seemed to tell 1930s America, lay much further back in history to a time of honesty, hard work and family values. Snow White's own path within the film was a mirror, and a glimpse into the American Way, where the past was viewed as more vital than dead.

Notes

1   Waldo Frank, quoted in Warren I Susman, *Culture as History – the Transformation of American Society in the Twentieth Century* (Washington: Smithsonian Institution Press, 2003), 28.

2 Ibid., 3.

3 Robert Harrison, *State and Society in Twentieth-Century America* (Harlow: Addison Wesley Longman, 1997), 169.

4 Susman, *Culture as History – the Transformation of American Society in the Twentieth Century*, 164.

5 Margaret Thorp, *America at the Movies* (New Haven: Yale University Press, 1939), 17.

6 Lawrence Levine, 'Hollywood's Washington: Film Images of National Politics During the Great Depression', in *The Unpredictable Past: Explorations of America's Cultural History*, ed. Levine (New York: Oxford University Press, 1993), 231, 253; Iwan Morgan and Philip John Davies, *Hollywood and the Great Depression* (Edinburgh: Edinburgh University Press, 2016).

7 John Belton, *American Cinema, American Culture*, 3rd edn (New York: McGraw-Hill, 2009), 22.

8 Ibid., 171.

9 David Eldridge, *American Culture in the 1930s* (Edinburgh: Edinburgh University Press, 2008), 65.

10 Steven Watts, 'Walt Disney: Art and Politics in the American Century', *Journal of American History*, 82 (1) (1995): 84, 101.

11 Susman, *Culture as History – the Transformation of American Society in the Twentieth Century*, 158.

12 Smithsonian American Art Museum, '1934: A New Deal for Artists', SAAM. Available at https://americanart.si.edu/exhibitions/1934 (accessed 30 October 2019).

13 Watts, 'Walt Disney: Art and Politics in the American Century', 96.

14 Janet Harbord, quoted in Chris Pallant, *Demystifying Disney* (London: Bloomsbury, 2011), 68; Henry Giroux, 'Animating Youth: The Disnification of Children's Culture', *Socialist Review* 94, no. 3 (1994): 68, 65–79.

15 Thomas Inge, 'Walt Disney's Snow White and the Seven Dwarves: Art Adaptation and Ideology', *Journal of Popular Film and Television* 32, no. 3 (2004): 140, 132–42.

16 Jack Doyle, 'Disney Dollars, 1930s' 'Prosperity Out of Fantasy,' Topics of the Times, *New York Times*, The Pop History Dig. Available at http://www.pophistorydig.com/topics/tag/new-york-times-magazine/ (accessed 19 July 2018).

17 Eldridge, *American Culture in the 1930s*, 78.

18 Tracey Mollet, *Cartoons in Hard Times: The Animated Shorts of Disney and Warner Brothers in Depression and War, 1932–1945* (London: Bloomsbury, 2017), 5.

19 T. D. Carroll, 'Men with Professions Were Only Too Glad to Clean the Yard to Make a Dollar', audio recording, Library of Congress. Available at https://www.loc.gov/item/afcwip003853 (accessed 20 July 2018).

20	Luther Clark, 'Looking Around with a Hay Farmer', *Life Histories*, Library of Congress. Available at https://www.loc.gov/resource/ wpalh0.07011806/?st=gallery (accessed 19 July 2018).

21	Susman, *Culture as History – the Transformation of American Society in the Twentieth Century*, 41.

22	Margaret King, 'The Audience in the Wilderness: The Disney Nature Films', *Journal of Popular Film and Television* 24, no. 2 (1996): 60–8.

23	Michael Kammen, *Mystic Chords of Memory: The Transformation of Tradition in American Culture* (New York: Vintage Books, 1993), 5.

24	Richard Gross, Rob McIlveen, *Aspects of Psychology: Memory* (London: Hodder and Stoughton, 1999), 1.

25	Karen Wheeler quoted in Steven Allen, 'Bringing the Dead to Life: Animation and the Horrific', *At The Interface/Probing the Boundaries* 61 (2010): 96.

26	Svetlana Boym, *The Future of Nostalgia* (New York: Basic Books, 2001), xiv.

27	Ibid., xix.

28	Susman, *Culture as History – the Transformation of American Society in the Twentieth Century*, 3.

29	Ibid., 164.

30	Daniel J. Czitrom, 'American Motion Pictures and the New Popular Culture', in *Popular Culture in American History*, ed. Jim Cullen (Oxford: Blackwell, 2001), 151.

31	Watts, 'Walt Disney: Art and Politics in the American Century', 87.

32	Inge, 'Walt Disney's Snow White and the Seven Dwarves: Art Adaptation and Ideology', 141.

33	David Whitley, *The Idea of Nature in Disney Animation* (Aldershot: Ashgate, 2008)

34	Boym, *The Future of Nostalgia*, xix.

35	Kammen, *Mystic Chords of Memory: The Transformation of Tradition in American Culture*, 7.

36	*Walt Disney – Part 1*, American Experience (2015), [TV programme] PBS, 14 September 2014.

37	Boym, *The Future of Nostalgia*, xiv.

9

Recasting *Snow White*: Parodic animated homages to the Disney feature

Terry Lindvall

Walt Disney's *Snow White and the Seven Dwarfs* (David Hand, 1937) premiered on 4 February 1938. Just three months later, on 4 May, Hollywood columnist (and future television host) Ed Sullivan quoted Mae West's quip from a vaudeville routine: 'I used to be Snow White, but I drifted.'[1] The throwaway line not only drew laughs, but it marked a moment when a great work of art had reached its apotheosis: it had been found worthy of burlesque. This chapter charts the cyclical journey of a fairy tale, from cinematic tour de force to follow a path meandering down to parody. If it is good enough, or popular enough, a celebrated text can eventually be transformed into a Fractured Fairy Tale. Cited and spoofed by other animators, *Snow White and the Seven Dwarfs* would become as iconic as the pope, with each new riff acknowledging the genius of the original.

As film scholar Ronald Gottesman so aptly put it in his study of film parody, parody functions as a sign 'that a culture is simultaneously maintaining continuity and making something new and valuable out of the eternal tension between imagination and reality'.[2] Parodic form demonstrates a delight that a culture has with its past and an ongoing creativity that can play with 'something old, something new; something borrowed, something *blue*' (i.e. transgressive). In this chapter I open up the ludic extensions of Walt Disney's successful folly, showing how several animation artists working within different national contexts and filmmaking traditions have borrowed from, paid homage to and ultimately parodied *Snow White and the Seven Dwarfs*. These playful works inspired by Disney's cel-animated adaptation showcase the nature of parody and intertextuality as organic adaptions of folklore itself and, in doing so, create a larger and more global community of shared pleasure.

Parody

Parody itself is etymologically derived from classic Greek sources παρῳδία (para – alongside or parallel, and oido – song), as a burlesque song. The term *parodia* appears in Aristotle's *Poetics* (ii: 5) and suggests more of a comic, or even carnivalesque, mask, making men look worse than they are.[3] Parody seeks to be funny, employing a fresh use of gags, especially old and running gags. With these gags, it can interrupt its imitation with a tactic of anomalous surprise, an unpredicted violation of audience expectation with anachronism and absurd logics. One such tactic would be in breaking the 4th wall and becoming self-reflexive, directly addressing the spectators. This Brechtian interruption can delve into a meta-cinematic commentary on film and filmmaking itself or appropriate what Steven Seidman has labelled 'Comedian Comedy'.[4] Parody can contain elements of satiric discourse, challenging the original even while honouring it.[5] Finally, and crucially, parody must, at its best, possess a playful affection, as it helps to be a fan of the target. Fleet Street wit, G. K. Chesterton argued, is 'mere derision, mere contempt, never produced or could produce parody'.[6] Admiration, even reverence, is necessary. Unlike much satire, one must love the object of parody. Unless one has understood and exulted in the ingenuity of a work, unless one has loved and embraced the form and the style, one cannot fully parody it. If imitation is, as Oscar Wilde quipped, the 'sincerest form of flattery that mediocrity can pay to greatness', we may assert that parody is the purest form of flattery that wit can play to greatness. For it innovates as it iterates; it creates while it copies; it emulates as it imitates.

As Martha Bayless observed about medieval parody, it is not invariably critical, even when it satirizes. While 'medieval satire on drinking and gluttony often regards these vices affectionately, with explicit or implicit indications that the satirists are drinkers and gluttons themselves'.[7] The animators who take Disney animation to task are likewise not engaged in critical assessment but as devotees of an art they cherish. As such, parodies are more entertaining than polemical. An essential characteristic of parody is additionally that it requires both an original narrative based on familiar work and one that simultaneously *imitates and exaggerates* the tropes of that work.[8] As such, to use French critic Gérard Genette's categories, parody offers a hypertextuality that directly transforms the hypotext in a playful way. Genette explains that the 'former is grafted onto the earlier in either transformative and imitative ways, with parody fitting more in the transformation technique marking difference over similarity, and pastiche being primarily imitative, stressing similarities rather than differences'. It often functions as an educational tool to define not only the recognizable codes of the hypotext but also to show forth the invisible qualities of that text's form and motive.[9]

In arguing how a text might be interpreted, Genette's primary neologism is transtextuality, which encompasses elements of imitation, transformation and classification of types of discourse; it is 'all that sets the text in relationship, whether obvious or concealed with other texts'.[10] Two key sets (out of five) that impact this study are intertextuality and hypertextuality. In his concern to understand the ways in which signs and texts function, Genette defined intertextuality as that relationship 'between two texts or among several texts' and as 'the actual presence of one text within another', consisting of homage, quotation, allusion and plagiarism of the original cinematic text, the hypotext.[11] Intertextual homages and burlesques offer shadows of parody. They quote and reference the original, often with an off-hand tribute or a cameo.

Abundant Snow Whites

Such intertextuality between Disney's *Snow White* and popular culture are ubiquitous. Quotations from the original appear in television shows (e.g. *M*A*S*H** [Larry Gelbart, 1972–83]; *Mystery Science Theatre 3000* [Joel Hodgson, 1988–99]). In feature films, *The Dark Knight* (Christopher Nolan, 2008) lists the Joker's seven dwarfs; Lily Tomlin appears as the eponymous heroine in *9 to 5* (Colin Higgins, 1980); *What's Up, Tiger Lily?* (Woody Allen, 1966) identifies sailors with the names of the dwarfs; and *Annie Hall* (Woody Allen, 1977) features an animated segment in which Alvy fantasizes about the Evil Queen. Animated series like *Veggie Tales* (Phil Vischer and Mike Nawrocki, 1993–) and *The Simpsons* (Matt Groening, 1989–) spoof it, with Lisa's Snow White forced to eat an apple by the witch – who is then mauled by the friendly animals and decapitated by a deer.[12]

Various films recycle and foreground certain tropes, such as the dwarfs, poisonous apples, the evil stepmother's mirror and Snow White's signature costume.[13] Two unique animated films tip the hat to several of these Disney tropes. In Monique Renault and Gerrit van Dijk's *Pas à deux* (1988), rotoscoped pop culture characters proliferate and metamorphose: Bardot and Popeye morph into Betty Boop and Mickey Mouse. As Tarzan swings with Tina Turner, a Disneyfied dwarf suddenly walks by, stops and gazes as Tina becomes Snow White in Tarzan's arms. However, the gyrating iconic character quickly transmogrifies through Grace Jones, Mona Lisa and finally into our animators Renault and van Dijk.

Osamu Tezuka's environmental short *Legend of the Forest* (1987) doubles as a clever history of the animated film, from early nineteenth-century cinematic toys through the excessive violence of television cartoons into computer animation and an environmental parable. Tezuka emulated Disney's use of classical music in *Fantasia* (James Algar et al., 1940) with Tchaikovsky's 4th symphony, while playing homage to various styles and directors: John Stuart Blackton, Émile Cohl, Winsor McCay, the Fleischers and the Zagreb studios, including fleeting allusions to Disney's *Flowers and Trees* (Burt Gillett, 1932). Two curiously juxtaposed scenes, symbolizing non-violent resistance and more sinister attempts, are derived from *Snow White*. Trying to keep one flower alive, seven dwarfs carry lantern bulbs through the beleaguered forest to an evil tyrant. In contrast, the old Disney witch offers an apple to destroy the human invaders. The dwarfs naively present the one last rose to a military–industrial Hitler-like authority who smashes it and the dwarfs with machinery. These two animated films incorporate allusion, repetition, pastiche and quotation and point back to the cultural production and practice of our hypotext, but they do not contribute any salient imitation suggested by the original.[14]

Almost parodies: The Italian connection

Parody fits most snugly in Genette's category of hypertextuality, a relationship that involves the connection 'uniting a text B (which I shall call *hypertext*) to an earlier text A (I shall, of course, call it the *hypotext*), upon which it is grafted in a manner that is not that of commentary'.[15] This particular relation will modify, elaborate, extend or transform with such results as producing a sequel, spoof or parody. Four animated films function as approximate parodic asymptotes of Disney's *Snow White*, exploiting its tropes and imitating its narrative structure for comic effect.

Although Italian animator Bruno Bozzetto would describe himself as an avid Disney fan, his admiration would be expressed though outrageous humour. His feature *Allegro Non Troppo* (1976) took on the high-brow *Fantasia* (1940) with authentic low-brow humour, a coarse and unpolished style with unrestrained slapstick and sexual imagery (breasts are ubiquitous). With a half-dozen classical pieces of music (including Ravel's Bolero) interspersed with live action farce, *Allegro non Troppo* parodies the overall cinematic form and elitist style of the Disney prestigious roadshow compilation. A pompous producer announces that audiences will experience classical music in marvellously novel ways. When an associate tries to explain that a 'Mr. Grisney' has already accomplished this feat, he ignores him. With a slight satiric social commentary on the labour-intensive work of animators, a poor artist is released from a dungeon to frantically animate symphonic pieces performed by an orchestra of old women (one of whom is later knocked out with a champagne cork). He brings Stravinsky's 'Firebird Suite' to life as his cartoons castigate a culture of consumerism. Disney's dignity is merrily subverted into an imaginative and carnivalesque work in its own right.

The allusion to the character of Snow White occurs with a scullery maid who works unceasingly to feed the women and tend to the onerous errands of the host producer and an overbearing conductor. The animator tries, vainly, to romance the girl, but is interrupted by the conductor. He rebels against his authority with escalating Laurel-and-Hardy slapstick violence. Ultimately, romance culminates as the maid with her bucket and animator with his easel are transformed via animation into Snow White and prince Charming, flying off together, leaving a frustrated producer behind. The action returns to the host and the conductor discussing their next project. After a bit of brainstorming the host reveals his latest 'original' idea of an asymmetrical love story of seven little men who work in a mine and one woman with the title 'Sleeping Beauty'. But the host warns him not to advertise, as 'some screenwriter hack might steal the idea. You can't trust anyone these days. He'll change the title, play up the sex. And give it some crazy name like *Snow White and the Seven Dwarfs*. And then, we'll be screwed.'

Bozzetto's co-writer, Guido Manuli exhibits a perversely erotic obsession with the Disney film. He is the Italian Tex Avery to Bozzetto's Disney, fulfilling the task of erecting 'something borrowed, something *blue*' (i.e. risqué) in his aesthetic parodies. He invests Disney with libidinous sexuality. In his sci-fi version of the Bible, *Fantabiblical* (1977), he constructs a quick homage to *Snow White*'s cackling witch, who shows up with a puppet snake offering Adam and Eve an apple. After a bite, they turn into Mickey and Donald Duck. In his *S. O. S.* (1979), Manuli inserts an image of the prince leaning over Snow White's bier to kiss the dead, smiling princess. Suddenly, he screams, spits and scrams away on his horse, leaving the seven dwarfs kneeling beside the coffin. In Manuli's *Just a Kiss* (*Solo un Bacio*, 1983), an artist even falls in love with the Disney version of Snow White (after first sitting at his drawing board doodling out large-breasted and assed women). He breathes heavily over his rendition of the Disney heroine, feeling her pencil drawn face. With colour paints and a hypodermic needle, he transforms himself into a sexist cartoon character who enters the drawing where she comes to life. However, when he kisses her and grabs her butt, she slaps him and kicks him in the groin. He offers her an apple and she screams. As Paul Wells has pointed out, Manuli's 'desire to debase and abuse is an intrinsically human quality'.[16] As the cartoonist continues to assault her, seven angry dwarfs with axes emerge out the Italian book, *Bianeaneue e I Sette nani*.[17] As they bully the cartoonist, a witch shows up with an apple of death. He begs for his life, holding up posters declaring 'I love Mickey

FIGURE 9.1 The transgressive animator lusts after Disney's fantasy only to be rewarded with the wages of his sin in *Solo un Bacio* (Guido Manuli, 1983).

Mouse and W. Disneyland.' The witch shoves the apple in his mouth and he comes out of the cartoon, dead (Figure 9.1).

In Manuli's later *Casting* (1997), a director, hiding behind a paper-bag face, interviews candidates to play the role of Snow White. The first aspirant holds an apple and a blue bird, then bites the apple. A second applicant eats the blue bird and sings. Other contenders, from a big-breasted Eve to a bald transvestite, play out their own riffing gags, until a final candidate appears pregnant, with photos of the seven dwarfs as possible fathers. Odd male candidates for the Prince fare no better, as an American tries to kiss Snow White while chewing bubble gum, a Hamlet-like character examines Snow White's head like Yorrick's skull and a doctor operates to extract the apple. Finally, a psychopath hides a chain saw and bloody axe under his raincoat. Auditioning for the Witch, characters exhibit large buttocks, muscular arms or an old, wrinkled face. The dwarfs, Goopy, Sabby, Snappy, Crabby, Blabby and Sneezy, are all too short. When they see the live-action animator, they chase him to the iconic cliff of the Disney film. The animator tries to push a rock on them, only to be struck by lightning. The dwarfs laugh.

The very funny and naughty Italian animators follow the great literary critic Mikhail Bakhtin's conception of parody only in the most superficial of ways, de-familiarizing the text and eliciting carnivalesque laughter. One recognizes a transgressive, even Dionysian tone to their allusions. As both Julia Kristeva and Roland Barthes interpreted parody as a 'new anti-traditional and anti-bourgeois conception of literary discourse', these animating rascals do create dynamic play of two texts that manifest quotations and heteroglossia.[18] The latter is linked to a festive spirit by a common, vulgar laughter, with roots harkening back 'deep into pre-class folklore'. Bakhtin's carnival evokes clownishness, where slave and jester supplant king and priest; a riotous confusion mixes all varieties of discourses; and merry rogues follow their most basic instincts. Their films treat those once-taboo topics like sex and death with abandon and hilarity.[19]

Bakhtin examined the carnivalesque literature as parodic, revealing his definition of the 'double-voiced discourse'. When the voice becomes travestying, a fresh text can secede from such classification and simply celebrate the comic intertextual deformation of the original text. Essentially, parody can become an end in itself, a hybrid of incongruity and caricature, composed of deforming images. Bakhtin sees parody as a 'dialogic interaction between two utterances, two languages' and one that allows 'grading various types and stages of parodicity: [as] merely superficial, shallow, rhetorical or deep'.[20] This consists of two languages: the language being parodied and the language that parodies (using low, familiar, conversational language). The parody of these two Italian animators remains wonderfully shallow. The analysis of the next film shows us how parody enables us to 'read the social context, society's conventions, positions of utterance, discourse, and the distribution of power from the text'.

In parody's double-voiced words or images, expressed by two speakers or texts, the second appropriates the utterance of the former and uses it 'for his own purposes by inserting a new semantic orientation into a word which already has – and retains – its own orientation'. We hear both points of view in the parody. For Gary Morson, a double-voiced view is best pictured as 'a special sort of palimpsest in which the uppermost inscription is a commentary on the one beneath it, which the reader can know only by reading through the commentary that obscures in the very process of evaluating'.[21] The Italians flourish in the realm of rude burlesque, which 'fools around with the material of high literature and adapts it to low ends'.[22] Where parody of *Snow White* becomes, what Linda Hutcheon called, a 'constructive principle in literary history' erupts out of another animated text from the unlikely confines of Termite Terrace.[23]

Playful parody: American and Dutch

Director Bob Clampett's hilarious, but controversial Warner Bros. Merrie Melody cartoon, *Coal Black and de Sebben Dwarfs* (1943), offers an apotheosis of Snow White parodies. Its working title, *So White and De Sebben Dwarfs*, was changed as its similarity to Disney came too close for litigious comfort.[24] A Warner Bros. sheet announced it as a 'dusky satire on *Snow White*', while Warren Foster, writing with Clampett on *Porky in Wackyland* (1938), scripted the manic and demented Grimm Brothers' story, with brazen connections to Disney's work.[25] Clampett and Foster envisioned their cartoon as a spoof of Snow White, but also as a tribute to the jazz musical features of the era. A fan of Duke Ellington's music (such as *Jump for Joy*), Clampett researched the 1940s black musical culture with visits to various Los Angeles clubs.[26] The former lead singer for the Spirits of Rhythm quartet, Leo Watson (nicknamed 'Zoot' Watson) gave his personality to Prince Chawmin'. Animator Virgil Ross, who worked on the Prince, recalled going downtown to nightspots like Club Alabam 'to watch the latest dances and pick up some atmosphere. Some of it was pretty funny stuff that we actually used in the picture: real tall guys dancing with real short little women, and they'd swing their legs right over the tops of their heads!' Ellington suggested that Clampett direct a musical cartoon that celebrated 'black' music.[27] The *Motion Picture Herald* reviewed the cartoon as 'a satire on *Snow White* done to black-face, set in modern swing' with some rotoscoped jitterbugging integrating black culture and marginalized jazz music from lowbrow culture into a celebration. In fact, Clampett tried to draft Eddie Beal and His Orchestra, an all-black musical group, to secure a more authentic jazz score, but producer Leon Schlesinger blocked the funding and forced Clampett to rely on the company's Carl W. Stalling, ironically a former Disney employee who had pioneered the innovative 'Mickey-Mousing' scoring of the *Silly Symphonies*. Beal's musician Roy Elderidge was used only for the gag finale, with Prince Chawmin's desperate kissing sequence of 'Waking-up-So-White' amid soaring trumpet blasts.

Opening with the warm glow of the hearth, a crackling fire silhouettes a large woman cuddling a young child in her lap. The child asks her 'Mammy' to tell the story of 'So White an' de Sebben Dwarfs'. Mammy's earthiness, both in warmth for her 'Honey Chile' and with unpredictably bawdy wit, creates an engrossing storyteller, like a Black Wife of Bath compelling her audience to listen and be taken for a ride. She ain't no Uncle Remus and she ain't gonna whitewash no children's story. As she begins amidst the tranquil setting, some lively jitterbug beats soon wake the hearer with a dazzling fanfare: 'Well, once there was a *mean* ol' queen. And she lived in a gorgeous castle. And was that ole' gal rich! She was just as rich as she was mean! She had *everythang*!'

A sly dig against affluent 'hoarders' depicts the Wicked Queen storing all manner of war-rationed goods: sugar, rubber tires, coffee and Eli Whitney's Cotton Gin (along with some Chattanooga Chew-Chews). Her gorgeous castle looks a lot like Xanadu from Orson Welles' *Citizen Kane* (1941), previewing a later allusion. Historian Michael Barrier noted that Disney's original queen was to be a comic foil, caricatured as a 'fat, batty, cartoon type, self-satisfied' Queen.[28] Disney did not crown such a grotesque for his villain; Clampett did. The heavy-set Queen orders the magic mirror to send her a 'prince about six feet tall'. Up drives the monocle stud of Prince Chawmin' in his flashy limousine wearing a white Zoot suit and holding a long, thin cigarette holder, presumably an effete phallic symbol and the epitome of a civilian shirking his wartime duty. On seeing the two ladies, he exclaims with a brazen grin flashing two diced teeth, a four and a three, 'that mean ol' queen sho' is a fright / but her gal So White is dyn-a-mite!' But he only has words and eyes for the Queen's scullery maid, So White.

Bent over a large pot washing the clothes all day (and getting the blues at night), So White sways her curvaceous behind like an unleashed Tex Avery Red. Disney would have had a coronary. Its excess is what makes it delightfully parodic. Clampett's extreme sexualized caricature fleshes out the original wholesome archetype. So White is the object of sexual desire for every male character in the picture. As a bouncy fry cook, she moves and wiggles with a rubber elasticity, shaking her booty. The implicit attraction of Disney's dwarfs to Snow White, especially Dopey who returns for a kiss, is hyperbolically exaggerated with the uninhibited libido of American soldiers. Its sheer flamboyance earned the film much of its notoriety.

The Warner Bros. humour 'played havoc with all human types, offering equal-opportunity burlesque'.[29] Parallels to the original regularly pop up. In an exquisite spoof of Snow White dreaming into the well, So White belts out, 'Some folks think I's kinda dumb, but I know some day my prince will come.' Prince Chawmin magically appears in the reflection, then leads her in a delicate minuet that suddenly swings into an ecstatic jitterbug. Seeing the 'sickening sight' of her potential lover with her maid, the scowling Queen phones Murder Inc. and demands they 'Black out So White!' Equal opportunity derision includes an ad on their van announcing 'We rub out anybody for $1.00; Midgets: 1/2-price; Japs: free.' As the thugs kidnap the damsel, the Prince falls on his face, revealing a yellow streak down his back, a stigma of those not fighting in the war. Like the huntsman, they take her into the dark woods, where she seemingly bestows lipstick 'favours' upon them. She wanders about stumbling until when a pair of eyes howls 'Whooo? … who goes there, friend or foe?' Seven little jive-talking army men, looking like 5 Fats Wallers dwarfs, a Stepin Fetchit and a potent 'Dopey' sing with swing-style rhythms, 'We're in the Army now; we're not behind the plow.' She kisses her rescuers who faint right down. She contrasts the boys in uniform with the zoot suits and opts for the former, becoming 'wacky of khaki nowwww!'

White finds work as the mess hall cook, 'fryin' up eggs an' pork chops too' (to the tune of Ella Fitzgerald's 1941 hit, 'Five O' Clock Whistle'). As a quick pun on the Second World War slogan 'Keep 'em flying,' a sign reading 'Keep 'em frying' hangs on the pipes of her makeshift stove. The egg eyes and bacon smile from the pan at the sizzling cook. Meanwhile, the queen has learned that So White is still alive, so pumps an apple full of poison. Driving a little cart, looking like a cross between Jimmy Durante and the wolf from the Three Little Pigs, the Queen pedals her Candied Apples on a Stick' treats. Disguised as an old peddler with a huge nose, the queen arrives at the Sebben Dwarfs' camp where she finds So White looking like the American flag herself, wearing red shoes, blue short skirt and white blouse. Identifying herself as a friend, with Durante's trademark 'ha cha cha cha', she offers So White the poisoned fruit. The 'Dopey' alerts the others that the queen has caused So White to 'kick the bucket', and the entire squad hops into its vehicles (a Jeep, a 'Beep' and, for 'Dopey', a 'Peep'). As the queen makes her escape over the hills, the dwarfs load a cannon with both a war shell and 'Dopey'. The shell sails over to the queen, stops in front of her in mid-air, opens and 'Dopey' appears, knocking the crone out with a mallet.

Even though the queen has been defeated, So White is still dead to the world. The dwarfs note, in spoken rhyme: 'She's outta this world! She's stiff as wood! She's got it bad, and that ain't good! There's only one thing that'll remedy this and dat's Prince Chawmin' and his Dynamite Kiss!' Chawmin' offers to 'give her that kiss, and it won't be a dud. It'll bring her to life with my special'. With an extreme close-up on his lips, Clampett delivers a reverberating anomalous gag: 'Rosebud.' Unfortunately, the Prince's slobbering kisses become desperate. Nothing he does can stir her. Frantic, with Eddie Beal's trumpet solo underscoring his impotence, he transforms into a pale-white, withered, old, balding dude who has lost it all and shrugs away. Moseying into the task, the Dopey dwarf unleashes an earth-shaking kiss that snaps her eyes wide open and causes her pigtails to spring to life twirling, launching her into the air. The effete Prince asks the potent dwarf, 'Man, what you got that makes So White think *you* so hot?!' He responds, 'well, *dat* is a military secret', kissing his lady again, making those pigtails fly erect with unfurled flags to a rousing leitmotif from John Philip Sousa's 'The Stars and Stripes Forever' soldier and his gal grin at each other.

Bakhtin defined parody as the 'creation of a decrowning double'.[30] In other words, it is a hybrid that both conserves and transforms the primary text, and a form of parody that 'celebrates bi-directionality by challenging the discourse that contains it'. The parody of *Coal Black* approximates Bakhtin's view of an author speaking in someone else's discourse 'with a semantic intention that is directly opposed to the original one'. The text thus becomes 'an arena of battle between two voices', namely Walt Disney and Robert Clampett. Norman Klein puts the cartoon in historical perspective as an anarchic wartime cartoon for the troops, especially black men in uniform. He writes how the humour for GIs in the animated *Private SNAFU* cartoons was 'racier and blunter' than regular theatrical releases that Disney distributed. No doubt, Clampett's cartoon addresses the mood, patriotism, anxieties and prejudices of the era, but it did so with an unleashed libido.

Both Klein and, indeed, Paul Wells saw *Coal Black* not only reflecting 'white anxiety about modernity' but also about 'big-band anarchy as a raunchier alternative to Disney'.[31]

Parody trumps racism in the sense that Clampett showed just how white Disney's fairy tale was. *Coal Black* was its cultural antithesis. Beyond racial caricature, it mocked the status quo aesthetic of Hollywood.[32] Wells articulated it cogently that 'Clampett used Warner Bros' more self-conscious dramatization of social tensions to release the stereotypes from their static, marginalized and naturalized condition.' The aggressive jazz, jitterbugging, violent, sexual humour (as well as the enthusiastic, embodied Pentecostal religion of *Tin Pan Alley Cats*) subverted the passive, conservative cultural aesthetic principles practiced by Disney. *Coal Black*, read against the grain, presented otherness with vitality and virility. *Snow White*'s polite kiss (as if Prince Charming had simply applied a napkin to his beloved's face) offered no sexual desire. *Coal Black* showed every GI what the passion of the little guy could offer. Even in vulgar caricatures, 'otherness' and 'difference' stood out as distinct and desirable. The parody worked to reconstruct the fairy tale according to young male imaginations. And, to top it off, against the stigma of short men, Coal Black presents Dopey as more sexually potent than the six-foot-tall prince that the Queen wants, a merry swipe at the ideal height of romantic leads. Ironically, the most passionate virile hero will be a miniature, a Tex Avery-sized dwarf, not your standard prince. Such parodic animation offers an exaggerated reality, exuberant and fully expressive, hyperbolic, especially in the world of Bob Clampett, with the characters just as overstated as any other Clampett cartoon character. In understanding the hypertext of *Coal Black*, it is key to recognize Genette's transtextual purpose, namely to help interpret this later text through its relation to the earlier hypotext. Clampett's cartoon must be seen as this elaboration and parody of the original, existing in its historical context and against the Disney classic.[33]

Conclusion

While animated parodies of *Snow White* draw upon its recognizable forms, characters and costumes, ultimately each bows in appreciation of its classic status. From the Italian masters of animated parodies, Bruno Bozzetto and Guido Manuli to hilariously controversial work of Bob Clampett's *Coal Black and the Sebben Dwarfs*, Snow White lives on, kissed by comic princes and animators. And with those parodic kisses, the classic is bestowed with immortality. Parody produces a resurrection of affectionate laughter for an old masterpiece. Film parodies provide a way that 'Western cultures have devised for talking to themselves about change – how difficult yet how unavoidable it is. ... [It] is a sign, in fact, that a culture is simultaneously maintaining continuity and making something new and valuable out of the eternal tension between imagination and reality.'[34] Transformations of the fairy tale offer an opportunity to look back and see 'with fresh eyes, enter an old text from a new critical direction'.[35] And parodies give us fresh, twinkling and laughing eyes.

Notes

1   Ed Sullivan, 'Hollywood', *Augusta Chronicle* (4 May 1938): 4; See 'Mae's Famous Sayings Are Part of Nation's Folklore', *Life Magazine* (23 May 1949): 105.

2   Ronald Gottesman, 'Film Parody: An Immodest Proposal', *Quarterly Review of Film and Video* 12, nos 1–2 (1990): 1

3   Aristotle, *Poetics* (USA: Dover, 1997), 3.

4   Steve Seidman, *Comedian Comedy* (USA: UMI Research, 1981).

5   Terry Lindvall, Dennis Bounds and Chris Lindvall, *Divine Film Comedies* (London: Routledge, 2016), 150–9.

6   G. K. Chesterton, *Varied Types* (Charleston: BiblioLife, 2009), 184.

7   Martha Bayless, *Parody in the Middle Ages* (Ann Arbor: University of Michigan, 1996), 7.

8   Michael Teuth, *Reeling with Laughter: American Film Comedies – From Anarchy to Mockumentary* (Plymouth: Scarecrow, 2012).

9   It takes other artists to parody it *and* to endow it with a cultural afterlife. This work does not deal with remakes or adaptations, many of which are clever and even allude to the original. Mere adaptations of the Grimm story do not count as parodies. The live-action screwball comedy *Ball of Fire* (Howard Hawks, 1941) also presents a variation of the *Snow White* tale, in which a gangster's moll (Barbara Stanwyck) on the run from the law seeks refuge with eight professors (teaching Cary Grant how to 'yum yum'). Snow White was never so promiscuous. Other works reflect Disney, but have no direct connection: Gottfried Kolditz's *Schneewittchen* (1962), Rupert Sanders's *Snow White and the Huntsman* (2012) and Joe Nussbaum's very clever *Sydney White* (2007) (with the immortal sing-song, punning parodic moment by one of the campus nerd dwarfs addressing the sinister sorority queen: 'Hi, Ho!'). Thomas Inge examines how Disney adapted the original tale in 'Walt Disney's *Snow White*: Art, Adaptation, and Ideology', *Journal of Popular Film and Television* 32, no. 3 (2004): 137–42.

10 Gérard Genette, *The Architect: An Introduction* (trans. Jane Lewin) (Berkeley: University of California Press, 1992), 84.

11 Ibid., 1–2.

12 Various catchphrases or allusions to the magic mirror, the poisoned apple, the music of Whistle While you Work, find their way into media. A poster of Dopey in *The Shining* (Stanley Kubrick, 1980) or a nursery wall picture of

Seven Dwarfs mourning at Snow White's coffin in *Akira* (Katsuhiro Otomo, 1988) attest to the international intertextuality. The *Gremlins* (Joe Dante, 1984) terrorize a movie theatre, but pause to watch Snow White's dwarfs singing on the screen; in *Gremlins 2: The New Batch* (Joe Dante, 1990), they take over the movie projector, interrupting the movie as they just want to see *Snow White and the Seven Dwarfs*. Robin Williams turns himself into several dwarfs from *Back to Neverland* (Jerry Rees, 1989). In *Enchanted* (Kevin Lima, 2007) many scenes are spoofed, where the queen disguises herself as an old crone and offers Giselle an apple. Prince Edwards mistakes a television for a magic mirror and Giselle offends an old man with dwarfism thinking he is Grumpy.

13   Snow White sings in *Shrek 2* (Andrew Adamson, Kelly Asbury and Conrad Vernon, 2004) and fights in *Shrek the Third* (Chris Miller and Raman Hui, 2007). Even Disney's *Ralph Breaks the Internet* (Rich Moore and Phil Johnston, 2018) alludes to the original. Here Snow White gets a 3-D animation makeover and appears when Vanellope von Schweetz, the little friend of video game character Ralph, goes into a restricted area of the internet and meets all the Disney princesses. She claims to be a princess, but Snow White challenges her: 'Were you poisoned?' Other princesses ask, 'Do people assume all your problems were solved because a big strong man showed up?' She responds, 'YES! What's up with that?' All the princesses respond: 'She is a princess!' and Snow White trills a warbling chirp.

14   See Simon Dentith, *Parody* (London: Routledge, 2000), 9.

15   Gérard Genette, *Palimpsests: Literature in the Second Degree* Lincoln: University of Nebraska Press, 1997), 5.

16   Paul Wells, *Understanding Animation* (London: Routledge, 1998), 81.

17   See Giannalberto Bendazzi, *Animation: A World History: Volume II* (Bloomington: Indiana University Press, 1996).

18   Heteroglossia rests upon his conception of language not as a static, communicable representation of the speaker's intention but as a system bearing the weight of centuries of intention, motivation and implication. See also Marko Juvan, 'The Parody and Bakhtin', in *Bakhtin and the Humanities*, ed. Miha Javornik, Marko Juvan, Aleksander Skaza, Jola Škulj and Ivan Verč (Ljubljana: Znanstveni inštitut Filozofske fakultete, 1997), 193–209.

19   Ibid., 198.

20   Juvan, 'The Parody and Bakhtin', 202.

21   Gary Morson and Caryl Emerson (eds), *Rethinking Bakhtin: Extensions and Challenges* (Evanston, IL: Northwestern University Press, 1989), 66.

22   John Gross (ed.) *Oxford Book of Parodies* (Oxford: Oxford University Press, 2010), xi.

23   Linda Hutcheon, *A Theory of Parody: The Teachings of Twentieth-Century Art Forms* (London: Methuen, 1985), 36.

24   Clampett's *Beany and Cecil Show* (1962) revived the fairy tale with his television parody version of 'So What and the Seven Whatnots' (ABC, 1962) in

Lost Wages (Las Vegas) show in a Dixieland Dive. He caricatured the 'dwarfs' with such diverse characters as Dizzy R. Nez (Desi Arnaz on the conga), Elfiz (Elvis Presley on guitar) and Stash-Do (Louis 'Satchmo' Armstrong on the trumpet), a blonde pig-tailed So What, impersonating nightclub singer Squeely Smith (Vegas performer Keely Smith) singing 'Scooby doo' (A 'French Review' show slyly features 'Take Me to your Lido'). Dishonest John delivers some poison apple juice and a martini to So What, who is laid out flat, until the Sea-serpent gives her a super-slurpy kiss, and her pigtails lift. And Cecil goes parading out to the tune of 'When the Saints Go Marching In'.

25   Christopher P. Lehman, *The Colored Cartoon: Black Representation in American Animated Short Films: 1907–1954* (Amherst: University of Massachusetts, 2007).

26   Another significant, if overlooked, influence was Clampett's commandeering of Al Hirschfeld's Harlem caricatures, with gold-toothed bucks, slinky chanteuses and Zoot-suited blacks. Hirschfeld, Al (and William Saroyan) *Harlem as Seen by Hirschfeld* (New York: Hyperion Press, 1941).

27   Trying to fill out an authentic casts of voices, Clampett hired singer Vivian to express 'So White' and her mother, Ruby Dandridge, to play the wicked Queen. He also scooped up Lou 'Zoot' Watson to become 'Prince Chawmin'.

28   Michael Barrier, *Hollywood Cartoons: American Animation in Its Golden Age* (New York: Oxford University Press, 1999), 125–6.

29   Terry Lindvall and Ben Fraser, 'Darker Shades of Animation: African-American Images in the Warner Bros. Cartoon', in *Reading the Rabbit*, ed. Kevin S. Sandler (New Brunswick: Rutgers University Press, 1998), 130–1.

30   Jeffrey S. Rush, 'Who's in on the Joke: Parody as Hybridized Narrative Discourse', *Quarterly Review of Film and Video* 12 (1–2) (1990): 5–12.

31   Norman M. Klein, *Seven Minutes: The Life and Death of the American Animated Cartoon* (London: Verso, 1993), 187.

32   Paul Wells, *Animation and America* (Edinburgh: Edinburgh University Press, 2002), 57.

33   Even the OWI described the cartoon as 'a vulgar parody' [with] 'some excellent boogie-woogie background music'. Michael Shull and David Wilt, *Doing Their Bit: Wartime American Animated Short Films, 1939–1945* (Jefferson, NC: McFarland, 1987), 90.

34   Ronald Gottesman, 'Film Parody: An Immodest Proposal', *Quarterly Review of Film and Video* 12, nos 1–2 (1990): 1–3. One other exceptional parody deserves mention: Paul Driessen's *3 Misses* (1998).

35   Stella Bolaki, 'Four Times upon a Time: "*Snow White*" Retold', in *Beyond Adaptation*, ed. Phyllis Frus and Christy Williams (Jefferson, NC: McFarland, 2010), 182.

PART THREE

International legacies

10

The indigenization of Disney's *Snow White and the Seven Dwarfs* (1937) in China: From 'Snow Sister' and 'Dolly Girl' to *Chinese Snow White* (1940) and *Princess Iron Fan* (1941)

Yuanyuan Chen

Introduction

Walt Disney's first animated feature film *Snow White and the Seven Dwarfs* (David Hand, 1937) was released in Shanghai in June 1938. Thanks to the localized advertising and promotional strategies, it was a massive box-office success in China. The blockbuster hit was watched by 400,000 people and made more than 7 million RMB across the country.[1] This chapter will explore how Disney's *Snow White* was interpreted and indigenized in China during the 1930s and 1940s by examining the following four areas. The first section will investigate how Shanghai during the 1930s and 1940s – as a mixed, dynamic and unstable cosmopolitan metropolis – offered a perfect stage for novelties such as Hollywood film and Disney animation. The second section will examine how localized advertising and marketing campaigns promoted *Snow White*, and how the film, in turn, bolstered the local economy and artistic creations. Third, by a short comparative analysis, I will rethink the film *Chinese Snow White*, a live-action remake of Disney's *Snow White* released in 1940. In the final section, the first Chinese animated feature *Princess Iron Fan* (Wan Guchan and Wan Laiming, 1941), which is widely considered as the Chinese version of *Snow White* in animation, will be compared with Disney's *Snow White*.

Shanghai: An encounter with Disney

The settlement of Disney in Shanghai started over eighty years ago, as early as the 1930s. Despite that fact that during the 1930s and 1940s the country was suffering the ravages of the Second World War, Shanghai was an exceptional city that accommodated Disney's animated films. Marie-Claire Bergère describes Shanghai as the cradle of Chinese modernity – 'the international settlement, with its trading companies, banks, naval yards, and factories that had turned Shanghai into a world metropolis; and the French concession, the international settlement's younger sister, whose shady streets, fashion houses, literary bohemia, and militant revolutionaries had caused the town to be known as "the Paris of the East" '.[2] Shanghai had been opened up to the West ever since the Treaty of Nanking was signed in 1842, and it soon became a popular place for overseas residents. These foreign influences bought to the city not only modern technologies, such as electricity, telephones and trams, but also the new industry of leisure and entertainment, including cafés, horse racing and the cinema. Shanghai quickly became the primary city where Hollywood distributed its films and, consequently, the city that was most influenced by Hollywood culture in China.

Disney's first discussion in print in China occurred on 6 February 1930, introduced in an article titled ' "Mickey the Mouse" Liked by Britons' which was published in *North China Daily News* (字林西報), an influential English-language newspaper in Shanghai. The author not only presented how much the critics in London enjoyed the film but also praised Mickey Mouse as 'a real creature of the present' that expresses a philosophy.[3] Afterwards, Disney and his cartoon stars soon became fashionable among the local population with a rapidly increasing presence in media from the period. The publications can be generally divided into two categories: those that introduce Walt Disney and the cartoon characters, such as the articles 'The Father of Mickey Mouse: Walt Disney's Successful Career' in *Movietone* (電聲) and 'Mickey Mouse Is Becoming a Star' in *Linglong* (玲瓏), and those serializing Disney's cartoon strips, which were vital ways to popularize their work in China prior to and alongside animated film screenings.[4]

Due to the fact that early animated shorts were usually screened before the feature film as a supplementary and the lack of reliable data, it is hard to know when Disney animation was first shown in China.[5] Based on the archives of *North China Daily News*, a screening of the animated short *Midnight in a Toy Shop* (Wilfred Jackson, 1930) from Disney's *Silly Symphonies* series was advertised on 23 December 1931, accompanying the feature film *Meet the Wife* (Leslie Pearce, 1931) as a bonus attraction for the Theatre Imprint in Shanghai (Figure 10.1), which would indicate that Disney's animated films appeared in Chinese theatres at least as early as 1931.[6] An increasing number of local theatres soon began to show Disney's animations, and the audience responded to these films exceptionally well. Until 1935, Mikey became a household name in Shanghai and was deeply loved by the local audience.[7]

During the period of the Republic of China, the expansion of Disney in China can be divided into three phases. The period from 1930 to 1941 was the first 'golden era', a time when Disney became better known in Shanghai. Although the city was semi-occupied by the Japanese from 1937 to 1941, Shanghai was a 'Solitary Island' where the foreign concessions largely remained intact. It created an enclave of prosperity for film industry and offered the possibilities for Disney's continuous expansion in China. Animated films such as *Snow White* and *Pinocchio* (Ben Sharpsteen and Hamilton Luske, 1940) were introduced in Shanghai during this period. From 1942 to 1945, the dissemination of Disney's work in Shanghai was severely interrupted due to the outbreak of the Pacific War. At the time only a very few articles in newspapers and magazines mentioned Disney. From the surrender of Japan in 1945, to when the Communist Party took over the mainland in 1949, was the second 'golden era' for Disney's expansion in China. Thanks to Kuomintang's pro-American stance Hollywood films regained a significant market share in Shanghai, and the import of Disney's animated films, such as *Bambi* (David Hand, 1942), *The Three Caballeros* (Norman Ferguson, 1944), *Song of the South* (Harve Foster and Wilfred Jackson, 1946) and *Fun and Fancy Free* (Jack Kinney, Bill Roberts, Hamilton Luske and William Morgan, 1947), appealed to local audiences.

The debut of *Snow White* in Shanghai

Snow White reached Shanghai in June 1938. Shanghai was a 'Solitary Island' at the time, where, fortunately, most cinema theatres were built in the foreign concessions and kept intact from Japanese invasion. The film was first released in Metropol Theatre (大上海大戲院) and Nanking Theatre (南京大戲院) in Shanghai on 2 June 1938 and soon screened in other local theatres. According to the archival records, *Snow White* attracted over 210,000 viewers in Shanghai, including 30,000 viewers in Metropol Theatre, 25,000 viewers in Nanking Theatre, 52,000 viewers in Rialto Theatre (麗都大戲院), 30,000 viewers in Uptown Theatre (平安大戲院), 20,000

FIGURE 10.1 Disney's *Midnight in Toyshop* advertised in *North China Daily News* on 23 December 1931.

viewers in Lafayette Cinema (辣斐大戲院), 18,000 viewers in The Capitol Theatre (光陸大戲院), 17,000 viewers in Zhejiang Theatre (浙江大戲院), 11,000 viewers in Empire Theatre (恩派亞大戲院) and 6,600 viewers in Willie's Theatre (威利大戲院).[8] It was such an unprecedented success that the theatres in Shanghai were filled to bursting with their audiences, despite five shows a day during the second round of the film's screening.[9] Metropol Theatre and Nanking Theatre, the two largest theatres in Shanghai, screened the same film simultaneously, which only happened once before when Charlie Chaplin's *Modern Times* (1936) was released.[10]

Snow White quickly became a critically acclaimed, commercial success in China. A film review in English published in *The China Press* on 3 June 1938, a major English-language newspaper in Shanghai of the time, recognizes it 'a masterpiece of color, photography and ingenuity … Every element essential in a drama, a comedy and a musical, are contained in this perfect co-ordination of all known forms of entertainment, with the result that "Snow White" is as a document as the screen has ever shown.'[11] The earliest film review on *Snow White* in Chinese was published in *Li Daily* (力報) on 9 June 1938. The author described how the long-awaited film shook the whole city, keeping the audience spellbound. Describing *Snow White* as a successful educational film teaching the young audience that jealousy is poisonous and only love conquers all, the author added that not only is every frame visually stunning, but that the sound effects are vivid, the music is pleasant and the depiction of dwarfs is impressive, especially the characters Grumpy and Dopey.[12]

Besides the charm of the film itself, the localized advertising and marketing campaigns also contributed to its significant box-office success within China. Wan Baiwu, the son of Wan Guchan, one of the Chinese animation's pioneers, recalled that during *Snow White*'s premiere in Shanghai, 'the film was advertised everywhere, in magazines, newspapers and broadcast programs'.[13] For example, *The China Press* advertised two posters of *Snow White* on 2 and 3 June 1938 when the film was just released (Figures 10.2 and 10.3).[14] *Nanhai Yinxing*, an influential cinema weekly newspaper in Shanghai, published a series of articles covering the different aspects of the film that it believed would amuse the local Chinese audience.[15] Some articles involved playfully teasing the characters of the seven dwarfs, such as 'Dwarfs are Too Lazy to Wash Faces' and 'Dopey Doesn't Want to Talk'.[16] Moreover, it is interesting to note that in those articles 'Snow White' was often translated from English into the local dialect 'Snow Sister' (雪姐兒 *xuě jiěr*) instead of a more literal translation such as the 'princess Snow White', which, as a phrasing strategy that advertised and promoted the film, made the character more appealing to the audience.

To promote *Snow White* in China, the Disney company issued a unique film handbook in Chinese on 5 May 1938, nearly one month before the film's release date. With over forty pages of content, the handbook includes

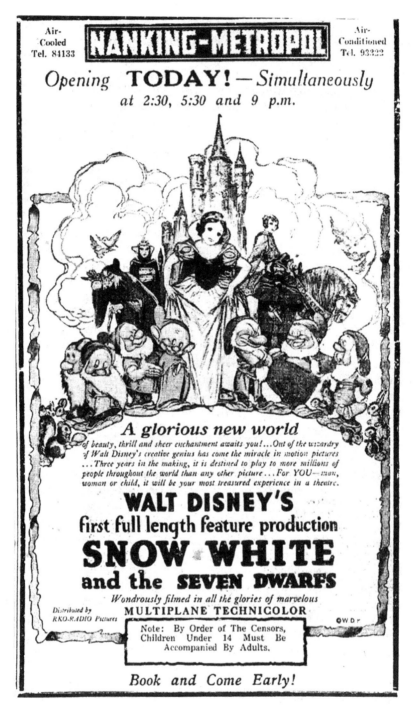

FIGURE 10.2 The poster of *Snow White* in *The China Press* on 2 June 1938.

FIGURE 10.3 The poster of *Snow White* in *The China Press* on 3 June 1938.

the music scores of three well-known theme songs, forty black-and-white images, fourteen colour images and the translated film transcripts, which could be purchased at the theatres and the main bookstores in Shanghai. Besides the handbook, some derivative products of the characters were distributed along with the film. For example, two fabrics printed with the figures of Snow White or the dwarfs were designed to easily transform into a puppet by being filled and stitched together. Printed on the top of the puppets, 'Snow White' was also translated via the local Shanghai dialect into the phrase 'dolly girl' (洋囡囡 *yáng nān nān*), in order to better accommodate and engage the Shanghai audience.

With Snow White and the dwarfs becoming publicly recognized in Shanghai in the late 1930s and 1940s, the local business began to utilize their images to attract customers. For instance, on the same day of *Snow White*'s release in Shanghai, there were at least eight advertisements published in *The China Press* that employed Snow White and the dwarfs as the celebrity endorsers to promote their brands and products, spanning from food and housewares to daily service (Figure 10.4).[17]

Besides this, various elements of the film, such as the sets and settings, costumes and props, lightings and music, were adopted by local children's playgrounds, ballrooms, restaurants and clubs, as the selling points that differentiated these venues from competitors. For instance, the Sincere company advertised its children's playground by highlighting that 'it is a happy world for children, where all the settings are as the same as the film *Snow White*'.[18] Park Hotel Shanghai also addressed in its advertisement that 'the music, lightings, settings and costumes in our Sky Terrace Hall are reproduced faithfully as what they appeared in the original film *Snow White*'.[19] Furthermore, some merchants even hired actresses for their venues to imitate Snow White to amuse the customers. Victory Ballroom, for instance, advertised in the local newspapers that 'Princess Snow White will be showing up on 22nd October night, and anyone who wants to meet her needs to come early to secure a place.'[20]

Moreover, during the late 1930s and 1940s, 'Snow White' was registered as a trademark for numerous local products, including 'Snow White' sweets, 'Snow White' Eskimo Toffee, 'Snow White' moisturizers, 'Snow White' fragrant powder, 'Snow White' linen, 'Snow White' cigarette and so forth. The use of these trademarks, of course, had never been granted by the Disney company, but usually they were announced through the local mainstream media. For example, the 'Snow White' Eskimo Toffee was first advertised in *The Sin Wan Pao* (新聞報) on 2 June 1938, the same day as the film's release. The advertisement is composed of an illustration of Snow White and the dwarfs carrying a large box of 'Snow White' Toffee and a slogan on the bottom 'Try a "Snow White" Eskimo Toffee when you go to watch *Snow White*.' The advertisement indeed was an ingenious design, which was placed right next to the film poster, maintaining the continuity with the image and, at the same time, opening up a dialogue with the customers.[21]

The 'Snow White' cigarette is another interesting example of how Snow White and the dwarfs were represented and utilized in local advertising. Advertisements of the 'Snow White' cigarette were extensively printed in

FIGURE 10.4 The advertisements utilizing *Snow White's* images published in *The China Press* on 2 June 1938.

various newspapers and magazines between December 1938 and April 1939. Borrowing the classic frame from the film where the dwarfs find Snow White sleeping in their bedroom, the earliest version altered the seven dwarfs from looking at Snow White to looking at two packets of 'Snow White' cigarettes. Another impressive version was published in January 1939 in *The Society Daily* (社會報), in which Snow White is seen holding a cigarette and enjoying smoking.[22]

In August 1938, the Jackson & Brothers company (吉遜行) made a formal announcement through the *Sin Wan Pao* about the registration of 'Snow White' as the trademark for its latest cosmetic powder. The 'Snow White' powder soon became popular throughout Shanghai, thanks to the effective endorsement by Snow White, who, as claimed by the film, had skin as white as snow. Aimed at young modern women, the manufacturer claimed that with its magic pink and white power all the skin imperfections would be corrected, which perfectly fitted the customers' impression of Snow White. In its first advertisement published in the *Sin Wan Pao* on 22 August 1938, the benefits of the powder were addressed by accompanying text, as well as by the images of Snow White and a modern woman.[23] A later version issued on 31 August 1938 employed the seven dwarfs surrounding a tin of 'Snow White' powder with different postures, accompanied by the slogan 'if you want to be as beautiful as Snow White, please apply the Snow White powder' (Figure 10.5).[24]

The incredible popularity of *Snow White* also aroused the interest of the local artists, and 'Snow White' became a heated topic in literary and artistic creation at the time. One of the most famous work was a caricature titled 'Snow White's Eight Immortals Crossing the Sea', created by Changmin Ni and published in *Shanghai Daily* on 25 December 1938 (Figure 10.6).[25] As indicated by the title, this work is based on a Chinese Taoist myth 'the Eight Immortals crossing the Sea', a story dating back to the Yuan Dynasty (1200 CE).[26] In Ni's caricature, Snow White, equipped with a magic lotus flower, stands at the stern of a boat, while the seven dwarfs hold the different magic weapons just like their counterparts in the 'Eight Immortals'. This image, in fact, perfectly symbolizes how the film *Snow White* crossed the Pacific Ocean from the United States and eventually arrived in China – a journey of resourcefulness, where the key players involved used their wits to make the most of what was available.

The remake *Chinese Snow White*

Filled with admiration about the tremendous commercial success of Disney's *Snow White*, Xinhua Film Company, the most significant film production company in Shanghai during the 1930s and 1940s, decided to invest a live-action remake, *Chinese Snow White* (also translated as *Chinese Princess Snow White*). Released in 1940, the film was directed by Wu Yonggang, while Chen Juanjuan, a well-known child star and marketed as the Chinese Shirley Temple, starred as Snow White.

To better accommodate a local audience and reflect the social circumstance of the time, there are two significant changes from Disney's *Snow White*. First, *Chinese Snow White* is a contemporary story set during the Republican period of China (1912–49), which is a complete departure from the original historical European setting. Consequently, instead of being a princess, Snow White is portrayed as a local girl who grew up in a wealthy family. Second, rather than mining for jewels, the seven dwarfs in the Chinese remake devote themselves to the act of 'removing' the mountains. This has potential associations with the well-known Chinese fable 'The Foolish Old Man

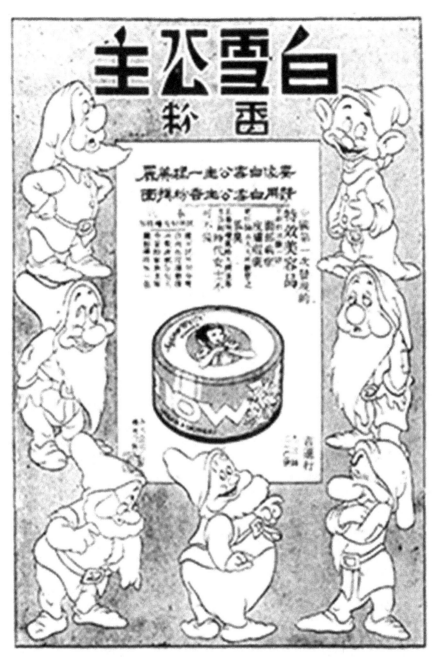

FIGURE 10.5 'Snow White' powder advertised in *The Sin Wan Pao* on 31 August 1938.

（作民長倪）　白雪公主的八仙過海

FIGURE 10.6 The caricature 'Snow White's Eight Immortals Crossing the Sea', 1938.

Removes the Mountains', which advocates perseverance, determination and willpower.

At the start of the film, with a definite educational purpose, *Chinese Snow White* attempts to teach the audience that only hard work, collaboration and selfless actions can bring happiness.[27] What is most striking is that the romantic plot between Snow White and the prince – which is so key to the Disney version of the narrative – is entirely removed in *Chinese Snow White*. For Chinese nationals in the period, a hard-working and revolutionary proletarian was a more convincing hero, as opposed to a love-struck prince. In the remake, the prince is therefore replaced by Xiao Yi, who, as a worker in the kitchen, not only saves Snow White but also indoctrinates her and the dwarfs with proletarian ideology.

Chinese Snow White was also made during the 'Solitary Island' period. This meant that the film, on the one hand, intended to deliver a message of anti-Japanese sentiment and national salvation and, on the other hand, had to be both entertaining and subtle to survive in the Japanese and foreign concessions which occupied Shanghai. If the stepmother and the cruel doctor symbolize both darkness and dictatorship, then the seven dwarfs and Xiao Yi represent the strengthening and collaboration of the proletariat. Working as mountain 'removers', the seven dwarfs were also an excellent metaphor that responded to the idea of Mao Zedong's 'New Democratic Revolution': a collaboration of proletarian workers, peasants, small business owners and the nationally based capitalists, which aimed to overcome the three mountains of imperialism, feudalism and bureaucrat capitalism weighing down on the Chinese people.

Although *Chinese Snow White* is visually realistic in many ways, the director maintained some degree of exaggeration as in Disney's original feature. Doors and windows are all blown open by the power of Sneezy's sneeze, Bashful blows a myriad of bubbles from his mouth after drinking soap water and the face in a photo – which appears in the background of the scene – changes to a dramatic expression whenever the antagonist appears on scene. Other parts of the film also stay faithful to the original, especially the interior of the dwarfs' cottage, the depiction of the forest and the lake. Moreover, just like Disney's *Snow White*, the Chinese remake was also influenced by German expressionism. Scenes such as when Snow White flees from home, and those which involve her murderous stepmother, use shadows to create a depressing atmosphere and reflect Snow White's fear. Interestingly, *Chinese Snow White* imitates the scene in the Disney film where the princess kisses the dwarfs. However, this scene loses the charm of the animated version once you realize that the dwarfs are actually played by seven full-size male adults, and the role of Snow White is performed by an 11-year-old girl.

At first glance it appears as if *Chinese Snow White* is a contradiction; this is a film that tries to copy Disney's *Snow White*, while also rejecting it. While the film kept the fidelity of the original animation in its setting, character movement and designs, it also removed certain elements and changed the story to suit its prospective audience in China. Despite its apparent irreconcilability, as an experiment and a film *Chinese Snow White* works well regardless, showing how successfully Chinese studios could imitate Hollywood films despite the difficulties and hardships of war faced by filmmakers and audiences in the period.

The first Chinese animated feature
Princess Iron Fan

Princess Iron Fan, directed by the Wan Brothers (Wan Guchan and Wan Laiming), and produced by Xinhua Film Company and Shangyuan Company (上元企業公司), is another example to show the influence and indigenization of Disney's *Snow White* in China. The eighty-minute-long film premiered in Metropol Theatre and Astor Theatre (滬光大戲院) on 19 November 1941, making it the first Asian animated feature-length film.[28] The film is based on the chapters 'Monkey King Makes Three Attempts to

Borrow the Plantain Fan' from the Chinese classical novel *Journey to the West* (西遊記). In Wan's memoirs *Money King and Me*, he recalled how Disney's *Snow White* motivated his creation of *Princess Iron Fan*, noting that 'since Americans could produce their western style *Snow White*, we, of course, can make our own Chinese style *Princess Iron Fan*. If we are successful, it will be fascinating for the audience to enjoy two princesses and compare them from the stories to the artistic styles.'[29] Information about the thought process behind the Wan Brothers' animation strategy can also be revealed through discussions in his memoirs. Wan claimed, 'in term of the content, my brothers and I believe that we should develop our own path, differentiating from Disney's. It is interesting to watch Disney's animations for the first time, but it soon becomes boring if you watch them more times. I do not like the stories, but I have to repeatedly watch them, because besides the stories there are too many techniques I want to borrow.'[30] Hence, in order to make *Princess Iron Fan*, the Wan Brothers decided to tell a Chinese story for a Chinese audience, while also employing the technologies from Disney's *Snow White*.

Princess Iron Fan, which was both a critical and commercial success, was screened in Shanghai for over a month. It was widely praised by numerous newspapers and magazines as the Chinese version of *Snow White*. For instance, *Popular Cinema News* (大眾影訊) commented that the Wan Brothers successfully imitated the methods of Disney's *Snow White*, producing the frames beautifully and vividly, just like a Hollywood film.[31] As the first animated feature film in China, an analysis of the film reveals the appropriation of techniques learned by observation of Disney's animation. First, just like Disney's *Snow White*, rotoscoping was partially applied in *Princess Iron Fan* to capture realistic gestures and movements. As Wan described, first they filmed the live-action performance by the actors and then drew the movements frame by frame based on their footage.[32] Second, the Wan Brothers applied the synchronization of sound and image in *Princess Iron Fan*, techniques which had been fully realized in Disney's own animated feature. For instance, a deep and slow melody played by trombone synchronizes with the appearance of the fatty Pigsy, a humorous effect achieved through the arrangement of the audio and visual elements. Accurate lip sync was also used in *Princess Iron Fan*, a topic of discussion that Wan introduced to *United China Movie News* when he pointed out that, if the dialogue of the character was 'I and you', a key frame of the mouth with the shape of 'I' would be drawn, as well as the frames 'and' and 'you'. Then the frames passed to the animation team, who completed the in-betweens. All the dialogues and songs in *Princess Iron fan* had been done by this way.[33]

Even though *Princess Iron Fan* appropriated various aspects of Disney's *Snow White*, it also explored Chinese culture, aesthetics and visual language. The landscape of *Princess Iron Fan* is a Chinese ink-and-wash painting,

FIGURE 10.7 The landscape of *Princess Iron Fan*.

in which trees and mountains are highly stylized through applying simple brushstrokes and by the faintness and pressure of ink (Figure 10.7). The character design of the film was heavily influenced by traditional Chinese opera. The Princess, who is wrapped in an armour-look dress, is very similar to the operatic costume typically used for military women in Peking opera (Figure 10.8). Just like *Chinese Snow White*, *Iron Fan* also carries anti-Japanese sentiments. As Wan pointed out, conquering Bull Demon King is a powerful metaphor that suggests the image of Chinese people triumphing over their Japanese invaders, eventually winning the war through the collaborations across the country.[34]

Princess Iron Fan certainly is not a flawless animation but given the time and circumstances under which it was produced, it is indeed an impressive animated feature film. Deeply influenced by Disney's *Snow White*, *Princess Iron Fan* borrowed a variety of animation techniques from the former film while telling a different, specifically Chinese, story. However, what is most significant about *Princess Iron Fan* is its uniquely Chinese approach to animation too, combining traditional Chinese aesthetics with the historical and political contexts of the period.

Conclusion

The 1930s and 1940s were a period of cultural and artistic prosperity and rapid political change in bustling Shanghai, during which time Disney

FIGURE 10.8 The Princess wears an armour-look dress similar to the operatic costume.

animation marched into the city and captured the hearts of the local audience. The importance of *Snow White* was recognized in Shanghai almost immediately and still provides inspiration to new animators and audiences, over eighty years after its initial release. The unique time period and social circumstances of the city provided possibilities for the popularization of *Snow White*, which in turn nourished the local economic, cultural and artistic innovations. Using historical examples and archives, in this chapter I have emphasized the significance of *Snow White* to Chinese film and animation. For those interested in the historical development of Chinese animation, the reinterpretation and indigenization of Disney's *Snow White* provides an early example of the relationship between Hollywood and China, illustrating how economics, society, culture and art are being continually developed and reshaped within the context of globalization.

Notes

1   See 'Snow White in China', *Movietone* 8, no. 29 (1939): 1204.
    (白雪公主在中國, 電聲); Shanghai Library Document Supply Centre, ed.,
    Retrospections of Walt Disney in Shanghai: A City Chronicle of ROC
    (Shanghai: Shanghai Scientific and Technological Literature Press, 2016), 45.
    (上海图书馆文献提供中心, 迪士尼上海往事: 民国时期的城市记忆, 上海科
    学技术文献出版社).

2   Marie-Claire Bergère, *Shanghai: China's Gateway to Modernity*, trans. Janet Lloyd(Stanford, CA: Stanford University Press, 2009), 2.

3   J. A. Van Brakle, 'Mickey the Mouse' Liked by Britons', *North China Daily News* (6 February 1930): 10.

4   See: The Father of Mickey Mouse: Walt Disney's Successful Career', *Movietone* 6, no. 7 (1937): 377. (米老鼠的製作者：華爾特狄斯耐成功經過，電聲); 'Mickey Mouse Becomes a Star', *Linglong* 3, no. 24 (1933): 1262. (米老鼠成明星，玲瓏) (This and all translations from Chinese are by the author.)

5   Chinese scholar Hong Guo believes that the earliest Disney animations began to be screened in Shanghai at the end of the 1920s. See: Hong Guo, *Shanghai: The Cradle of Modern Chinese Animation Movie* (Shanghai: Zhongxi Book Company, 2017), 97. (郭虹, 上海：中国动画电影的摇篮, 上海：中西书局)

6   'Midnight in Toyshop', Advertisement, *North China Daily News* (23 December 1931): 25.

7   Gang Qin, 'Disney's Animation in Shanghai in the Republic of China during the Era of 'Sound Animation': Based on Lu Xun's Dairy', *Modern Chinese Literature Studies*, no. 7 (2017): 38–49. (秦刚, 有声卡通'时代的迪士尼动画在民国上海——以鲁迅日记为线索, 中国现代文学研究丛刊).

8   'Snow White in China', *Movietone* 8, no. 29 (1939): 1204. (白雪公主在中國, 電聲).

9   'The Most Popular Film and Star by Shanghai Audience', *Silver Flower Monthly*, no. 13 (1939): 16. (上海觀眾最歡迎的影片及明星, 銀花集).

10 '*Snow White*', *Nanhai Yinxing* 1, no. 7 (1938): 2. (白雪公主, 南海銀星).

11 "Snow White' Said Screen Masterpiece', *China Press* (3 June 1938): 5.

12 Cang Luo, 'Review: Snow White and the Seven Dwarfs', *Li Daily* (9 June 1938): 2. (滄洛, 影評：白雪公主和七侏儒, 力報).

13 Xinyi Zheng, 'I Watched *Snow White* 78 Years ago', *Global People* (7 July 2016). Available at http://www.hqrw.com.cn/2016/0707/53171.shtml (accessed 9 July 2018) (郑心仪, 78年前我看《白雪公主》, 环球人物网).

14 '*Snow White*', Advertisement, *China Press* (2 June 1938): 5; '*Snow White*', Advertisement, *China Press* (3 June 1938): 5.

15 Nanhai Yinxing, the cinema weekly newspaper, advertised the film *Snow White* on its front pages for three issues from 21 May to 4 June 1938.

16 See: He, 'Dwarfs Are Too Lazy to Wash Faces', *Nanhai Yinxing* 1, no. 5 (1938): 1. (赫, 矮子懶洗面, 南海銀星); Wei Ming, 'Dopey Doesn't Want to Talk', *Nanhai Yinxing* 1, no. 6 (1938): 1. (煒明, 不想講話的啞子, 南海銀星).

17 'ALOHA BALLROOM', Advertisement, *China Press* (2 June 1938): 10; 'Chang Seng Tailor', Advertisement, *China Press* (2 June 1938): 10; 'Commercial Equipment Co.' Advertisement, *China Press* (2 June 1938): 8; 'E-Z Dry Cleaning Co.', Advertisement, *China Press* (2 June 1938): 8; 'Handkerchiefs', Advertisement, *China Press* (2 June 1938): 8; TYNG YU BROTHERS', Advertisement, *China Press* (2 June 1938): 8; 'VIENNA

GARDEN', Advertisement, *China Press* (2 June 1938): 9; 'YUEN TAI & CO.', Advertisement, *China Press* (2 June 1938): 9.

18   'Sincere Company's Children Playground', Advertisement, *Sin Wan Pao* (17 December 1938): 19. (兒童世界，新聞報).

19   'The Park Hotel's Sky Terrace Hall', Advertisement, *Oriental Daily* (25 June 1945): 2.

20   'Victory Ballroom', Advertisement, *Li Daily* (22 October 1938): 6.

21   'Snow White' Eskimo Toffee, Advertisement, *Sin Wan Pao* (2 June 1938): 13. (白雪公主北極太妃，新聞報).

22   'Snow White' cigarette, Advertisement, *Sin Wan Pao* (21 December 1938): 16. (白雪公主香煙，新聞報); 'Snow White' cigarette, Advertisement, *Society Daily* (24 January 1939): 2. (白雪公主香煙，社会報).

23   'Snow White Powder', Advertisement, *Sin Wan Pao* (22 August 1938): 14. (白雪公主香粉，新聞報).

24   'Snow White Powder', Advertisement, *Sin Wan Pao* (31 August 1938): 1. (白雪公主香粉，新聞報).

25   Changmin Ni, 'Snow White's Eight Immortals Crossing the Sea', Caricature, *Shanghai Daily* (25 December 1938): 15. (倪長民，白雪公主的八仙過海，申報).

26   In the original story of 'the Eight Immortals crossing the Sea', the eight immortals, including He Xiangu, Cao Guojiu, Li Tieguai, Lan Caihe, Lü Dongbin, Zhang Guolao, Han Xiangzi and Han Zhongli, decide to use their magic weapons to cross the sea when they come back from a banquet. Li Tieguai uses his walking stick, Han Zhongli uses his palm-leaf fan, Zhang Guolao uses his paper donkey, Lan Caihe uses his basket, Lü Dongbin uses his long sword, Han Xiangzi uses his flute, Han Xiangzi uses his jade and He Xiangu uses her lotus flower. Thanks to their ingenuity, they all successfully cross the sea. The combination of Snow White and the seven dwarfs and the eight immortals is ingenious. Not only because both the stories have eight characters but also because Snow White and He Xiangu are the only females in both groups.

27   Yuhua Li, 'Film Review for *Chinese Snow White*', *Women Weekly* 2, no. 3 (1940): 20–1. (李玉華，中國的白雪公主影評，婦女界).

28   'Princess Iron Fan', *Movie Daily New* (19 November 1941): 3 (鐵扇公主，電影日報).

29   Laiming Wan and Guohun Wan, *Monkey King and Me* (Taiyuan: Beiyue Literature & Art Press, 1985), 88. (万籟鸣，万国魂，我与孙悟空，太原: 北岳文艺出版社).

30   Ibid., 70.

31   Zuixia Jin, '*Princess Iron Fan* Animated Film', *Popular Cinema News* 2, no. 21 (1941): 583. (金醉霞，'鐵扇公主'卡通片，大眾影訊).

32 'The First Chinese Animated Feature Film: *Princess Iron Fan*', *Creation Monthly* 1, no. 1 (1941): 64. (中國第一部長篇卡通電影: 鐵扇公主，萬象).

33 'The Experience of Making *Princess Iron Fan*', *United China Movie News* 1, no. 9 (1941): 67. (*我們繪製 '鐵扇公主'的經過，國聯影訊*).

34 Wan and Wan, *Monkey King and Me*, 90.

11

Unearthing *Blanche-Neige*: The making of the first made-in-Hollywood French version of *Snow White* and its critical reception

Greg Philip and Sébastien Roffat

The first French version of *Snow White and the Seven Dwarfs* has never been the object of a full analysis.[1] This chapter is an attempt to present new information regarding the first French dubbing made in Hollywood, alongside its production and its reception when first shown in Paris on 6 May 1938. As long-time enthusiasts of the film, our alternate goal was to be able to find, screen and preserve that lost version. This raised several questions: What are the technical and artistic merits of this specific version? What was the creative process? How was it critically received? And why was this version replaced in subsequent releases?

The making of the first French version

In the silent era, movies were usually shot with two cameras. One negative was used for domestic release and the other one for foreign adaptations. Alternate takes were also used for that second version, which was similar but not identical to the first, and that was used as a basis for all foreign versions. Intertitles were translated in the appropriate language, reshot and inserted in the movie: that was enough to achieve a foreign (say French) or international version.[2]

When talkies arrived, the basic principle was retained: although musicals flourished because they required few adaptations for foreign release, the need to have spoken dialogue adapted in the native language of the country of release demanded a solution. Subtitles as we know them today were archaic and inadequate. In any case, in France, the demand for French talking pictures was growing, as well as the rejection of the English language. Studios reacted by shooting their movies in multiple versions. In Germany, England and Hollywood, several films were produced using the same sets, same costumes, same script, sometimes the same crew but with a different cast, each speaking a different language. One rather famous example of that is Tod Browning's *Dracula* (1931), whose English-speaking crew was working during the day, while the Spanish crew took over at night. The result was two productions of the same script, with the Spanish version costing far less ($66.000) than the American one ($355.000).[3]

This system of multiple language versions (or MLVs) was phased out by 1934 due to the development of a technique that started as early as 1931 with better and better results as time went by: *dubbing*.[4] With sound recording having more and more fidelity with the RCA 'noiseless' system, there was no more concern about surface noise when mixing various tracks together. In order to improve these versions, studios eventually prepared an international soundtrack with only music and effects ready to be mixed with new dialogue to complete the illusion that the on-screen actor actually spoke a foreign language.

Critics and audiences initially disliked dubbing in France as it was Critics and audiences initially disliked dubbing in France as it was considered cheating, since the real voice of the American actor was not heard anymore and because of the bad quality of the first attempts.[5] However, dubbing was eventually preferred because multiple versions were much more expensive, and because they prevented the audience from seeing the Hollywood stars that could only speak English. Of course, by the time *Snow White* was released, dubbing had become an industry standard. However, Disney wanted things done fast yet still keep complete control over that alternate version.

The early Disney sound shorts did not need adaptation for foreign countries as the soundtrack comprised of merely music and sound effects, but with dialogue and songs came the need for adaptation. That is where expatriates who had come to Hollywood to shoot movies in French came in useful: the studio could hire some of them to record a French version in Hollywood, without the added expense of recording abroad or importing actors. Disney planned to use this system with their first feature. Even though France had passed a law that compelled filmmakers to dub their movies in France, a special permit was delivered for *Snow White* because it was a cartoon and therefore that French version was not really considered dubbing.[6]

Two foreign versions were hastily prepared: Spanish and French. Paul Stuart Buchanan was made head of foreign adaptations. After those two essential versions were made, Buchanan then travelled to Paris and from there prepared all other foreign recordings which were then shipped back to the United States to be mixed to the international soundtrack.[7] But the first two versions were recorded right there in California, so he had to pick a translator and artistic director – a job requiring a perfect knowledge of the French language, so surprisingly he chose a Chilean: Marcelo Ventura.

Born in 1901, Ventura was fluent in Spanish, English, French and Greek, so became a diplomat for the King of Spain, and in that capacity, he directed a documentary called *Barcelona Trailer* (1929) and travelled to the United States to show it as the Delegate of the 1929 International Exposition of Barcelona, a trip during which he met the director of Paramount Adolf Zukor.[8] Ventura became Mae West's personal assistant and made cameo appearances in some of her movies. He changed his name to Marcel Ventura on 13 May 1938. His duty on these international versions of *Snow White* was to pick actors for various parts, ultimately casting himself as the Prince.[9]

The main criterion for the performers' selection was how close they sounded to the original US actors. Even when there was no dialogue such as in *Snow White*'s forest scene, some of the human sound effects were mixed differently from one version to another. At the end of the forest scene, more screams were added in subsequent mixes for each version, so that Snow White screams twice in the original US version, three times in French and up to five times in Italian (that difference has been wiped from all new versions since they are mixed with the same international track which is identical to the original US version). Just like in the original Disney feature, no actors were credited in that version. It was Disney's will to maintain the illusion by not revealing who the actors behind the performance were. In the original programme, no actors are mentioned, only the characters.

François Justamand, on the website *la gazette du doublage*, published an article in 2009 revealing that the Disney archives in Burbank had kept a document about 'outside salaries' paid in September 1938 to a group of twenty-three artists to make a 'Snow White French version'. He gave a few of the names, but based on what he found in the press and interviews of French artists, he was unsure if this was actually a list of the cast of the first French version. More research was needed about these artists, and comparing their voices across as many movies as possible makes it possible to link each character with the corresponding actor. The actors that played the dwarfs have an impressive filmography, with mostly uncredited cameos in famous or not so famous movies. Louis Mercier is a very familiar face in any Hollywood production that features French-speaking characters, such as Alfred Hitchcock's *The Man Who Knew Too Much* (1956) where he plays the policeman in Marrakech, or *To Catch a Thief* (Alfred Hitchcock, 1955) (playing a Croupier), as well as *Casablanca* (Michael Curtiz, 1942), *To Have and Have Not* (Howard Hawks, 1944) and *The Razor's Edge* (Edmund Goulding, 1946), to name a few. Likewise, Eugene Borden – who had featured in *The Mark of Zorro* (Rouben Mamoulian, 1940), *Gilda* (Charles Vidor, 1946) and *All About Eve* (Joseph L. Mankiewicz, 1950) – had a very distinctive nosy voice that perfectly fit the part of Doc.

All of these voices were rather close to their American counterparts. However, even so, some creative choices were still possible: the actor who played Happy was Charles de Ravenne, who came from a family of actors that originated in Nice in the south of France and had a very strong southern accent that, to any listener with a good knowledge of France, might evoke associations of sunny skies. As in other dubbings, one actor at least did double duty. Veteran actor André Cheron played both Grumpy and the Hunter, while the Queen and the hag here are also both played by the same actress. Two artists were also needed for Snow White: Christiane Tourneur, wife of director Jacques Tourneur, for the speaking part. However, she could not sing and a professional singer had to take care of the songs. Ventura had to find a lyric soprano who spoke French and whose voice matched Adriana Caselotti's in California. It is not surprising that he eventually chose an American girl. It was probably decided that a slight American accent, especially in the singing, would not be a problem. Actually, problematic accents seem to plague every early version of *Snow White*: the speaking voice in the Spanish version has a very heavy US accent, while most members of the German cast were actually Austrian. In the French version, Snow White thus sings with the voice of Beatrice Hagen who was voted in 1936 'first Hollywood radio baby star', not exactly your average Paris girl. During her short time at the studio in early 1938, she also recorded the brief singing part of the farmer in the Disney Silly Symphony titled *Farmyard Symphony* (Jack Cutting, 1938).

Technical and artistic merits of the first French version

Translation

As far as quality is concerned, the translation is rather good, although some phrases are not grammatically correct. For instance, when Snow White goes to sleep, she inquires if the dwarfs will be comfortable downstairs. In that French version, she utters 'êtes-vous sûrs que vous serez confortables?'.

Unfortunately, the word 'confortable' in French can only be applied to something, not someone. A couch can be 'confortable', not a person. This kind of mistake, ironically enough, must have sounded unacceptable when first released but sounds almost modern today given the influence of English upon the French language. In fact, even in laudatory reviews of this version, critics often regret the bizarre accents of some of the characters and the few mistakes in the translation, even in the programme of the premiere![10]

A critic published on 12 May 1938 in *Candide* notes that 'The dialogue – especially in the French version – is bad and hurts the film. The image is light, detached from contingencies, but these precise words spoken with pronounced and fake dictions, with slang accents and mistakes, bring us back to reality.'[11] Likewise, the opening line in the book translates 'Once upon a time' as 'Il y avait une fois' unlike the more common and modern 'Il était une fois' which has been digitally replaced in 1992 and used until the 2001 DVD release, after which the English version was subtitled and used instead. However, the translation of songs was so successful in that version that it was kept with very minimal changes throughout all subsequent versions.

Technical quality

Although most of the film's soundtrack is quite successful for a 1938 recording, for some reason, only the quality of the recording of the singing voice of the main character leaves a lot to be desired, as Buchanan and Roy Disney privately regretted.[12] The sound is so unsuccessful that it is hard to understand the lyrics, which is not helped by Beatrice Hagen's accent. Indeed, several records were cut directly from the American and Spanish soundtracks but none from the French version. Only re-recordings of the French songs were issued by many different singers and bands, the original soundtrack was only heard in theatres.[13] However, one thing that is common to all foreign versions of *Snow White* made in 1938 is that only the wordless choirs are used. Choirs with actual translated lyrics were only recorded from the 1960s. Other than that, the Technicolor copies of the time are of the same quality as the US prints.

Visual adaptation

Great care was taken to give the impression that the film had been made almost especially for the French, so instead of adapting only the soundtrack, every visual element that contained writing on-screen was also changed. That obviously included the main and end titles. These were simply translated and shot over the same backgrounds and, like the original Disney film, emphasized the fact that this was a feature-length animation.

Domestic   **French**

FIGURE 11.1 On the left, the US version, on the right the French version.

A tougher job was to reshoot animated segments with translated backgrounds. They either had to erase them, such as the flour bowl when Snow White is baking or the Vault sign at the dwarfs' mine, or translate them (such as the many books belonging to the Queen). The camera department occasionally made it easier for themselves by removing some of the cel layers when they were not absolutely necessary: so in the bedroom sequence, when Snow White reads the names of the dwarfs off of their beds, there are fewer animals running around (Figure 11.1). An even tougher job involved working with the visible animated writing. When Snow White bakes a pie for the dwarfs, the birds grab a piece of pastry and write the name Grumpy on the top. For the French version, the animators had to reanimate the whole sequence. This is the only instance where they undertook this task: for all other versions, the birds merely make a whirl with the paste (Figure 11.2).

With later translations, some of the dialogues differed from what is seen onscreen. When the Queen reads 'mummy dust', the translation on the book and in her dialogue is 'magic powder', probably with the aim of not scaring children. But the new translation from 1962 onwards remains 'mummy dust', yet since the book had not changed, the Queen appeared to read the line wrong. In 1958, Snow White was reissued in the United States for the first time without the RKO distribution deal, meaning that every mention of RKO had to be erased from the credits. New main and end titles were shot for the film with a new background, and it is that background that was also used to make new versions of the foreign titles. The credits were smaller so that the top and bottom of the film could be matted (as was the industry standard then), and the credits could still be read. One important change took place: the new cast was listed. In 1992, some of these French inserts were altered to modernize the film. Finally, when the Blu-ray was released, they were completely removed and any copy of Snow White shown in France today is the American version with a voiceover for the book opening. Little by little, what was left of this first French version has been completely

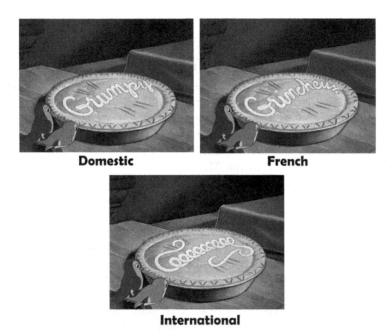

Domestic   **French**

International

FIGURE 11.2 US version (left), French version (right) and international version (centre).

erased. However, given the fragile nature of nitrate film, its preservation is essential as this is how the contemporary French audience saw the film.

Disney's aesthetic triumph: *Snow White and the Seven Dwarfs*

The American press was unanimous in its praise for a film that had been hailed as 'Disney's Folly'.[14] Walt Disney appeared on the cover of *Time*, and *Snow White* was screened five weeks in a row at Radio City Music Hall in New York. For the first time in American film history, a movie earned more money in the second week than in its previous one. In the first three weeks, Radio City Music Hall sold 521,000 tickets.[15] It was estimated that in three months, 20 million spectators saw the film. One of the first reviews to appear in France was that of John W. Garner, who had seen the film in the United States in January. His review could not have been more enthusiastic: 'He is a spectator still under the impression of the adorable fairytale conceived by this magician whose imagination has never been more fertile in poetic discoveries. … We can predict for Snow White a posterity equal to the one of her young brother Mickey.'[16] On 30 April 1938, Raoul d'Ast in the newspaper *Liberté* wrote that 'In New York, the film was so successful that the tickets worth a dollar ten at the ticket office were sold [on the black market] for up to five dollars at the doors of Radio City Music Hall. It is to be expected that all Paris will want to see this extraordinary achievement, which will be a milestone in the history of cinema.'[17]

It was the Pathé-Cinéma company that ensured the exclusivity of Disney's *Snow White* for a duration of six months and who would also project it on the screens of its circuit of Paris and the rest of France. The French release was set for 6 May 1938 in the Marignan cinema Paris on the Champs-Elysées (the film was due out in mid-April, but the French dubbing was not finished in time). The release in France of *Blanche Neige* was also a first: whereas the habit in France was to show two feature films together, the American producer demanded that this animated feature-length film be shown with just a short documentary. The reason given by the producer was that '*Snow White* does not need any supplements. The film is self-sufficient. Any other film shown at the same time would only diminish its value.'[18] This comment revealed the confidence that the Americans had in the success of this film. The programme proposed in Marignan was thus: 'Pathé-Journal, world news; *A story of penguins*, documentary about the life of penguins; Walt Disney's *Snow White and the Seven Dwarfs*'.[19] RKO France also published a very detailed advertising notice intended exclusively for cinema operators.[20] The title is explicit: 'An exceptional film requires exceptional publicity. For this movie you MUST do a MAXIMUM of advertising to get the MAXIMUM turnover.' It also explained that

> You can never give too much attention to the aesthetics and advertising appeal of your façade. Always ensure it is very well lit, well maintained and well cared for. The advertising elements that make up it must be well disposed and their artistic layout must attract the eye of the passer-by. Some of the advertising suggestions included Singing Competition for Children, Snow White Cake, Hiring a dwarf dressed as Dopey in front of the theater.

Snow White attracted the attention of the French press from 30 April 1938, exactly a week before its release on 6 May . Rarely would a film enjoy so such enthusiasm and unanimity on the part of French press reviews. A month after its release in Paris, there were already 100,000 spectators for the Marignan alone.[21] The film was screened for thirty-one weeks in Paris (four months in Marignan, then in Imperial and until December). Success followed in Lyon and throughout France. Indeed, the film was a global success. According to estimates for foreign countries and the United States, *Snow White*'s revenues amounted to $8 million in 1938, making it the greatest success at that time. The first release of the film in the United States earned $4.2 million; in Great

Britain the figure was $2 million; France contributed half a million dollars; the rest of the world for a million and a half.

France was therefore the third country in the world in which *Snow White and the Seven Dwarfs* had the most success. We can estimate the number of the French audience at around 3.5 million. *Snow White* achieved seven times more revenue and attracted eight times more viewers than was average. The top ten films in 1938 in France according to the magazine *La Cinématographie française* were:

1) *Snow White and the seven dwarfs*, Disney studios

2) *Le Quai des brumes* [*Port of Shadows*], Marcel Carné

3) *Katia*, Maurice Tourneur

4) *La femme du boulanger* [*The Baker's Wife*], Marcel Pagnol

5) *Alerte en Méditerranée* [*Alert in the Mediterranean*], Léo Joannon

6) *The Adventures of Robin Hood*, Michael Curtiz and William Keighley

7) *Barnabé*, Alexandre Esway

8) *La Maison du Maltais* [*Sirocco*], Pierre Chenal

9) *Les Trois Valses* [*Three Waltzes*], Ludwig Berger

10) *Prison sans barreaux*, Léonide Moguy[22]

For the first time since 1936, two American films were ranked in the top ten productions of the year. *Snow White* won the first place that had gone to *La Grande Illusion* (Jean Renoir, 1937) the year before. It is the first time in history that an American movie ranked the first place in France (in the same magazine, French actor Jean Gabin was elected the most popular star in French cinema). A rare occurrence, *Snow White and the Seven Dwarfs* was even shown in French in New York at the Waldorf Theater from April 1939. Walt Disney himself made a short appearance.[23] *Snow White and the Seven Dwarfs* was certainly an extraordinary success with both the public and the critics. However, this did not stop an interesting debate starting in the French press: by wanting to reach photographic realism in his first feature-length film, did Walt Disney contribute to the destruction of the very essence of the cartoon?

Photographic realism: Killing or reinventing cartoons?

From the outset, *Snow White and the Seven Dwarfs* was described as a masterpiece by the French press. Yet a debate was emerging: some press reviews considered that by copying the model of film in real shots, Disney was moving away from their prior 'plasmaticness' as defined by Sergei Eisenstein.[24] Animated cartoons had been hailed by French critics exactly because they seemed to be the first cinematographic genre to clearly move away from filmed theatre. Was it a new beginning or the beginning of the end for animated movies? That was the question which in part agitated the small world of the French film press in 1938.

Unlike filmed theatre, the cartoon exploits to the full the new possibilities of its technique. This 'masterpiece' (the term itself comes back more than thirty times in the corpus of reviews) was generated by a drawing factory. This was also what French critics admired. What was also surprising for many observers was the mastered technique of drawing human beings attained by the cartoon industry in only a few years. In just a decade, Disney passed from embryonic drawings of Mickey in the first cartoons to a perfect animation of animals and men. In 1935, Walt Disney himself explained: 'I definitely feel that we cannot do the fantastic things, based on the real, unless we first know the real.'[25] As Paul Wells remarks,

[Disney] wanted animated figures to move like real figures and be informed by a plausible motivation. As Disney's studio grew and embarked on ever more ambitious projects, most notably the creation of a full-length animated feature, Disney's animators undertook programmes of training in the skills and techniques of fine arts in the constant drive towards ever greater notions of realism. Animals had to move like real animals.[26]

The level of reality was further enhanced by the development of the multi-plane camera, which enabled the creation of the illusion of perspective. This camera costs $75,000 in a total budget of $1.5 million, more than four times the average budget of a feature film in 1937 (more than six times over the original estimate).

As Disney advanced towards the development of what had been called an aesthetic of the 'illusion of life' – that the public accepts, recognizes and even finds comfortable – critical opinion had begun to change. While Snow White and the Seven Dwarfs was unanimously hailed in the United States as an important date both for the feature film and for its realistic effects, in 1941 the American critical climate had clearly changed. Even Siegfried Kracauer, a fervent theorist of cinematic realism, criticized the Disney animated features because they began to 'imitate the technique of the realistic films', emphasizing three-dimensional space, camera movement and characterization. In a declaration that suggests his preference for early animation's avant-garde, Kracauer argues that the cartoon should work differently from live-action film, that it should emphasize 'the dissolution rather than the reinforcement of conventional reality' since 'its function is not to draw a reality which can better be photographed'.[27] There is a kind of consensus among the Anglophone scholars from 1941 that offer the first real reproach about Disney's 'photographic realism', such as the particular critique of Kracauer for *Dumbo* (Ben Sharpsteen, 1941). Esther Leslie even goes as far as to devote a whole chapter to this.[28] However, several French critics had already echoed such an opinion as early as the release of *Snow White* in 1938.

These criticisms of *Snow White* were rather marginal, but nevertheless present enough evidence that reflect the ambiguity with which the film was received. One reviewer noted that 'It's legitimate to ask ourselves if we do not witness the death of the cartoon [because] this cartoon is constructed like a "real film." '[29] Pierre Brisson from *Le Figaro* similarly argued 'As soon as the cartoon seeks to supplant photography, it goes astray and loses its meaning.'[30] François Vinneuil in *L'Action française* gave an interesting analysis in the same vein, noting, 'With the queen, we see the cartoon looking for models in the photographic cinema, … in the manner of Greta Garbo.'[31] Louis Chéronnet in *Beaux-Arts* also agreed that 'Every servile imitation of movement is as false as the search for photographic truth in a painting … In *Snow White*, the evil queen and the young Prince Charming, "credible characters," seem unfeasible and in fact become unacceptable'.[32] Fauteuil 22 writing in *La Croix* also admitted that 'the characters of Snow White and Prince Charming did not quite satisfy me. They lack stylization, they are too much like reality.'[33] Another critic in *Notre Temps* said he was 'afraid, very afraid' because 'For a few minutes into Walt Disney's film, I thought he was abandoning stylization to faithfully recompose the photographic reality. … May filmmakers open their films even more to fantasy and poetry, make our dreams possible, never copy the truth, but reinvent it!'[34] Even the famous French author, journalist and historian Robert Brasillach argued that 'We regret a little the charming madness of olden days which has disappeared from the screens.'[35]

Among these reviews focused on *Snow White*'s realist style, Marcel Arland from *La Nouvelle Revue Française* (NRF) delivered (much later, more than five months after its release) one of the most violent reviews of *Snow White*. While the previous comments are incorporated into more positive remarks, for Arland 'Everything in this film, or almost everything, is savourless, boring and silly. … *Snow White* is a failure.'[36] One senses in Arland's argument all the weight of Walter Benjamin who wrote in 1935 *The Work of Art in the Age of Mechanical Reproduction* several criticisms of Disney and Mickey. Arland condemned the film as a 'meticulous copy of life', noting that 'In its appetite to embrace everything, to replace everything, the cinema destroys itself. Look, we are told, the gestures, words and colors, our films are the meticulous copy of life.' Arland's virulent criticism was absolutely unique in the corpus of the 234 press articles studied on Disney's *Snow White*. Bearing the weight of the Frankfurt School, he was the very archetype of the conflictual relationship that Disney maintained with the intellectuals, especially after the Second World War.

In March 1939, Etienne Fuzellier in *Les Cahiers du Sud* also used harsh terms to describe the film through its 'insidious blandness', 'sneaky tartuferie', 'marshmallow style', 'enormous flaws in taste' and painful and annoying impressions'.[37] The weekly Paris-based French news magazine *Marianne* noted 'the film is long, colour often turns into chromolithography'.[38] *Le Figaro* concurred: 'The landscapes resemble chromolithographs. Colours often remain vulgar,' while Jean Fayard in *Candide* also shared this point of view by arguing 'Snow White. This little doll-headed lady is as bland as real movie stars.'[39] These critiques echoed that of filmmaker Jean Cocteau at the first showing of the film. He was present at the gala organized for the release of *Blanche Neige* on 26 April 1938 and found the film 'awful'.[40]

Walt Disney himself had always been suspicious regarding the studies undertaken on his films. In 1937, he noted that 'We just try to make a good picture. And then the professors come along and tell us what we do.'[41] After *Snow White*, if the general press and the audience were enthusiastic, this was hardly the case of the academics or the great French museums. In the 1930s or 1940s, no book about Disney was published in France, and no French publisher translated Harvard Professor Robert D. Feild's book *The Art of Walt Disney* or *Art from the Mayas to Disney*, written by artist Jean Charlot in 1939, a collection of essays in which he saw Disney as the heir of Cubism. Likewise, no French museum bought or exhibited works from Disney Studios, and no French academic study was interested in Disney.[42] For the first time, in 1959 the Exhibition 'The Art of Animation' opened in a small room of the Parisian Department Stores Le Printemps. Only half of the works exhibited in the United States were in France because the vast halls of the Musée des Arts Décoratifs, Rue de Rivoli, near the Louvre, refused to host the exhibition (whereas Belgium had welcomed it at the Musée des Beaux-Arts of Brussels). This was the only major event in France before the 1985-6 Centre Georges Pompidou exhibition and the Grand Palais exhibition in 2006–7. In spite of the public success of this French version, it was returned only three times (1938, 1944, 1951), after which a new version was created and the original disappeared, never to be seen or heard again.

Three versions, discovery of the first version

There are three French versions of *Snow White*. A studio can have many reasons to record a new soundtrack for a film: the improvement of its technical qualities, legal reasons, the addition of new or previously cut scenes, voice consistency of a character throughout various sequels or modernization of the vocabulary. In the case of *Snow White*, the subsequent versions were mainly motivated by the first two reasons. The first version was recorded early in 1938, was released on 6 May 1938 at the Marignan Theater in Paris and then was reissued in 1944 and 1951. The film was re-recorded in 1962 because the quality of the original recording at the time was considered too old to meet the 1960s standards. Lucie Dolène was chosen for both the singing and speaking parts. That version was reissued in 1973, 1983 and 1992 in a restored version, and finally released on VHS in 1994.

In 1996, Lucie Dolène sued Disney for use of her voice in these tapes since she was not receiving any residuals (like Peggy Lee had done before her regarding the use of her voice in *Lady and the Tramp* [Clyde Geronimi, Wilfred Jackson and Hamilton Luske, 1955]). Dolène won the case but considered it a personal failure not only because the sum that she won was relatively disappointing, but more importantly because she was blacklisted from further Disney productions (a loss for fans who already heard her in *The Jungle Book* [Wolfgang Reitherman, 1967] as the little girl, and later *Beauty and the Beast* [Gary Trousdale and Kirk Wise, 1991] as Mrs. Potts). In those films, her voice was meticulously replaced by other actors. In the case of *Snow White*, obviously, the whole feature had to be changed.

For that reason and in order to meet the standards of DVD (5.1 surround sound), yet another new version was recorded in 2001 with actress Valérie Siclay in the speaking part and Rachel Pignot in the singing role. It is this version that is now widely distributed on DVD, Blu-ray and in theatres. The previous version can still be found legally on VHS and Laserdisc. Only the first version has remained unavailable ever since its last release in 1951. This led to speculations over who the actors were. Even in articles of the time, one really needs to look hard to find actual information about the cast. When such information was included, it was often incorrect or incomplete. Various actresses and singers such as Lily Pons are rumoured to be the voice of Snow White, yet while unconfirmed some of these rumours persist to this day.

In an era of multitrack media, DVDs and Blu-rays, the inclusion of an old track would perhaps not take too much disc space. However, there is no apparent commercial reason to restore and release these old versions of *Snow White*. The public does not even suspect that they ever existed, and French film experts usually deny any artistic or historical value to any French version since they almost unanimously prefer original versions. However, overlooking the importance of dubbed versions is a serious mistake as these are the versions that most French viewers actually saw and heard and that, to this day, remain the most viewed versions in the country. The original versions (most often in English) remain a niche in France.

After repeated calls to private collectors through our own personal blogs, eventually, in February 2013, a private collector who actually owned a 16mm copy agreed to have it digitized. He played an extract of his copy over the phone so we could confirm this was what we were looking for: we had never heard that version before. We were able to capture the sound of the film as he was playing it for us. We also filmed the screen in order to have a visual reference to synchronize the sound to a restored image, because the copy had numerous cuts and missing frames. We then set out to work with our modest digital means to restore the track, removed some of the hiss, bleeps and pops and synchronized it to the restored DVD image. A few years later, we discovered that a 35mm copy was kept in the vaults of the Archives françaises du film at Bois D'Arcy. We could not use it for the restoration, but were happy to see another copy with some scenes intact where they were in poor shape in 16mm. Finally, we found a collector who happened to own a very rare 35mm nitrate copy, possibly the only one in private hands, and was able to scan the titles and other shots from that. The end result is an HD file of that long-lost French version.

Re-recording a new version of a film to meet with new standards is a good opportunity to see it in a new light, discover new talents. Unfortunately, it is the current policy of the Disney studio to replace previous versions by the latest one. In very few cases do they see a commercial reason to release an 'old' version, though it can occur: the Italian Blu-ray of *Peter Pan* (Clyde Geronimi, Wilfred Jackson and Hamilton Luske, 1953) has a track for each of the two Italian versions, while the first French version of *The Little Mermaid* (Ron Clements and John Musker, 1989) has recently been re-released. Some collectors hold on to their old VHS tapes in order to keep 'their' version of a film, while it is not hard to find among social media pages certain requests for the release of a specific version. Unfortunately, in the case of *Snow White*, the two first versions are not commercially available anymore, and the first one has not even been seen since 1951! The contempt of film buffs and disinterest of general audience are reasons for the lack of demand, and there is little commercial interest for the studio to release that version.

Conclusion

Clearly, in 1938, *Snow White* marked a break concerning the reception of Walt Disney movies in France. Very soon there grew an irremediable gap between Walt Disney and France: on the one hand an undeniable popular success and very favourable reviews (before the Second World War at least) and on the other hand the absolute scorn from French intellectuals both for Disney and for its millions of spectators. From the moment when Walt Disney sought absolute realism as part of his visual style, he cut himself off from a part of the French intelligentsia. Even though for the French viewing public *Snow White* marked the beginning of a new era and a series of successful feature films such as *Pinocchio* (Ben Sharpsteen and Hamilton Luske, 1940), *Bambi* (David Hand, 1942) or *Dumbo* (that was released after the war in France), the film marked an irreconcilable split between Disney and the intellectual movements, especially of the French left.

Walt Disney is undoubtedly the filmmaker who has suffered the most incredible reversal of opinion of the twentieth century at the hands of French critics, passing from the position of genius to that of impostor in a relatively short time: sometimes seen as 'the old uncle Walt', the greatest storyteller of the twentieth century, a genial, fascinating, popular beloved figure and a respected purveyor of innocent imagination, edifying fantasy and moral instruction. Yet among French circles, he is sometimes seen as Disney the artistic fraudster, an imperialist, a cynical manipulator of cheap commercial formulas, a mushy sentimentalist, vulgar and abject, an object of intellectual disdain, a manipulator of the industrial machine for mass culture with strongly conservative ideas.[43]

Notes

1   The study of the film's reception is based on the 234 press articles issued at the time of release in 1938. Even though several articles on the subject were published (with a few errors), most notably François Justamand's 2001 article for DVD Vision, republished on his website La gazette du doublage called '*Blanche Neige et les sept nains: Ses trois doublages*', http://www.objectif-cinema.com/horschamps/040.php, as well as '*Le mystère Blanche Neige*', La gazette du doublage, November 2009 http://www.objectif-cinema.com/spip.php?article5235. In 2013, Rémi Carémel, '*Le premier doublage de Blanche-Neige enfin retrouvé!*', http://danslombredesstudios.blogspot.com/2013/03/le-premier-doublage-de-blanche-neige.html. Also in 2013, Greg Philip, '*Snow White's First French Version*', http://www.alostfilm.com/2013/03/snow-whites-first-french-version.html. Rémi Carémel and Greg Philip, 'Films d'animation Disney: à la recherche des doublages perdus et le cas *Blanche Neige et les sept nains*', in *Archives et acteurs des cinémas d'animation en France*, ed. Sébastien Denis, Chantal Duchet, Lucie Merijeau, Marie Pruvost-Delaspre, Sébastien Roffat (Paris: L'Harmattan, 2014), 167–74. Karl Derisson includes some of the information already published in his book *Blanche Neige et les sept nains: la création du chef-d'œuvre de Walt Disney* (Paris: L'Harmattan, 2014), 83. Pierre Lambert, in his 2000 book *Blanche Neige* (Rozay-en-Brie: Démons et Merveilles) or in the 2009 reissue (ed. La Martinière), does not even mention the original dubbing.

2   Davide Pozzi, with the collaboration of Claudine Kaufmann, 'Koenigsmark, Journal d'une Restauration', in *Léonce Perret*, ed. Bernard Bastide and Jean A. Gili (AFRHC, 2013), 223.

3   Bryan Senn, *Golden Horrors: An Illustrated Critical Filmography of Terror Cinema, 1931–1939* (Jefferson, NC: McFarland, 2006), 440.

4   Ginette Vincendeau, 'Hollywood Babel: The Coming of Sound and the Multiple-Language Version', in '*Film Europe' and 'Film America': Cinema,*

Commerce and Cultural Exchange, 1920–1939, ed. Andrew Higson and Richard Maltby (Exeter: University of Exeter Press, 1999), 207–24.

5   Martin Barnier, *Des Films Français Made in Hollywood, Les Versions Multiples 1929–1935* (Paris: L'Harmattan, 2005), 10–11.

6   Anon., 'Snow White Is Exempted from French Dubbing Rule', *Film Daily* (20 May 1938): 10.

7   J. B. Kaufman, *The Fairest One of All: The Making of Walt Disney's Snow White and the Seven Dwarfs* (California: The Walt Disney Family Foundation Press, 2012), 255.

8   As explained on the back of a press picture of the two men. Personal collection Greg Philip.

9   Kaufman, *The Fairest one of All*, 255.

10   *L'intransigeant*, 7 May 1938. 'Admittedly, the voices given to the legendary characters too often have Anglo-Saxon accents which are shocking.'

11   Jean Fayard, '*Blanche-Neige et les Sept Nains*', *Candide* (12 May 1938).

12   Kaufman, *The Fairest one of All*, 255.

13   The programme of the Marignan Theater which ran the film exclusively for months in Paris only mentions the English soundtrack and re-recordings of the songs by Lucienne Dugard, Ray Ventura and various British band leaders.

14   Beverly Hills, '"*Disney's Folly*" Makes History', *Liberty Magazine* (12 February 1938): 43.

15   Anon., 'Vendredi au Marignan, un très grand évènement cinématographique: Blanche Neige et les sept nains.' *Paris-midi* (4 May 1938): 6.

16   John W. Garner, 'De New York. *Blanche-Neige*. Ce qu'est la féerie de Walt Disney', *le Jour* (3 February 1938): 6.

17   Raoul d'Ast, 'Nous verrons le 6 mai au Marignan *Blanche-Neige et les sept nains*', *Liberté* (30 April 1938): 4.

18   Edmond Epardaud, 'Une parfait oeuvre d'art, une déplorable affaire commerciale: Blanche Neige', *La griffe* (11 November 1938) (Rondel collection held at the Bibliothèque des Arts et Spectacle).

19   For more details, see Greg Philip, 'The French *Snow White* premiere', 15 November 2011, http://www.alostfilm.com/2011/11/french-snow-white-premiere.html.

20   Our thanks go to Jacqueline Dana-Mounier, daughter of Jean Mounier, advertising manager for RKO France, who kept some his archives (and donated a part of them to the Cinémathèque française). She also published some documents on her website: https://www.cinema-jeanmounier.com/cinema/rko-19371939/blanche-neige/.

21   Anon., 'Cette charmante petite fille n'est autre que le 100.000ème spectateur de Blanche Neige et les sept nains que l'on a fêté, l'autre jour, au Marignan', *Le Figaro* (7 June 1938): 5.

22   A. T., 'Référendum français, *Blanche Neige* et Jean Gabin … sont d'après les directeurs le meilleur film de l'année et la vedette la plus populaire de 1938', *Le jour – Echo de Paris* (13 April 1939): 6.

23 Kaufman, *The Fairest one of All*, 257.

24 Serguei Eisenstein, *Walt Disney*, Circé, 1991.

25 Walt Disney Productions. Inter-Office Communication. Date 23 December 1935. To Don Graham from Walt. http://www.lettersofnote.com/2010/06/how-to-train-animator-by-walt-disney.html.

26 Paul Wells, *Understanding Animation* (London: Routledge, 1998), 24.

27 Siegfried Kracauer, quoted in J. P. Telotte, *Animating Space: From Mickey to WALL-E* (Lexington: University Press of Kentucky, 2010), 133.

28 Esther Leslie, 'Dumbo and Class Struggle', in *Hollywood Flatlands: Animation, Critical Theory and the Avant-Garde* (New York: Verson, 2002), 200–18.

29 'Le cinéma. *Blanche-Neige et les sept nains*' (5 May 1938) (Rondel collection held at the Bibliothèque des Arts et Spectacle).

30 Pierre Brisson, 'Chronique des spectacles. *Blanche-Neige* de Walt Disney', *le Figaro* (8 May 1938): 5.

31 François Vinneuil [Lucien Rebatet], 'L'écran de la semaine. *Blanche-Neige et les sept nains*', *l'Action française* (13 May 1938): 5.

32 Louis Chéronnet, 'Au cinéma. *Blanche-Neige et les sept nains*', *Beaux-Arts* (20 May 1938): 6.

33 Fauteuil 22, '… Dans un fauteuil. *Blanche-Neige et les sept nains*', *La Croix* (15/16 May 1938): 6.

34 'Blanche-Neige', *Notre temps* (17 June 1938): 3.

35 Robert Brasillach, 'Les Spectacles: Petite histoire du dessin animé', *la Revue Universelle* (15 May 1938) (Rondel collection held at the Bibliothèque des Arts et Spectacle).

36 Marcel Arland, *Nouvelle Revue Française* (1 October 1938): 610.

37 Etienne Fuzellier, 'De Méliès à Blanche-Neige', *Cahiers du Sud* (March 1939): 276.

38 Mezzanine, 'La semaine à l'écran. Blanche-Neige', *Marianne* (18 May 1938): 17.

39 Pierre Brisson, 'Chronique des spectacles. *Blanche-Neige* de Walt Disney', *le Figaro* (8 May 1938); and Jean Fayard, '*Blanche-Neige et les Sept Nains*', *Candide* (12 May 1938): 5.

40 Jean Cocteau, *Cahiers Jean Cocteau*, no. 10 (Paris: Gallimard, 1985), 182.

41 'Mouse and Man', *Time* (27 December 1937): 21.

42 There was, however, the exhibition at la Cinémathèque française, *Exposition du dessin animé*, from December 1945 to February 1946, not specifically about *Snow White* or Disney, but some of his characters appear on the poster next to Grimault's or Emile Cohl's. This exhibition was directly followed by another, *Emile Reynaud, inventeur du dessin animé*, which also lasted three months.

43 Sébastien Roffat, 'Disney Walter Elias', in *Dictionnaire de la pensée du cinéma*, dir. Antoine de Baecque and Philippe Chevallier (Paris: Presses Universitaires de France, Paris, 2012), 233–6.

12

From Disney to LGBTQ tales: The South-American Snow White in *Over the Rainbow: Um Livro de Contos de Fadxs*

Priscila Mana Vaz, Janderson Pereira Toth and Thaiane de Oliveira Moreira

In that cruel mirror, she began to see her deformed face and hated herself more than ever, even more than the stepmother, who had left her.

'THE RESURRECTION OF JULIA', LORELAY FOX.[1]

Across the internet one finds a huge number of memes highlighting the wealth of Disney animated characters connecting them to LGBTQ motifs. However, despite a strong popular desire to see such progressive characterizations, the Disney studio has not yet produced any animated films with a LGBTQ theme or character. However, in 2016 a book came to the attention of Disney fans titled *Over the Rainbow: Um Livro de Contos de Fadxs* (Over the Rainbow: A Book of Fairy Tales). The book, written by a group of Brazilian authors, blends famous stories such as *Snow White* and *Cinderella* together with LGBTQ motifs, answering something of a popular desire among Disney fan culture to see this engagement with identity. The book has no connection with Disney in institutional terms, but, as social media revealed, it proved to be 'a mind blow to fans'.[2]

The mixing of Disney characters with LGBTQ themes had certainly proliferated on the internet since the release of the film *Frozen* (Chris Buck and Jennifer Lee, 2013). The narrative of a princess who comes to the throne without having to marry a prince was well-received by the LGBTQ community, who saw it as an opportunity to be represented in Disney's animated movies. Due to Elsa's attitudes and actions in the film, some fans suggested that the princess could be gay.[3] This movement resulted in a lot of related content circulating on the web produced by Disney fans that began to explore LGBTQ identities through the Disney style of animation. It is in this context in which the story *A Ressurreição de Júlia – Branca de Neve* (The Resurrection of Julia – Snow White) was released. The story is the last tale in the *Over the Rainbow* book and concerns a transsexual girl by the name of Júlia. The narrative is based on a mix of references from the Brothers Grimm version as well as Disney's 1937 animated feature. However, to understand the context of *Over the Rainbow*'s release, it is first necessary to look back at the historical relationship between Disney's films and fairy tales, as well as the international release of *Snow White* outside of Hollywood.

Disney's *Snow White* first arrived in Brazil in 1938. The film had an impressive worldwide circulation and was re-released several times in the United States.[4] Due to its positive reception, Disney's feature-length animated cartoon strengthened the circulation of the *Snow White* tale across various parts of the world. In fact, the film began a tradition in the Disney studios of adapting the fairy tales to the cinema and helped to construct what would become the great empire of Disney, albeit in a sanitized and infantilized mode. Jack Zipes considers how Disney subverts the original fairy-tale stories as part of his adaptations, by bringing together moralizing questions with utopian universes. However, in doing so, Disney conquers viewers from around the world and consolidates, once and for all, animation's place in the twentieth century. The success of Disney's adaptations therefore depends not only on the tale but also on its use and distribution in society, as we will see in the Brazilian case analysed in the following paragraphs.

In *Over the Rainbow*, the creative universe that the authors inhabit is imbued with multiple references and allusions to Disney animation. One of the authors, Lorelay Fox, who also is a YouTuber, shows her references in a video produced to coincide with the release of *Over the Rainbow*. Alongside Disney's moralizing subversion of established fairy tales, its animated productions have been further re-appropriated by different audiences and in different contexts, including LGBTQ communities. The purpose of this chapter is therefore to understand how Disney's fairy-tale features have been adapted by the LGBTQ community and across Brazilian social media and to examine how online users represent LGBTQ narratives through the Disney animated style.

Fairy tales, entertainment, LGBTQ and the need to be represented

According to a study presented by GLAAD, an organization that aims to analyse how the media portrays LGBTQ communities, Disney still has multiple steps to take in the process of building a more inclusive image of LGBTQ characters.[5] Their study, called the Studio Responsibility Index Report, examines how the major film studios represent LGBTQ people/characters in their productions.[6] One of the interesting points highlighted in this study is the 'straightwashing' phenomenon, where there is the omission of a character's LGBTQ experience by turning it into heterosexual one and/or eliminating their identities or love interests. A good example of this practice is adaptations of the characters who are openly LGBTQ in comic books, yet who end up straightjacketed in heteronormative roles, such as the characters of Valkyrie and Korg in the recent Marvel adaptations of *Thor: Ragnarok* (Taika Waititi, 2017) and Ayo and Aneka in *Black Panther* (Ryan Coogler, 2018).

For Disney as a corporation, it is strategic to think of multiple markets, creating productions that are successful both in the East and in the West. An example of this differing acceptance can be detected in responses to their live-action version of *Beauty and the Beast* (Bill Condon, 2017), which featured the character LeFou, and was banned in several markets, mainly those in Asian, after the director Bill Condon declared in the premiere that the character was gay.[7] The PinkNews portal conducted an analysis suggesting that the movie *Beauty and the Beast* was heavily impaired in conservative markets compared to the release of *Spider-Man: Homecoming* (Jon Watts, 2017), for example, although the first film surpassed the latter in more liberal markets, for example, the first movie made $504 million at the US box office and the second made 'just' $278 million.[8]

According to the GLAAD survey, in 2017 Walt Disney Studios released eight films, of which only one included LGBTQ representation. The only movie that has passed on the Vito Russo Test (a kind of adaptation of the Bechdel test for the LGBTQ cause, named in honour of LGBTQ activist and filmmaker Vito Russo) was their version of *Beauty and the Beast*. The report insists that Disney historically has the worst market history when it comes to the representation of LGBTQ characterization from all the studios tracked in the report.

The adoption of policies for the insertion of LGBTQ characters is something that Disney needs to apply in its productions, in addition to the possibility of profiting from sales of products for LGBTQ consumers, a practice known as Pink Money.[9] One example of this capitalization is the sale on the official website of Mickey Mouse ears in the colours of the rainbow flag, a symbol created by Gilbert Baker and adopted by the LGBTQ community shortly before the month of LGBTQ pride. Another example of pink money capitalization is the 'Gay Days' at Disney events. These events take place every first Saturday in June and bring more than 100,000 people to Disney's theme parks and resorts annually (CLOUD, 2010). With its first edition being held in 1991, the event brings together thousands of people dressed in red shirts, a proud symbol of a non-normative presence at Disney.

It is interesting to think of this displacement of LGBTQ community representation that is often linked to Pride Parades and now, with many having children, are occupying traditional spaces of family fun, such as Disney. As much as the event brings thousands of people to the Disney theme parks, the event was not recognized officially in the Disney calendar until 2019. However, while Gay Days have long been an unofficial tradition at Disney parks in the United States, Disneyland Paris will host the company's first official LGBTQ pride event.[10] The issues presented in this chapter have as their main point the representation of LGBTQ people in literary or media works. The story chosen to be analysed in this chapter helps us reflect on these needs of public representation for certain kinds of identity. As pointed out by Fox,

> It's cool that we always look at the movies trying to see something beyond the obvious that they show. I believe that nowadays more and more drawings shows this kind of thing [representativeness]. They try to be more inclusive. They talk about various issues of gender, sexuality, even in an almost subliminal way. But who is affected, perceives the marks and identifies itself and feels happy.[11]

In this sense, it is interesting to observe how the culture of films and other works permeates consumption by linking a sense of community, belonging and sharing of affections. Fox continues that 'I think the big difference when you read fairy tales and you are the LGBTQ audience, you never really identify with those tales. You see a little boy who met the little girl and they lived happily ever after, but you want to find a little boy too. But there was never a stories like that, so we rewrote the stories.'[12]

Among the strategies to meet this need for representation, fanfictions (better known by the abbreviated forms 'fanfic' or 'fic') that are, as the name intuitively indicates, 'fictions created by fans' appear as the best alternative. These are stories that appropriate the characters and/or universe existing in an already published work (a book, an anime, a manga, a movie, a TV series and so forth) but follow a different script, created by a fan of such work and made available in online spaces.[13] As they do not depend on the original author's permission, these stories are spreading faster and faster on the internet and can give the dimension of success of a work based on the amount of fanfics it produces or inspires. One of the points in creating these fanfics is the creation of relationships that are not present in the original work. The new interweaving of characters can reconfigure the story giving new perspectives, including the creation of LGBTQ couples. Through an analysis of these materials on social media platforms (such as Twitter) and video sharing site YouTube, it is possible to identify the creation of such threads and videos, respectively, that mix Disney stories by changing the sexual orientation of characters (Figure 12.1).[14]

The launch of *Over the Rainbow* presented similarly creative possibilities for the representation of characters and the transformation of their narrative. Through a search on Twitter for the references to the book (in Portuguese), few direct mentions were found, since the name of the book is long and diffuse, but qualitatively the main observation in all the social media mentions is that of representation. Tweets mention reactions like 'Oh my god! I can't believe a just found a book that mix fairy tales and LGBTQ motifs!' and 'Over the rainbow: a book of fairy tales is a Brazilian book that mix fairy tales and real life. It was written by the LGBTQ community and it is GREEAT!'[15] The editorial decision to invite only members of the LGBTQ community to write the book made it possible to write and describe characters and stories that contained personal experiences of members of the community, providing greater connections between the characters and the author of the story.

As a starting point for the investigation of the LGBTQ themes in relation to Disney, data collection and analysis methods were developed based on social networks analysis. Such analysis marks an intersection of Sociology, Social Psychology and Anthropology, and seeks to highlight the structures which represent actors (which can be any relational entity, though in the case of this chapter, videos) and the relations between them, understood as edges that represent the interactions between nodes.[16] We next set out to go beyond the metrics offered by YouTube, such as 'likes' and dislikes of a video, to understand how networks of content related to the LGBTQ universe and Disney are formed and consolidated. We also tried to understand what types of content are being offered and what languages are involved in these productions. For these fans, Disney and fairy tales become correspondent terms as most know fairy tales through their adaptation by the Disney studio into animated features.

To acquire the data needed, we used YouTube Data Tools, a collection of tools for extracting data from YouTube via API (v3), created by Bernhard Rieder of the University of Amsterdam and researcher of the Digital Methods Initiative. The first phase consisted of a survey of the 175 videos considered most relevant by the algorithm of YouTube itself from the search for the terms 'Disney' and 'LGBT'. Based on this data, we used the Video

FIGURE 12.1 Disney animated characters as gay couples created by fans.

Network tool with a 0-depth search depth to understand the formation of connections made by YouTube between relevant videos and videos linked through the 'recommended videos' functionality of these videos. This survey also allowed the identification of video communities from the profiles used, offering insights concerning the circulation of content related to the theme in different networks of authority. By using algorithms that identified the connectivity of the clusters, we identified four communities (or clusters) of videos. To better understand these clusters, we categorized them from behaviours and profiles, which Fábio Malini presents as one of the aspects of network perspectivism.[17] For grid perspectivism, this aspect allows us to analyse the clusters from the point of view based on affinity relations, 'which analyzed separately operate discourses, images, social bonds and internal discussions'.[18] Thus, clusters were identified by their profile strengths and/or behaviours (Figure 12.2).

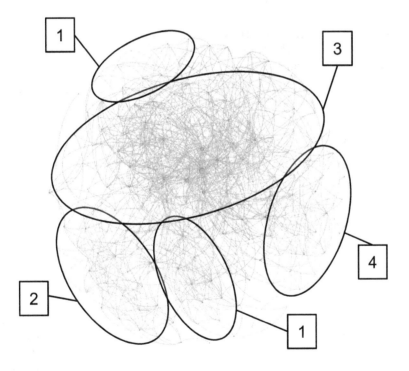

FIGURE 12.2 Cluster from YouTube data collection from 175 videos related to the terms 'Disney' and 'LGBT'.

Although the search parameters were set to Portuguese, the largest cluster, labelled as cluster 3, and with ninety-two videos, is formed by videos in English. This cluster has the most viewed and most central videos on the network.

Title	Channel	Views Count
10 Famous People Who Recently Came Out	TheTalko	5.006.525
10 Gay Characters on Disney Channel and in Disney Movies	TheTalko	4.119.437
10 Disney Channel Stars Who EMBARRASSED Disney	TheTalko	2.891.505
Did Disney Cut a Gay Kiss from Descendants 2?	Clevver News	2.384.588
6 Disney Stars You Didn't Know Are GAY!	Celebrity Statz	1.857.180

The fourth cluster comprises expressions of affection and LGBTQ community themes, such as drag queens presentations and wedding requests, most of which have taken place during Gays Days at Disney.

Title	Channel	Views Count
Beauty and the Beat Boots by Todrick Hall	todrickhall	9.550.594
Patrick and Gavin's Disney World Proposal	Gavin&Patrick	705.888
GAY DAYS! – Jun 1	shep689	180.982
One Magical Weekend 2018 – LGBTQ Pride at Walt Disney World!	One Magical Weekend	170.914
Disney World Gay Proposal Streamed on Facebook Live	Gregory Gaige	156.838

Cluster 2 represents the videos made mostly in Portuguese. At the top of this in terms of number of views is a video about a Brazilian pastor and his views on Disney, released by the Brazilian Felipe Neto channel, one of the most popular YouTubers in the world according to the list of subscribers published by *Watchin' Today*.[19] The contents are very close to that represented in cluster 3, with the creation of lists of LGBTQ characters.

Title	Channel	Views Count
DISNEY E O SILAS MALAFAIA [+13]	Felipe Neto	3.250.252
In a Heartbeat – A Film by Beth David and Esteban Bravo	TheEllenShow	991.144
A Evolução e a Polêmica das Princesas da Disney	imaginago	732.238
5 PERSONAGENS GAYS EM FILMES DA DISNEY	Teoria TV	259.715
CASAIS NÃO OFICIAIS DA DISNEY! 🌈	Jessica Ballut	225.567

The first clusters at the top and bottom present an informational dynamic similar to the second cluster, changing only the language, in this case, to Spanish. In this analysis it is possible to observe how the lack of non-normative representation causes fans to find ways to represent themselves in stories without becoming official content producers.

Title	Channel	Views Count
7 Personajes Gays en Películas de Disney	Luan Palomera	1.440.585
10 famosos que recientemente SALIERON DEL CLOSET	nalisita	1.307.905
DISNEY CHANNEL PRESENTA a SU PRIMER PERSONAJE ABIERTAMENTE 64Y en UNA SERIE	Chicas Cosmo	1.070.301
HOMOSEXUALIDAD EN DISNEY	De Película ATV	1.026.365
Disney Channel Censura Escena Gay en Descendientes 2	NeiterAll	796.551

Disney's disinclination to properly represent this community of its consumers results in them coming together to build their own venues and events, such as the Gay Days at Disney. However, this also causes a lack of legitimacy in the company to create products using LGBTQ symbols without being questioned by its exclusionary trading strategies.

'The Resurrection of Júlia' and Disney's Snow White

A new version of the Snow White tale appeared in Brazil in 2016, with an idea that is, perhaps, far from traditional. In 'The Resurrection of Júlia' tale from *Over the Rainbow*, Snow White is now named Julia, a transgender girl, who is abandoned by her stepmother a day before her sex change surgery. After being lost in the streets (the modern forest), she is welcomed by a group of seven transsexual characters. The insertion of LGBTQ representation into the story brings a dimension to the narrative that helps to maintain similarities with the Disney version, but places the question of identity into a space not previously explored by Disney. This adaptation also does not engage with Snow White as told by the Brothers Grimm, the version that inspired Disney's cel-animated feature.

The tale begins by presenting Júlia's stepmother Lorena and her obsession with her body and her beauty. With a very descriptive approach, we are led to the ritual of beauty that she undertakes every night. Her body, not so young, shows her age and the problems caused by her smoking addiction. Lorena is 47 years and has to take care of her stepdaughter, but does not like the girl. Lorena wakes up in a very bad mood, looks at herself in the mirror and sees her face getting older every day. As the time goes by and Júlia grows closer to adulthood, her stepmother begins to despise her even more. She looks at the girl's beauty and becomes fixated on her own wrinkled face. Both the Disney version and 'The Resurrection of Júlia' share a similar focus on the envy that the stepmothers feel for the girls. In the latter, the motivation for the stepmother to send the girl away is the same as in Disney's animated version: she hates the fact that the young girl is more beautiful than her.

The changes in the stories begin when we examine the main characters. Despite the name of the films, the Evil Queen holds a more prominent place in the narrative than Snow White, who is presented with no great emphasis in her personality or backstory. We only met a dreamy girl who sings while doing her chores, while a Prince sings about his love for the character without complication. The sequence showing the Prince's arrival is depicted as rapid, showing too the anger of the Evil Queen. From this point the Queen decides to have Snow White killed. Despite the Queen's central place in the narrative, the fairy-tale structure as proposed by Vladimir Propp shows how Snow White remains the protagonist.[20]

The Queen is the villain of the story and remains in opposition to Snow White. She occupies an important role into the narrative, motivating the princess to become a heroine. As Zipes argues,

> In contrast to the humble characters, the villains are those who use words and power intentionally to exploit, control, transfix, incarcerate, and

destroy for their own benefit. They have no respect or consideration for nature and other human beings, and they actually seek to abuse magic by preventing change and causing everything to be transfixed according to their interests.[21]

In the next sequence, the Evil Queen asks one of her employees – The Huntsman – to take Snow White into the forest to meet her death. The Queen demonstrates 'no respect for other humans', asking The Hunter to bring Snow's heart in a box.[22] At this moment she consolidates herself as a villain.

However, in 'The Resurrection of Júlia', the duality between the girl and her stepmother is not what guides the narrative. The tale is more concerned with Júlia's journey to find herself than any battle with a villain. From this perspective, the story begins to connect more directly and effectively with LGBTQ themes. When the tale presents Júlia, about nine pages of the story are used just to introduce the girl and her backstory. We are introduced to a young rich girl who attended the best schools. She begins to find (and identify) herself as different when she travels with her father to Disneyland. Here is the first direct reference to the Disney universe. The girl meets the Disney Princess and returns to her school telling her friends that she wants to be a princess. From this moment on, we (and Júlia) understand her desire to be a transgender girl. Júlia is impacted because of the bullying she suffers, but at her home, her mother and father accept her as she is. However, when her parents die, she is forced to live with her stepmother.

For Tzvetan Todorov a fairy tale is a story where 'the hero has a superiority over the reader and the laws of nature'.[23] In this sense, 'The Resurrection of Júlia' does not qualify outright as a fairy tale. But as Zipes tells us of such stories,

> It is the transgression that makes the tale exciting; it is the possibility of transformation that gives hope to the teller and listener of a tale. Inevitably in the course of action there will be a significant or signifying encounter. Depending on the situation, the protagonist will meet either enemies or friends.[24]

Given Zipes's definition and emphasis on the 'possibility of transformation' and despite the absence of magic in the narrative, 'The Resurrection of Júlia' can be understood as much a fairy tale as Disney's own adaptation of *Snow White*. This is because what the story presents next is a complete change in Júlia's life. From this point on, Júlia is poisoned by her stepmother (as in Disney's version) but with drugs, not with an apple laced with poison, and she is abandoned on the streets. In Disney's telling of the tale, the poisoning of Snow White occurs only at the end of the narrative and leads to the 'happy ending' and her awakening by the Prince. By comparison, Júlia suffers throughout as she is poisoned twice, and her life is in danger during almost the entire tale.

In Disney's version, and after the hunter refuses to kill Snow White, she lives in the forest where she meets the seven dwarfs. Júlia, instead, experiences very difficult situations, including living on the streets, until she gets help. But again, there are similarities between the two representations. Both girls spend some time alone and lost. In Disney's film, Snow White is scared by the forest animals, while Júlia is scared about being alone in a different, foreign city. At this point, it is clear that Disney's adaptation is designed more for children, because the animals are welcoming and become Snow White's friends. 'The Resurrection of Júlia', however, develops more adult themes in a story that relies on the dangers of living on the street.

After eleven pages describing Júlia's difficulties, the book brings to us to the 'Seven Dwarfs': the transsexual girls who welcome Júlia to live with them. The LGBTQ community corresponds to the dwarves as they are framed as a marginalized group. It is only after meeting the girls that Júlia begins her journey towards her 'happy ending'.

The 'happy endings' are very different in the two versions discussed here. *Snow White*'s ending is satisfactory because she meets a handsome Prince who saves her life with a kiss of true love. As such, this happy ending is centred on a heterosexual union. In Júlia's tale, the character's happy ending is also motivated by a male figure, and she also get married. But in this case, her own individual happiness becomes the focus. Júlia achieves her happy ending by meeting a man (a doctor) who performs her sex change surgery. They then fall in love and marry. Júlia then returns home and her stepmother is arrested. Only at the end of the tale do we learn that Lorena wanted to kill Júlia because of her homophobic behaviour towards her own stepdaughter.

Conclusion

The issue of representation is vital for social groups that are historically and structurally marginalized in society. Given their international influence, the Disney studio can play a pivotal role in building and giving a voice to these otherwise invisible parts of society. However, the LGBTQ audience is not represented in Disney's productions, opening the possibility for creating parallel narratives (including in fanfiction) in which alternative and non-normative sexuality, as well as themes of identity, can be explored. The release of *Over the Rainbow* in 2016 – and in particular its tale 'The Ressurrection of Júlia' – quickly drew the attention of Disney LGBTQ's fans and communities, taking on Disney's *Snow White* not only by borrowing its narrative structure but also by exposing the need for greater representation of the minority audiences. 'The Resurrection of Júlia' functions successfully as a contemporary actualization of Disney's film, responding to the LGBTQ audience and their desire to be visibly represented. Despite an unofficial and unlicensed Disney version, the story was positively championed by non-normative audiences for taking the familiar story and providing an alternative vision of love, romance and identity. As one YouTuber who presents himself as gay commented, 'I had never read a book with transvestites. And I think this is very, very important, that every transvestite community can get book once at least and see themselves represented there, even if just in a fairy tale, to see their story being told.'[25]

Despite these positive shifts towards LGBTQ representation, some questions still remain: How much longer will big companies like Disney need to incorporate the plurality of identity we see in our society? When will these companies realize the power of visibility, and that being represented makes a difference to those who watch and enjoy their products? Society has already changed. Now it is time for the dominant narratives to change too.

Notes

1 'Nesse espelho cruel, começou a enxergar sua face deformada e se odiou mais do que nunca, mais até mesmo do que a madrasta, que a havia deixado'. A Ressurreição de Júlia (Branca de Neve), Lorelay Fox.

2 Comment extracted from Twitter about the book launch.

3 https://www.gaystarnews.com/article/14-disney-characters-you-had-no-idea-were-gay051013/#gs.sm8zgt and https://www.buzzfeed.com/br/alisoncaporimo/o-pessoal-no-twitter-esta-pedindo-para-a-disney-da. Accessed 30 August 2020.

4 According to the website IMDB.com, the movie has earned more than $415 million around the world.

5 Gay and Lesbian Alliance Against Defamation.

6 https://www.glaad.org/sri/2018/walt-disney-studios. Accessed 30 August 2020.

7 https://www.todayonline.com/singapore/gay-moment-beauty-and-beast-totally-unnecessary-national-council-churches. Accessed 30 August 2020.

8 https://www.pinknews.co.uk/2018/04/24/avengers-infinity-war-disney-rainbow-ears-mickey-blockbusters/. Accessed 30 August 2020.

9 The amount of money earned by the companies from the LGBTQ consumption.

10 Tim Fitzsimons, 'Magical Pride: Disney to host its first official LGBTQ pride event this year', NBC News (31 January 2019). Available at https://www.nbcnews.com/feature/nbc-out/magical-pride-disney-host-its-first-official-lgbtq-pride-event-n965396. Accessed 30 August 2020.

11 Repensando filmes Disney – com Lorelay Fox, https://www.youtube.com/watch?v=uXaWYbu0Rg8.

12 Como você imagina seu contos de fadas?, https://www.youtube.com/watch?v=PgaMqEwIoiQ&t=723s.

13 Beatriz D'Oliveira and Marina Romanelli. 'Fanfictions e o Papel do Fã na Era da Transmídia', *Revista Hipertexto* 3, no. 1 (January/June) (2013): 1–14.

14 https://twitter.com/harleivy/status/952252485195968512.

15 https://twitter.com/ltdramababy/status/1041097024710561792 and https://twitter.com/paolastefanyy/status/959197951909335044.

16 Linton C. Freeman, 'Some Antecedents of Social Network Analysis', *Connections* 19, no. 1 (1996): 39–42.

17 Fábio Malini, *Um método perspectivista de análise de redes sociais: cartografando topologias e temporalidades em rede.* XXV Encontro Anual da Compós, Universidade Federal de Goiás, Goiânia, 2016.

18 'que analisados separadamente operam discursos, imagens, laços sociais e discussões internas' (Malini, *Um método perspectivista de análise de redes sociais*, 12).

19 https://watchin.today/charts/channel/top. Accessed 30 August 2020.

20 Vladimir Propp, *Morphology of the Folktale* (Bloomington: Indiana University, 1958).

21 Jack Zipes, *Why Fairy Tales Stick: The Evolution and Relevance of a Genre* (New York: Routledge, 2006), 51.

22 Ibid.

23 Tzvetan Todorov, *Introduction à la littérature fantastique* (Paris: Éditions du Seuil, 1970), 15.

24 Jack Zipes, *Why fairy tales stick*, 49.

25 Contos de fadas LGBTQ | Over the rainbow | Vitor Martins, https://www.youtube.com/watch?v=C_bREOgkuUQ.

13

Snow White's censors: The non-domestic reception and censorship of *Snow White and the Seven Dwarfs* with a case study on the Low Countries

Daniël Biltereyst

The popularity of "Snow White" is certainly a reflection of the better tastes and desires of American audiences.[1]

Although *Snow White and the Seven Dwarfs* (David Hand, 1937) is now conceived as a landmark movie in the history of modern children's cultural industry and its exploitation of childhood innocence, it remains remarkable to observe how Walt Disney's first feature-length cartoon did not receive the unproblematic reception the company had hoped for at the time of its release.[2] Whereas *Snow White* did not encounter real problems in getting a seal of approval from Hollywood's internal censorship system, after which it became an immediate international box-office hit, the feature's release outside the United States was not completely trouble-free, especially among foreign censorship boards.

This chapter examines *Snow White*'s non-domestic reception and censorship by concentrating on a case study around its censorial problems and obstacles in Belgium and the Netherlands, aka the Low Countries. As Annette Kuhn argued in her analysis of the British reception of the movie, *Snow White* faced the problem that 'it was seen as both a frightening film and as a film suitable for children'.[3] In Britain, but also in the Low Countries and in other foreign territories, local censorship boards struggled with the possible impact of particular scenes on children's imagination, in particular those where Snow White flees into the forest that produces monstrous trees, or where the Queen transforms into a witch. Some censorship boards like those in Belgium, Britain and the Netherlands saw the movie as dangerous and even nightmarish for children so that they imposed age restrictions, in some cases even combined with cuts in order to allow children to see Disney's intensively hyped cinematic fairy tale.[4]

This chapter starts with a short introduction to *Snow White*'s preliminary censorial experiences with Hollywood's Production Code Administration (PCA, 1934–68), an organization that did its best to consolidate all of the possible censorship problems from the United State and the rest of the world, so that American films could play everywhere. Before zooming in on the movie's censorship in the Low Countries, I examine what happened in Britain and in a few other European countries where the movie was shown before being released in Belgium and the Netherlands. Besides being a comparative study on cross-national/cultural differences in the reception and censorship of the movie, this chapter uses *Snow White* as a case study in the context of wider discussions around Hollywood's hegemony and its conflictual relationship with Europe. One of the hypotheses, which is part of a larger project on the historical reception and censorship of US movies in the old continent, is that many European censors were probably less tolerant, liberal or progressive than the ones in the United States – hence reconceptualizing common knowledge on US and Hollywood's internal censorship as being paternalist, conservative or more restrictive than their European counterparts.

'I cannot see (…) any censorable parts in the picture'

As with all motion pictures produced by members of the Motion Picture Producers & Distributors of America (MPPDA), Walt Disney Productions submitted the project to produce a feature cartoon based on Grimms' fairy tale to the PCA.[5] PCA, often referred to as the Breen Office (after its head, Joseph I. Breen), operated as the internal board for members of the MPPDA, which required producers and filmmakers to submit their projects for approval, often including the supervision of treatments, detailed screenplays with dialogue and the final film, eventually leading to the PCA's seal.[6] The first traces of the correspondence between Disney and the PCA goes back to early March 1936, when the script was not yet completed, but when the company suggested to 'spend a few moments with Walt discussing the picture from the censorship angle'.[7] Although *Snow White* was presented by William E. Garity from the Disney company as 'an experiment on our part', he argued that he could not see 'any censorable parts in the picture'.[8]

Looking at the correspondence in the PCA file, which is kept in the Margaret Herrick Library, Los Angeles, *Snow White* was a relatively easy project to be accepted by the PCA. In early November 1937, John Rose of the Walt Disney Productions' story department sent the synopsis and dialogue script of the movie to the administration in order to obtain a temporary approval certificate.[9] In his letter to Walt Disney a few days later, Breen answered that he was happy to report that after reading the script, the PCA was convinced the story complied with the provisions of Hollywood's internal censorship system, and that Disney's feature cartoon 'should encounter no reasonable censorship difficulties'.[10] Whereas many Hollywood pictures, which were submitted to the PCA in order to receive its seal, had encountered several difficulties, *Snow White*'s censorship history was a swift and easy one, resulting in a certificate of approval issued on 14 December 1937.

One week later, on 21 December, *Snow White* premiered at the Carthay Circle Theatre in Los Angeles, then in New York where it broke all popularity records. In his memoirs, the head of the MPPDA Will H. Hays looked back at the New York premiere as an unforgettable event, praising Disney's *Snow White* as a great 'tribute to the spirit of the American people', noting:

> As *Snow White* spread like wildfire across the screens of the nation it hung up records that were as fantastic as the picture itself. Railroads ran special excursions; early daily openings in city theatres were ordered; police had to be called to prevent stampedes; in Tennessee, the governor led a parade from the State House to the theatre. This response was perhaps as great a tribute to the spirit of the American people as to the genius of Walt Disney.[11]

Snow White's general release in February 1938, and its unprecedented popularity in the United States in the months to follow, inspired more representatives from the industry to think about the movie as reflecting quintessential American tastes and values. In a letter to Breen in early February 1938, the novelist, producer and screenwriter Val Lewton of Selznick International Pictures described Disney's first feature-length animated film as 'a reflection of the better tastes and desires of American audiences'.[12] In the meantime, *Snow White* was ready to be released abroad, with the British market the first to be conquered.

'They are more easily upset by fairy stories than their "tougher" American cousins'[13]

The first major non-domestic market where Disney's cartoon feature was to be released was Britain, where *Snow White* premiered on 24 February 1938 in the New Gallery cinema in London. In her sophisticated analysis of the British reception of Disney's picture, Kuhn describes *Snow White*'s release and subsequent success as a unique, remarkable and highly memorable event, one that coincided 'with a moment of change in Britain's cinema culture'.[14] According to Kuhn, the film arrived at a time when discourses on cinema and its audiences were undergoing significant shifts, with, in this case, unprecedented media coverage and wider discussions on consumerism, horror films and the impact of cinema on children. A key trigger for these discussions was the decision by the British Board of Film Censors (BBFC), on 14 January 1938, to give the film an adult rating (A certificate) so that under 16s needed to be accompanied by an adult. This decision understandably did not please Disney and its UK distributor, RKO Radio Pictures, who had hoped for an unrestricted all-audience category. The BBFC's A certificate prompted a debate in the British press on cinema and the question 'on how far children should be protected from terror'.[15]

In his memoirs on his experiences as a BBFC examiner, chief film censor and later secretary, John Trevelyan referred to the British censors' troubles with *Snow White*. Being warned by parents who had told that their children were scared by the witch and some other scenes in the movie, Trevelyan testified that the BBFC 'had anticipated this and for this reason had given the film an "A" certificate in order to convey a warning'.[16] Upon seeing the movie, the Board felt that the dark forest scenes and those with the old witch were too frightening for children.

It remains unclear whether these censorial problems added an extra layer to the hype around *Snow White*, but one of the results of the public discussions in the press was that many local authorities ignored the BBFC's recommendation and gave the picture an all-audience 'U' category (universal).[17] *Snow White*'s censorial obstacles in Britain obviously also troubled Disney and the PCA, which closely tried to ensure a swift release of the picture. This was, for instance, the case in the beginning of March 1938 when Breen himself wrote a letter to Mary W. Burd, who had dealt with *Snow White*'s overseas censorial troubles in a column which was published in a magazine for the Delphian Society, which promoted education of women in the United States. In her 'March Thoughts', Burd explicitly referred to the BBFC's decision:

Another news-item from Britain which may surprise most readers is that no British child under sixteen is to be admitted to cinema houses showing *Snow White and the Seven Dwarfs*, unless accompanied by an adult. The reason for this ban is that the film censors think the picture will give children the nightmare. English young folk are unused to excitement, so that, as one British paper says, 'they are more easily upset by fairy tales than their "tougher" American cousins.'[18]

Breen was far from interested in any cross-cultural difference in American and British children's psyche. What troubled the PCA chief was that this information on the British censors' reservations and difficulties with *Snow White* could awaken more conservative forces in the United States. In fact, Breen had been approached with questions on the British censorship problems by Mary Hearn from the powerful Catholic National Legion of Decency (LoD), who argued that 'it is our duty to foster and encourage the production of good pictures, as it is our duty to condemn bad ones'.[19] Hoping that this might calm down the discussion on *Snow White*, Breen answered Hearn's question on the British 'ban' by (mis)informing her about the fact that 'the picture has been given a "U" Certificate in England, which means that it may be shown universally'.[20]

Whereas the movie continued to break all-time records in the United States, Disney prepared the movie's international release with the help of the PCA. One of the tasks of the MPPDA's censorship administration and moral arbiter was to monitor the reception and censorship of the members' movies in foreign territories. In some of those markets the picture had to be cut, like in Australia, where one deletion was demanded in order to allow children to watch the movie, but in other territories *Snow White* passed without any significant problem.[21] This was the case in one of the biggest foreign markets for Hollywood films, France, where a French dubbed version of the movie was made and where it enjoyed a broad release. Disney's feature cartoon didn't encounter any problems with France's state censor, so that *Blanche Neige et les Sept Nains* premiered on 6 May 1938 in Paris, attracting wide press coverage. In 1938 *Snow White* became the big money maker of American films in France, as one of the internal PCA reports mentions, and it was one of the few films which is 'expected to gross more than the best French film' (see Chapter 11 in this volume).[22]

La Grande Muette's scissors

It was the same French dubbed version of *Snow White and the Seven Dwarfs* that was used by RKO Radio Films S.A.B., the Belgian branch of RKO Radio Pictures, for the Kingdom of Belgium. Given the small size (8 million inhabitants) and the bilingual character of its film market (French and

Dutch), it was common practice to distribute French versions of Hollywood pictures in Belgium, especially in the multilingual capital Brussels and in the French-speaking south. The first step in RKO's release scheme was to submit the movie to the Belgian Board of Film Control (BeBFC) in order to try to attract a large, family-oriented audience.

In terms of film censorship, Belgium was one of the few countries in the world without a system of obligatory film control.[23] This policy was inspired by the liberal Belgian Constitution of 1831, which explicitly forbids any form of censorship. Confronted with criticism on cinema's impact on children, however, the Belgian Parliament had adopted after the Great War a film control law which stated that, in principle, all films were forbidden for children under 16 years old, unless the film had been approved by a film control board. One of the implications of this September 1920 law was that no adult film censorship was ever installed in the country and that many controversial movies like revolutionary Soviet pictures could in principle be released for adults and adolescents above 16 years.[24] When distributors wanted to attract children and families for their movies, however, they needed to submit their pictures before the board, which mainly consisted of representatives of the judicial system, the film industry, politicians and (high) school teachers and pedagogues. One option for the BeBFC was to forbid a film for children under 16 ('children not allowed', 'enfants non admis'/'kinderen niet toegelaten') on the basis of a list of criteria which explicitly aimed at protecting children (political censorship was explicitly forbidden). The other option for the members of the BeBFC was to grant a 'children allowed' certificate ('enfants admis'/'kinderen toegelaten'). In the latter case the board could eventually make suggestions to the distributor for cuts to be made in the movie – a practice that the board often applied (around one-third of the movies controlled by the BeBFC were subjected to cuts in the 1930s). It was up to the distributor then to either follow this advice or not. But economic concerns cast a shadow over Belgium's liberal conception of film regulation, since fear of income loss made distributors comply with almost any cut the board asked for.[25]

This was exactly what happened during the control board meeting of 7 May 1938 (one day after the Parisian premiere), when the BeBFC stated that *Snow White* contained too many frightening scenes of terror. In order to be able to receive a 'children allowed' seal the board requested five cuts to be made by RKO. Although the official report of the board meeting (Figure 13.1) is quite short, it mentions that one of the five members of the board (probably a representative of the local film industry) had some hesitations about requesting cuts, but the board finally decided unanimously about where to cut the movie in order to be allowed for children. The board minutes state that the requested deletions were imposed due to 'the fairy-tale scenes which could upset younger children'.[26]

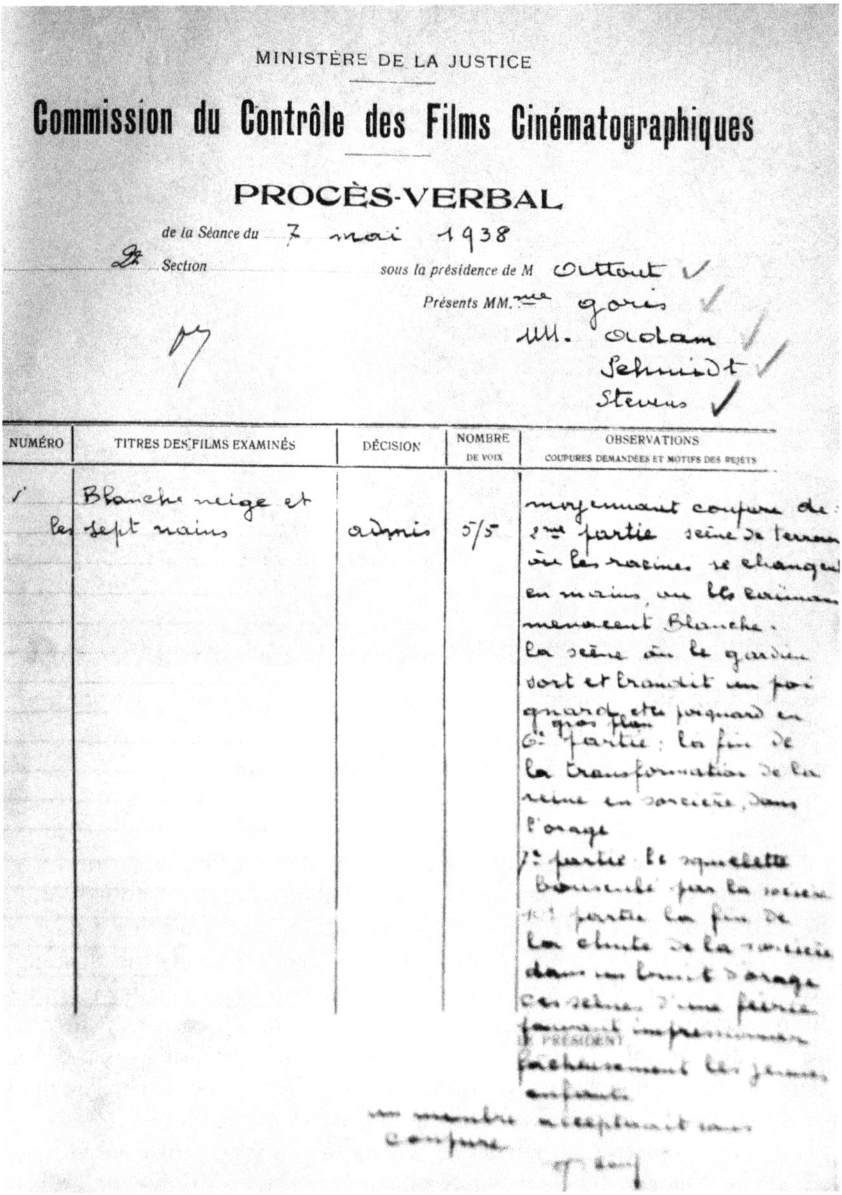

MINISTÈRE DE LA JUSTICE

Commission du Contrôle des Films Cinématographiques

PROCÈS-VERBAL

de la Séance du 7 mai 1938

2e *Section* *sous la présidence de M* Ottout ✓

*Présents MM.*mes Goris ✓

MM. Adam ✓

Schmidt ✓

Stevens ✓

NUMÉRO	TITRES DES FILMS EXAMINÉS	DÉCISION	NOMBRE DE VOIX	OBSERVATIONS COUPURES DEMANDÉES ET MOTIFS DES REJETS
1	Blanche neige et les sept nains	admis	5/5	moyennant coupure de: 2me partie scène de terreur où les racines se changent en mains, où les animaux menacent Blanche. La scène où le gardien sort et brandit un poignard, cette poignard en gros plan 6e partie: la fin de la transformation de la reine en sorcière, dans l'orage 7e partie le squelette bousculé par la reine. 8e partie la fin de la chute de la sorcière dans un bruit d'orage. Ces scènes d'une féerie pourront impressionner fâcheusement les jeunes enfants.

LE PRÉSIDENT

un membre acceptant sans coupure.

FIGURE 13.1 Procès-Verbal (minutes) of the Belgian Board of Film Control meeting, 7 May 1938, on *Blanche Neige et les Sept Nains.*

Source: Blanche Neige et les Sept Nains file, Archive of the BeBFC, State Archives of Belgium.

FIGURE 13.2 Second cut in the Belgian print of *Blanche Neige et les Sept Nains* with the hunter's dagger in close-up.

Source: Snow White and the Seven Dwarfs, Disney Company.

  According to the minutes, the first cut referred to the long 'scene of terror where branches change into hands and caimans threaten Snow White'. The second one shortened the scene where the hunter is waving a dagger (Figure 13.2), but the BeBFC minutes specify that 'especially the close-up' had to be deleted. The third cut, which was also controversial in other countries, related to the end of the scene where the queen is transformed into a witch during the storm, whereas the fourth deletion was the one where the skeleton in the prison is mashed together by the witch. The final one is the fall of the witch in the storm at the end of the film.[27]

  It is not completely clear whether it was this heavily shortened version of *Blanche Neige et les Sept Nains* which was shown during the official Brussels premiere (a major gala event in one of the most prestigious Brussels film palaces) on 19 May 1938. But, although the newspapers and movie magazines closely followed the movie already before the Belgian release, the censorial problems with the BeBFC were never mentioned. This fully corresponded with the BeBFC's general policy not to communicate about suggested cuttings, whereas for distributors, who were mainly interested in getting the all-audience certificate, any public information about cuts could be harmful for their commercial and artistic credibility. The BeBFC acting as 'la grande muette' (the big silent) and imposing cuts, however, didn't seem to harm the commercial success and popularity of *Snow White* in Belgium where the movie also secured a big audience, was highly promoted and became an exclusive event. After its Brussels premiere, *Snow White* was released on several copies and subsequently shown for many months in the biggest first-run film palaces in the major cities (Brussels, Antwerp, Liège and Ghent, see Figure 13.3), followed by screenings in most of the other minor cities.[28]

In hindsight, one might argue that the requested deletions did not prevent the movie becoming a major blockbuster in 1938 and into 1939, and also later when *Snow White* was re-released. Given that newspapers and magazines did not mention the cuts and the movie's mutilation in a handful of key scenes, the Belgian censors were perhaps quite efficient in taking the sting out of a picture that they considered too frightening for children. Besides objections related to artistic integrity, however, it is clear that the deleted scenes significantly weakened the picture's narrative strength and affective tensions. Some of these cuts also heavily modified Disney's art of animation and his worldview in general. An example here is the sequence of the anthropomorphized forest, heavily cut in the Belgian version; the cut not only destroyed one of the most impressive parts of the movie, it also weakened Disney's view upon wild nature as fundamentally ambiguous.[29]

The censors' dilemma with a gruesome cinematic masterpiece

In the Netherlands, newspapers also closely followed the international hype around *Snow White*. Between the Los Angeles premiere and the Dutch release in November 1938 many hundreds of articles appeared in the Dutch press. The British, French and Belgian releases were closely followed, often with the question of when the movie would finally be shown in the Netherlands. The British censorship troubles were also widely covered, with articles on how 'England censors fairy tales'.[30] In early March 1938, newspapers also started to report on the reasons why Dutch audiences were so late to have the opportunity to see the movie, noting that the making of a Dutch version of *Snow White and the Seven Dwarfs* (as *Sneeuwwitje en de Zeven Dwergen*) was a difficult and costly enterprise that took several months to be completed.

Two weeks before the Dutch version's release on Armistice Day (11 November 1938) the Dutch branch of RKO in Amsterdam, RKO Films NV,

FIGURE 13.3 *Blanche Neige et les Sept Nains* shown in the most prestigious film palace in Ghent, Cinema Capitole, with a clear indication of 'children allowed' ('enfants admis').

Source: Sofexim-Cinex Archive, State Archives of Belgium.

finally submitted the picture to the Dutch censorship board, the *Centrale Commissie voor de Filmkeuring* (CCF). In the Netherlands, censorship was launched in 1928 and was an obligatory system with a board consisting of representatives from different religious and ideological strands in Dutch society. Similar to the Belgium system, the Dutch CCF could impose age ratings (including a 14 years certificate), in some cases accompanied with cuts, while the distributor could appeal and ask for additional rounds of film control. Similar to the BeBFC, distributors could start negotiations with the censors, but it mostly resulted in distributors having only a minor say in this negotiation process.

Looking at *Snow White*'s censorship history in the Netherlands, it is surprising how RKO heavily invested in getting the all-audience seal. Between the first submission of the movie before the CCF on 21 October 1938 and the final decision by the board on 1 February 1939, six screenings were held before the censorship board, who mostly reconfirmed the 14 years rating and demanded cuts.[31] The first screening and discussion on October 21 resulted in the curious decision which not only imposed a 14 years limit but also recognized that *Snow White* was both 'a gruesome film' and a 'cinematic masterpiece'. The censors argued that, as a consequence, no cuts could be demanded because that would disturb the viewing experience.

RKO immediately appealed, but the censors reconfirmed their decision (24 October 1938). After accepting the trailer (85 metres, 4 November 1938) and the official release of the movie (11 November), RKO kept on resubmitting the picture in order to remove the age restriction which had now also become a topic of discussion in the press. Besides discussing the CCF's firm decision, film critics started writing about the movie's gruesome character and its possible impact on children, even before *Snow White* had been shown on Dutch screens. In one of those articles with the title 'A story for children and a film for adults' (*Haagsche Courant*, 3 November 1939), the journalist referred to the censors' dilemma:

The generation for whom the film is intended, the children under 14, will not be able to see *Snow White*. We have noticed that the decision by the CCF came as a surprise for many. Many have asked the question: why? A fairy tale is meant to be for children. ... We now have more information from the CCF about the reason for making Disney's famous cartoon inaccessible for children under 14. The answer was that the board was unanimous in its opinion that certain parts of Disney's film had to be considered so creepy and frightening for children that two things had to be faced: or to put the scissors in it and simply cut these fragments out of the film, or to make the film as a whole accessible to an audience over 14. The first option was just unimaginable because cutting into Disney's masterpiece would entail a mutilation of the work as a whole.[32]

One week later, *Sneeuwwitje* was released in most of Holland's major cities, including Amsterdam, Utrecht and The Hague, followed by Rotterdam, Leiden and Groningen (Figure 13.4). In Amsterdam, the movie was shown in cinema Nöggerath where it stayed on the programme for more than four months. According to data on the Cinema Context platform, with information on film programming for a wide selection of Dutch cities, *Snow White* was screened in the Netherlands till March 1940, just before the German invasion and the start of the Second World War in this part of Europe.[33]

On 22 November 1938, RKO tried to get a better age rating again, resubmitting a picture that they seemed to have cut by 54 metres, but, although a new commission with other members watched this version,

FIGURE 13.4 Advertising for the first screenings of *Sneeuwwitje en de Zeven Dwergen* in Cinema Metropole Palace in The Hague.

Source: Haagsche Courant, 10 November, 1938.

the CCF reconfirmed its decision due to the 'many gruesome images'. One month later, another screening was organized and the censors referred to cuts that should be made, such as the transformation of the queen into a witch and the hunter's dagger. In early February 1939 (1 February 1939), the CCF was asked to watch another version again, one which seemed to have been shortened by RKO once more, and the censors finally granted the movie an 'all-audience' certificate, on the condition that some cuts were to be made. RKO finally got what it wanted and the censors' dilemma was resolved, but the deletions needed to make the film admissible for children, however, were so extreme that a total of 100 metres of film was cut out of *Snow White*.

Censorship as negotiation, manoeuvring and power

The Low Countries, obviously, were only small pieces in Disney's European marketing and release puzzle, especially compared to Germany where the film producer and its distributor encountered a complex set of censorial, cultural and geopolitical problems of a completely different order. Although the Disney company saw Germany as a key element in its European marketing strategy, it finally failed to release *Snow White* in Nazi Germany, mainly due to the anti-Hollywood and anti-American policies at the time.[34] This relatively limited case study on comparing cross-national reception and censorship of *Snow White* at the time of its release, however, brings forward many questions. One of them relates to the different types of censorship with which a seemingly innocent cultural product might be confronted with. This chapter has not referred to internal or pre-production censorship at the time of conceiving, writing and producing the movie, when the Disney company tried to take into account, and deal with, possible future censorship problems in the different exploitation territories.[35] This kind of pre-production censorship activities also refers to negotiations with the PCA, which was not only a moral arbiter but also served as a sort of a central intelligence agency with specialized knowledge on foreign legal systems and their censorship sensitivities and strategies. From this perspective, the censorial problems that Disney encountered in the Low Countries and elsewhere may appear to be a failure for the PCA.

The case of Disney's *Snow White* also illustrates the different types, traditions and values of censorship that an American producer had to face when trying to release their film products. In their battles with all these different censorship boards, distributors like RKO often only had a quite restricted space for manoeuvring and negotiating the best possible conditions for getting their pictures in the best possible conditions on the local screens.

Snow White shows that commercial strategies were often more important than issues related to artistic integrity, respect for an author's world view or those linked to audience's experiences in terms of narrative coherence, or affects and emotions related to watching a movie.

Distributors and the PCA also needed to closely monitor changes in the boards' strategies, practices and sensitivities, as well as shifts in the wider political–economic context in which they operated. After the Second World War, *Snow White* was re-released several times again, leading to more censorship interventions which tried to keep track with changing moral and political values.[36] This did not mean, however, that *Snow White* had an unproblematic post-war re-release. In Britain, for instance, RKO resubmitted the picture before the BBFC in 1953 for a proposed re-release in 1954. After another inspection of the movie, the BBFC informed RKO that the film remained most appropriately classified at A; a U certificate could be achieved by making cuts in a few sequences (e.g., deleting sounds of screaming and sight of clutching hands during the scene with Snow White's journey through the woods; the removal of the sight of a skeleton; the deletion of the witch's screams as she falls from rocks). RKO declined the offer and instead appealed against the BBFC's decision to the various local authorities. For another re-release in 1964, the distributor received an all-audience certificate (U, 31 July 1964) only when a set of cuts were made in the movie (the scene where Snow White flees into the forest, or the queen as hag kicks over the bones of a skeleton reaching for a water jug).[37] In Belgium, in October 1973, *Snow White* was resubmitted by a new local distributor, Elan Films, who argued that 'we think that the control board will now look differently at the movie than the one who did it in 1938'. This time, the film was admitted as children allowed without cuts.[38]

This comparison between US and European censorship practices, though, brings forward more complex questions on how to interpret censorial similarities and differences across time and space. Could we argue that, based on this case study, European boards like the official state censors in the Low Countries were less tolerant than their American industrial counterparts? Were differences and shifts in censorship decisions and practices indicative of wider changes in the respective societies and their hegemonic socio-ideological and normative values? One part of the answer on these complex questions resides in examining power structures in and around those boards, with questions on who decided, why, as well as how these censorship decisions tried to keep track (or not) with wider shifts in society. Another part of the answer probably is to reject any idea of censorship practices reflecting societal values and norms at all, but rather to conceive the practice of censorship as a site of struggle and negotiation where various discourses and interests compete. Notwithstanding their differences in terms of censorship aims, practices and strategies, it is clear as well that (probably apart from the BBFC) the censorship boards examined in this case study were heavily criticized, at times even condemned and finally dismantled.[39]

Notes

1 Quote from a letter by Val Lewton (Selznick International Pictures) to Joseph Breen (Production Code Administration, hereafter PCA), 9 February 1938, *Snow White and the Seven Dwarfs* file, PCA archives, Margaret Herrick Library, Los Angeles.

2 Henry Jenkins, 'Introduction: Childhood Innocence and Other Modern Myths', in *The Children's Culture Reader*, ed. Henry Jenkins (New York: New York University Press, 1998), 1–37. See also Henry A. Giroux, *The Mouse That Roared: Disney and the End of Innocence* (Lanham, MD: Rowman and Littlefield, 2001); and Eric Smoodin, *Snow White and the Seven Dwarfs* (London: Palgrave, 2012).

3 Annette Kuhn, 'Snow White in 1930s Britain', *Journal of British Cinema and Television* 7, no. 2 (2010): 188.

4 See on the British case Kuhn, 'Snow White in 1930s Britain', 189–93.

5 Kerry Segrave, *American Films Abroad: Hollywood's Domination of the World's Movie Screens from the 1890s to the Present* (Jefferson, NC: McFarland, 1997). See also MPPDA Digital Archive, record #2353, https://mppda.flinders.edu.au/records/2353 (accessed 30 August 2020).

6 Thomas Doherty, *Hollywood's Censor: Joseph I. Breen & The Production Code Administration* (New York: Columbia University Press, 2007).

7 Letter by E. Garity (Walt Disney Corporation) to Douglas Kinnon (Association of Motion Picture Producers), 2 March 1936, *Snow White and the Seven Dwarfs* file, PCA archives, Margaret Herrick Library, Los Angeles.

8 Quote from a Letter by William E. Garity (Walt Disney Corporation) to Douglas Kinnon (Association of Motion Picture Producers), 2 March 1936, *Snow White and the Seven Dwarfs* file, PCA archives, Margaret Herrick Library, Los Angeles.

9 Letter by John Rose (Story Department, Walt Disney Corporation) to Douglas McKinnon (Production Code Administration/PCA), 1 November 1937, *Snow White and the Seven Dwarfs* file, PCA archives, Margaret Herrick Library, Los Angeles.

10 Letter by Joseph Breen (PCA) to Walt Disney (Walt Disney Corporation), 3 November 1937, *Snow White and the Seven Dwarfs* file, PCA archives, Margaret Herrick Library, Los Angeles.

11 Will H. Hays, *The Memoirs of Will H. Hays* (New York: Doubleday, 1955), 488.

12 Letter by Val Lewton (Selznick International Pictures) to Joseph Breen (PCA), 9 February 1938, *Snow White and the Seven Dwarfs* file, PCA archives, Margaret Herrick Library, Los Angeles.

13   Quote from 'March Thoughts' by Mary W. Burd (Delphian Society), March 1938, *Snow White and the Seven Dwarfs* file, PCA archives, Margaret Herrick Library, Los Angeles.

14   Kuhn, 'Snow White in 1930s Britain', 197.

15   Ibid., 186.

16   John Trevelyan, *What the Censor Saw* (London: Michael Joseph, 1973), 82.

17   On the British censorship and reception of *Snow White and the Seven Dwarfs*, see Kuhn, 'Snow White in 1930s Britain', Trevelyan, *What the Censor Saw*, 83, as well as a special file on the movie on the BBFC website, https://www.bbfc.co.uk/case-studies/snow-white-and-seven-dwarfs-1937.

18   'March Thoughts' by Mary W. Burd (Delphian Society), March 1938, *Snow White and the Seven Dwarfs* file, PCA archives, Margaret Herrick Library, Los Angeles.

19   Letter by Mary W. Hearn (National Legion of Decency) to Mary W. Burd (Delphian Society), 3 March 1938, *Snow White and the Seven Dwarfs* file, PCA archives, Margaret Herrick Library, Los Angeles.

20   Letter by J. I. Breen (PCA) to Mary W. Hearn (LoD), 7 March 1938, *Snow White and the Seven Dwarfs* file, PCA archives, Margaret Herrick Library, Los Angeles. 'Universally' underlined in the original letter.

21   The cut referred to the elimination of the 'incident of witch kicking skeleton out of the way'. See Report 15 April 1938, *Snow White and the Seven Dwarfs* file, PCA archives, Margaret Herrick Library, Los Angeles.

22   Letter by Harold L. Smith to Colonel F. L. Herron, 24 January 1939, *Snow White and the Seven Dwarfs* file, PCA archives, Margaret Herrick Library, Los Angeles.

23   Daniël Biltereyst, 'Film Censorship in a Liberal Free Market Democracy: Strategies of Film Control and Audience's Experiences of Censorship in Belgium', in *Silencing Cinema: Film Censorship around the World*, ed. Daniël Biltereyst and Roel Vande Winkel (New York: Palgrave Macmillan, 2013), 275–93.

24   See Daniël Biltereyst, '*Will We Ever See Potemkin?* The Historical Reception and Censorship of S.M. Eisenstein's *Battleship Potemkin* (1925) in Belgium, 1926–1932', *Studies in Russian and Soviet Cinema* 2, no. 1 (2008): 5–19.

25   For a case study on the Belgian censorship of the American *Tarzan* series, see Liesbet Depauw and Daniël Biltereyst, 'The Belgian Board of Film Control and the Tarzan Films, 1932–1946', *Historical Journal of Film, Radio and Television* 38, no. 1 (2018): 1–19.

26   Procès-verbal (minutes) of the BeBFC meeting of the 7th of May, 1938, *Blanche Neige et les Sept Nains* file, Archive of the BeBFC, State Archives of Belgium, Brussels.

27   For an illustration of these cuts, see Kevin Giraud, '*Blanche Neige et les Sept Nains* face à la censure', *Koregos*, http://www.koregos.org/fr/kevin-giraud-blanche-neige-et-les-sept-nains-face-a-la-censure/ (accessed 30 August 2020).

28 See for a case study on the distribution, exploitation and reception history of Disney's animated feature films in the Belgian city of Ghent between 1937 and 1982, Liesbeth Van de Vijver, 'Going to the Exclusive Show: Exhibition Strategies and Moviegoing Memories of Disney's Animated Feature Films in Ghent (1937–1982)', *European Journal of Cultural Studies* 19, no. 4 (2016): 403–18.

29 Kevin Giraud, '*Blanche Neige et les Sept Nains* face à la censure'. See also David Whitley, *The Idea of Nature in Disney Animation* (Aldershot: Ashgate, 2008).

30 'Engeland Censureert Sprookjes', *Het Vaderland* (28 February 1938): 8.

31 See *Sneeuwwitje en de Zeven Dwergen* file, Archive Centrale Commissie voor de Filmkeuring, Nationaal Archief, The Hague (file numbers F1947, F2119, F2436, G0269). See also the summaries on *Sneeuwwitje en de Zeven Dwergen* on www.cinemacontext.nl (accessed 30 August 2020).

32 'Het Sprookje van Sneeuwwitje en de Zeven Dwergen: Een verhaal voor kinderen en een film voor ouderen', *Haagsche Courant* (3 November 1939): 11.

33 See 'Programmes' for *Sneeuwwitje en de Zeven Dwergen* on www. cinemacontext.nl (accessed 30 August 2020).

34 On the German reception of *Snow White and the Seven Dwarfs* in the 1930s, see Rolf Giesen and J. P. Storm, *Animation under the Swastika: A History of Trickfilm in Nazi Germany, 1933–1945* (Jefferson, NC: McFarland, 2012); Markus Spieker, *Hollywood untern Hakenkreuz: Der amerikanische Spielfilm im Dritten Reich* (Trier: Wissenschaftlicher Verlag Trier, 1999), 123, 280, 289, 325; Dirk Alt, *Der Farbfilm marschiert!: Frühe Farbfilmverfahren und NS-Propaganda 1933–1945* (Munchen: Belleville, 2013), 193–4.

35 See Smoodin, *Snow White and the Seven Dwarfs*.

36 See Janet Wasko, *Understanding Disney: The Manufacture of Fantasy* (Cambridge: Polity, 2001); Janet Wasko, Mark Pillips and Eileen R. Meehan (eds), *Dazzled by Disney: The Global Disney Audiences Project* (London: Leicester University Press, 2001).

37 See http://www.bbfc.co.uk/releases/snow-white-and-seven-dwarfs-1937 (accessed 30 August 2020).

38 See *Blanche Neige et les Sept Nains* file, Archive of the BeBFC, State Archives of Belgium, Brussels.

39 I would like to thank Kristine Krueger, Eric Smoodin, Tomaso Subini and Roel Vande Winkel.

14

Snow White in the Spanish cultural tradition: Analysis of the contemporary audiovisual adaptations of the tale

Irene Raya Bravo and María del Mar Rubio-Hernández

Introduction – Snow White, an eternal and frontier-free tale

As one of the most popular fairy tales, *Snow White and the Seven Dwarfs* has international transcendence. Not only has it been translated into numerous languages around the world, but it has also appeared in several formats since the nineteenth century. However, since 2000, an increase in both film and television adaptations of fairy tales has served to retell this classic tales from a variety of different perspectives. In the numerous *Snow White* adaptations, formal and thematic modifications are often introduced, taking the story created by Disney in 1937 as an influential reference but altering its narrative in diverse ways. In the case of Spain, there are two contemporary versions of Snow White that participate in this trend: a film adaptation called *Blancanieves* (Pablo Berger, 2012) and a television adaptation, included as an episode of the fantasy series *Cuéntame un cuento* (Marcos Osorio Vidal,

2014). Both exhibit characteristics of the *Postmodern Fairy Tale*, since they are contemporary narratives that rewrite and revise 'classic' fairy tales.[1]

This chapter studies the connections between these two Spanish adaptations of *Snow White* and the Disney production, as well as the original Brothers Grimm fairy tale.[2] To contextualize the connections between these versions, the folk-tale tradition in Spain is explained to emphasize the many literary versions of the tale that appeared throughout the nineteenth century. The focus of this discussion will include the variant production contexts; the historical moment where the action takes place; the adding or elimination of passages or characters; the staging, production design and visual style; the similarities and differences between character personalities, their narrative arcs and roles within the story; and the structural variations that determine the end of the tale. Furthermore, the appearance of cultural topics within the Spanish adaptations will also be taken into account with the aim of studying possible aspects related to national identity.

Snow White and the folk-tale tradition in Spain

Spain has an extensive tradition of short-storytelling that goes back centuries. Such traditions refer not only to poietics (the creation of new stories) but also to the work on compilation and its derivative process of translating, adapting and versioning already existing tales, fables and legends that belong to different cultural contexts and historical moments. In fact, the country has performed a significant role in this sense. A rich flow of Eastern tales and legends was spread to the rest of Europe through Spain, since many of them date back to the millenary Indian literature and Buddhist tradition.[3] The compilation of tales began around the high Middle Ages, when fables that originated in the Eastern civilizations started to be translated into Latin or old Castilian. The first example known is *Disciplina clericalis*, written in the twelfth century by Petrus Alphonsi. The book is composed by a collection of fables and tales with moralizing goals – known at the time as *exempla* – coming from the Christian, Arabic and Jewish oral folkloric traditions, which had a relevant impact within the European context of the time due to their multicultural perspective.

The case of Fernán Caballero, one of the representatives of the literary movement called *costumbrismo*, is especially outstanding, since the name stands for the pseudonym adopted by the writer Cecilia Böhl de Faber. She focused on the recovery of the folkloric tale, moved by a folklorist spirit that was inspired by the conscientious labour of the Brothers Grimm.[4] She therefore included some traditional tales in novels like *La Gaviota* (1849) and combined them with popular poems in compilation works such as *Cuentos y poesías populares andaluzas* (1859).

Working in a different mode, Vicente Barrantes was an author who wrote his own versions, creating, in 1853, a unique version of Snow White called 'El espejo de la verdad' ('The Mirror of Truth'). Despite the fact that the tale was substantially transformed (the main character is the queen, called Teodolinda, who gives away her daughter when she is told by the mirror that the girl would be prettier than her), this version still presents several motives and elements in common with the Brothers Grimm version, such as the magic mirror.[5] One of the most interesting features about this tale is that Barrantes includes ferocious criticism against some social aspects of the period, such as the popular press (the queen gets married to a gossip columnist) and the traditional institution of marriage, considered as a fatal mistake for men, since it would bring madness. As Montserrat Amores highlights, the tale can be understood as 'mocking entertainment in which social criticism prevails', which somehow anticipates those contemporary versions that also present critiques against conservative aspects of the original tale.[6]

There are numerous versions of Snow White that can be traced across and throughout the Hispanic tradition, which might explain why they are known under a great variety of titles. Amores argues that the main character is sometimes called Blanca Flor ('White Flower'), and that there are several differences with the European version.[7] For example, in some of the adaptations, such as 'Cuento de los ladrones', compiled by J. Camarena, the dwarfs have been substituted with thieves. The work of Espinosa is especially significant in this sense, since not only does he identify thirty-eight Hispanic versions of Snow White, but he also establishes five variations of the tale.[8] In his analysis, he determines the main elements that constitute this type of story:

A. The story is about a heroine, who is pale as the snow and red as the blood.

B. Her beauty provokes the envy from her mother or stepmother.

   (B1. who might have a magic mirror which reveals who's the prettiest).

C. The mother orders some hunters or servants to bring the girl into the forest and kill her, but they take pity of her and let her live. She finally finds protection with dwarfs or thieves and stays in their house.

   C2, C3, C4. The persecutor tries to kill the heroine by getting the help of a witch or someone else with a magic object such as an apple, a comb, a corset, a ring …

D. The dwarfs or thieves put the heroine inside a crystal box. (D1. The dwarfs or thieves throw the crystal box into the sea).

E. She is found by a prince who extracts the magic object that makes her faint, and she comes back to life (sometimes, the object is extracted by a servant or someone else).

    E1. The prince marries the heroine ...

F. The prosecutor is punished.[9]

In the same way, Amores presents a detailed study of nineteenth-century versions of folkloric tales in order to highlight their influence on the literary context of the period and the interest that they generated among writers. The author catalogues the versions of popular tales in the Spanish context, establishing a chronology and following a systematic analysis for their classification. This way, she identifies numerous versions of the tale, such as 'La buena hija', 'La madrastra envidiosa' or 'Nevadita', including several Catalonian and Basque versions.[10] Her contribution is, therefore, enriching since it continues the work by authors like Espinosa or Maxime Chavalier.[11]

The existence of certain folktales – such as Snow White – and their evolution into different versions should be understood as a proof of their ties within the Hispanic tradition and their extensive diffusion in the Peninsula.[12] In fact, the relevance of this tale is not restricted to nineteenth-century literature but remains alive through different media expressions. The two versions analysed in the following pages show its continuous adaptation in the current popular culture context since the turn of the millennium, a phenomenon that ultimately alludes to the idea of hypertextuality and the plurality of readings and reinterpretations that can derive from the same text.[13]

Blancanieves (Pablo Berger, 2012)

After several decades without any presence in the big screen, 2012 was a prolific year for the adaptation of the tale *Snow White and the Seven Dwarfs*. The Spanish version by Pablo Berger, which was recognized with ten Goya awards, was released simultaneously with the two American productions about the princess.[14] Despite the fact that *Snow White and the Huntsman* (Rupert Sanders, 2012) maintains a medieval fantasy atmosphere with a gothic aesthetic style, the princess is given an epic and decisive role, whereas *Mirror Mirror* (Tarsem Singh, 2012) also represents Snow White as a fighter, but in a colourful, festive ambiance, much closer to the children's stories setting. Lucía Ugarte del Campo considers all three films as perfect cases to exemplify the multiplicity of stories that can emerge from the same tale, since they are created within different genres (the epic genre, comedy and drama-thriller) even though they originate from the same fairy-tale source.

Since 2010, numerous translations of iconic fairy tales, which are not usually aimed at young audiences, have expanded the original stories by the introduction of variations in the traditional roles, especially in the case of female representation.[15] The Spanish version is perhaps the most daring in its style, since it is filmed in black and white and is completely silent (with the exception of musical accompaniment). Furthermore, several resources from early cinema, such as intertitles, transitions with fading effects, iris shots at the start or end of scenes, as well as a certain tendency to exaggerate the actors' characterization and interpretation, are also used. These creative choices also demonstrate a stylistic fusion among German expressionism, Soviet avant-garde cinema and Hollywood styles.[16]

Blancanieves tells the story of the young Carmen, the daughter of the famous bullfighter Antonio Villalta and the famous singer Carmen de Triana, who died in childbirth. Villalta, who is unable to get over his wife's death and is physically incapable due to a fateful bullfight, seeks refuge in the care provided by a manipulative nurse called Encarna – who will take advantage of his weaknesses to keep him away from his daughter after their marriage. The stepmother's efforts do not impede the father–daughter relationship, until it is cut short when the stepmother assassinates her husband to take all his money and remove his daughter, Carmen. Even though the young lady manages to escape from the attacker sent by the stepmother, she loses her memory during the attack and is rescued by six 'bullfighter dwarfs', who belong to a travelling artists company and embrace her as one of the family's member. With them, Carmen discovers her vocation as a bullfighter, hailed by the public, under the name of Blancanieves. Her debut takes place in the same arena where her father met his fateful destiny and, although she recovers her memory, she is deceived by her stepmother, who makes her bite a poisoned apple that puts her to sleep eternally.

The use of symbolic objects such as the poisoned apple, the crystal coffin or the mirror that reinforces the stepmother's vain behaviour, works as iconic connections between the film and the classic Snow White tale. Nevertheless, the iconography is profoundly linked to the cultural tradition of *la españolada*. *La españolada* is a specific genre of the Spanish cinematography (considerably present in specific historical moments) that comprehends those films that exploit certain elements of national folklore.[17] Numerous aspects belonging to this movement are visualized in the film. The bullfighting iconography is visible and shown through the images of bullfighting arenas, brave bulls, bullfighter's outfits, the death liturgy and the celebration of two bullfights that mark the beginning and the end of the story. These images have a significant influence on both Carmencita's past and future as a bullfighter. In much the same way, the folkloric tradition is also present in the story, embodied in her mother – a copla (traditional folk music) singer – the popular dancing and the apparel (*mantilla*). The story likewise portrays the traditional sentimental relationship between the bullfighter and the folkloric singer, reproducing a typical motive in popular productions such as *El último cuplé* (Juan de Orduña, 1957), *Solo los dos* (Luis Lucia Mingarro, 1968) and *El relicario* (Rafael Gil, 1970). Another aspect that strengthens the film's ties with *la españolada* is the story's setting. From the first scenes, the action takes places in the Seville of the 1920s, although there are no historical, social or political references that connect the movie representations to the real reference. Rather, the representation of the Andalusian capital is confirmed, which is based on a long process of identification between *la españolada* and Seville that dates back to eighteenth-century popular legends and that continues during Romanticism. The consequence of said association is a metonymic process that unites the image of Seville to the image of Andalusia and, by extension, to the rest of Spain.[18]

In particular, *Blancanieves* can be located within the post-españolada, since it takes the clichés inherited from *la españolada*, combined with extra Hispanic references, in order to be freed from the universalizing timelessness of the Brothers Grimm tale.[19] The movie is historically contextualized within a creative postmodern climate in which Spanish cinema is remodelling its own topics, and it is characterized by the recycling of references, the interactivity of languages and the culture mix.[20] This postmodern approximation to the story allows the characters to perform outside the parameters of *la españolada* through alternative gender roles. For instance, a fundamental difference is introduced regarding Carmencita, since her ability as a bullfighter, a profession which has been traditionally linked to the male context, makes her role transgressive within the story. Nevertheless, Carmencita is also a traditional Snow White in the sense that she is depicted with all the features given to the classical character, being beautiful, kind and profoundly innocent, which ultimately means her downfall.

The characterization within the film more broadly is also subject to modification. A new character is included in the story: her grandmother, a strong attachment figure for Carmen during her childhood in the absence of her parents, whose death provokes the girl's movement to the family home. Another essential difference concerns the incarnation of the prince figure in the dwarf Rafita, completely in love with Carmen, who performs as her protector and support during the whole time. Jesusín is likewise identified as the grumpy dwarf, who breaks the family harmony by betraying Blancanieves's confidence trying to make her face a brave bull. However, in the same way as in Disney's animated version, he joins the rest of dwarfs to revenge the villain stepmother, who is symbolically killed by a bull. Regarding the stepmother, her relevance as a main character in the story is also justified by production motives.[21] She performs the role of an absolute villain without any nuance or humanizing features, a 'cruel and beautiful dominatrix'.[22] Not only did she try to get rid of Carmencita, but she also subjected her to a terrible childhood, more similar to Cinderella's infancy than to Snow White's. From a narrative perspective, a 'structural inversion variation' is also established.[23] The end reproduces the contrary of what is expected at the beginning of the film, since Carmen never gets to wake up from the poisoning and she is exhibited as an attraction in travelling fairs, despite Rafita's cares, who remains by her side and looks after her during her eternal sleep. Even though he tries to wake her up by kissing her, as in the Disney version, Carmen does not come back to life, and she is just able to express her pain through a furtive tear that makes this version distant from the fairy-tale happy ending.

Cuéntame un cuento: 'Blancanieves' (Iñaki Peñafiel, 2014)

Two years after Pablo Berger's film was released, a new version of the Blancanieves tale for TV was produced, this time a self-contained chapter of the miniseries *Cuéntame un cuento* and broadcast on Antena 3 Televisión, a generalist channel of the Spanish television market. *Cuéntame un cuento* is composed of five chapters that reinterpret several folk tales from a modern point of view: The Three Little Pigs, Little Red Riding Hood, The Beauty and the Beast, and Hansel and Gretel. Directed by Iñaki Peñafiel, *Blancanieves* stands as the second-most watched episode (after the release of The Three Little Pigs), achieving an audience share of 13.4 per cent, with 2,468,000 spectators.[24]

The fact that a production like this appeared on Spanish television is not unremarkable, since *Cuéntame un cuento* is a response to the adaptation of tales produced for American television, such as *Once Upon a Time* (ABC: 2011–18) or *Grimm* (NBC: 2011–17). All these programmes of tales share a common feature in their translation to the small screen, mixing present-day elements from the urban context with traditional aspects linked to folk tales. In this regard, and even though the analysed miniseries do not introduce supernatural elements, as it takes place in an urban fantasy, its atmosphere connects with the fundamental aspects of this subgenre, since it 'carefully transfigure apparatus traditionally associated with rural settings in order to adapt it to modern cities, often redesigning it to fit specific locations'.[25]

In this TV version, Blancanieves is called Blanca (meaning 'white' in Spanish), and she lives happily in a big mansion with her father, her stepmother and her stepmother's son, until Eve, the stepmother, discovers that her husband wants to divorce. In order not to lose her economic patrimony, based on a great cosmetic empire, the stepmother decides to hire a murderer to kill her husband and Blanca. Although the father is finally killed by the murderer, he takes pity on Blanca in the last moment and lets her live. Blanca loses her memory in the escape and is rescued by a group of seven thieves named with pseudonyms, who rename her as Nieves (meaning 'snow'). There are clear connections that can be established between this contemporary adaptation and some earlier Spanish versions of the tale from the nineteenth century, by recovering a unique narrative element such as the replacement of dwarfs by thieves. The girl grows up in an orphanage and, when she becomes an adult, works in a casino at the same time that she collaborates with the thieves in several frauds, until destiny reunites her with her stepbrother Diego. From that moment on, her present meets her past while she tries to rebuild her life. Once more, she becomes her stepmother's victim when she discovers Blanca's real identity.

Some iconic elements are maintained in the story, such as the apple (Blanca has a beautiful apple tree in her garden, and she is poisoned with an apple pie), as well as the mirror as an identifying object linked to the villain. However, both items are devoid of magical features since the story is developed as a plausible fiction with little trace of fantasy. Both stories do use very similar metaphors, as the Evil Queen and Eve share an obsession with maintaining power and with beauty as an inherent feature of youth, displaying narcissistic and vain personalities that are reinforced through their personal fascination with mirrors. Egoism is usually a feature given to villains in folk and fairy tales, since it is understood as a synonym of evil incarnated in the main character's opponent. Thus, the exemplary nature of tales warns against the egoism hidden under beauty, while mirrors become a recurring element to symbolize this moral.[26] However, in opposition to other adaptations, the stepmother in this version is humanized, since she is able to love, and presents a weak point in regard to her son, whose death means her real destruction.

Much of the action takes place in a specific urban place akin to Madrid, but there are not enough geographical anchors for the spectator to easily identify the nationality of the city.[27] In this sense, the television show does not include any identifying element of Spanish culture, which allows the audience to connect it with any other foreign space. The theory of cultural domination or destruction of a local cultural perspective is an appropriate frame to explain the creation of such a disconnected audiovisual product. Its neutral appearance makes the programme more accessible to the public, becoming a 'travelling narrative' that can be easily exported internationally without generating any rejection based on a cultural shock.[28] Moreover, the fact that it depicts worldwide known stories also favours its exportable dimension. Consequently, the product has turned into a very exportable format, which has resulted in its adaptation within other countries – such as the Mexican production *Érase una vez, lo que no te contaron del cuento* (Blim/Canal 5, 2017) and the American *Tell Me a Story* (CBS All Access, 2018–). However, even though the series does not settle down in any specific spatial context, it does cling to contemporaneity, since it functions as an excuse to show the less savoury aspects of modern and urban life such as criminality, prostitution and physical abuse, which are very common topics in any urban fantasy formula.[29]

The most palpable connection with the folk-tales context is the introduction of an extradiegetic narrator who tells the story as a fable, creating a strong contrast with the miniseries iconography and thriller structure that runs throughout. There are also several links with the police genre, such as the inclusion of thieves, the use of firearms, persecutions and the multiple scenes of action. While all these elements tie the story with the current times, the association with folk tales is managed through the voice-over narration. This genre mix creates a hybrid fiction, following current TV tendencies that also influence the national context.[30] This is especially significant for generalist channels in Spanish broadcast television that compete in the prime time, which traditionally require attractive products to attract a large market share.

Blancanieves and her role as a princess – as Bonachón (Happy) calls her – can be understood from a dualist perspective.[31] On the one hand, in order to adapt to contemporaneity as Nieves, she loses her innocence acting as bait in the committed frauds by consciously using her seductive and beauty charms and living her sexuality freely. This attitude makes her distant from the usually naive personality assigned to the princess. On the other, Blanca maintains certain naivety regarding her trust in others, since she does not suspect her stepmother's real intentions until she is poisoned. Blanca is the folk-tale princess' alter ego, who, in opposition to Nieves, perpetuates the crystallized image of Blancanieves as the epitome of the natural woman exempt from artifices.[32] Concerning her arch transformation, the main difference with the Disney version is Blancanieves's decision to achieve revenge against her opponents, going back home with the dwarfs to make Eve and her son face the truth and consequently breaking the traditional role of Blancanieves as an 'innocent persecuted heroine' by becoming the persecutor.[33]

The two main modifications in relation to the original text concern the representation of characters. First, the adviser-mirror is embodied in Sonia, a consultant who warns Eva about possible threats. The connection between this character and the magic object is made evident, since she is portrayed through her reflection in the mirror in most of the scenes. Second, the prince's role is split into two characters: Diego, Blancanieves's stepbrother, with whom she shares a special bond since their childhood and starts a sentimental relationship, and Bonachón, one of the thieves-dwarfs, who turns into the real emotional support for Blancanieves and is ultimately chosen by her. In opposition with other versions, loyalty and commitment are rewarded over the Prince archetype, since Bonachón differs from the prince as he is not wealthy or gallant, but he remains next to Blancanieves when her stepmother and stepbrother betray her. Their story is sealed with a kiss and an escape together, similar to the Disney movie, in that it fulfils the 'structural variation of saturation'[34] by which the expected end becomes real.

Conclusion: Blancanieves's survival in the contemporary Spanish context

Even though the characters in the two texts analysed in this chapter maintain many similarities with the classical versions, they both show (post) feminist features associated with modern times. Carmen voluntarily choses a profession usually reserved for men, and Nieves performs with initiative, assuming the role of avenger. Nevertheless, while it is true that female roles are somewhat transgressive, there are no other positive or long-lasting female characters who support the heroine, since the grandmother dies too soon in the movie and the orphanage nuns who take care of Blanca in the television series only show an incidental relevance. This noteworthy absence of female heroines seems to reinforce Bruno Bettelheim's psychological analysis about the *Snow White* tale that bases the princess' salvation on waiting for a male character – first, the dwarfs and second the prince.[35] Thus, they both would seem to consolidate the idea that it is necessary that a man rescues or takes care of women. Nonetheless, regarding Carmen's case, not even her prince is able to bring her back to life.

The fact that one of the dwarfs performs as the authentic blue prince for Snow White in both cases seems significant, not just because of the romantic interest shown in each production but because of the loyalty and support demonstrated by the characters until the end. Parallel to the reimagination of the princess role, these actualizations about the prince can be inserted in the historical conjunction regarding the development of new masculinities, in which man is not a saviour anymore but a partner in adventure, acquiring an auxiliary role instead of a rescuer.[36] Another similarity between both versions is the fact that Snow White is betrayed by Grumpy; in the movie, Jesusín is moved by jealousy and in the television series due to economic reasons, which introduces danger inside the trust circle and puts the stability of the family core in danger.[37]

Regarding the *españolización* (or `Hispanization') of the tale, the approach shown in both media examples is diametrically opposed. While Berger's film feeds from stereotypes deeply rooted in 'la españolada' folklore, the representation of space in the *Cuéntame un cuento* episode is neutral, disconnected from a specific context: a decision that can be explained by distribution motives, since the television programme has become an increasingly exportable format to other countries. In contrast, the fundamental and unique quality in Berger's work relies on its adhesion to the Hispanic culture. This establishes a parallelism between today's script writers and producers' work and nineteenth-century writers' labour. Not only do they recover folk tales from the past and bring them to current generations as compilers used to do, but they also reinterpret original tales by adapting them to the present context, in the same way as writers such as Barrantes and his unique version of Blancanieves. In this regard, the updating of traditional tales, plus the reference to childhood memories which connect to the public's affective dimension, seem effective techniques when creating attractive audiovisual products for an extensive audience.[38]

Despite the modification of certain elements, the tale's essence remains recognizable. The story's recognizable structure is thus respected, as two magical objects stand as the key elements that allow the identification of Snow White, even with the licences taken: the mirror, as a symbol of the villain's narcissism and selfishness, and the apple, which symbolizes misfortune since it triggers Blancanieves's fall into temptation.

Notes

1 Cristina Bacchilega, *Postmodern Fairy Tales: Gender and Narrative Strategies* (Philadelphia: University of Pennsylvania Press, 1997).

2 Jacob and Wilhelm Grimm were academics and folklorists who developed an exhaustive cultural research by collecting and publishing German legends, fables and tales from the oral tradition. In opposition to popular belief, and despite the fact that they finally had to alter certain details to satisfy the bourgeoisie requests, their tales' collections were not originally targeted for children; they were guided by a scientific rigour instead in order to respect their primitive nature – Moisés Selfa Sastre, 'Siete cuentos inéditos traducidos al español de los Hermanos Grimm: ejemplo de relatos poco moralizantes', *MediAzioni* 17 ('Perspectivas multifacéticas en el universo de la literatura infantil y juvenil') (2015): 2.

3 Aurelio M. Espinosa, *Cuentos populares españoles recogidos de la tradición oral de España. Tomo I* (Stanford, CA: Stanford University Press, 1923), 12.

4 Monserrat Amores, 'Cuentos de vieja, de Juan Ariza. La primera colección de cuentos folclóricos españoles', in *El cuento español en el siglo XIX. Autores raros y olvidados*, ed. Jaume Pont (Lleida: Scriptura, Edicions Universitat de Lleida, 1998), 10.

5 Montserrat Amores, '"El espejo de la verdad" de Vicente Barrantes. Una versión libre del cuento de Blancanieves', *Revista Garoza*, no. 8 (2008): 13.

6 Ibid., 22.

7 Ibid., 13.

8 Aurelio M. Espinosa, *Cuentos populares españoles recogidos de la tradición oral de España. Tomo III* (Madrid: CSIC, 1946–7), 431–41.

9 Ibid., 434–5.

10   Monserrat Amores, *Catálogo de cuentos folclóricos reelaborados por escritores del Siglo XIX* (Madrid: CSIC, 1997), 120–1.

11   Maxime Chavalier wrote *Cuentos folklóricos españoles del Siglo de Oro*, in 1983.

12   Amores, *Catálogo de cuentos folclóricos*, 10.

13   Gérard Genette, *Palimpsestos: la literatura en segundo grado* (Madrid: Taurus, 1989).

14   The Goya Awards are given annually by the Academia de las Artes y las Ciencias Cinematográficas de España (Spanish Academy of Cinematographic Arts and Sciences), being the major recognition for the film works in Spain.

15   Irene Raya and Pedro García, 'El camino hacia Juego de Tronos: Nuevas tendencias en la fantasía cinematográfica y televisiva del nuevo milenio', in *Reyes, espadas, cuervos y dragones. Estudio del fenómeno televisivo Juego de Tronos*, ed. Irene Raya and Pedro García (Sevilla: Fragua, 2013), 44.

16   Diane Braco, 'El hechizo de las imágenes: Blancanieves, el cuento espectacular de Pablo Berger (2012)', *Fotocinema. Revista científica de cine y fotografía*, no. 11 (2015): 42.

17   Nancy Berthier, 'Espagne folklorique et Espagne éternelle: l'irrésistible ascension de l'espagnolade', *Bulletin d'histoire contemporaine de l'Espagne*, no. 24 (1996): 245–54; Marta García Carrión, 'Españoladas y estereotipos cinematográficos: algunas consideraciones sobre su recepción en la España de los años veinte', *Revue Iberic@l, Revue d'études ibériques et ibéro-américaines* (dossier monographique: Les stéréotypes dans la construction des identités nationales depuis une perspective transnationale), no. 10 (2016): 123–35. Although it is usually recognized as a film genre, the origin of the term 'españolada' is linked to the French literature of mid-nineteenth century, which constructed a romantic and orientalist stereotype, combined with the Andalusian folklore, to define Spain as an exotic country. Its defining iconographic elements are: beautiful dark haired and dark eyed women, the presence of bulls and bullfighters, as well as bandits and wild passages, and the exhibition of regional singings and dances. García Carrión, 'Españoladas y estereotipos cinematográficos: algunas consideraciones sobre su recepción en la España de los años veinte', 124–5.

18   José Luis Navarrete Cardero, 'La españolada y Sevilla', *Cuadernos de EICHEROA*, 4 (2003), 9–11.

19   Braco, 'El hechizo de las imágenes', 30.

20   José Luis Navarrete Cardero, *Historia de un género cinematográfico: la españolada* (Madrid: Quiasmo, 2009), 279–90.

21   In the same way as Julia Roberts turned out as an essential key in the promotion of *Mirror, Mirror*, Maribel Verdú, a Spanish cinema star, is the most important actress of this production. This indicates why both villains enjoy a privileged space in the promotional covers of their respective films.

22   Cristina Colombo, 'Blancanieves: De la ficción al empoderamiento', in *VII Jornadas de Poéticas de la Literatura Argentina para Niñas* (Ensenada: *Memoria Académica*, 2016), 8.

23 Francesco Casetti and Federico Di Chio, *Cómo analizar un film* (Barcelona: Paidós, 1991), 204.

24 The poor audience figures reached by the TV show dismissed its renovation, since it achieved a global share of 12.7 per cent on average, with 2,337,000 spectators, opposite to the 13 per cent averaged by the channel Antena 3 in Mondays primetime during 2014. Available at https://www.formulatv.com/series/cuentame-un-cuento/foros/2/1/audiencias/, https://www.elespanol.com/bluper/noticias/cuentame-un-cuento-despide-127-de-media.

25 Brian Stableford, *The A to Z of Fantasy Literature* (Lanham, MD: Scarecrow Press, 2009); Alexander Irvine, 'Urban fantasy', in *The Cambridge Companion to Fantasy Literature*, ed. Edward James and Farah Mendlesohn (Cambridge: Cambridge University Press, 2012), 200–13.

26 The constant presence of mirrors and this type of characters can be conceived, from a symbolic perspective, as an allusion to the myth of Narcissus, which illustrates the fatal consequences of self-love. In this sense, it is important to note that, in most versions, the Evil Queen receives a brutal final punishment, although the Grimm Brothers themselves lessened the severity of their first edition, where she was forced to wear a pair of red-hot iron shoes and dance in them.

27 The actor who plays Bonachón, Félix Gómez, explains in an interview that 'the magic forest was changed for a dark and thug Madrid' in the production. However, the truth is that the identification with the Spanish capital is hidden, except for subtle details such as a sign of the parking Princesa, the view of the Schweppes building in the Gran Vía through a window and so on. Available at https://www.antena3.com/series/cuentame-un-cuento/blancanieves/felix-gomez-cambiamos-bosque-magico-madrid-oscuro-macarra_20141114571b4ee c4beb287a291789b7.html. Accessed 30 August 2020.

28 Milly Buonanno, *The Age of Television: Experiences and Theories* (Bristol: Intellect Books, 2008), 108.

29 Stefan Ekman, 'Urban Fantasy: A Literature of the Unseen', *Journal of the Fantastic in the Arts* 27, no. 3 (2016): 466.

30 Maite Ribés Alegría, 'La hibridación de géneros y la crisis de la calidad televisiva: consejos audiovisuales en el panorama televisivo', *Comunicar: Revista científica iberoamericana de comunicación y educación*, no. 25 (2005): 1–10; Inmaculada Gordillo, *La hipertelevisión: géneros y formatos* (Ecuador: Ciespal, 2009); Irene Raya Bravo, 'La tendencia hacia la hibridación en el macrogénero extraordinario durante la era hipertelevisiva. Casos de estudio: Galáctica: estrella de combate, Juego de Tronos y American Horror Story', *Revista de la Asociación Española de Investigación de la Comunicación* 3, no. 6 (2016): 11–18.

31 The fact that the main character is created as a dual figure is revealing and it can be related to an extensive cultural tradition representing, through a diversity of expressions, the concept of duality, which is present in the collective imaginary. Albert Chillón, 'La urdimbre mitopoética de la cultura mediática', *Anàlisi: quaderns de comunicació i cultura*, no. 24 (2000): 156.

32 Bacchilega, *Postmodern Fairy Tales*, 29.

33 Ibid.

34 Casetti and Di Chio, *Cómo analizar un film*, 204.

35 Bruno Bettelheim, *Psicoanálisis de los cuentos de hadas* (Barcelona: Grijalbo Mondadori, 1994), 20.

36 This change of roles is also shown in other film versions of Snow White; for example, in the representation of the hunter and the prince in *Snow White and the Huntsman,* or the prince in *Mirror Mirror*, as well as in other recent Disney productions like *Tangled* (Nathan Greno and Byron Howard, 2010) or *Frozen* (Chris Buck and Jennifer Lee, 2013).

37 Jordi Balló and Xavier Pérez, *Yo ya he estado aquí: ficciones de la repetición* (Barcelona: Anagrama, 2005), 80.

38 Rovira Collado and Pomares Puig, `Clásicos infantiles para adultos. Últimas adaptaciones cinematográficas de cuentos tradicionales', in *1st International Conference: Teaching Literature in English for Young Learners*, ed. Agustín Reyes Torres, Luis S. Villacañas de Castro and Betlem Soler Pardo (Facultat de Magisteri: Universitat de València, 2012), 199.

15

The adventures of *Snow White* in Turkish cinema

Zeynep Gültekin Akçay

Introduction

To track the footsteps of Disney cartoons in Turkish cinema is to gain insight into the global role of fairy tales introduced by the Brothers Grimm and led by Disney's *Snow White and Seven Dwarfs* (David Hand, 1937), their impact on cultural productivity and stylistic and ideological differences between how they are built. This chapter looks into the historical journey of *Snow White* in Turkish cinema, tackling adaptations of the film to offer a discussion of transnational textual references and hybridity of style. Domestic adaptations of Disney animated movies within Turkish film production include titles such as *Sovalye, Pamuk Prenses ve Hain/Knight Snow White and Traitor* (Orhan Oguz, 1996), *Ali Baba ve 7 cüceler/Ali Baba and Seven Dwarfs* (Cem Yılmaz, 2015) and *Pamuk Prens/Snow Prince* (Birol Güven and Hasan Tolga Pulat, 2016). This chapter addresses three particular domestic productions inspired by both the Brothers Grimm story and Disney's first animated feature: *Pamuk Prenses ve 7 cüceler/Snow White and Seven Dwarfs* (Ertem Göreç, 1971), *Komser Sekspir/Police Chief Shakespeare* (Sinan Çetin, 2000) and *Anlat Istanbul/Istanbul Tales* (Selim Demirdelen, Kudret Sabancı, Ümit Ünal, Yücel Yolcu and Ömür Atay, 2004).

Snow White and Seven Dwarfs adapted: Ertem Göreç

Movies had been promoted by the Turkish government in the aftermath of the First World War, while Turkish cinema underwent a transformation in both quantity and quality as more and more professional filmmakers emerged. Cinema turned out to be extremely profitable as a business, and the number of movies with a focus on melodrama, comedy and fantasy began to rise in line with commercial interests. The ever-growing demand in movies called for references to literary works as a source, and adaptations came into prominence.[1] As set out by Gilbert Adair, the American people and many other international communities discovered the Brothers Grimm's *Snow White* from Walt Disney.[2] In Turkey, on the other hand, Disney's animated movie did not arrive until as late as the 1970s, after television became more mainstream. However, before this period, Disney's feature-length adaptation of *Snow White* was faithfully adapted for Turkish audiences by the director Ertem Göreç in 1970 (Figures 15.1 and 15.2). Göreç's movie was successful at the Turkish box office upon its initial release. In fact, it was sold to Italy for $8,500 and went on to win several awards, coming third at the International Antalya Film Festival (1971). The film also raised awareness about Walt Disney's original animated version of *Snow White*, as audiences who used to hear stories about the feature now became its viewers.[3]

For the majority of adapted movies in Turkish cinema, the director or screenwriter takes the initiative, as there are no Hollywood-style 'book hunters' or professionals who play the part of agencies.[4] It was the screenwriter Hamdi Degirmencioglu who began the process of adapting *Snow White and Seven Dwarfs*, which triggered a trend of folk tales across Turkish cinema. Göreç explains:

> Playing the part of Snow White, Zeynep Degirmencioglu is the daughter of the screenwriter Hamdi. As a father, Hamdi had a good faith belief in his daughter, and came up with scripts that befitted her. For instance, when Zeynep turned eight, he wrote the script for Aysecik touted as the origin of movies for kids. Zeynep was sixteen once this trend of movies came to an end. Having sought themes that fitted for her age, he watched the Snow White by Walt Disney, and wrote an adapted script. The screenwriter Degirmencioglu told me and our producer Ozdemir Birsel about how he wanted to shoot a movie for her daughter to star as a young girl rather a kid as she was getting older.[5]

In addition to the screenwriter's daughter playing the leading role, the producer Ozdemir Birsel's spouse and actress Belgin Doruk played the part as the mother of Snow White. Göreç's version also made effective use of

FIGURE 15.1 Poster for *Pamuk Prenses ve 7 cüceler.*

FIGURE 15.2 Various scenes from *Pamuk Prenses ve 7 cüceler.*

narrative structures adopted by Disney in his cel-animated feature.[6] In fact, the Evil Queen and the Witch were played by the same actress in Göreç's movie as it was the case in Disney's *Snow White*. Played by Suna Selen, both characters underwent an extensive makeup and a meticulous costume selection process so that audiences would not notice that both characters are played by the same actress. Costume design was quite affordable, as Göreç described in a recent interview: 'Another element that alleviated our aesthetic concerns apart from cost-related ones was the assistance of Belgin Doruk, the wife of our producer, and the actress playing the part of birth mother, to design and manufacture the costumes.'[7]

Turkish cinema has always been loyal to Hollywood-style popular movie narratives amid commercial concerns, and the adaption of *Snow White* consciously made use of recognizable stars.[8] The movie featured the child star Zeynep Değirmencioglu (Snow White), known for her role as Aysecik, as well as Belgin Doruk (Mother Queen), Salih Guney (Prince) and Suna Selen (Evil Queen).[9] Göreç notes that 'We were trying to make sure that the leading roles were played by stars as we shot movies in line with the needs of the audience.'[10] Göreç's *Snow White* grew into a highly popular movie, inspired by Disney's animated adaptation rather than the original Brothers Grimm story, and interlaced with local elements as part of its move to Turkish cinema screens.[11]

The dwarfs were the most striking components of this localization process, and the producer and screenwriter took the liberty of casting performers with dwarfism as a way of creating a degree of realism for the audience. Ahead of shooting, an advertisement was placed in national newspapers with the phrase 'wanted to perform in a movie'. The advertisement attracted applications from all over Turkey, with the process resulting in the selection of seven dwarf performers who were not professional actors when they were cast.

Snow White marked a breakthrough for Turkish cinema as for the first time performers of diminutive stature were cast in a primary role, and they went on to become famous stars following the release of the movie. Göreç sought to make his dwarfs more comedic than Disney's presentation of the dwarfs, arguing that 'Our movie is the version of an animated cartoon shot with actors. However, we incorporated Turkish jokes and patterns of behavior into the Disney's movie so that we could attract families.'[12] In particular, Göreç pushed the envelope for the most humorous dwarf by turning him into Keloğlan, one of the primary Turkish folkloric story protagonists. Keloğlan the dwarf is a man of his word, a little bit clumsy, brave, cunning and fair. In typical Turkish stories, Keloğlan is a character who outsmarts opponents, demonstrating dexterity, craftiness and tricks that one could not assume from his small size, frailness, posture and appearance.[13] Göreç's use of the culturally specific Keloğlan character is an invention for its period, helping to present a Western tale to a Turkish audience.

Another element of localization that plays a role in the adaptation of the Disney movie is the use of melodramatic narration. Elements of comedy and scenes with several songs incorporated into the melodramatic narration through supporting characters become indispensable to the narrative. For example, the Queen sees the Prince and Princess talking to one another and becomes jealous. She then sends her soldiers to catch them, following which the Prince is confronted by the soldiers, fighting against ten soldiers on his own. Meanwhile, a child comes to his rescue, and they are able to defeat the soldiers. These scenes reference local heroes that challenge an entire army on their own as a part of the historical fantasy trend that dominated contemporary Turkish cinema. Another addition to Disney's narration is a boy who accompanies the Prince and occasionally even imparts advice. This boy is the kind of element that Vladimir Propp describes as an auxiliary and a wise person of Turkish folkloric stories, giving advice to a protagonist as events become difficult.[14]

Göreç's adaptation of Snow White, which certainly appealed to Turkish viewers, was consistent with Disney's formulaic narrative structures and ticked all the boxes in embracing elements such as family, the bonds of matrimony and power.[15] However, Göreç's adaptation is quite simple in structure, not only evoking but also simplifying Disney's version and its organization into nine discrete chapters: Origin (birth of the protagonist),

Jealousy, Dismissal, Acceptance, Jealousy Again, Death, Exhibition, Animation and Solution.[16] Unlike the Disney version, Göreç does not cover the first chapter so extensively, and so does not dwell on the birth and background of Snow White as a character. However, Göreç attached importance to the diversity of animals in a similar manner to Disney's animated adaptation.

Shakespeare and Snow White: Sinan Çetin

The lack of capital to shoot movies in the late 1980s, the attachment of priority to anomalistic and innovative movies seeking commercial return and the ever-growing popularity of television all paved the way for pursuing non-cinematic capital resources. These resources enabled the industry to employ a variety of directors. Some figures such as Erden Kıral, Yavuz Ozkan and Sinan Çetin who had shot only a few short movies became pioneers of the Turkish cinema.[17] Directed by Çetin in 2000, *Komser Sekspir* is an absurd freestyle adaptation of Disney's *Snow White*.[18] Film critic Cumhur Cambazoglu argues, 'The movie is a story where Sinan Çetin, who loves taking an amusing look at the relation between the system and citizens, takes a swipe at narrating it in the heart of Beyoglu and tries to find an absurd discourse and a sense of conditioning and come up with an act that goes beyond battle cries.'[19] The film became a blockbuster, attracting 1.332 million viewers and remaining in theatres for a total of thirty-seven weeks. *Komser Sekspir* made a total box-office return of TRY 2.867.678.000, ranking fourth among the top viewed movies in the past decade, and also won the cinematographer and the best artist of the year awards.[20]

Çetin adopted an elliptic narrative for his adaptation. He excluded many chapters, characters and themes from Disney's animated version, perhaps explaining why *Komser Sekspir* has gone relatively unnoticed as an adaptation of Disney's *Snow White* in much literature on Turkish cinema. On the other hand, *Komser Sekspir* forged a completely new narrative ranging from new chapters, characters and themes, to new dialogue, set and costume details. Çetin adopted a melodramatic narrative in his unique style, while also bringing up the country's problems as part of his interpretation of the fairy tale. He worked collectively with friends (the directors Mustafa Altıoklar and Tevfik Baser), who provided Çetin with assistance to write the script and even shoot the finished film. A particular set of Turkish filmmaking traditions concerning the role of collaborative labour put to use during the production of *Komser Sekspir* are outlined by Mesut Ceylan, the screenwriter of the movie, who explains:

After I tried to get my point across for almost ten days, Sinan Çetin agreed to listen to what I had to say. I asked him if it would not be funny to have a rehearsal for Snow White and Seven Dwarfs at a police station. Mr. Çetin also found this idea interesting, so we started to discuss the details. Mr. Çetin also told me that a few changes would be necessary. The script, which I originally thought to be based on a father & son story, morphed into a father & daughter story thanks to the director Tevfik Başer's inputs. Upon the recommendation by the director Mustafa Altıoklar, we decided that the daughter should have cancer.[21]

Ceylan recounts too how he has developed the script, noting that 'Snow White and Seven Dwarfs was a book I read crying on a number of occasions when I was just a kid. It was a book read by my teacher as it if had been a rite and we had been crying about. And I think it is one of the most classic aspects of humor: Playing such a delicate story at a police station ... That was the foundation.'[22] Another common Turkish tradition manifested in *Komser Sekspir* through having multiple roles played by one person. In this respect, the film's screenwriter was also the Prince, the Commissioner Cemil became the Evil Queen, the Commissioner Cemil's father became a hunter and the director of the film made an appearance at the end of the movie.

Some tales such as Snow White are repackaged over and over again.[23] In *Komser Sekspir*, this repackaging process takes place through parody and pastiche as understood by Fredric Jameson.[24] The film comprises a set of skits with no thematic integrity and easily narrated and intelligible tales that turn into a more anecdote format. Main figures and characters (the Police Commissioner, Prostitute and Drug Dealer) are all protagonists who are evocative of comic and cartoon typecasting. One of Çetin's pastiche patterns is that he displays Disney's book on the screen as a direct reference to the studio's film. With a focus on eccentricity and idiosyncrasy to create imitation and amusement, parody is a frequent element of *Komser Sekspir*.[25] One of the most significant scenes that define such parodic intent occurs when Cemil the police commissioner has the playwright Shakespeare's monument built in the courtyard of the police station and then pours out her grief to Ataturk in a monologue that is dually eccentric and ridiculous.

As is the case in Disney's animated film, main characters must face a variety of foes or challenges to achieve their ultimate goals. The climactic confrontation is followed by a happy ending at the closure of the movie. In *Komser Sekspir*, however, there are various problems involved in the creation of a happy ending: The woman who plays the Queen breaks her foot, while the theatre team arranges a holiday to the chief commissioner as an outstanding service award so that he does not return to the police station. While the rehearsals continue at the police station, the delegation representing the European Commission of Human Rights arrives as an observer. At the same time, Snow White's evil friends report the incident to the prosecutor. The prosecutor comes to the police station after the complaint seeking to have everyone arrested. The prosecutor is threatened with a gun by the father of Commissioner Cemil and thrown behind bars. Immediately afterwards, the rival mafia's men arrive, wounding the mafia father and the hunter with a gun. In the meantime, after the disappearance of one of the seven dwarfs, the drug dealer becomes a dwarf. In the show, the Queen is commissioned by Cemil, and the hunter was played by his father. Against all odds, the cast puts the play on stage, the girl dies and the father goes to jail, and once he serves his time, all his criminal entourage take a step towards a more blissful life.

Disney's dominant gender roles are also highlighted throughout *Komser Sekspir*. As pointed out by Janet Wasko, Disney's princesses are constructed as beautiful, naive, well-mannered, obedient and 'honourable'.[26] As in Disney's version of *Snow White*, *Komser Sekspir*'s Snow White appears in need of male protection. Yet while the Prince is a perfect choice, Snow White's father is omitted. In the Disney version, the dwarfs aid Snow White, while a bunch of criminals provide the character with assistance in the Turkish adaptation. Disney's heterosexual and monogamous image of marriage is also continued in Çetin's film. The commissioner's wife dies, and he never contemplates getting married again. He never lets any other woman in his life until he meets the prostitute he casts for the Snow White play. *Komser Sekspir* uses the reflexivity of a play to engage with the discourse of marriage, including the commissioner's relationship with a prostitute who becomes honourable via her transformation (late into the film, the duo have an affair). The family concept central to the Disney formula is also continually emphasized. Cemil's emphasis on phrases such as 'my daughter' and 'my father' can be understood as an extension of ownership within his personal relationships. Family and heterosexuality, which are Disney narrative constants, are fully embraced in *Komser Sekspir* too. Such strategies are clear to see in Cemil's wrongful misconduct for the sake of his family's well-being and how he ends up in jail.

Çetin's film also features contrasts such as good and evil, as well as class distinctions between the rich and the poor. Sureyya Cakır argues that *Komser Sekspir* offers an objective account for the evil or good about life in general, as wealth and poverty are presented as a natural part of life outside socio-economic circumstances.[27] This is a means to make ideological masking within the film possible. The narrative underlines the fact that one can be good through affection, obedience and conventional values. Erich Fromm's concepts of extrovert and introvert obedience are important to how *Komser Sekspir* represents Cemil and his father, who both obey police work and are thus public authorities.[28] They waive their autonomy and allow an external power to shape their judgements, replacing their own will and power, and resign themselves to its will. However, Cemil's decision to put a theatre play on stage at the police station with a cast of criminals marks an effort to make his daughter happy after finding out about her terminal illness. This decision makes him renounce his extrovert obedience and drives him to his faith, that is to say, his introvert obedience. Such introvert obedience is not a submission but a coming to terms, just as Cemil comes to terms with the death of his daughter and the idea of making her happy for one last time. The Police Commissioner Cemil's acts of introvert obedience go on and on all the way to the final scenes of the movie. Sinan Çetin underscores the fact that this is just a tale by killing the girl and sending the commissioner to prison for challenging the state apparatus, and there is no way to condone such acts of rebellion. In addition, all the evil criminals become more mature at the police station that serves as the venue of the status quo, where they obey the kinds of dominant values associated with Disney (such as kindness and morality).[29] Even though some ideological predicaments and elements of social threat are forged in Çetin's film, the story comes to a conclusion in the way emphasized by Disney storytelling traditions (rehabilitation of criminals thanks to the play, and the happy ending for the police commissioner after serving his time in jail).

Snow White and her eighth dwarf in the dark forest aka Istanbul

As an adaptation of Grimm tales, *Anlat Istanbul* morphs what lies between the lines in folk tales into an account of Istanbul in the 2000s. The screenwriter Ümit Ünal notes that 'The wealthy, the poor, the pretty, the ugly, the criminals, the innocents, the marginals, the power holders, and the Istanbulites from every walk of life and gender transform into tale heroes in a panorama embracing Istanbul in its entirety from Beyoglu to Aksaray, from the Bosphorus to the underground.'[30] *Anlat Istanbul* thus offers a portrayal of others, choosing to depict mafia members and the criminal network that operates in the city.

Anlat Istanbul manipulates Disney's tale just as Disney have been criticized for attacking the Grimms' original story.[31] The heroes in Disney's adaptation have their own unique story of progression, whereas this Turkish tale does not culminate in a happy ending in ways that disrupt Disney's narrative formula. The conventional Disney characters become contrary in the film. For instance, Snow White (Azra Akın) is the spoiled grown-up daughter of a crime boss (Çetin Tekindor). However, she falls into the hands of the Witch Queen (Vahide Gordum) after her father is killed as a result of a feud, and then a hunt begins in the underground tunnels of Istanbul. A dwarf, who ends up on the streets, assists Snow White (Hilal Arslan) during the hunt.[32] Hulya Alkan argues that *Anlat Istanbul* features characters who wish to escape from the city and who are alienated from their neighbourhood.[33] All of the protagonists who happen to end up in the city by accident or coincidence try to escape Istanbul, and thus take revenge on the city for their defeats in life.

Jonathan Frome highlights how it is a mistake to consider Disney's *Snow White* as a film movie for children, as it is replete with tumultuous and dramatic narrative events.[34] *Snow White* certainly abounds with malicious acts, such as the threat of murder, the terror of the nocturnal forest, the Queen's magic, her pursuit of Snow White and even her death. *Anlat Istanbul* also directs its tale to adults, doing so by making use of tropes and conventions of the fairy tale. For example, the ambiguous notion of 'over the hills and far away' is used to turn time and space upside down. This convention captivates the space and time in the tale. By doing so, it is intended to attract viewers to the supernatural universe of the tale. *Anlat Istanbul*'s Snow White presents this trope as remorse. The Hunter's line 'we went over the hills and far away, but it seems we could not go nowhere fast' expresses his serving of the King as remorse. The magical time and space of Disney is therefore itself turned upside down, making the viewers face the brutal facts of the real world rather than being enchanted by their framing as fantasy. The conflicts between the naive and innocent archetype, alongside the female witch character, are just several of the tropes of tale. *Anlat Istanbul* features both in its combination of Hurrem the stepmother with Idil the Snow White. Additionally, the fact that the name of the stepmother is Hurrem makes direct reference to the film's historical context.[35] The dialogue between Idil the Snow White and her stepmother Hurrem for the opening scene of the movie both attracts the audience into the universe of the tale and leaves them alone with insecurity and a feeling of restlessness in a desperate and paralysed state in a deserted corner of life.

In *Anlat Istanbul*, the princess is defined by her character and physical state. Figured as the 'Snow White' character in the film, Idil resembles Disney's depiction of the princess through her beauty and vulnerability. While analysing the Snow White fairy tale, Clarissa P. Estés argues that the metaphor of sleep points to the state of unconsciousness, but additionally signifies creation and renovation.[36] The fact that Idil actually progresses towards being adult, while trying to regain her consciousness under the influence of a tranquilizer, is what separates her from Disney's construction of the Princess character.

The film's eighth dwarf puts Idil through Istanbul's underground construction sites. Once Idil emerges from the ground, she becomes mature and reborn, now set for a new life. The representation of Idil approaches closely the Brothers Grimm's 7-year-old princess rather than Disney's princess, particularly in the scene when she defies the hunter and struggles with him. Idil (as Snow White) is victorious in her escape, at which point Disney value of 'morality' and the victory of good against evil manifest.[37] Disney's *Snow White* features the evil stepmother as someone diabolic in character. Disney's evil stepmother is matched in the attractive and beautiful queen of *Anlat Istanbul* too. When Idil asks the stepmother gazing at herself in the mirror of a hospital room 'What do you see, the queen of the stages, the former miss Turkey?', she makes a direct reference to the stepmother's long-disappeared beauty.

In its narrative structure and representation of characters, *Anlat Istanbul* bears a resemblance to Disney's version while diverging from it in several aspects. Of the nine chapters that organize its narrative (Origin, Jealousy, Dismissal, Acceptance, Jealousy, Death, Exhibition, Animation and Solution), only five (Jealousy, Dismissal, Acceptance, Animation and Solution) are used. Unlike Disney's adaptation, the tale begins with Snow White rushing to the hospital as soon as she hears about the murder of her father, before running into her stepmother. The stepmother (playing the role of the Evil Queen) had Snow White's father killed, and in the stepmother's effort to now kill her, she gets assistance from the hunter. This narrative process takes the same course as Disney's version of the tale. However, Disney's forest laden with secrets is here portrayed as the dark streets of Istanbul. The Turkish city is displayed on screen with all its ruthlessness, misdeeds and challenges to Idil. To emphasize the darkness of the city, a large proportion of the film features scenes that take place at night. Ünal connects each element of the story through images of Istanbul, spatial and cultural links that are established as central to the characters' experience. In *Anlat Istanbul*, the city is shown by its negative face, its darkness formed by the fearsomeness of the mafia that operate beneath the city.

Conclusion

The mutual exchange between literature and cinema and the adaptation of a novel, a play or any other literary work into a movie dates back to the early years of Turkish cinema. Adaptation is favoured in Turkish cinema as a way of overcoming creative difficulties and to mitigate script costs. Ertem Göreç, Sinan Çetin and Ümit Ünal all rose to prominence in Turkish cinema through their adaptation of the *Snow White* story. Each of the three directors opted to adapt Walt Disney's cel-animated feature, rather than the original Brothers Grimm tale. Each made use of some of Disney's classic narrative characteristics, and each emphasized the role of women in line with the Disney formula. In these three retellings, women were addressed as too naive, beautiful or evil. Disney's deserted forest is another element featured in each of the three movies. The dwarfs that went relatively unnoticed in the Brothers Grimm tale are now placed at the forefront of the narrative, just as central as in Disney's film. Even Disney's conservative ideologies and obedience to moral values, patriotism, individualism, a strict commitment to work ethic, loyalty to family institution and unequal distribution of social powers are elements covered in different ways in each of the three Turkish adaptations. Justice is dispensed by distinction between the good and the evil. One is rewarded, while the other is punished.

Disney's many adherences to the *Snow White* fairy tale, as well as its numerous deviations, are similarly put to use by the Turkish directors. The dwarfs are the best examples of where such transformation occurs. Göreç cast dwarf performers, transforming one into the figure of the Keloğlan, a common folkloric protagonist. In Çetin's film, the dwarfs are portrayed as criminals detained at a police station, while Ünal's version *Anlat Istanbul* features only one female dwarf. Following the narrative of Disney's adaptation, the background of Snow White as a character, that is to say, her mother and familial information, is not presented in any of the three versions, while each illustrates the theme of jealousy more so than in Disney's cel-animated feature. Despite these various animated adaptations by Turkish filmmakers, Disney's *Snow White*, as this chapter argues, did enjoy success in Turkish Cinema, but not until its arrival in the 1970s. Following its release, Disney's tale was repeatedly returned to over the next fifty years in a form that would attract Turkish audiences, yet with filmmakers careful not to lose any of the story's unique elements and, with it, parts of its attraction.

Notes

1   Zeynep Çetin Erus, *Amerikan ve Turk Sinemalarında Uyarlamalar (Adaptations in American and Turkish Cinemas)* (Istanbul: Es, 2005).

2   Gilbert Adair, *Postmodernci Kapıyı İki Kere Calar (The Postmodernist Always Rings Twice)*, trans. N. Dikbas (Istanbul: Iletisim, 1993).

3   Ayse Sasa, *Yesilcam Gunlugu (Yesilcam Diary)* (Istanbul: Dergah, 2002).

4   Çetin Erus, *Uyarlamalar (Adaptations)*.

5   Ertem Göreç, *Interview with Ertem Göreç*, February 2018, Sanatcı Yasam Evi, Kartal-Istanbul.

6   Kristian Moen, *Film and Fairy Tales: The Birth of Modern Fantasy* (London: I.B. Tauris, 2013), 180.

7   Göreç, *Interview with Ertem Göreç*, 2018.

8   Nilgun Abisel, *Populer Sinema ve Turler (Popular Cinema and Genre)*, 2nd edn (Istanbul: Alan, 1999).

9   *Aysecik* is the leading actress of *Aysecik* film adapted by director Memduh Un from the novel *Kemalettin Tugcu's Aysecik*.

10   Göreç, *Interview with Ertem Göreç*, 2018.

11   Filiz Bilgic, *Turk Sinemasında 1980 Sonrası Uslup Arayısları (Post-1980 Style Intervals in Turkish Cinema)* (Ankara: Kultur Bakanlığı, 2002).

12   Göreç, *Interview with Ertem Göreç*, 2018.

13   Tahir Alangu, *Keloglan Masalları (Keloglan Fairytales)*, 11th edn (Istanbul: Yapı Kredi).

14 Vladimir Propp, *Masalın Bicimbilimi ve Olaganustu Masalların Donusumu (Morphology of the Folktale)*, trans. M. Rıfat and S. Rıfat, 3rd edn (Istanbul: Is Bankası, 2017).

15 Dilek Tunalı, 'Populer Masallardan Sinemaya Yapılan Uyarlamalarda Kulturel Antropolojik Sureklilik ve Donusum' (Cultural Anthropological Continuity and Transformation in Adaptations from Popular Tales to Cinema), *Uluslararası Sosyal Arastırmalar Dergisi* 10, no. 49 (2017): 368.

16 M. Thomas Inge, 'Walt Disney's Snow White Art, Adaptation and Ideology', *Journal of Popular Film and Television* 32, no. 3 (2004): 137.

17 Burcak Evren, *Turk Sinemasında Yeni Konumlar (New Positions in Turkish Cinema)* (Istanbul: Broy, 1990), 6.

18 After fainting in a school rehearsal, little Su is diagnosed with leukaemia. As a result she is forced to give up the *Snow White* role she wanted so badly. Police Chief Cemil decides to stage the production of *Snow White and the Seven Dwarfs* at his oppressive police station. He hopes to win a TV competition in order to save his dying daughter. The directorial duties are assumed by drug dealer Tatu who claims to have been a star in his youth. Prince Charming is played by a drug addict, homeless kids play the dwarfs and a prostitute plays the Queen. As the rehearsals go on at the police station, Cemil tries to hide the hostile environment of the police station from her daughter, causing a series of tragicomic events like the arrival of UN delegates who mistake the rehearsal for a rehabilitation programme.

19 Cumhur Cambazoglu, 'Komser Sekspir' Sinema Ansiklopedisi, https://sinemaansiklopedisi.wordpress.com/2017/12/26/kolay-para-kulhan-aski/, 2001 (accessed 5 August 2018).

20 Mesut Ceylan, 'Komser Sekspir', NTV Arsiv, http://arsiv.ntv.com.tr/news/64082.asp#BODY, 16 February 2001 (accessed 2 August 2018).

21 Ibid.

22 Ibid.

23 Ayse Dilara Bostan and Serpil Kırel, 'Postmodern Donem Disney Prenses Anlatılarında İnsa Edilen Kadın Temsilinin Moana Ornegi Uzerinden Incelenmesi' (The Analysis of Women Presentation Built in Disney Princess Narrative in Postmodern Era through the Case of Moana), *TRT Akademi 5*, no. 3 (2018): 12.

24 Fredric Jameson, 'Postmodernizm ya da Kapitalizmin Kulturel Mantigi (Postmodernism, or, the Cultural Logic of Late Capitalism)', trans. G. Nalis, D. Sabuncuoglu and D. Erksan, in *Postmodernizm (Postmodernism)*, ed. Necmi Zeka (Istanbul: Kıyı, 1994), 59–116.

25 Fredric Jameson, *Kulturel Donemec (The Cultural Turn)*, trans. K. İnal (Ankara: Dost, 2005), 16.

26 Janet Wasko, *Understanding Disney: the Manufacture of Fantasy* (Cambridge: Polity Press, 2007), 115.

27 Sureyya Cakır, 'Yesilcam Sineması ve Masal Formu: Aysecik' (Yesilcam Cinema and Tale Form: Aysecik), *Turkish Studies* 12, no. 21 (2017): 133–50.

28 Erich Fromm, *Itaatsizlik Uzerine Denemeler (On Disobedience)*, trans. A. Sayın (Istanbul: Yaprak, 1987).

29 Pubescence is hero's growth, maturation, becoming another human being [see Tunalı, *Populer Masallardan Sinemaya (Popular Tales to Cinema)*, 363].

30 Atilla Dorsay, *100 Yılın 100 Turk Filmi (100 Turkish Films of the Year 100)* (Istanbul: Remzi, 2013).

31 See Jack Zipes, *Fairy Tales and the Art of Subversion: The Classical Genre for Children and the Process of Civilization*, 2nd edn (New York: Routledge, 2006).

32 Evinc Dogan and Evren Dogan, 'Kent ve Anti-Gosteri: Istanbul'un Sine-masal İmgeleri' (City and Anti-Show: Cine-fairy Images of Istanbul), *Sinecine* 2, no. 9 (2018): 123.

33 Hulya Alkan, 'Kent ve Sinema Iliskisi Baglamında 90 Sonrası Turk Sinemasında Istanbul' (Istanbul in Turkish Cinema after 90 in the Context of City and Cinema Relations), MA diss. Dokuz Eylul University Graduate Schools of Fine Arts, Izmir, 2007.

34 Jonathan Frome, 'Snow White: Critics and Criteria for the Animated Feature Film', *Quarterly Review of Film and Video* 30, no. 5 (2013): 462–73.

35 The name of Suleyman the Magnificent's wife remembered with her intrigues is also Hurrem Sultan.

36 Clarissa Pinkola Estés, *Kurtlarla Kosan Kadınlar: Vahsi Kadin Arketipine Dair Mit ve Oykuler (Woman Who Run with the Wolves: Myths and Stories of the Wild Woman Archetype)*, trans. H. Atalay (Istanbul: Ayrıntı, 2003), 171–2.

37 Wasko, *Understanding Disney*, 119.

GUIDE TO FURTHER READING

As noted throughout this book, while there is a wealth of extant scholarship on both *Snow White* and the Disney studio more generally, these texts tend to follow well-established lines of enquiry, which returns us to the purpose of this collection: to extend discussions of Disney's *Snow White* in new directions. To this end, the handful of sources highlighted here offer a variety of starting points that may lead readers to explore *Snow White* in a number of specific ways.

Archives

Story-Conference Notes for *Snow White and the Seven Dwarfs*, Dated 26 July 1934 through 8 June 1937. Transcription from the Original California, copied by David R. Williams, August 1987, and held in the collection of the British Film Institute, London.

This collection of production papers, held in the British Film Institute's Special Collections, provides rare access to materials ordinarily kept locked away in 'The Disney Morgue' (Disney's extensive studio archive). These papers record both the developing industrial practices at Disney in the mid-1930s and a range of individual creative contributions beyond those of Walt Disney.

Production

Richard Holliss and Brian Sibley's *Snow White and the Seven Dwarfs & the Making of the Classic Film* (New York: Simon & Schuster, 1987).

An accessibly written and presented book, which, despite its age, holds up well. This book provides useful coverage of pre- and post-release ephemera, such as merchandise and spin-offs. The book is also generously illustrated and provides a glimpse of the production artwork generated during the making of *Snow White*.

Identity

Amy M. Davis's *Good Girls and Wicked Witches: Women in Disney's Feature Animation* (Eastleigh: John Libbey, 2006).

Davis's book engages with a variety of Disney texts (1937–2004) and in doing so offers a useful analysis of how female identity is constructed within the film *Snow White*. Davis's book is certainly not the only example of scholarship interested in unpicking the question of Disney's (frequently stereotypical) identity politics, but given the breadth of Davis's work it does represent a good starting point.

Marginalized voices

Mindy Johnson's *Ink & Paint. The Women of Walt Disney's Animation* (Glendale: Disney Editions, 2017).

Like Davis, Johnson also takes a wide-angle view of Disney, covering approximately eighty years of the studio's history. Using a combination of archival access and oral history, Johnson works hard to reclaim a space within Disney history for the many talented women who have worked at the studio over the years, but whose stories were frequently pushed to the margins of the Disney narrative.

Disney style

Frank Thomas and Ollie Johnston's *The Illusion of Life* (New York: Disney Editions, 1984).

Being two of Disney's famous 'Nine Old Men', both Thomas and Johnston reflected upon their vast experience working at Disney when writing *The Illusion of Life*. Setting out a number of principles that took root at the Disney studio during the 1930s and 1940s, their book articulates the conscious process of promoting this house style – a style that would come to define and dominate hand-drawn animation for several decades. Many of the examples offered are linked to the production of *Snow White*.

Looking back

Eric Smoodin's *Snow White and the Seven Dwarfs* (London: Palgrave, 2012).

A compact but impressively wide-ranging illustrated book that fully identifies the landmark status of *Snow White* within global film history and contemporary popular culture, but also its more immediate contribution to the Disney studio's company narrative. Smoodin's largely industrial approach takes in the film's pre-production through to its critical response upon its release, situating Disney's inaugural feature film within the context of Walt's position as a highly influential Hollywood filmmaker. The book is a terrific introduction to *Snow White* that covers multiple bases, one that in its scope perhaps belies its shorter length. Smoodin's book was also chosen to be reprinted and reissued as a special edition in 2012 to celebrate the twentieth anniversary of the BFI Film Classics series.

BIBLIOGRAPHY

Works cited

Archival documents

Procès-verbal (minutes) of the BeBFC meeting of the 7th of May, 1938. *Blanche Neige et les Sept Nains* file. Archive of the BeBFC, State Archives of Belgium, Brussels.

Record #2353, MPPDA Digital Archive. Available at https://mppda.flinders.edu.au/records/2353 (accessed 14 March 2020).

Sneeuwwitje en de Zeven Dwergen file. Archive Centrale Commissie voor de Filmkeuring. Nationaal Archief, The Hague.

Snow White and the Seven Dwarfs file. PCA Special Collections. Margaret Herrick Library, Los Angeles.

Story-Conference Notes for *Snow White and the Seven Dwarfs*. LOC-435. British Film Institute, London.

Bibliography

A. T. 'Référendum français, *Blanche Neige* et Jean Gabin … sont d'après les directeurs le meilleur film de l'année et la vedette la plus populaire de 1938'. *Le jour – Echo de Paris*, 13 April 1939: 6.

Abisel, Nilgun. *Populer Sinema ve Turler (Popular Cinema and Genre)*, 2nd edn. Istanbul: Alan, 1999.

Adair, Gilbert. *Postmodernci Kapıyı İki Kere Calar (The Postmodernist Always Rings Twice)*, trans. N. Dikbas. Istanbul: Iletisim, 1993.

Alangu, Tahir. *Keloğlan Masalları (Keloğlan Fairytales)*, 11th edn. Istanbul: Yapı Kredi, 2016.

Alkan, Hulya. 'Kent ve Sinema Iliskisi Baglamında 90 Sonrası Turk Sinemasında Istanbul' (Istanbul in Turkish Cinema after 90 in the Context of City and Cinema Relations). MA diss., Dokuz Eylul University Graduate Schools of Fine Arts, Izmir, 2007.

Allan, Robin. 'The Fairest Film of All'. In *The Walt Disney Film Archives: The Animated Movies 1921–1968*, edited by Daniel Kothenschulte, 60–89. Cologne: Taschen GmbH, 2016.

Allan, Robin. '50 Years of *Snow White*'. *Journal of Popular Film and Television*, 15, no. 4 (1988): 156–63.

Allan, Robin. *Walt Disney and Europe: European Influences on the Feature Films of Walt Disney*. Bloomington: Indiana University Press, 1999.

Allen, S. 'Bringing the Dead to Life: Animation and the Horrific'. *At the Interface/ Probing the Boundaries*, 61 (2010): 87–108.

Alt, Dirk. *Der Farbfilm marschiert!: Frühe Farbfilmverfahren und NS-Propaganda 1933–1945*. Munchen: Belleville, 2013.

Amores, Monserrat. '*Cuentos de vieja*, de Juan Ariza. La primera colección de cuentos folclóricos españoles'. In *El cuento español en el siglo XIX. Autores raros y olvidados*, edited by J. Pont, 25–46. Lleida: Scriptura, Edicions Universitat de Lleida, 1998.

Amores, Monserrat. '"El espejo de la verdad" de Vicente Barrantes. Una versión libre del cuento de Blancanieves'. *Revista Garoza*, no. 8 (2008): 9–26.

Amores, Monserrat. *Catálogo de cuentos folclóricos reelaborados por escritores del Siglo XIX*. Madrid: CSIC, 1997.

Aristotle. *Poetics*. USA: Dover, 1997.

Arland, Marcel. *Nouvelle Revue Française* (1 October 1938): 610.

Audissino, Emilio. 'A Gestalt Approach to the Analysis of Music in Film'. *Musicology Research – Music on Screen: From Cinema Screens to Touchscreens*, 1 (Spring 2017): 69–88.

Bacchilega, Cristina. *Postmodern Fairy Tales: Gender and Narrative Strategies*. Philadelphia: University of Pennsylvania Press, 1997.

Balló, Jordi, and Xavier Pérez. *Yo ya he estado aquí: ficciones de la repetición*. Barcelona: Anagrama, 2005.

Barnes, Brooks. 'Her Prince Has Come: Critics, Too'. *New York Times*, 29 May 2009. Available at https://www.nytimes.com/2009/05/31/fashion/31disney.html (accessed 12 March 2020).

Barnier, Martin. *Des films français Made in Hollywood, Les versions Multiples 1929–1935*. Paris: L'Harmattan, 2005.

Barrier, Michael. 'The Animated Man: A Life of Walt Disney'. *Sight and Sound*, 17, no. 7 (2007): 92.

Barrier, Michael. *The Animated Man: A Life of Walt Disney*. London: University of California Press, 2007.

Barrier, Michael. *Hollywood Cartoons: American Animation in Its Golden Age*. New York: Oxford University Press, 1999.

Barrios, Richard. *A Song in the Dark: The Birth of the Musical Film*. New York: Oxford University Press, 1995.

Batkin, Jane. *Identity in Animation: A Journey into Self, Difference, Culture and the Body*. London: Routledge, 2017.

Bayless, Martha. *Parody in the Middle Ages*. Ann Arbor: University of Michigan, 1996.

BBFC website. 'Snow White and the Seven Dwarfs (1937)'. Available at https://www.bbfc.co.uk/case-studies/snow-white-and-seven-dwarfs-1937 (accessed 13 March 2020).

Bell, Elizabeth, Lynda Haas and Laura Sells, eds. *From Mouse to Mermaid: The Politics of Film, Gender, and Culture*. Indianapolis: Indiana University Press, 1995.

Belton, John. *American Cinema American Culture*. New York: McGraw-Hill, 2005.

Bendazzi, Giannalberto. *Animation: A World History: Volume II*. Bloomington: Indiana University Press, 1996.

Bergère, Marie-Claire. *Shanghai: China's Gateway to Modernity*, trans. J. Lloyd. Stanford, CA: Stanford University Press, 2009.

Berthier, Nancy. 'Espagne folklorique et Espagne éternelle: l'irrésistible ascension de l'espagnolade'. *Bulletin d'histoire contemporaine de l'Espagne*, no. 24 (1996): 245–54.

Bettelheim, Bruno. *Psicoanálisis de los cuentos de hadas*. Barcelona: Grijalbo Mondadori, 1994.

Bilgic, Filiz. *Turk Sinemasinda 1980 Sonrasi Uslup Arayislari (Post-1980 Style Intervals in Turkish Cinema)*. Ankara: Kultur Bakanligi, 2002.

Biltereyst, Daniël. 'Film Censorship in a Liberal Free Market Democracy: Strategies of Film Control and Audience's Experiences of Censorship in Belgium'. In *Silencing Cinema: Film Censorship around the World*, edited by Daniël Biltereyst and Roel Vande Winkel, 275–93. New York: Palgrave Macmillan, 2013.

Biltereyst, Daniël. '*Will We Ever See Potemkin?* The Historical Reception and Censorship of S.M. Eisenstein's *Battleship Potemkin* (1925) in Belgium, 1926–1932'. *Studies in Russian and Soviet Cinema*, 2 no. 1 (2008): 5–19.

Boeckenhoff, Katharina, and Caroline Ruddell. 'Lotte Reiniger: The Crafty Animator and Cultural Value'. In *The Crafty Animator: Handmade, Craft-Based Animation and Cultural Value*, edited by Caroline Ruddell and Paul Ward, 75–98. London: Palgrave Macmillan, 2019.

Bohn, James. *Music in Disney's Animated Features: Snow White and the Seven Dwarfs to the Jungle Book*. Jackson, USA: University Press of Mississippi, 2017.

Bolaki, Stella. 'Four Times upon a Time: "*Snow White*" Retold'. In *Beyond Adaptation: Essays on Radical Transformations of Original Works*, edited by Phyllis Frus and Christy Williams, 181–93. Jefferson, NC: McFarland, 2010.

Bordwell, David, and Kristin Thompson. *Film Art: An Introduction*, 10th edn. New York: McGraw-Hill, 2013.

Bostan, Ayse Dilara, and Serpil Kırel. 'Postmodern Donem Disney Prenses Anlatilarinda İnsa Edilen Kadın Temsilinin Moana Ornegi Uzerinden Incelenmesi' (The Analysis of Women Presentation Built in Disney Princess Narrative in Postmodern Era through the Case of Moana), *TRT Akademi*, 5, no. 3 (2018): 6–27.

Bouldin, Joanna. 'The Body, Animation and the Real: Race, Reality and the Rotoscope in Betty Boop'. *Conference Proceedings: Affective Encounters Rethinking Embodiment in Feminist Media Studies*. University of Turku, 2001.

Boym, S. (2001) *The Future of Nostalgia*. New York: Basic Books.

Braco, Diane. 'El hechizo de las imágenes: Blancanieves, el cuento espectacular de Pablo Berger (2012)'. *Fotocinema. Revistacientífica de cine y fotografía*, no. 11 (2015): 26–49.

Brasillach, Robert. '*Les Spectacles: Petite histoire du dessin animé*'. *La Revue Universelle*, 15 May 1938 (Rondel collection held at the Bibliothèque des Arts et Spectacle).

Brisson, Pierre. 'Chronique des spectacles. *Blanche-Neige* de Walt Disney'. *le Figaro*, 8 May 1938: 5.

Brode, Douglas. *From Walt to Woodstock: How Disney Created Counterculture.* Austin: University of Texas Press, 2004.

Brode, Douglas, and Shea T. Brode, eds. *Debating Disney: Pedagogical Perspectives on Commercial Cinema.* Lanham, MD: Rowman & Littlefield, 2016.

Bronfen, Elisabeth. 'Speaking with Eyes: Tod Browning's *Dracula* and Its Phantom Camera'. In *The Films of Tod Browning*, edited by Bernd Herzogenrath, 151–71. London: Black Dog, 2006.

Bronner, Simon J. *Following Tradition: Folklore in the Discourse of American Culture.* Logan: Utah State University Press, 1998.

Bryman, Alan. *The Disneyization of Society.* New Jersey: Blackwell, 1999.

Bucksbaum, Sydney. 'The Evolution of Disney Princesses, from *Snow White* to *Frozen 2*'. *Entertainment Weekly.* 21 November 2019. Available at https://ew.com/movies/disney-princesses-evolution/ (accessed 10 March 2020).

Buhler, James, Rob Deemer and David Neumeyer. *Hearing the Movies: Music and Sound in Film History.* New York: Oxford University Press, 2010.

Buonanno, Milly. *The Age of Television: Experiences and Theories.* Bristol: Intellect Books, 2008.

Burns, William F. 'From the Shadows: Nosferatu and the German Expressionist Aesthetic'. *Mise-en-scène: The Journal of Film & Visual Narration*, 1, no. 1 (2016): 62–73.

Byrne, Eleanor, and Martin McQuillan. *Deconstructing Disney.* London: Pluto Press, 1999.

Cocteau, Jean. *Cahiers Jean Cocteau*, no. 10, Paris: Gallimard, 1985.

Cakir, Sureyya. 'Yesilcam Sineması ve Masal Formu: Aysecik' (Yesilcam Cinema and Tale Form: Aysecik)', *Turkish Studies*, 12, no. 21 (2017): 133–50.

Cambazoglu, C. 'Komser Sekspir'. *Sinema Ansiklopedisi (Cinema Encyclopedia).* Available at https://sinemaansiklopedisi.wordpress.com/2017/12/26/kolay-para-kulhan-aski/ (accessed 5 August 2018), 2001.

Cameron, Kate. 'Disney Masterpiece at the Music Hall'. *New York Daily News*, 14 January 1938, 50.

Campbell, Joseph. *The Hero with a Thousand Faces.* London: HarperCollins, 1993.

Canemaker, John. *Before the Animation Begins: The Art and Lives of Disney Inspirational Sketch Artists.* New York: Hyperion, 1997.

Canemaker, John. *Walt Disney's Nine Old Men and the Art of Animation.* New York: Disney Editions, 2001.

Care, Ross. 'Make Walt's Music: Music for Disney Animation, 1928–1967'. In *The Cartoon Music Book*, edited by Daniel Goldmark and Yuval Taylor, 21–36. Chicago: A Capella Books.

Carémel, Rémi. '*Le premier doublage de Blanche-Neige enfin retrouvé!*'. Available at http://danslombredesstudios.blogspot.com/2013/03/le-premier-doublage-de-blanche-neige.html (accessed 20 March 2020).

Carémel, Rémi, and Greg Philip. 'Films d'animation Disney: à la recherche des doublages perdus et le cas Blanche Neige et les sept nains'. In *Archives et acteurs des cinémas d'animation en France*, edited by Sébastien Denis, Chantal Duchet, Lucie Merijeau, Marie Pruvost-Delaspre and Sébastien Roffat, 167–74. Paris: L'Harmattan, 2014.

Carroll, T. D. 'Men with Professions Were Only Too Glad to Clean the Yard to Make a Dollar', audio recording, Library of Congress. Available at https://www.loc.gov/item/afcwip003853 (accessed 20 July 2018).

Caselotti, Adrianna. 'Snow White Speaks', *People Weekly* (18 May 1987): 104.

Casetti, Francesco, and Federico Di Chio. *Cómo analizar un film*. Barcelona: Paidós, 1991.

Casetti, Francesco. *Les théories du cinéma depuis 1945*. Paris: Nathan, 1999.

Cavanagh, Patrick. 'The Artist as Neuroscientist'. *Nature*, 434 (March 2007): 301–7.

Çetin Erus, Z. *Amerikan ve Turk Sinemalarında Uyarlamalar (Adaptations in American and Turkish Cinemas)*. Istanbul: Es, 2005.

Ceylan, M. 'Komser Sekspir', *NTV Arsiv*, 16 February. Available at http://arsiv.ntv.com.tr/news/64082.asp#BODY (accessed 2 August 2018).

Chan, Crystal. 'How to Write a Film on a Piano: Norman McLaren's Visual Music', *BFI*, 23 November 2016. Available at https://www.bfi.org.uk/news-opinion/sight-sound-magazine/features/how-write-film-piano-norman-mclaren-s-visual-music (accessed 31 December 2019).

Chang, Justin. '*The Princess and the Frog*', *Variety* (24 November 2009). Available at https://variety.com/2009/digital/features/the-princess-and-the-frog-1200477289/ (accessed 12 March 2020).

Chéronnet, Louis. 'Au cinéma. *Blanche-Neige et les sept nains*'. *Beaux-Arts*, 20 May 1938: 6.

Chesterton, G. K. *Varied Types*. Charleston: Bibliolife, 2009.

Chillón, Albert. 'La urdimbre mitopoética de la cultura mediática'. *Anàlisi: quaderns de comunicació i cultura*, no. 24 (2000): 21–159.

Churchill, Douglas. 'Disney's "Philosophy"'. *New York Times*, 6 March 1938: 9, 23.

Churchill, Douglas. 'Now Mickey Mouse Enters Art's Temple'. *New York Times*, 3 June 1934: 12 sect. 6

Churchill, Douglas. 'Walt Disney Signs for more Whirls'. *New York Times*, 9 January 1938: 5 sect. 10.

Churchill, Douglas. 'West-Coasting along'. *New York Times*, 30 January 1938: 5 sect. 10.

Clark, L. 'Looking Around with a Hay Farmer', *Life Histories*, Library of Congress. Available at https://www.loc.gov/resource/wpalh0.07011806/?st=gallery (accessed 19 July 2018).

Cloud, John. 'How Gay Days Made a Home at Disney World'. *Time*, 21 June 2010. Available at http://www.time.com/time/magazine/article/0,9171,1995839-1,00.html.

Coates, Paul. *The Gorgon's Gaze: German Cinema, Expressionism, and the Image of Horror*. Cambridge: Cambridge University Press, 1991.

Colombo, Cristina. 'Blancanieves: De la ficción al empoderamiento'. In *VII Jornadas de Poéticas de la Literatura Argentina para Niñas*, 13–14 May 2016, Ensenada, Argentina, in *Memoria Académica*. Available at www.memoria.fahce.unlp.edu.ar/trab_eventos/ev.7517/ev.7517.pdf.

Colt, S. 'Walt Disney – Part 1', *American Experience* (2015), Sarah Colt Productions [TV programme] PBS. Available at https://www.pbs.org/video/american-experience-walt-disney-part-1-chapter-1/ (accessed 25 July 2018).

Coons, Richard. '"Snow White", Disney's First Full-Length Film, Rated 'Movie of the Month' for Artistry and Charm'. *Washington Post*, 9 January 1938: 1.

Coplan, Amy. 'Catching Character's Emotions: Emotional Contagion Response to Narrative Fiction Film'. In Film Studies, no 8 été 2006, Manchester University Press, 2007.

Corliss, Richard. '*Tangled*: Disney's Ripping Rapunzel'. *TIME*, 26 November 2010. Available at http://content.time.com/time/arts/article/0,8599,2033166,00.html (accessed 10 March 2020).

Correspondence from Walt Disney to Don Graham, 23 December 1935. Available online at http://www.lettersofnote.com/2010/06/how-to-train-animator-by-walt-disney.html (accessed 14 March 2020).

Coyle, Rebecca. 'Audio Motion: Animating (Film) Sound'. In *Drawn to Sound: Animation Film Music and Sonicity*, edited by Rebecca Coyle, 1–22. London: Equinox.

Crafton, Donald. *Before Mickey: The Animated Film 1898–1928*. Chicago: University of Chicago Press, 1993.

Crafton, Donald. *The Talkies: American Cinema's Transition to Sound 1926–1931*. London: University of California Press, 1997.

Creation Monthly. 'The First Chinese Animated Feature Film: *Princess Iron Fan*', 1, no. 1 (1941): 64.

Crisler, B. R. 'Film Gossip of the Week: Walt Disney and His Galaxy of Fauna'. *New York Times*, 30 May 1937: 7.

Croxton, Katie. 'Snow White, the Grimm Brothers and the Studio the Dwarfs Built'. In *Walt Disney, from Reader to Storyteller: Essays on the Literary Inspirations*, edited by Kathy Merlock Jackson and Mark I. West, 21–30. Jefferson, NC: McFarland, 2015.

Culhane, John. 'Snow White at 50: Undimmed Magic'. *New York Times*, 12 July 1987: 243–55.

Cunningham, J. P. 'The Play and Screen: "Snow White and the Seven Dwarfs"'. *Commonwealth*, 28 January 1938: 386.

Cupchick, Gerald C. "Emotion in Aesthetics: Reactive and Reflective Models'. *Poetics*, no. 23 (1994): 183.

Czitrom, D. J. 'American Motion Pictures and the New Popular Culture, 1893–1918'. In *Popular Culture in American History*, edited by Jim Cullen, 131–56. Oxford: Blackwell, 2001.

d'Ast, Raoul. 'Nous verrons le 6 mai au Marignan *Blanche-Neige et les sept nains*'. *Liberté*, 30 April 1938: 4.

D'Oliveira, Beatriz, and Marina Romanelli. 'Fanfictions e o Papel do Fã na Era da Transmídia'. *Revista Hipertexto*, 3, no. 1 (January/June 2013): 1–14.

Daugherty, Frank. 'Mickey Mouse Comes of Age'. *Christian Science* Monitor, 2 February 1938: 8–9.

Davis, Amy M., ed. *Discussing Disney*. Bloomington: Indiana University Press, 2019.

Davis, Amy M. *Good Girls and Wicked Witches: Women in Disney's Feature Animation*. Eastleigh: John Libbey, 2006.

deCordova, Richard. 'The Mickey in Macy's Window: Childhood, Consumerism, and Disney Animation'. In *Disney Discourse: Producing the Magic Kingdom*, edited by Eric Smoodin, 203–13. London: Routledge, 1994.

Deja, Andreas. *The Nine Old Men: Lessons, Techniques, and Inspiration from Disney's Great Animators*. Boca Raton, FL: CRC Press, 2015.

Dentith, Simon. *Parody*. London: Routledge, 2000.

Depauw, Liesbet, and Daniël Biltereyst. 'The Belgian Board of Film Control and the Tarzan films, 1932–1946'. *Historical Journal of Film, Radio and Television*, 38, no. 1 (2018): 1–19.

Derisson, Karl. *Blanche Neige et les sept nains: la création du chef-d'œuvre de Walt Disney*. Paris: L'Harmattan, 2014.

Disney, Walt. 'Deeds Rather Than Words'. In *Faith Is a Star*, edited by R. Gammon, 6–10. New York: E. P. Dutton, 1963.

Do Rozario, Rebecca-Anne C. *Fashion in the Fairy Tale Tradition*. London: Palgrave Macmillan, 2018.

Dogan, Evinc, and Evren Dogan. 'Kent ve Anti-Gosteri: Istanbul'un Sine-masal İmgeleri' (City and Anti-Show: Cine-fairy Images of Istanbul), *Sinecine*, 2, no. 9 (2018): 111–30.

Doherty, Thomas. 'This Is Where We Came In: The Audible Screen and the Voluble Audience of Early Sound Cinema'. In *American Movie Audiences: From the Turn of the Century to the Early Sound Era*, edited by Melvyn Stokes and Richard Maltby, 143–62. London: British Film Institute, 1999.

Doherty, Thomas. *Hollywood's Censor: Joseph I. Breen & The Production Code Administration*. New York: Columbia University Press, 2007.

Dorsay, Atilla. *100 Yılın 100 Turk Filmi* (100 Turkish Films of the Year 100), Istanbul: Remzi, 2013.

Doyle, J. 'Disney Dollars, 1930s' "Prosperity Out of Fantasy," Topics of the Times, *New York Times*, The Pop History Dig. Available at http://www.pophistorydig.com/topics/tag/new-york-times-magazine/ (accessed 19 July 2018).

Dury, Richard. 'The Hand of Hyde'. In *Robert Louis Stevenson Reconsidered: New Critical Perspectives*, edited by William B. Jones, Jr., 101–16. Jefferson, NC: McFarland, 2013.

Dyer, Richard. 'Entertainment and Utopia'. *Movie*, no. 24 (Spring 1977): 2–13.

Eisenstein, Sergei (trans. Jay Leyda). *Eisenstein on Disney*. London: Methuen, 1988.

Eisner, Lotte H. *The Haunted Screen: Expressionism in German Cinema and the Influence of Max Reinhardt*. London: Thames and Hudson, 1969.

Ekman, Stefan. 'Urban Fantasy: A Literature of the Unseen'. *Journal of the Fantastic in the Arts*, 27, no. 3 (2016): 452–69.

Eldridge, D. *American Culture in the 1930s*. Edinburgh: Edinburgh University Press, 2008.

Elsaesser, Thomas. *BFI Film Classics: Metropolis*. London: BFI, 2000.

Elsaesser, Thomas. *Weimar Cinema and After: Germany's Historical Imaginary*. London: Routledge, 2000.

Epardaud, Edmond. 'Une parfait oeuvre d'art, une déplorable affaire commerciale: Blanche Neige'. *La griffe*, 11 November 1938 (Rondel collection held at the Bibliothèque des Arts et Spectacle).

Espinosa, Aurelio M. *Cuentos populares españoles recogidos de la tradición oral de España. Tomo III*. Madrid: CSIC, 1946–7.

Espinosa, Aurelio M. *Cuentos populares españoles recogidos de la tradición oral de España. Tomo I*. California: Stanford University Press, 1923.

Estes, Clarissa Pinkola. *Kurtlarla Kosan Kadınlar (Woman Who Run with the Wolves)*, trans. H. Atalay, Istanbul: Ayrıntı, 2003.

Evren, Burcak. *Turk Sinemasında Yeni Konumlar (New Positions in Turkish Cinema)*, Istanbul: Broy, 1990.

Fauteuil 22, '... Dans un fauteuil. *Blanche-Neige et les sept nains*'. *La Croix*, 15–16 May 1938: 6.

Fayard, Jean. '*Blanche-Neige et les Sept Nains*.' *Candide*, 12 May 1938: 17.

Film Daily. 'Snow White Is Exempted from French Dubbing Rule'. 20 May 1938: 10.

Finch, Christopher. *The Art of Walt Disney: From Mickey Mouse to the Magic Kingdoms and Beyond*. New York: Abrams, 2011.

Finn, John C. 'Review – *Film Snow White and the Seven Dwarfs*'. *Variety*, 28 December 1937.

Fitzsimons, Tim. 'Magical Pride: Disney to Host Its First Official LGBTQ Pride Event This Year'. *NBC News*, 31 January 2019. Available at https://www.nbcnews.com/feature/nbc-out/magical-pride-disney-host-its-first-official-lgbtq-pride-event-n965396. Magical Pride: Disney.

Foster, Amy. 'Futuristic Medievalisms and the U.S. Space Program in Disney's *Man in Space* Trilogy and *Unidentified Flying Oddball*'. In *The Disney Middle Ages: A Fairy-Tale and Fantasy Past*, edited by Tison Pugh and Susan Aronstein, 153–70. New York: Palgrave, 2012.

Frampton, Daniel. *Filmosophy*. London: Wallflower press, 2006.

Franks-allen, Sara. 'See the Real Life Models for Your Favourite Disney Characters'. *The FW*, 2014, thefw.com/real-life-disney-models/.

Freeberg, Gallese. 'Motion, Emotion and Empathy in Esthatic Experience'. *Trends in Cognitive Sciences*, 11 no. 5 (2007): 199.

Freeman, Linton C. 'Some Antecedents of Social Network Analysis'. *Connections*, 19, no. 1 (1996): 39–42.

Freud, Sigmund. *The Uncanny*, trans. David McLintock. London: Penguin, 2003.

Frome, Jonathan. '*Snow White*: Critics and Criteria for the Animated Feature Film'. *Quarterly Review of Film and Video*, 30, no. 5 (2013): 462–73.

Fromm, Erich. *Itaatsizlik Uzerine Denemeler (On Disobedience)*, trans. A. Sayın, Istanbul: Yaprak (1987).

Furniss, Maureen. *Art in Motion: Animation Aesthetics*. Revised Edition. Bloomington: Indiana University Press, 2014.

Fuzellier, Etienne. 'De Méliès à Blanche-Neige'. *Cahiers du Sud*, March 1939: 276.

Gallese, Guerra. "Embodying Movies: Embodied Simulation and Film Studies". *Cinema*, 3 (2012): 1–27

García Carcedo, Pilar. *La literatura infantil en el ámbito de lo hispánico: tradición y renovación*, 2004. Available at www.liceus.com (accessed 24 July 2018).

García Carrión, Marta. 'Españoladas y estereotipos cinematográficos: algunas consideraciones sobre su recepción en la España de los años veinte'. *Revue Iberical, Revue d'études ibériques et ibéro-américaines* (dossier monographique: Les stéréotypes dans la construction des identités nationales depuis une perspective transnationale), coordinated by G. Galéote, no. 10 (2016): 123–35.

Gardner, B. T., and L. Wallach. 'Shapes of Figures Identified as a Baby's Head'. *Perceptual and Motor Skills*, 20, no. 2 (1965): 135–42.

Garner, John W. 'De New York. *Blanche-Neige*. Ce qu'est la féerie de Walt Disney'. *Le Jour*, 3 February 1938: 6.

Genette, Gérard. *Narrative Discourse: an Essay in Method*. Ithaca: Cornell University Press, 1980.

Genette, Gérard. *Palimpsests: Literature in the Second Degree*. Lincoln: University of Nebraska Press, 1997.

Genette, Gérard. *The Architect: An Introduction*, trans. Jane Lewin. Berkeley: University of California Press, 1992.

Giesen, Rolf, and J. P. Storm. *Animation under the Swastika: A History of Trickfilm in Nazi Germany, 1933–1945*. Jefferson, NC: McFarland, 2012.

Giraud, Kevin. '*Blanche Neige et les Sept Nains* face à la censure'. *Koregos*. Available at http://www.koregos.org/fr/kevin-giraud-blanche-neige-et-les-sept-nains-face-a-la-censure/ (accessed 10 March 2020).

Giraux, Henry A. *The Mouse That Roared: Disney and the End of Innocence*. Lanham, MD: Rowman and Littlefield, 2001.

Giroux, Henry A. 'Animating Youth: The Disnification of Children's Culture'. *Socialist Review*, 94 no. 3 (1994): 65–79.

Gomery, Douglas. *The Coming of Sound: A History*. New York: Routledge, 2005.

Good Housekeeping. 'Walt Disney's Snow White and the Seven Dwarfs: Adapted from Grimm's Fairy Tales'. November 1937: 35.

Gorbman, Claudia. *Unheard Melodies: Narrative Film Music*. London: Indiana Jones University, 1987.

Gordillo, Inmaculada. *La hipertelevisión: géneros y formatos*. Ecuador: Ciespal, 2009.

Göreç, Ertem. Interviewed by Sanatcı Yasam Evi (Artist Nursing Home), Kartal-Istanbul, February 2018.

Gottesman, Ronald. 'Film Parody: An Immodest Proposal'. *Quarterly Review of Film and Video*, 12 (1990): 1–3.

Gould, Stephen Jay. 'Mickey Mouse meets Konrad Lorenz'. *Natural History*, 88 (1979): 30–6.

Gross, John. *Oxford Book of Parodies*. Oxford: Oxford University Press, 2010.

Gross, R., McIlveen, R. *Aspects of Psychology: Memory*. London: Hodder and Stoughton, 1999.

Guo, Hong. *Shanghai: The Cradle of Modern Chinese Animation Movie*. Shanghai: Zhongxi Book, 2017.

Haagsche Courant. 'Het Sprookje van Sneeuwwitje en de Zeven Dwergen: Een verhaal voor kinderen en een film voor ouderen'. 3 November, 1939: 11.

Harmetz, Aljean. 'Disney's "Old Men" Savor the Vintage Years'. *New York Times*, 4 July 1993: 9.

Harries, Dan. *Film Parody*. London: BFI, 2000.

Harrison, Paul. '"Snow White," $1,600,000 Disney Screen Creation, Now Ready for Public'. *Washington Post*, 9 January 1938: 1.

Harrison, R. *State and Society in Twentieth-Century America*. Harlow: Addison Wesley Longman, 1997.

Hays, Will H. *The Memoirs of Will H. Hays*. New York: Doubleday, 1955.

He. 'Dwarfs are Too Lazy to Wash Faces'. *Nanhai Yinxing*, 1, no. 5 (1938): 1.

Heldt, Guido. *Music and Levels of Narration in Film: Steps Across the Border*. Bristol: Intellect Ltd, 2013.

Het Vaderland. 'Engeland censureert sprookjes'. 28 February, 1938: 8.

Hirschfeld, Al, and William Saroyan. *Harlem as Seen by Hirschfeld.* New York: Hyperion Press, 1941.

Holliss, Richard, and Brian Sibley. *Snow White and the Seven Dwarfs & the Making of the Classic Film.* New York: Simon & Schuster, 1987.

Holt, Nathalia. *The Queens of Animation: The Untold Story of the Women.* London: Little, Brown, 2019.

Huron, David. *Sweet Anticipation: Music and the Psychology of Expectation.* London: MIT Press, 2007.

Hutcheon, Linda. *A Theory of Parody: The Teachings of Twentieth-Century Art Forms.* London: Methuen, 1985.

Inge, T. 'Walt Disney's Snow White and the Seven Dwarves: Art Adaptation and Ideology'. *Journal of Popular Film and Television*, 32, 3 (2004): 132–42 (140).

Irvine, Alexander. 'Urban Fantasy'. In *The Cambridge Companion to Fantasy Literature*, edited by Edward James and Farah Mendlesohn, 200–13. Cambridge: Cambridge University Press, 2012.

Jameson, Fredric. 'Postmodernizm ya da Kapitalizmin Kulturel Mantığı' (Postmodernism, or, the Cultural Logic of Late Capitalism), trans. G. Nalis, D. Sabuncuoglu, D. Erksan, in N. Zeka (eds), 59–116, *Postmodernizm (Postmodernism),* Istanbul: Kıyı, 1994.

Jameson, Fredric. *Kulturel Donemec (The Cultural Turn),* trans. K. İnal, Ankara: Dost, 2005.

Jenkins, Eric. *Special Affects: Cinema, Animation and the Translation of Consumer Culture.* Edinburgh: Edinburgh University Press, 2014.

Jenkins, Henry. *The Children's Culture Reader.* New York: New York University Press, 1998.

Jin, Zuixia. '*Princess Iron Fan* Animated Film'. *Popular Cinema News*, 2, no. 21 (1941): 583.

Johnson, David. 'Dick Lundy (1909–1990)'. In *Snow White's People: An Oral History of the Disney Film Snow White and the Seven Dwarfs, Volume 1*, edited by Didier Ghez, 31–52. USA: Theme Park Press, 2017.

Johnson, David. 'Grim Natwick (1890–1990)'. In *Snow White's People: An Oral History of the Disney Film Snow White and the Seven Dwarfs, Volume 1*, edited by Didier Ghez, 53–74. USA: Theme Park Press, 2017.

Johnson, David. 'Wilfred Jackson'. In *Snow White's People: An Oral History of the Disney Film Snow White and the Seven Dwarfs, volume 1*, edited by Didier Chez, 1–21. Theme Park Press.

Johnson, Mindy. *Ink & Paint: The Women of Walt Disney's Animation.* Glendale: Disney Editions, 2017.

Justamand, François. 'Le mystère Blanche Neige'. *La gazette du doublage.* November 2009. Available at http://www.objectif-cinema.com/spip. php?article5235 (accessed 10 March 2020).

Justamand, François. 2001 article for DVD Vision, republished on his website La gazette du doublage called '*Blanche Neige et les sept nains : Ses trois doublages*', http://www.objectif-cinema.com/horschamps/040.php.

Juvan, Marko. 'The Parody and Bakhtin'. In *Bakhtin and the Humanities*, edited by Miha Javornik, Marko Juvan, Aleksander Skaza, Jola Škulj and Ivan Verč, 193–209. Ljubljana: Znanstveni inštitut Filozofske fakultete, 1997.

Kalmakurki, Maarit. '*Snow White and the Seven Dwarfs*, *Cinderella* and *Sleeping Beauty*: The Components of Costume Design in Disney's Early Hand-Drawn Animated Feature Films'. *animation: an interdisciplinary journal*, 13, no. 1 (March 2018): 7–19.

Kalmus, Natalie M. 'Color Consciousness'. *Journal of the Society of Motion Picture Engineers*, 25 (August 1935): 139–47.

Kammen, M. *Mystic Chords of Memory: The Transformation of Tradition in American Culture*. New York: Vintage Books, 1993.

Kassabian, Anahid. *Hearing Film: Tracking Identifications in Contemporary Hollywood Film Music*. New York: Routledge, 2011.

Kaufman, J. B. *The Fairest One of All: The Making of Walt Disney's Snow White and the Seven Dwarfs*. California: Walt Disney Family Foundation Press, 2012.

Kaufman, J. B. 'Before Snow White'. *Film History*, 5, no. 2 (June 1993): 158–75.

Kelly, Katherine Coyne. 'Disney's Medievalized Ecologies in *Snow White and the Seven Dwarfs* and *Sleeping Beauty*'. In *The Disney Middle Ages: A Fairy-Tale and Fantasy Past*, edited by Tison Pugh and Susan Aronstein, 189–207. London: Palgrave Macmillan, 2012.

King, C. R., C. R. Lugo-Lugo and M. K. Bloodsworth-Lugo. *Animating Difference: Race, Gender, and Sexuality in Contemporary Films for Children*. Plymouth: Rowman & Littlefield, 2011.

King, Margaret J. 'The Audience in the Wilderness: The Disney Nature Films'. *Journal of Popular Film and Television*, 24 (1996): 60–8.

Klein, Norman M. *Seven Minutes: The Life and Death of the American Animated Cartoon*. London: Verso, 1993.

Koehler, Dorene. *The Mouse and the Myth: Sacred Art and Secular Ritual of Disneyland*. East Barnet: John Libbey, 2017.

Kokas, Aynne. *Hollywood Made in China*. Oakland: University of California Press, 2017.

Kracauer, S. *From Caligari to Hitler: A Psychological History of the German*. Revised and expanded edition, edited by Leonardo Quaresima. Princeton: Princeton University Press, 2004.

Kuhn, Annette. 'Snow White in 1930s Britain'. *Journal of British Cinema and Television*, 7 no. 2 (2010): 132–42.

L'intransigeant. 7 May 1938. 'Admittedly, the Voices Given to the Legendary Characters too Often Have Anglo-Saxon Accents Which Are Shocking'.

Lambert, Pierre. *Blanche Neige*. Rozay-en-Brie: Démons et Merveilles, 2000.

Laneyrie–Dagen, Nadeije. *L'invention du corps. La représentation de l'homme du Moyen Age à la fin du XIX*. Paris: Flammarion, 2006.

Le Cinéma. 'Blanche-Neige et les sept nains'. 5 May 1938 (Rondel collection held at the Bibliothèque des Arts et Spectacle).

Le Figaro. 'Cette charmante petite fille n'est autre que le 100.000ème spectateur de Blanche Neige et les sept nains que l'on a fêté, l'autre jour, au Marignan'. 7 June 1938: 5.

Lee, Newton, and Krystina Madej. *Disney Stories: Getting to Digital*. New York: Springer, 2012.

Lehman, Christopher P. *The Colored Cartoon: Black Representation in American Animated Short Films: 1907–1954*. Amherst: University of Massachusetts, 2007.

Leslie, Esther. *Hollywood Flatlands: Animation, Critical Theory and the Avant-Garde*. New York: Verson, 2002.

Levine, L. *The Unpredictable Past: Explorations of America's Cultural History*. New York: Oxford University Press, 1993.

Li, Yuhua. 'Film Review for *Chinese Snow White*'. *Women Weekly*, 2, no. 3 (1940): 20–1.

Liberty Magazine. ' "Disney's Folly' Makes History (Snow White and the Seven Dwarfs)'. 12 February 1938: 43.

Life Magazine. 'Mae's Famous Sayings Are Part of Nation's Folklore'. 23 May 1949, 105.

Lindvall, Terry, and Ben Fraser. 'Darker Shades of Animation: African-American Images in the Warner Bros. Cartoon'. In *Reading the Rabbit: Explorations in Warner Bros. Animation*, edited by Kevin S. Sandler, 121–36. New Brunswick: Rutgers University Press, 1998.

Lindvall, Terry, Dennis Bounds and Chris Lindvall. *Divine Film Comedies*. London: Routledge, 2016.

Lipscomb, Scott D., and David E. Tolchinsky. 'The Role of Music Communication in Cinema'. In *Musical Communication*, edited by Dorothy Miell, Raymond MacDonald and David J. Hargreaves, 383–404. New York: Oxford University Press, 2005.

Literary Digest. 'M.M. Is Eight Years Old'. 3 October 1936, v. 22, 19.

Literary Digest. 'Movies: Walt Disney Goes Feature Length'. 22 January 1938, 23.

Lorenz, Konrad. *Essais sur le comportement animal et humain, 1965*. Paris: Seuil, 1970.

Luo, Cang. 'Review: Snow White and the Seven Dwarfs'. *Li Daily*, 9 June 1938: 2.

MacQueen, Steve. 'Walt Disney's Unseen Animation: Rare Treasures from the Vault'. *Smithsonian Institution* (14 March 1998): speech given at the National Museum of Natural History.

Malini, Fábio. *Um método perspectivista de análise de redes sociais: cartografando topologias e temporalidades em rede*. XXV Encontro Anual da Compós, Universidade Federal de Goiás, Goiânia, 2016.

Maltby, Richard. *Hollywood Cinema*. Oxford: Blackwell, 2003.

Maltin, Leonard. *Of Mice and Magic: A History of American Animated Cartoons*. New York: McGraw-Hill, 1980.

Mccormack, David. "The real-life models that helped to inspire some of Walt Disney's best-loved and most iconic characters". *Daily Mail*, March 2013. Available at https://www.dailymail.co.uk/news/article-2299738/The-real-life-models-helped-inspire-Walt-Disneys-best-loved-iconic-characters.html.

Merritt, Russell, and J. B. Kaufman. *Walt Disney's Silly Symphonies: A Companion to the Classic Cartoon Series*. Glendale: Disney Editions, 2016.

Mezzanine. 'La semaine à l'écran. Blanche-Neige'. *Marianne*, 18 May 1938: 17.

Miller family, 'The Entire Family Reviews "Snow White"'. *Los Angeles Times* (2 January 1938): 1 part III.

Minor Jose Gaytan Shares Disney Animation Progression Reels, *On Animation*, July 2018. Available at https://onanimation.com/2018/07/15/minor-jose-gaytan-shares-disney-animation-progression-reels/ (accessed 10 March 2020).

Mitchell, M. *Gone with the Wind*. New York: Macmillan, 1936.

Moen, Kristian. *Film and Fairy Tales: The Birth of Modern Fantasy*. London: I.B. Tauris, 2013.

Mollet, Tracey. "'With a Smile and a Song...'": Walt Disney and the Birth of the American Fairy Tale'. *Marvels and Tales*, 27, no. 1 (2013): 109–24.

Mollet, Tracey. *Cartoons in Hard Times: The Animated Shorts of Disney and Warner Brothers in Depression and War, 1932–1945*. New York: Bloomsbury, 2017.

Morgan, I., and P. J. Davies. *Hollywood and the Great Depression*. Edinburgh: Edinburgh University Press, 2016.

Morson, Gary, and Caryl Emerson (eds). *Rethinking Bakhtin: Extensions and Challenges*. Evanston, IL: Northwestern University Press, 1989.

Movie Daily New. 'Princess Iron Fan'. 19 November 1941: 3.

Movietone. 'How Is Snow Sister and the Seven Dwarfs Created?', 7, no. 11 (1938): 212–13.

Movietone. 'Snow Sister and the Seven Dwarfs Will Make a Profit of Fifteen Million', 7, no. 13 (1938): 254.

Movietone. '*Snow White* in China'. 8, no. 29 (1939): 1204.

Muller, John. 'Fred Astaire and the Integrated Musical'. *Cinema Journal*, 24, no. 1 (1984): 28–40.

Murray, Robin L., and Joseph K. Heumann, *That's All Folks?: Ecocritical Readings of American Animated Features*. Lincoln: University of Nebraska Press, 2011.

Nanhai Yinxing. '*Snow White*', no. 7 (1938): 2.

Navarrete Cardero, José Luis. 'La españolada y Sevilla', *Cuadernos de Eicheroa*, no. 4, Sevilla, 2003.

Navarrete Cardero, José Luis. *Historia de un género cinematográfico: la españolada*. Madrid: Quiasmo, 2009.

Nelson, Thomas A. 'Darkness in the Disney Look'. *Literature/Film Quarterly*, 6, no. 2 (1978): 94–103.

Nesbet, Anne. 'Inanimations: "Snow White" and "Ivan the Terrible".' *Film Quarterly*, 50, no. 4 (1997): 20–31.

Neumeyer, David. 'Diegetic/Nondiegetic: A Theoretical Model'. *Music and the Moving Image*, 2, no. 1 (2009): 26–39.

Neupert, Richard. 'Painting a Plausible World: Disney's Color Prototypes'. In *Disney Discourse: Producing the Magic Kingdom*, edited by Eric Smoodin, 106–17. London: Routledge, 1994.

Ni, Changmin. 'Snow White's Eight Immortals Crossing the Sea'. *Shanghai Daily*, 25 December 1938: 15.

North China Daily News. 'Midnight in Toyshop [Advertisement]'. 23 December 1931: 25.

Notre temps. 'Blanche-Neige'. 17 June 1938: 3.

Nugent, F. S. 'Disney Is Now Art–But He Wonders'. *New York Times*, 26 February 1939: 4.

Oriental Daily. 'The Park Hotel's Sky Terrace Hall [Advertisement]'. 25 June 1945: 2.

Pallant, Chris. *Animated Landscapes: History, Form, and Function*. New York: Bloomsbury, 2015.

Pallant, Chris. *Demystifying Disney: A History of Disney Feature Animation*. New York: Continuum Books, 2011.

Pantouvaki, Sofia. 'Experiencing Visual Metaphors: The Perception of the Theatre and Imagery by Children and Youth in Oppressive Situations'. In *Engaging Children Creatively and Critically*, edited by Mary A. Drinkwater, 39–60, Oxford: Inter-Disciplinary Press, 2013.

Paris-midi. 'Vendredi au Marignan, un très grand évènement cinématographique: Blanche Neige et les sept nains'. 4 May 1938: 6.

Philip, Greg. '*Snow White's First French Version*'. Available at http://www.alostfilm.com/2013/03/snow-whites-first-french-version.html (accessed 20 March 2020).

Philip, Greg. 'The French *Snow White* Premiere'. 15 November 2011. Available at http://www.alostfilm.com/2011/11/french-snow-white-premiere.html.

Pierce T. J. 'Wow, We've Got Something Here: Ward Kimball and the Making of Snow White'. *New England Review-Middlebury Series*, 37, no. 1 (2016): 123–36.

Power, Patrick. 'Character Animation and the Embodied Mind–Brain'. *animation: an interdisciplinary journal*, 3, no. 1 (2008): 25–48.

Pozzi, Davide with the collaboration of Claudine Kaufmann, 'Koenigsmark, journal d'une restauration', *Léonce Perret*, AFRHC, 2013, 223.

Prendergast, Roy. M. *Film Music: A Neglected Art*. New York: W. W. Norton, 1992.

Propp, Vladamir. *Masalın Bicimbilimi ve Olaganustu Masalların Donusumu (Morphology of the Folktale)*, trans. M. Rıfat and S. Rıfat, 3rd edn, Istanbul: Is Bankası, 2017.

Propp, Vladimir. *Morphology of the Folktale*. Bloomington: Indiana University, 1958.

Pryor, T. M. '"Snow White' Sidelights: Censors Toppled and Business Boomed as the Dwarfs Went Round the World'. *New York Times* (February 5, 1939): 4 sect. 9.

Pugh, Tison, and Susan Aronstein, eds. *The Disney Middle Ages: A Fairy-Tale and Fantasy Past*. Hampshire: Palgrave Macmillan, 2012.

Qin, Gang. 'Disney's Animation in Shanghai in the Republic of China during the Era of "Sound Animation" – Based on Lu Xun's Dairy'. *Modern Chinese Literature Studies*, no. 7 (2017): 38–49.

Raitt, E. I. 'What Can Business Do to Remove Consumer Suspicion?'. *Journal of Home Economics*, 28 (January, 1936): 5–8.

Ramachandran, V. S., Hirstein William. 'The Science of Art: A Neurological Theory of Aesthetic Experience'. *Journal of Consciousness Studies*, 6, nos 6–7 (1999): 15–51.

Raya Bravo, Irene, and García, Pedro. 'El camino hacia Juego de Tronos. Nuevas tendencias en la fantasía cinematográfica y televisiva del nuevo milenio'. In *Reyes, espadas, cuervos y dragones. Estudio del fenómeno televisivo Juego de Tronos*, edited by Irene Raya Bravo and Pedro García, 33–60. Sevilla: Fragua, 2013.

Raya Bravo, Irene. 'La tendencia hacia la hibridación en el macrogénero extraordinario durante la era hipertelevisiva. Casos de estudio: Galáctica: estrella de combate, Juego de Tronos y American Horror Story'. *Revista de la Asociación Española de Investigación de la Comunicación*, 3, no. 6 (2016): 11–18.

Rémi, Carémel, and Greg Philip. 'Films d'animation Disney: à la recherche des doublages perdus et le cas *Blanche Neige et les sept nains*'. In *Archives et acteurs des cinémas d'animation en France*, edited by Sébastien Denis, Chantal Duchet, Lucie Merijeau, Marie Pruvost-Delaspre and Sébastien Roffat, 167–74. Paris: L'Harmattan, 2014.

Rhodes, Gillian. *Superportaits: Caricatures and Recognition*. Oxfordshire: Psychology Press, 1996.

Ribés Alegría, Maite. 'La hibridación de géneros y la crisis de la calidad televisiva: consejos audiovisuales en el panorama televisivo'. *Comunicar: Revista científica iberoamericana de comunicación y educación*, no. 25 (2005): 1–10.

Robbins, L. H. 'Mickey Mouse Emerges as Economist'. *New York Times Magazine*, 10 March 1935, VI, 8.

Roberts, Ian. *German Expressionist Cinema: The World of Light and Shadow*. London: Wallflower Press, 2008.

Robinson, Tasha. '*Moana* Review: After 80 Years of Experiments, Disney Has Made the Perfect Disney Movie'. *The Verge*. 26 November 2016. Available at https://www.theverge.com/2016/11/26/13749060/moana-film-review-walt-disney-animation-dwayne-johnson-diversity (accessed 10 March 2020).

Roffat, Sébastien. 'Disney Walter Elias'. In *Dictionnaire de la pensée du cinema*, edited by Antoine de Baecque and Philippe Chevallier, 233–6. Paris: Presses Universitaires de France, 2012.

Rovira Collado, Joan M., and Pomares Puig, Pilar. 'Clásicos infantiles para adultos. Últimas adaptaciones cinematográficas de cuentostradicionales'. In *1st International Conference: Teaching Literature in English for Young Learners*, edited by Agustín Reyes Torres, Luis S. Villacañas de Castro and Betlem Soler Pardo, 199–206. Facultat de Magisteri: Universitat de València, 2012.

Rush, Jeffrey S. 'Who's in on the joke: Parody as Hybridized Narrative Discourse'. *Quarterly Review of Film and Video*, 12, nos 1–2 (1990): 5–12.

Salt, Barry. 'From Caligari to Who?' *Sight and Sound*, 48, no. 2 (1979): 119–23.

Sammond, Nicholas. *Babes in Tomorrowland: Walt Disney and the Making of the American Child, 1930–1960*. Durham: Duke University Press, 2005.

Sandlin, Jennifer A., and Julie C. Garlen. *Disney, Culture, and Curriculum*. London: Routledge, 2016.

Sasa, Ayse. *Yesilcam Gunlugu (Yesilcam Diary)*. Istanbul: Dergah, 2002.

Sayim, Bilge, Patrick Cavanagh. 'What Line Drawings Reveal about the Visual Brain'. *Frontiers in Human Neuroscience*, 5, Article 118 (October 2011): 1–4.

Schallert, Edwin. '"Snow White Achievement in Film Art'. *Los Angeles Times*, 22 December 1937: 11.

Schallert, Edwin. 'Cartoon Actors Claim Spotlight'. *Los Angeles Times*, 12 December 1937: 1.

Schallert, Edwin. 'Dwarf Dopey Hailed as Newest Scene Stealer'. *Los Angeles Times* 11 December 1937, 7 part II.

Schickel, Richard. *The Disney Version: The Life, Times, Art and Commerce of Walt Disney*. Revised and updated edn. London: Pavilion Michael Joseph, 1986.

Schreibman, Myrl A., and Max Steiner. 'On Gone with the Wind, Selznick, and the Art of "Mickey Mousing": An Interview with Max Steiner'. *Journal of Film and Video*, 56, no. 1 (Spring 2004): 41–50.

Segrave, Kerry. *American Films Abroad: Hollywood's Domination of the World's Movie Screens from the 1890s to the Present*. Jefferson, NC: McFarland, 1997.

Seidman, Steve. *Comedian Comedy*. USA: UMI Research, 1981.

Selfa Sastre, Moisés. 'Siete cuentos inéditos traducidos al español de los Hermanos Grimm: ejemplo de relatos poco moralizantes', *MediAzioni* 17 ('Perspectivas multifacéticas en el universo de la literatura infantil y juvenil') (2015): 1–11.

Senn, Bryan. *Golden Horrors: An Illustrated Critical Filmography of Terror Cinema, 1931–1939*. Jefferson, NC: McFarland, 2006.

Shull, Michael, and David Wilt. *Doing Their Bit: Wartime American Animated Short Films, 1939–1945*. Jefferson, NC: McFarland, 1987.

Silver Flower Monthly. 'The Most Popular Film and Star by Shanghai Audience', no. 13 (1939): 16.

Smith, Murray, 'Empathy and the Extended Mind'. *Aesthetic Research Group Seminar Series 2006–2007*, Research Paper, University of Kent.

Smithsonian American Art Museum. '1934: A New Deal for Artists', SAAM. Available at https://americanart.si.edu/exhibitions/1934 (accessed 30 October 2019).

Smoodin, Eric. *Disney Discourse: Producing the Magic Kingdom*. London: Routledge, 1994.

Smoodin, Eric. *Snow White and the Seven Dwarfs*. London: Palgrave, 2012.

Snow White Archive. '1937 Snow White Photoplay School Study Guide'. *Snow White School Study* (1938). Available at http://filmic-light.blogspot.com/2013/03/1937-snow-white-photoplay-school-study.html (accessed 12 March 2020).

Solalinde, Antonio G. 'Prólogo'. In *Calila e Dimna*, 9–13. Barcelona: Red Ediciones, 2018.

Solomon, Charles. *The Art of the Animated Image: An Anthology*. Los Angeles: AFI, 1987.

Solomon, Charles. *The Disney That Never Was: The Stories and Art from Five Decades of Unproduced Animation*. New York: Hyperion, 1995.

Solomon, Charles. *The History of Animation: Enchanted Drawings*. New York: Wings Books, 1994.

Spieker, Markus. *Hollywood untern Hakenkreuz: Der amerikanische Spielfilm im Dritten Reich*. Trier: Wissenschaftlicher Verlag Trier, 1999.

Stableford, Brian. *The A to Z of Fantasy Literature*. Lanham: Scarecrow Press, 2009.

Starosielski, Nicole. '"Movements That Are Drawn": A History of Environmental Animation from *The Lorax* to *FernGully* to *Avatar*'. *International Communication Gazette*, 73, nos 1–2 (2011): 145–63.

Steinbeck, J. *The Grapes of Wrath*. New York: Viking Press, 1939.

Sternglanz, S. H., J. L. Gray and M. Et Murakami. 'Adult Preferences for Infantile Facial Features: An Ethological Approach'. *Animal Behaviour*, 25 (1977): 108–15.

Stillwell, Martin. 'The Story Behind Snow White's $10,000,000 Surprise Party'. *Liberty* (9 April 1938): 39.

Stilwell, Robynn J. 'The Fantastical Gap between Diegetic and Nondiegetic'. In *Beyond the Soundtrack: Representing Music in Cinema*, edited by Daniel Goldmark, Lawrence Kramer and Richard Leppert, 184–202. Berkeley: University of California Press.

Stilwell, Robynn J. 'The Silly Symphony'. *Fortune*, 10, no. 5 (November 1934): 88–95.

Stover, Cassandra. 'Damsels and Heroines: The Conundrum of the Post-Feminist Disney Princess'. *LUX: A Journal of Transdisciplinary Writing and Research*, 2, no. 1 (2013): 1–10.

Sullivan, Ed. 'Hollywood'. *Augusta Chronicle*, 4 May 1938: 4.

Susman, W. *Culture as History – the Transformation of American Society in the Twentieth Century*. Washington: Smithsonian Institution Press, 2003.

Tatar, Maria, ed. and trans. *The Annotated Brothers Grimm*. London: W. W. Norton, 2014.

Telotte, J. P. 'Ub Iwerks' (Multi)Plain Cinema'. *animation: an interdisciplinary journal*, 1, no. 1 (July 2006): 9–24.

Telotte, J. P. *Animating Space: From Mickey to WALL-E*. Lexington: University Press of Kentucky, 2010.

Telotte, J. P. *The Mouse Machine: Disney and Technology*. Urbana: University of Illinois Press, 2008.

Teuth, Michael. *Reeling with Laughter: American Film Comedies – From Anarchy to Mockumentary*. Plymouth: Scarecrow, 2012.

The China Press. '"Snow White" Said Screen Masterpiece'. 3 June 1938: 5.

The China Press. 'ALOHA BALLROOM'. 2 June 1938: 10.

The China Press. 'Chang Seng Tailor [Advertisement]'. 2 June 1938: 10.

The China Press. 'Commercial Equipment Co [Advertisement]'. 2 June 1938: 8.

The China Press. 'Film Poster of *Snow White*'. 3 June 1938: 5.

The China Press. 'Handkerchiefs [Advertisement]'. 2 June 1938: 8.

The China Press. '*Snow White*'. 2 June 1938: 5.

The China Press. 'Tyng Yu Brothers [Advertisement,]'. 2 June 1938: 8.

The China Press. 'VIENNA GARDEN [Advertisement]'. 2 June 1938: 9.

The China Press. 'YUEN TAI & CO. [Advertisement]'. 2 June 1938: 9.

The Household Magazine. '"Snow White" [Advertisement]'. June and July 1938: 12.

The Los Angeles Times. 'Disney Creates New Starts'. 17 December 1937, 11 part II.

The Los Angeles Times. '"Snow White" Sets Mark with $6,740,000 Gross'. 2 May 1939: 29.

The Los Angeles Times. '"Snow White" [Advertisement]'. 27 December 1937: 12.

The Los Angeles Times. '"Snow White" [Advertisement]'. 31 December 1937: 14.

The Los Angeles Times. '"Snow White" Premiere Due Tonight'. 21 December 1937: 10.

The Los Angeles Times. '"Snow White" Timely Fare for Christmas'. 25 December 1937: 14 part II.

The Los Angeles Times. 'Cartoon Characters Score Hit'. 2 January 1938: 10 part 1.

The Los Angeles Times. 'Disney Creates New Stars'. 17 December 1937: 11 Part 2.

The Los Angeles Times. 'Gala Premiere Assured for "Snow White"'. 20 December 1937: 9.

The New York Times. 'British Fear "Snow White" Will Cause Nightmares'. 6 February 1938: 37.

The New York Times. 'Disney Joins the Masters in the Metropolitan'. 24 January 1939: 21.

The New York Times. 'Film Critics Here Vote Year's "Best"'. 3 January 1939: 18.

The New York Times. 'M. Mouse Poorly Paid'. 12 March 1934: 20.

The New York Times. 'New Dwarf Industry'. 2 May 1938: 16.

The New York Times. 'Walt Disney Returns: Creator of "Mickey Mouse" Back from Tour of Europe'. 2 August 1935: 15.

The Shanghai Mercantile Press. 'Wu Yonggang Talks about *Chinese Snow White*'. 1 May 1940: 5.

The Sin Wan Pao. 'Children's Playground [Advertisement]'. 17 December 1938: 19.

The Sin Wan Pao. 'Snow White Cigarette [Advertisement]'. 21 December 1938: 16.

The Sin Wan Pao. 'Snow White Eskimo Toffee [Advertisement]'. 2 June 1938: 13.

The Sin Wan Pao. 'Snow White Powder [Advertisement]'. 22 August 1938: 14.

The Sin Wan Pao. 'Snow White Powder [Advertisement]'. 3 December 1938: 14.

The Sin Wan Pao. 'Snow White Powder [Advertisement]'. 31 August 1938: 1.

The Society Daily. 'Snow White Cigarette [Advertisement]'. 24 January 1939: 2.

Thomas, Frank, and Ollie Johnston. *The Illusion of Life: Disney Animation.* New York: Hyperion Press, 1981.

Thomas, Frank. "Can Classic Disney Animation Be Duplicated on the Computer?'. *Computer Pictures* (July 1984): 20–5.

Thomas, Joyce. *Inside the Wolf's Belly: Aspects of the Fairy Tale.* Sheffield: Sheffield Academic Press, 1989.

Thompson, Kristin. *Eisenstein's Ivan the Terrible: A Neoformalist Analysis.* Princeton: Princeton University Press, 1982.

Thorp, M. (1939) *America at the Movies.* New Haven: Yale University Press.

Tietyen, David. *The Musical World of Walt Disney.* Milwaukee: Hal Leonard Publishing Corporation, 1990.

Tiffin, Jessica. *Marvelous Geometry: Narrative and Metafiction in Modern Fairy Tale.* Detroit: Wayne State University Press, 2009.

Time. 'Mouse and Man'. 27 December 1937: 21.

Time. 'Mouse & Man'. 27 December 1937: 19.

Tinbergen, Niko. *The Study of Instinct.* Oxford: Clarendon Press, 1951.

Todd, C., Sonkin, R. 'Interview about Dust Storms, Sleet Storms and Tall Stories: Arvin FSA Camp July 28 1940'. Audio recording, Library of Congress. Available at https://www.loc.gov/item/toddbib000002/ (accessed 20 July 2018).

Todorov, Tzvetan. *Introduction à la littérature fantastique.* Paris: Éditions du Seuil, 1970.

Trevelyan, John. *What the Censor Saw.* London: Michael Joseph, 1973.

Tunalı, Dilek. 'Populer Masallardan Sinemaya Yapılan Uyarlamalarda Kulturel Antropolojik Sureklilik ve Donusum' (Cultural Anthropological Continuity and Transformation in Adaptations from Popular Tales to Cinema), *Uluslararası Sosyal Arastırmalar Dergisi,* 10, no. 49 (2017): 362–72.

U.S. Bureau of the Census. 'Estimated Median Age at First Marriage, by Sex: 1890 to Present'. Available at https://www.census.gov/population/socdemo/hh-fam/tabMS-2.pdf (accessed 25 September 2018).

Ugarte del Campo, Lucía. 'La Cuestión de la transposición en Blancanieves'. *Revista Lindes, Estudios Sociales del arte y de la cultura,* no. 6 (2013): 1–12.

United China Movie News. 'The Experience of Making *Princess Iron Fan*'. 1, no. 9 (1941): 67.

Valentine, Tim, Stephen Darling and Mary Donnelly. 'Why Are Average Faces
    Attractive? The Effect of View and Averageness on the Attractiveness of Female
    Faces'. *Psychonomic Bulletin & Review*, 11, no. 3 (2004): 482–7.
Van Brakle, J. A. '"Mickey the Mouse" Liked by Britons'. *North China Daily
    News*, 6 February 1930: 10.
Van de Vijver, Liesbeth. 'Going to the Exclusive Show : Exhibition Strategies and
    Moviegoing Memories of Disney's Animated Feature Films in Ghent (1937–
    1982)'. *European Journal of Cultural Studies*, 19, no. 4 (2016): 403–18.
Variety. '"Snow White' $100,000 on 5th N.Y. wk: Out of Town B.O. Astonishes
    Trade'. 16 February 1938: 11.
Variety. 'Disney's Princesses: From Snow White to Frozen'. 26 November 2013.
    Available at https://variety.com/gallery/disneys-princesses-from-snow-white-to-
    frozen/ (accessed 12 March 2020).
Variety. '"B'dcast,' vaude good $18,000 in Wash'. 2 March 1938: 7.
Variety. '"Snow White' OK $17,000'. 16 February 1938: 8.
Variety. '"Snow White' Panics L'ville, Wow $15,000'. 16 February 1938: 8.
Variety. 'Breakdown of Network Plugs'. 12 January 1938: 45.
Variety. 'Disney $42,000 Will Be the New Hub Record'. 16 February 1938: 8
Variety. 'Disney's Big B.O. kayoes vauders'. 23 February 1938: 1.
Variety. 'Film Reviews: 'Snow White and the Seven Dwarfs' ". 29 December
    1937: 17.
Variety. 'London OK's "Snow White"'. 23 February 1938: 5.
Variety. "Snow White $110,000 Bigger 3rd Week'. 2 February 1938: 9.
Variety. 'Unusual Re-Playdating Demand for "Snow White" before It Opens'. 9
    February 1938: 7.
Vincendeau, Ginette. 'Hollywood Babel: The Coming of Sound and the Multiple-
    Language Version'. In *'Film Europe' and 'Film America': Cinema, Commerce
    and Cultural Exchange, 1920–1939*, edited by Andrew Higson and Richard
    Maltby, 207–24. Exeter: University of Exeter Press, 1999.
Vinneuil, François. 'L'écran de la semaine. Blanche-Neige et les sept nains'. *l'Action
    française*, 13 May 1938: 5.
Walker, Michael. *Hitchcock's Motifs*. Amsterdam: Amsterdam University
    Press, 2014.
Walt Disney Productions. 'Making of a Masterpiece: Snow White and the Seven
    Dwarfs'. *Walt Disney Home* video, 1994.
Wan, Laiming, and Guohun Wan. *Monkey King and Me*. Taiyuan: Beiyue
    Literature & Art Press, 1985.
Wasko, Janet. *Understanding Disney: The Manufacture of Fantasy*.
    Cambridge: Polity Press, 2001.
Wasko, Janet, Mark Phillips and Eileen R. Meehan. *Dazzled by Disney: The Global
    Disney Audiences Project*. London: Leicester University Press, 2001.
Watts, S. 'Walt Disney: Art and Politics in the American Century'. *Journal of
    American History*, 82, no. 1 (1995): 84–110.
Webber, Andrew. 'Canning the Uncanny: The Construction of Visual Desire in
    Metropolis'. In *Fritz Lang's 'Metropolis': Cinematic Visions of Technology
    and Fear*, edited by Michael Minden and Holger Bachmann, 251–69.
    Suffolk: Camden House, 2000.
Webster, Chris. *Action Analysis for Animators*. Independence: CRC Press, 2012.

Weiming. 'Dopey Doesn't Want to Talk'. *Nanhai Yinxing*, 1, no. 6 (1938): 1

Wells, Paul. *Animation and America*. New Brunswick: Rutgers University Press, 2002.

Wells, Paul. *Animation: Genre and Authorship*. London: Wallflower Press, 2002.

Wells, Paul. *Understanding Animation*. London: Routledge, 1998.

Whitley, David. 'Learning with Disney: Children's Animation and the Politics of Innocence'. *Journal of Educational Media, Memory & Society*, 5, no. 2 (2013): 75–91.

Whitley, David. *The Idea of Nature in Disney Animation*. Aldershot: Ashgate, 2008.

Winters, Ben. 'The Non-Diegetic Fallacy: Film, Music, and Narrative Space'. *Music and Letters*, 91, no. 2 (2010): 224–44.

Zheng, Xinyi. 'I Watched *Snow White* 78 Years Ago', *Global People*, 7 July 2016. http://www.hqrw.com.cn/2016/0707/53171.shtml (accessed 9 July 2018).

Zimmer, Hans. 'Hans Zimmer Teaches Film Scoring'. *MasterClass*. Available at https://www.masterclass.com.

Zipes, Jack. 'The Great Cultural Tsunami of Fairy-Tale Films'. In *Fairy-Tale Films Beyond Disney: International Perspectives*, edited by Jack Zipes, Pauline Greenhill and Kendra Magnus-Johnson, 1–17. London: Routledge, 2016.

Zipes, Jack. *Fairy Tales and the Art of Subversion: The Classical Genre for Children and the Process of Civilization*. New York: Routledge, 2006.

Zipes, Jack. *Why Fairy Tales Stick: The Evolution and Relevance of a Genre*. New York: Routledge, 2006.

FILMOGRAPHY

Adventures of Robin Hood, The (1938), [Film] Dir. Michael Curtiz and William Keighley, USA: Warner Brothers.

African Cats (2011), [TV] Dir. Alistair Fothergill and Keith Scholey, USA: Walt Disney Studios Motion Pictures.

Air Circus, The (1928), [Film] Dir. Howard Hawks, USA: Fox Movietone.

Akira (1988), [Film] Dir. Katsuhiro Otomo, Japan: Toho.

Alerte en Méditerranée/Alert in the Mediterranean (1938), [Film] Dir. Léo Joannon, France: Compagnie Commerciale Française Cinématographique.

Ali Baba ve 7 Cüceler/Ali Baba and Seven Dwarfs (2015), [Film] Dir. Cem Yılmaz, Turkey: CMYLMZ Fikirsanat.

Alice Comedies (1923–7), [Film] Dir. Walt Disney and Ub Iwerks, USA: Walt Disney Productions.

Alice in Wonderland (1951), [Film] Dir. Clyde Geronimi, Wilfred Jackson and Hamilton Luske, USA: Walt Disney Productions.

All About Eve (1950), [Film] Dir. Joseph L. Mankiewicz, USA: 20th Century Fox.

Allegro Non Troppo (1976), [Film] Dir. Bruno Bozzetto, Italy: Roxy International.

Anlat Istanbul/Istanbul Tales (2004), [Film] Dir. Selim Demirdelen, Kudret Sabancı, Ümit Ünal, Yücel Yolcu and Ömür Atay, Turkey: Ishak Films.

Annie Hall (1977), [Film] Dir. Woody Allen, USA: United Artists.

Aristocats, The (1970), [Film] Dir. Wolfgang Reitherman, USA: Walt Disney Productions.

Autumn (1930), [Film] Dir. Ub Iwerks, USA: Walt Disney Productions.

Babes in the Woods (1932), [Film] Dir. Burt Gillett, USA: Walt Disney Productions.

Back to Neverland (1989), [TV] Dir. Jerry Rees, USA: Walt Disney Productions.

Ball of Fire (1941), [Film] Dir. Howard Hawks, 1941, USA: Samuel Goldwyn Productions.

Bambi (1942), [Film] Dir. David Hand, USA: Walt Disney Productions.

Band Concert, The (1935) [Film] Wilfred Jackson, USA: Walt Disney Productions.

Barcelona Trailer (1929), [Film] Dir. Marcelo Ventura, Spain.

Barnabé (1938), [Film] Dir. Alexandre Esway, France: Gray-Film.

Beany and Cecil Show (1962), [TV] Dir. Bob Clampett, USA: Paramount Television Network.

Beauty and the Beast (1991) [Film] Dir. Gary Trousdale and Kirk Wise, USA: Walt Disney Productions.

Beauty and the Beast (2017), [Film] Dir. Bill Condon, USA: Walt Disney Studios Motion Pictures.

Betty Boop's Bamboo Isle (1932), [Film] Dir. Dave Fleischer, USA: Fleischer Studios.

Black Panther (2018), [Film] Dir. Ryan Coogler, USA: Marvel Studios.

Blancanieves (2012), [Film] Dir. Pablo Berger, Spain: Wanda.

Bringing Up Baby (1938), [Film] Dir. Howard Hawks, USA: RKO Radio Pictures.

Brother Bear (2003) [Film] Dir. Aaron Blaise and Robert Walker, USA: Walt Disney Productions.

Cabinet of Dr. Caligari, The (1920), [Film] Dir. Robert Wiene, Germany: Decla-Bioscop.

Casablanca (1942), [Film] Dir. Michael Curtiz, USA: Warner Bros. Pictures.

Casting (1997), [Film] Dir. Guido Manuli, Italy.

Caught in the Fog (1928), [Film] Dir. Howard Bretherton, USA: Warner Bros. Pictures.

Chimpanzee (2012), [TV] Alistair Fothergill and Mark Linfeld, USA: Walt Disney Studios Motion Pictures.

China Plate, The (1931), [Film] Dir. Wilfred Jackson, USA: Walt Disney Productions.

China Shop, The (1934), [Film] Dir. Wilfred Jackson, USA: Walt Disney Productions.

Chinese Snow White (1940), [Film] Dir. Wu Yonggang, China: Xinhua Film Company.

Citizen Kane (1941), [Film] Dir. Orson Welles, USA: RKO Radio Pictures.

Clock Store, The (1931), [Film] Dir. Wilfred Jackson, USA: Walt Disney Productions.

Coal Black and de Sebben Dwarfs (1943), [Film] Dir. Bob Clampett, USA: Warner Bros.

Cookie Carnival, The (1935), [Film] Dir. Ben Sharpsteen, USA: Walt Disney Productions.

Cuéntame un cuento (2014–), [TV] Dir. Marcos Osorio Vidal, Spain: Cuatro Cabezas TV.

Dark Knight, The (2008), [Film] Dir. Christopher Nolan, USA: Warner Bros. Pictures.

Dracula (1931), [Film] Dir. Todd Browning, USA: Universal Pictures.

Dr. Jekyll and Mr. Hyde (1931), [Film] Dir. Rouben Mamoulian, USA: Paramount Pictures.

Dumbo (1941), [Film] Dir. Ben Sharpsteen, USA: Walt Disney Productions.

Earth (2007), [TV] Dir. Alistair Fothergill and Mark Linfeld, USA: Walt Disney Studios Motion Pictures.

Elmer Elephant (1936), [Film] Dir. Wilfred Jackson, USA: Walt Disney Productions.

El relicario/The Locket (1970), [Film] Dir. Rafael Gil, Spain: Paramount Films de España.

El Terrible Toreador (1929), [Film] Dir. Walt Disney, USA: Walt Disney Studios.

El último cuplé/The Last Torch Song (1957), [Film] Dir. Juan de Orduña, Spain: Producciones Orduña Films.

Enchanted (2007), [Film] Dir. Kevin Lima, USA: Walt Disney Studios Motion Pictures.

Érase una vez, lo que no te contaron del cuento (2017), [TV] Dir. Pedro Ybarra, Mexico: Televisa.

Fantabiblical (1977) [Film] Dir. Guido Manuli, Italy.

Fantasia (1940), [Film] Dir. James Algar, Samuel Armstrong, James Algar, Bill Roberts, Paul Satterfield, Ben Sharpsteen, David D. Hand, Hamilton Luske, Jim Handley, Ford Beebe, T. Hee, Norman Ferguson and Wilfred Jackson. USA: Walt Disney Productions.

Farmyard Symphony (1938), [Film] Dir. Jack Cutting, USA: Walt D isney Productions.

Father Noah's Ark (1933), [Film] Dir. Wilfred Jackson, USA: Walt Disney Productions.

Femme du boulanger, La/The Baker's Wife (1938), [Film] Dir. Marcel Pagnol, France: Les Films Marcel Pagnol.

Ferdinand the Bull (1938), [Film] Dir. Dick Rickard, USA: Walt Disney Productions.

Flowers and Trees (1932), [Film] Dir. Burt Gillett, USA: Walt Disney Productions.

Flushed Away (2006), [Film] Dir. David Bowers and Sam Fell, USA/UK: Aardman Animations.

Flying Mouse, The (1934), [Film] Dir. David Hand, USA: Walt Disney Productions.

Fox and the Hound, The (1981), [Film] Dir. Ted Berman, Richard Rich and Art Stevens, USA: Walt Disney Productions.

Frozen (2013), [Film] Dir. Chris Buck and Jennifer Lee, USA: Walt Disney Studios Motion Pictures.

Frozen 2 (2019), [Film] Dir. Chris Buck and Jennifer Lee, USA: Walt Disney Studios Motion Pictures.

Fun and Fancy Free (1947), [Film] Dir. Hamilton Luske Jack Kinney, Hamilton Luske, William Morgan and Bill Roberts, USA: RKO Radio Pictures.

Gilda (1946), [Film] Dir. Charles Vidor, USA: Columbia Pictures.

Goddess of Spring, The (1934), [Film] Dir. Wilfred Jackson, USA: Walt Disney Productions.

Gone with the Wind (1939), [Film] Dir. Victor Fleming, USA: Selznick International Pictures, Metro-Goldwyn-Mayer.

La Grande Illusion (1937), [Film] Dir. Jean Renoir, France: Réalisations d'Art Cinématographique (RAC).

Grasshopper and the Ants, The (1934), [Film] Dir. Wilfred Jackson, USA: Walt Disney Productions.

Gremlins (1984), [Film] Dir. Joe Dante, USA: Warner Bros.

Grasshopper and the Ants, The (1934), [Film] Dir. Joe Dante, USA: Warner Bros.

Grimm (2011–17), [TV] Dir. Stephen Carpenter, Jim Kouf and David Greenwalt, USA: Universal Television/NBC.

Grimm's Snow White (2012), [Film] Dir. Rachel Lee Goldenberg, USA: Asylum.

Gulliver's Travels (1939), [Film] Dir. Dave Fleischer, USA: Fleischer Studios.

Happily N'Ever After 2: Snow White – Another Bite at the Apple (2009), [Film] Dir. Steven E. Gordon and Boyd Kirkland, USA: Kickstart Productions.

Head of Janus, The (1920), [Film] Dir. F. W. Murnau, Germany: Lipow Film Company.

Huntsman: Winter's War, The (2016), [Film] Dir. Cedric Nicolas-Troyan, USA: Universal Pictures.

Informer, The (1935), [Film] Dir. John Ford, USA: RKO Radio Pictures.

Jazz Singer, The (1927), [Film] Dir. Alan Crosland, USA: Warner Bros. Pictures.

Jungle Book, The (1967), [Film] Dir. Wolfgang Reitherman, USA: Walt Disney Productions.

Just Dogs (1932), [Film] Dir. Burt Gillett, USA: Walt Disney Productions.

Katia (1938), [Film] Dir. Maurice Tourneur, France: Metropa Films.

King Kong (1933), [Film] Dir. Merian C. Cooper and Ernest B. Schoedsack, USA: Radio Pictures.

King Neptune (1932), [Film] Dir. Burt Gillett, USA: Walt Disney Productions.

Komser Sekspir/Police Chief Shakespeare (2000), [Film] Dir. Sinan Çetin, Turkey: Plato Film Production.

Lady and the Tramp (1955), [Film] Dir. Clyde Geronimi, Wilfred Jackson and Hamilton Luske, USA: Walt Disney Productions.

Legend of the Forest (1987), [Film] Dir. Osamu Tezuka, Japan: Tezuka Productions Co., Ltd.

Lilet Never Happened (2012), [Film] Dir. Jacco Groen, Philippines: Film and Music Entertainment (F&ME).

Little Mermaid, The (1989), [Film] Dir. Ron Clements and John Musker, USA: Walt Disney Feature Animation.

Living Desert, The (1953), [Film] Dir. James Algar, USA: Walt Disney Productions.

Lullaby Land (1933), [Film] Dir. Wilfred Jackson, USA: Walt Disney Productions.

Maison du Maltais, La/Sirocco (1938), [Film] Dir. Pierre Chenal, France: Compagnie Cinématographique de France.

Man-Proof (1938), [Film] Dir. Richard Thorpe, USA: Metro-Goldwyn-Mayer.

Man Who Knew Too Much, The (1956), [Film] Dir. Alfred Hitchcock, USA: Paramount Pictures.

Mark of Zorro, The (1940), [Film] Dir. Rouben Mamoulian, USA: 20th Century Fox.

M*A*S*H* (1972–83), [TV] Dir. Larry Gelbart, USA: 20th Century Fox Television.

Meet the Wife (1931), [Film] Dir. Leslie Pearce, USA: Columbia Pictures.

Metropolis (1927), [Film] Dir. Fritz Lang, Germany: UFA/Parufamet.

Midnight in a Toy Shop (1930), [Film] Dir. Wilfred Jackson, USA: Columbia Pictures.

Mirror Mirror (2012), [Film] Dir. Tarsem Singh, USA: Relativity Media.

Moana (2016), [Film] Dir. Ron Clements and John Musker, USA: Walt Disney Animation Studios.

Modern Times (1936), [Film] Dir. Charles Chaplin, USA: Charles Chaplin Productions.

Mother Goose Melodies (1931), [Film] Dir. Burt Gillett, USA: Walt Disney Productions.

Mr. Bug Goes to Town (1941), [Film] Dir. Dave Fleischer, USA: Fleischer Studios.

Mr. Smith Goes to Washington (1939), [Film] Dir. Frank Capra, USA: Columbia Pictures.

Mystery Science Theatre 3000 (1988–99), [TV] Dir. Joel Hodgson, USA: HBO Downtown Productions.

Nature's Half Acre (1951), [Film] Dir. James Algar, USA: Walt Disney Productions.

Night Before Christmas, The (1933), [Film] Dir. Wilfred Jackson, USA: Walt Disney Productions.

9 to 5 (1980), [Film] Dir. Colin Higgins, USA: 20th Century Fox.

Nosferatu: A Symphony of Horror (1922), [Film] Dir. F.W. Murnau, Germany: Prana Film.

Old King Cole (1933), [Film] Dir. David Hand, USA: Walt Disney Productions.

Old Mill, The (1937), [Film] Dir. Wilfred Jackson, USA: Walt Disney Productions.

Once Upon a Time (2011–18), [TV] Dir. Edward Kitsis and Adam
  Horowitz, USA: ABC Studios.
Out of the Inkwell (1918–29), [Film] Dir. Dave Fleischer and Max
  Fleischer, USA: Fleischer Studios.
Pamuk Prens/Snow Prince (2016), [Film] Dir. Birol Güven and Hasan
  Tolga Pulat, Turkey: MinT Motion Pictures.
Pamuk Prenses ve 7 cüceler/Snow White and Seven Dwarfs (1971), [Film]
  Dir. Ertem Göreç, Turkey: Hisar Film.
Pas à deux (1988), [Film] Dir. Monique Renault and Gerrit van Dijk,
  Netherlands: Haghefilm BV/Dutch Film Fund.
Peter Pan (1953), [Film] Dir. Clyde Geronimi, Wilfred Jackson and
  Hamilton Luske, USA: Walt Disney Productions.
Pied Piper, The (1933), [Film] Dir. Wilfred Jackson, USA: Walt Disney
  Productions.
Pinocchio (1940), [Film] Dir. Ben Sharpsteen and Hamilton Luske,
  USA: Walt Disney Productions.
Porky in Wackyland (1938), [Film] Dir. Bob Clampett, USA: Leon
  Schlesinger Productions.
Princess and the Frog, The (2009), [Film] Dir. Ron Clements and John
  Musker, USA: Walt Disney Animation Studios.
Princess Iron Fan (1941), [Film] Dir. Wan Guchan and Wan Laiming,
  China: China United Film Company.
Prison sans barreaux (1938), [Film] Dir. Léonide Moguy,
  France: Compagnie Internationale de Productions Cinématographiques.
Quai des brumes, Les/Port of Shadows (1938), [Film] Dir. Marcel Carné,
  France: Franco London Films.
Raggedy Anne & Raggedy Andy (1941), [Film] Dir. Dave Fleischer,
  USA: Fleischer Studios.
Ralph Breaks the Internet (2018), [Film] Dir. Rich Moore and Phil
  Johnston, USA: Walt Disney Animation Studios.
Razor's Edge, The (1946), [Film] Dir. Edmund Goulding, USA: 20th
  Century Fox.
Red Shoes and the Seven Dwarfs (2019), [Film] Dir. Sung Ho Hong and
  Moo-Hyun Jang, South Korea: Locus Creative Studios.
Rescuers, The (1977), [Film] Dir. Wolfgang Reitherman, John Lounsbery
  and Art Stevens, USA: Walt Disney Productions.
Robin Hood (1973), [Film] Dir. Wolfgang Reitherman, USA: Walt Disney
  Productions.
Santa's Workshop (1932), [Film] Dir. Wilfred Jackson, USA: Walt Disney
  Productions.
Schneewittchen (1959), [Film] Dir. Fritz Genschow, Germany: Fritz
  Genschow Films.

Schneewittchen und die 7 Zwerge (1955), [Film] Dir. Erich Kobler,
 Germany: Jugendfilm-Verleih.
Schneewittchen und die sieben Zwerge (1962), [Film] Dir. Gottfried
 Kolditz, Germany: DEFA (Deutsche Film-Aktiengesellschaft).
7 Dwarves – Men Alone in the Wood (2004), [Film] Dir. Otto Waalkes,
 Germany: Zipfelmützen GmbH & Co. KG.
7 Dwarves: The Forest Is Not Enough (2006), [Film] Dir. Sven Unterwaldt,
 Germany: Zipfelmützen GmbH & Co. KG.
Seventh Dwarf, The (2014), [Film] Dir. Boris Aljinovic and Harald
 Siepermann, Germany: Zipfelmützen GmbH & Co. KG.
Seven Dwarfs to the Rescue, The (1951), [Film] Dir. Paolo W. Tamburella,
 Italy: PWT Produzione.
Shining, The (1980), [Film] Dir. Stanley Kubrick, USA: Warner Bros.
Shrek 2 (2004), [Film] Dir. Andrew Adamson, Kelly Asbury and Conrad
 Vernon, USA: DreamWorks Animation.
Shrek the Third (2007), [Film] Chris Miller and Raman Hui, USA:
 DreamWorks Animation.
The Simpsons (1989–), [TV]. Dir. Matt Groening, USA: 20th Century Fox
 Television.
Sleeping Beauty (1959), [Film] Dir. Clyde Geronimi, USA: Walt Disney
 Productions.
Snow White (1902), [Film] Dir. Siegmund Lubin, USA: S. Lubin.
Snow White (1916), [Film] Dir. J. Searle Dawley, USA: Paramount Pictures.
Snow White (1933), [Film] Dir. Dave Fleischer, USA: Fleischer Studios.
Snow White: A Deadly Summer (2012), [Film] Dir. David DeCoteau,
 USA: Rapid Heart Pictures.
Snow White and the Huntsman (2012), [Film] Dir. Rupert Sanders,
 USA: Universal Pictures.
Snow White and the Seven Dwarfs (1937), [Film] Dir. David Hand
 (supervising), William Cottrell, Wilfred Jackson, Larry Morey, Perce
 Pearce and Ben Sharpsteen,Walt Disney Productions.
Snow White: A Tale of Terror (1997), [Film] Dir. Michael Cohn,
 USA: PolyGram Filmed Entertainment.
Snow White: The Sequel (2007), [Film] Dir. Picha, France: YC
 Alligator Film.
Solo los dos (1968), [Film] Dir. Luis Lucia Mingarro, Spain: Guión
 Producciones Cinematográficas.
Solo un Bacio/Just a Kiss (1983). [Film] Dir. Guido Manuli, Italy.
Song of the South (1946), [Film] Dir. Wilfred Jackson, USA: Walt Disney
 Productions.
S. O. S. (1979), [Film] Dir. Guido Manuli, Italy.
Sovalye, Pamuk Prenses ve Hain/Knight Snow White and Traitor (1996),
 [Film] Dir. Orhan Oguz, Turkey: Sinema Vakfi.

Spider-Man: Homecoming (2017), [Film] Dir. Jon Watts, USA: Marvel Studios.

Springtime (1929), [Film] Dir. Ub Iwerks, USA: Walt Disney Studios.

Stagecoach (1939), [Film] Dir. John Ford, USA: Walter Wanger Productions.

State Street Sadie (1928), [Film] Dir. Archie Mayo, USA: Warner Bros.

Steamboat Willie (1928), [Film] Dir. Ub Iwerks, USA: Walt Disney Studios.

Sunrise: A Song of Two Humans (1927), [Film] Dir. F. W. Murnau, USA: William Fox Studio.

Sword in the Stone, The (1963), [Film] Dir. Wolfgang Reitherman, USA: Walt Disney Productions.

Sydney White (2007), [Film] Dir. Joe Nussbaum, USA: Universal Pictures.

Synchromy (1971), [Film] Dir. Norman McLaren, Canada: National Board of Canada (NFB).

Tangled (2010), [Film] Dir. Nathan Greno and Byron Howard, USA: Walt Disney Animation Studios.

Tarzan (1999), [Film] Dir. Kevin Lima and Chris Buck, USA: Walt Disney Feature Animation.

Tell Me a Story (2018–), [TV] Dir. Kevin Williamson, USA: Outerbanks Entertainment.

Thor: Ragnarok (2017), [Film] Dir. Taika Waititi, USA: Marvel Studios.

Three Caballeros, The (1944), [Film] Dir. Norm Ferguson and Harold Young, USA: Walt Disney Productions.

Three Little Pigs (1933), [Film] Dir. Burt Gillett, USA: Walt Disney Productions.

3 Misses (1998), [Film] Dir. Paul Driessen, Netherlands: CinéTé Filmproductie BV.

To Catch a Thief (1955), [Film] Dir. Alfred Hitchcock, USA: Paramount Pictures.

To Have and Have Not (1944), [Film] Dir. Howard Hawks, USA: Warner Bros.

Trois Valses, Les/Three Waltzes (1938), [Film] Dir. Ludwig Berger, France: SOFROR.

True Confessions (1937), [Film] Dir. Wesley Ruggles, USA: Paramount Pictures.

Ugly Duckling, The (1931), [Film] Dir. Wilfred Jackson, USA: Walt Disney Productions.

Ugly Duckling, The (1939), [Film] Dir. Jack Cutting and Clyde Geronimi, USA: Walt Disney Productions.

Veggie Tales (1993–), [TV] Dir. Phil Vischer and Mike Nawrocki, USA: Big Idea Productions.

Walt Disney – Part 1, American Experience (2015), [TV] Dir. Sarah Colt, USA: Sarah Colt Productions.

Warming Up (1928), [Film] Dir. Fred C. Newmeyer, USA: Paramount Pictures.

What's Up, Tiger Lily? (1966), [Film] Dir. Woody Allen, USA: Benedict Pictures Corp.

Wise Little Hen, The (1934), [Film] Dir. Wilfred Jackson, USA: Walt Disney Productions.

NOTES ON CONTRIBUTORS

Zeynep Gultekin Akcay is an assistant professor at the Department of Radio, Television and Cinema, Sivas Cumhuriyet University, Turkey. She wrote her master's thesis on popular culture and television. She later received her PhD with a thesis titled 'Peasantry in Written Cultural Products from the Early Years of the Turkish Republic to Present Days: The Image of Peasantry in Turkish Novels'. She is one of the editors of the book titled *Ideology and Communication Symbolic Reflections of Intellectual Designs*. Her research area is television studies, popular culture, media and children. Fairy tale and ideology, cartoon music and ideology, hybridized children's plays through screens, gender in cartoons are recent topics of her study.

Jane Batkin is the author of *Identity in Animation: A Journey into Self, Difference, Culture and the Body*, which was published in 2017. Her chapter *Mirrors and Shadows: Duality, Illusion and the Divided Self in Toy Story* was published in the edited book *Toy Story: How Pixar Reinvented the Animated Feature* in 2018 and her chapter 'A Darker Heartland: A Study of Otherness, Dysfunction and the Uncanny in Aardman's Animated Short Films' was published in the edited book *Aardman Animations: Beyond Stop Motion* in 2020. Jane gained a PhD in 2020 for her work on identity in animated film and teaches film and animation at the University of Lincoln, where she is Programme Leader of the BA (Hons) Animation and Visual Effects course. She has previously taught at Ravensbourne College.

Daniël Biltereyst is director of the Cinema and Media Studies research center (CIMS) at Ghent University, Belgium. Besides exploring new approaches to historical media and cinema cultures, he is engaged in work on film and screen culture as sites of censorship, controversy, public debate and audience engagement. Biltereyst has published widely on these matters in edited volumes and academic journals. He recently published *The Routledge Companion to New Cinema History* (2019, with R. Maltby and Ph. Meers), *Mapping Movie Magazines* (2020, with L. Van de Vijver) and is finalizing a monograph on film control and censorship in Belgium.

Irene Raya Bravo holds a PhD from the University of Seville, where she currently teaches. Her main research lines focus on audiovisual narrative and television history. Besides participating in several publications about filming, television, narrative, genre and gender, she has coordinated three books: *Reyes, espadas, cuervos y dragones. Estudio del fenómeno televisivo Juego de Tronos* (2013), *De la estaca al martillo. Un viaje por los universos de Joss Whedon de Buffy a Los Vengadores* (2015) and *El viaje de la heroína. 10 iconos femeninos épicos del cine y la televisión* (2019). She is a member of the research group ADMIRA (Analysis of media, images and audiovisual tales in its history for social change. SEJ496).

Yuanyuan Chen is lecturer in animation history and theory at Ulster University, UK. Her research focuses on contemporary Chinese animation, with particular interest in the influence of modernism and postmodernism on Chinese animation after the 1980s. Her broader research interests span animation theory, Asian animation, experimental animation, modernism and postmodernism, non-fiction animation, virtual reality and animation. Her articles have been published in international peer-reviewed journals, such as *Modernism/Modernity, Journal of Chinese Cinemas, Alphaville: Journal of Film and Screen Media*, and so on.

Stéphane Collignon has been lecturing on animation theory, art history, image analysis and transmedia as well as teaching writing workshops at Haute École Albert Jacquard, in Namur, Belgium. He has a background in Journalism, Film Studies and Film Writing. His PhD dissertation focused on animation aesthetics and its ties to print cartoon, caricature and the uncanny valley theory. His research interests include phenomenology of cinema, empirical aesthetics, genres, visual narrative (including cartoons, comics, etc.), transmedia and pro wrestling (cuz it's awesome!).

Amy M. Davis is a lecturer in Film History at the University of Hull. She teaches modules on (among other things) American Animation History and Disney Studies and is the author of a number of papers on Disney and Animation. These include the books *Good Girls & Wicked Witches: Women in Disney's Feature Animation* (2006) and *Handsome Heroes & Vile Villains: Men in Disney's Feature Animation* (2013). She also edited the book *Discussing Disney*, which was released by John Libbey Publishing and the University of Indiana Press in December 2019 (and includes several people to be found in Pallant & Holliday's book, too!).

Sadeen Elyas is a PhD candidate in Film Studies–Film Musicology at the University of Hull. She has a bachelor's degree in Media and Screen Studies from the University of Hull, and her PhD builds upon research begun in her undergraduate dissertation. Her research interests are film music/sound (including the early use of sound in Hollywood cinema), animation studies, especially Disney, and depiction of food/cookery in film music. Her PhD research combines her interests and looks at the use of sound and music as a storytelling agent in silent cinema and sound film, focusing on Disney films and Disney theme parks. Sadeen is a composer who worked with different organizations in composing music for various projects. She is currently composing music for a stage musical.

Ian Friend has wide-ranging professional experience, having worked in the animation industry for over 20 years. He has worked as a 2D/3D Animator, Compositor, Character Designer and Storyboard Artist for animated series, video games and commercials for companies such as Sony, BBC, Channel 4, Dreamworks and Fox Kids. He has been working predominantly in Higher Education for the last nine years teaching animation theory and production techniques and is currently a senior lecturer in Animation and VFX at the University of Gloucestershire. He has recently presented papers at Anifest, CFP Media Journeys and the Manchester Animation Festival.

Christopher Holliday teaches Film Studies and Liberal Arts at King's College London specializing in Hollywood cinema, animation history and contemporary digital media. He has published several book chapters and articles on digital technology and computer animation, including work in *Animation Practice, Process & Production* and *animation: an interdisciplinary journal* (where he is also associate editor). He is the author of *The Computer-Animated Film: Industry, Style and Genre* (2018) and co-editor of *Fantasy/Animation: Connections between Media, Mediums and Genres* (2018) that examines the historical, cultural and theoretical points of intersection between fantasy and animation. He is also the co-founder and curator of *fantasy-animation.org*.

Maarit Kalmakurki, MA, is a costume and set designer with design credits across theatre, opera and film productions. Maarit is currently a Doctoral candidate at Aalto University School of Arts, Design and Architecture, Finland. Her doctoral research investigates the notions of digital character costume design in computer animated films. In Addition, Maarit's diverse research interests range between stage and film costume history and design, dress history and the use of technological tools in design and research processes.

Terry Lindvall (PhD, University of Southern California) occupies the C. S. Lewis Chair of Communication and Christian Thought at Virginia Wesleyan University in Virginia Beach, Virginia. He has taught at Duke University, the College of William and Mary, and several other universities; was a consultant for Dreamworks' *The Prince of Egypt*; and has authored twelve books including *God on the Big Screen* (2019), *Divine Film Comedies* (2016) and *God Mocks: A History of Religious Satire from the Hebrew*

Prophets to Stephen Colbert (2015). He is currently researching a book on *Seven Deadly Cartoon Sins: Short Animated Films as Parables, Proverbs and Fables* and is also producing a documentary feature on *A History of Prayers in Hollywood Films from the Silent Era to Today.* He is married to Karen Lindvall, a musician, and identifies with the dwarf Sleepy.

Thaiane de Oliveira Moreira has a PhD in Social Communication and is Professor of the Graduate Program in Communication of the Fluminense Federal University. She is the coordinator of the Research Group on Experiences of Audience Engagement and Transformations (LEETA). She has researched the circulation of communication in different spheres and its interactional processes in the production of knowledge, from a perspective aimed at strategic development of communication.

Victoria Mullins is currently undertaking her PhD at the University of Cambridge. Her doctoral research is funded by the Arts and Humanities Research Council and she explores the relationship between Disney (and Pixar) animation and cinematic horror. She is particularly interested in examining the construction, maintenance and implications of the boundaries between the adult and the child as presented within popular culture.

Pamela C. O'Brien is currently the acting dean of the School of Arts, Sciences and Business at Notre Dame of Maryland University. Prior to moving to the dean's role, she was the chair of the Communication Arts department at the University for two years. In addition, she taught for ten years at Bowie State University where she served as chair and associate professor in the Department of Communications and as program coordinator for the M.A. in Organizational Communication. Dr O'Brien also taught for nine years at the George Washington University in the Electronic Media major. Her research interests are the critical/cultural and historical study of animation, advertising law and the impact of communication technology change.

Chris Pallant, Reader in Creative Arts and Industries at Canterbury Christ Church University, is the author of *Demystifying Disney* (2011), *Storyboarding: A Critical History* (2015) and editor of *Animated Landscapes: History, Form and Function* (2015). He also founded and edits Bloomsbury's *Animation: Key Films/Filmmakers* series. Chris has published on a range of topics, including the 'cartoonism' of Tarantino's films, performance capture technology, the animated landscape of New York and the work of Rockstar Games. He currently serves as president for the Society for Animation Studies and is festival director for Canterbury Anifest.

Greg Philip is a French independent scholar and blog writer. He studied languages in Avignon. Fascinated by the film *Snow White and the Seven Dwarfs* ever since he saw it at age 4, he has collected Snow White items for years. This led to his participation in several magazines, websites, including his own blog, alostfilm.com, about lost films, forgotten stars and deleted scenes. Along with blog writer Rémi Carémel, he found a copy of the lost first French version on film through a private collector. He also took part in the 2013 seminar at La Sorbonne 'Archives et acteurs des cinémas d'animation en France', published the year after by L'Harmattan. He is currently co-writing the memoirs of actress and singer Lucie Dolène, who dubbed the voice of Snow White in the 1962 French version of the film.

Sébastien Roffat is a French historian specializing in animation. A PhD in Film Studies, a graduate of the Sorbonne Nouvelle University (Paris 3), he is winner of Aguirre-Basualdo Arts and Humanities Prize awarded by the Chancellor of the Universities of Paris in 2013 for his thesis 'The emergence of a French school of cartoon under the German Occupation (1940–1944)'. He is an associated researcher at the Institut de recherche sur le cinéma et l'audiovisuel (IRCAV), Sorbonne Nouvelle University, Paris 3. Teacher and lecturer, he is the author of eight books on animation, its history and its aesthetic but also political, economic and sociological aspects: 'Animation and propaganda cartoons during World War II' (2005), 'Disney and France: twenty years Euro Disneyland' (2007), 'Animated propaganda. Animated political cartoons between 1933 and 1945' (2010), 'The Truth about the invention of the moving picture. Émile Reynaud, his life and work' (a critical edition book by Maurice Noverre dated 1926), 'History of the French cartoon from 1936 to 1940: a cultural state policy?' (2014), 'Political and economic history of the French animated film under the Occupation: a golden age?' (2014), 'Aesthetics and reception of French cartoon under the Occupation: the emergence of a French school?' (2014).

María del Mar Rubio-Hernández holds a PhD in Communication Studies from the University of Seville (obtaining the Outstanding Doctorate Award), where she also earned an Advertising and Public Relations degree in 2007. She has visited foreign universities, such as the Erasmushoge School in Brussels and the University of Michigan, where she developed a special interest in the analysis of the advertising discourse. She is a member of the research group IDECO. Her scientific activity focuses on collaborations with international communication magazines and conferences; moreover, she has also participated in several collective books about popular TV shows and has also co-edited two books about advertising: *Branding cultural. Una teoría aplicada a las marcas y a la publicidad* (2019) and *Géneros narrativos audiovisuales en publicidad* (2019). She combines said research work with teaching at the Department of Communication Studies at the University of Seville since 2011.

Janderson Pereira Toth is a master's student in Computer Science at the Federal University of Rio de Janeiro (UFRJ) and graduated in Media Studies from Fluminense Federal University (UFF). He is a member of the Laboratory of Social Computing and Social Network Analysis (LABCores), where he studies psychological operations of dissemination of misinformation.

Priscila Mana Vaz is a PhD student in Communication at Fluminense Federal University (PPGCOM/UFF). She is a member of the Research Group on Experiences of Audience Engagement and Transformations (LEETA), whose development involves an international cooperation partnership with the University of Uppsala (Sweden); she is also a member of the Research Group Media_Müthos, with focus on Narrative Studies, Aesthetics and Fiction. She researches the relationship between narratives and brands and expanding storytelling universes in audiovisual productions. She has experience in communication, with emphasis on Communication Theory, working mainly in the following subjects: serial fiction and narrative genres.

INDEX